Library of Congress Cataloging in Publication Data

```
Linger, R      C        1941-
    Structured programming.

    (The Systems programming series)
    1.  Structured programming.  I.  Mills,
Harlan D., 1919-     joint author.  II.  Witt,
Bernard I., 1929-    joint author.  III.  Title.
QA76.6.L55           001.6'42           78-18641
ISBN 0-201-14461-1
```

ISBN 0-201-14461-1
ABCDEFGHIJ-HA-79

To Juyne
Lolly
Carol

THE SYSTEMS PROGRAMMING SERIES

Foreword

The field of systems programming primarily grew out of the efforts of many programmers and managers whose creative energy went into producing practical, utilitarian systems programs needed by the rapidly growing computer industry. Programming was practiced as an art where each programmer invented his own solutions to problems with little guidance beyond that provided by his immediate associates. In 1968, the late Ascher Opler, then at IBM, recognized that it was necessary to bring programming knowledge together in a form that would be accessible to all systems programmers. Surveying the state of the art, he decided that enough useful material existed to justify a significant publication effort. On his recommendation, IBM decided to sponsor The Systems Programming Series as a long term project to collect, organize, and publish principles and techniques that would have lasting value throughout the industry.

The Series consists of an open-ended collection of text-reference books. The contents of each book represent the individual author's view of the subject area and do not necessarily reflect the views of the IBM Corporation. Each is organized for course use but is detailed enough for reference. Further, the Series is organized in three levels: broad introductory material in the foundation volumes, more specialized material in the software volumes, and very specialized theory in the computer science volumes. As such, the Series meets the needs of the novice, the experienced programmer, and the computer scientist.

The Editorial Board

Preface

THE MATHEMATICAL CHARACTER OF SOFTWARE

The objective of this book is to show practicing programming professionals how to be more powerful, how to design more reliable and efficient software by the use of systematic methods of program analysis and synthesis. The central theme of these methods is the mathematical correctness of programs. There are two important by-products of this theme; namely, 1) the discipline of mathematical correctness provides a check and balance for the free and creative inventions that are so necessary in software design, and 2) the ability to create logically correct designs can be parlayed into actual programs that require little or no debugging. Since debugging is the most error prone and expensive activity in software development, its sharp reduction leads to more reliability and productivity simultaneously. The additional intellectual control of the design process allows more concentration on questions of software efficiency, and more capability for tuning program designs with execution experience.

Software began as an afterthought to hardware, and as long as hardware was small and simple, software could be handled informally by scientifically trained people as a by-product of the use intended for the hardware. As hardware grew in size and complexity, richer software possibilities emerged and software specialists appeared, to produce inventions such as assemblers, compilers, operating systems, and data management systems. Although there was an early recognition of mathematical ideas in computing, for example, in mathematical logic, linguistics, and automata theory, the approach of most software specialists was pragmatic rather than mathematical. Thus, although it may seem surprising, the rediscovery of software as a form of mathematics in a deep and literal sense is just beginning to penetrate university research and teaching, as well as industry and government practices. The forcing factor in this rediscovery has been the growth of software complexity, and the inability of informal software practices and management to cope with the complexity of today's challenges in software.

Of course, software is a special form of mathematics, with totally new demands in the sheer volume of logical precision required in its application. A single software project may occupy hundreds, even thousands, of people over several years, so that unique requirements exist for documentation, communication, and management of the development. These unique requirements lead to almost all of the jargon in software and, in fact, this jargon tends to obscure the mathematical character of software, as people get caught up in implementation and management details. But not understanding this mathematical character leads to an overly complex, *ad hoc* view of software based on historical and accidental ideas, which are often reinvented in ignorance and haste.

The work of E. W. Dijkstra and C. A. R. Hoare has been a major force in this rediscovery of software as mathematics.† Dijkstra has given an argument that sums up the case we want to make here:‡

> As soon as programming emerges as a battle against unmastered complexity, it is quite natural that one turns to that mental discipline whose main purpose has been for centuries to apply effective structuring to otherwise unmastered complexity. That mental discipline is more or less familiar to all of us, it is called Mathematics. If we take the existence of the impressive body of Mathematics as the experimental evidence for the opinion that for the human mind the mathematical method is indeed the most effective way to come to grips with complexity, we have no choice any longer: we should reshape our field of programming in such a way that, the mathematician's methods become equally applicable to our programming problems, for there are no other means.

---

† See, for example,
O.-J. Dahl, E. W. Dijkstra, and C. A. R. Hoare, *Structured Programming* (London and New York, Academic Press) 1972; and C. A. R. Hoare, "An Axiomatic Basis for Computer Programming," *Communications of the ACM*, vol. 12, no. 10 (October 1969): pp. 576–583.
‡ E. W. Dijkstra, "On a Methodology of Design," MC-25 Informatica symposium, MC Tract 37, Mathematisch Centrum, Amsterdam, Holland, 1971: pp. 4.1–4.10.

MENTAL WEIGHT LIFTING

Fifty years ago swimming champions were products of long hours of swimming practice—swimming and swimming and swimming. But these days, when the varsity swimming team assembles in the fall, emphasis is also placed on running and weight lifting to build stamina and muscles more effectively.

There is a similar lesson to learn in programming. A previous generation of programmers learned by programming and programming and programming—sometimes this led to one year of experience repeated ten times, rather than ten years of experience. For this reason, we will stress mental weight lifting for programming that develops capabilities for precise logical expression. Precise logical expression requires a discipline of thought that is invaluable in programming but that is easily bypassed in simple programming problems through ignorance or intent. In either case, the result is frustration and inability in more complex programming problems because of simple lessons bypassed.

We all learned in elementary mathematics courses that it wasn't enough just to get the right answers if we couldn't show how we got them. There was good reason: Though we might guess the answers on simple problems, we won't be able to do so on complex ones. But a systematic process for getting answers to simple problems will scale up to the complex ones. Structured programming provides a systematic process for creating correct programs, but the steps require mental precision rather than clever guesses. There is still room and reason for insight and ingenuity, but they should be addressed to the strategy of programming and not to its mechanics.

ABOUT THIS BOOK

This book is organized into seven chapters. Chapters 1 through 3 deal with context-setting, and concepts and notation for precise communication in the software development process. Chapter 4 defines key mathematical properties of programs, which are elaborated and applied to program reading, program verification, and program writing in Chapters 5, 6, and 7, respectively.

Chapter 1 introduces the idea of programs as mathematical objects whose correctness is subject to rules of logic and reason. A central thesis is that, by applying the principles of structured programming and its mathematics, programmers can expect to consistently write error-free programs. The chapter concludes with a discussion of the need for conceptual integrity and rigor in program design. Chapter 2 summarizes principles of logical expression, both in writing good English and in the use of mathematical logic, sets, functions, and grammars. Effective logical expression is essential for precise communication in software development. A process design language (PDL) is introduced in Chapter 3 as a means for precise expression of program designs. PDL is composed of a prescribed outer syntax of control, data, and system structures with important mathematical properties, and a flexible inner syntax of operations and tests.

Chapter 4 introduces a particular understanding of program designs in PDL as expressions in an algebra of functions. Such an approach permits mathematical rigor and precision in the design and development of software systems of any size. In the Structure Theorem, a small set of PDL control structures is shown to be sufficient to represent the logic of any arbitrarily complex program, and the concept of a structured program is defined. The proof of the Structure Theorem prescribes a methodology for converting any arbitrary program into a structured program.

We believe that the quality and clarity of one's own writing, whether for programs or prose, benefits from critical analysis of the works of others, and so in this book we introduce principles of program reading before program writing. In Chapter 5, function concepts are used to develop systematic reading and documentation techniques for structured programs, which are applied in a case study to the analysis of a published program.

Chapter 6 develops a function-theoretic basis for the correctness of structured programs. Correctness verification of loop-free programs is carried out by case analysis and substitution, and the Iteration–Recursion Lemma is introduced to reduce the verification of looping programs to the verification of loop-free programs. The Correctness Theorem summarizes verification requirements for the structures of PDL, and both formal and informal proof techniques are shown. The Invariant Status Theorem gives a systematic means for deriving loop invariants, and an alternate proof technique based on invariants is described. Finally, theoretical techniques for the derivation of structured programs are defined, for insight into the program design process.

Chapter 7 describes function-based techniques for designing structured programs. A central theme is the need to keep complexity intellectually manageable in program design. The processes of stepwise refinement and stepwise reorganization are illustrated as means to limit complexity, by localizing design decisions and correctness arguments. The chapter concludes with case studies of the critical differences between program detailing and program design, and between heuristic and rigorous design methods.

TO THE READER

Writing this book has been an adventure of some duration, during which time we have come to entirely new understandings about both the subject matter and effective means for teaching it. We have not exhausted either of these topics, so what is here is a summing up for now. But we do have the conviction that the subject matter is deep; we have observed that it gives people new power to deal with complexity in software design. This new power is crucial because, with the advent of structured programming, the standards of achievement have changed radically, just as the standards for doing engineering changed with the introduction of calculus.

This book is dedicated first to the new programmer beginning a professional career in software engineering, who already knows how to program computers and presumably has been well taught in structured programming from the beginning. But a beginning programmer needs a deeper foundation to cope with pressures that lie ahead—pressures from the complexities of ill-defined problems and poorly conceived software development tools, and most of all, pressures from large-scale, difficult deadline projects. All of these pressures will cry out for shortcuts and compromises. But many of these siren calls are pitfalls that lead to more difficulties and frustrations than can be imagined. Without strong inner discipline, based on a deep understanding of how to deal with massive logical designs and their complexities, the best of intentions and techniques are soon swamped. So take heed. This book begins with elementary notions, but just knowing about them is not enough; it is necessary to know them deeply and to understand their relation to the practice of large-scale logical design.

This book is also dedicated to the professional development of those more-experienced programmers who have already made or are about to make the transition to structured programming. The motivation for going to structured programming is easy to see with a healthy firsthand appreciation for the complexities and frustrations of sizable programming projects. A new look at the very foundations of programming discipline can help experienced programmers to recognize opportunities for simplification and rigor in such large and complex projects.

Finally, this book is dedicated to programming managers. The management of programming projects is a difficult and rewarding job. But the lack of sound technical direction is as disastrous as the lack of good organization or personnel motivation in programming management. This book can help with the technical part of the management problem. We believe it is vital that management be sensitive about the need to simplify requirements and the need for adequate time to develop conceptually sound designs. We also believe it is vital that management be well informed about technical problems and that managers be at ease with the language of the problem-solvers. Programmers should know more than this book covers in programming, and managers should know more than this book covers in strategies for system development. What this book does promote is a common methodology for precise communication between programmers and managers. For in the final analysis, there is no such thing as technical or management communication, only human communication.

ACKNOWLEDGEMENTS

We have benefitted from the encouragement and helpful suggestions of many people in writing this book. We wish especially to thank the following people for their valuable comments: Joel Aron, Terry Baker, Victor Basili, Richard Case, Jeffrey Gishen, David Gries, Matthew Hecht, Roy Maddux, Matthew Perriens, and K. S. Shankar. It is also our pleasure to acknowledge Penny Troutman, who did the major share of typing on the manuscript, as well as the typing support provided by Sharon Deason, Carolyn Duter, Sonja Ouellette, Debbie Shraga, and Sharon Warren. Finally, we are grateful to IBM for allowing much of the work on the book to be done using company time and resources. We emphasize, however, that the views expressed are our own and in no way constitute an official statement on the part of IBM.

Gaithersburg, Maryland   R. C. L.
February 1979   H. D. M.
                                                            B. I. W.

Contents

1
Precision Programming

1.1 PROGRAMMING IN THE SMALL

1.1.1 How to Write Correct Programs and Know It

There is an old myth about programming today, and there is a new reality. The old myth is that programming must be an error prone, cut-and-try process of frustration and anxiety. The new reality is that you can learn to consistently design and write programs that are correct from the beginning and that prove to be error free in their testing and subsequent use.

By practicing principles of structured programming and its mathematics, you should be able to write correct programs and convince yourself and others that they are correct by logic and reason, rather than by trial and error. Your programs should ordinarily execute properly the first time you try them, and from then on. If you are a professional programmer, errors in program logic should be extremely rare, because you can prevent them from entering your programs by positive action on your part. Programs do not acquire bugs as people do germs—just by being around other buggy programs. They acquire bugs only from their authors.

There is a simple reason why you should commit yourself to writing programs that are free of errors from the very start. It is that you will never be able to establish that a program has no errors in it by testing. Since there is no way to be certain that you have found the *last* error, your real opportunity to gain confidence in a program is to never find the *first* error. The ultimate faith you can have in one of your programs is in the thought process that created it. With every error you find in testing and use, that faith is undermined. Even if you have found the last error left in your program, you cannot be certain it is the last one.

1

Now the new reality is that ordinary programmers, with ordinary care, can learn to write programs which are error free from their inception. Just knowing that this is possible is half the battle. Learning how to write such programs is the other half. And gaining experience in writing correct programs, small ones at first, then larger ones, provides a new psychological basis for sustained concentration in programming that is difficult to appreciate without direct personal experience.

It will be difficult (but not impossible) to achieve no first error in a thousand-line program. But, with theory and discipline, it will not be difficult to achieve no first error in a fifty-line program nine times in ten. The methods of structured programming will permit you to write that thousand-line program in twenty steps of fifty lines each, not as separate subprograms, but as a continuously expanding and executing partial program. If eighteen of those twenty steps have no first error, and the other two are readily corrected, you can have very high confidence in the resulting thousand-line program.

The basis for this new precision in programming is neither human infallibility, nor being more careful, nor trying harder. The basis is understanding programs as mathematical objects that are subject to logic and reason, and rules for orderly combination (whether a program operates in numbers, text, or whatever). People still make mistakes doing mathematical reasoning, because people are fallible. But they make fewer mistakes, and they can check each other's work, to let even fewer mistakes through. The result is enough added precision in reasoning and communication to change programming from a cut-and-try ad hoc process to an orderly technical process.

1.1.2   What Is a Correct Program?

A correct program defines a procedure for a stated processor to satisfy a stated specification. Programs may require changes or corrections from three kinds of difficulties:

1. Specification changes
2. Programming errors
3. Processor discrepancies

By processor we mean any complex of hardware and software that converts programs into their executions, through compiling, assembling, and so forth, as necessary.

If you don't know what a program is supposed to do or don't know how the processor is supposed to work, then you can't write a correct program. So we presume a known specification and a known processor throughout. Even so, a practicing programmer must be prepared to deal with incomplete

and changing specifications and with processors that do not behave the way
their software/hardware manuals say. For these external difficulties we have
no simple remedy. But a radical reduction in programming errors can help
isolate difficulties in the other areas. Nevertheless, the usual experience in
programming often fails to separate these three sources of difficulty, so that
programming errors—lumped in with everything else—seem much more
inevitable than they really are. And the logical precision you develop as a
professional programmer serves well to improve your skills in recognizing
the need for, and in developing, good specifications, and in being able to
read, understand, and anticipate difficulties in processor descriptions.

Writing correct programs does not mean that programs can be written
once and for all. It means that they can be written to do exactly what is
intended of them. But as intentions change, program changes are required as
well. The same opportunities and principles apply to the program changes; if
programs are well designed and explained, you should be able to modify
them correctly as well as to write them correctly to begin with.

1.1.3   Proofs of Program Correctness

It is possible for professional programmers, with sufficient care and concentration, to consistently write correct programs by applying the mathematical
principles of structured programming. Those same principles also permit
mathematical proofs of program correctness to be carried out to any desired
degree of rigor, both during and after program construction.

A mathematical proof is an agenda for a repeatable experiment, just as
an experiment in a physics or chemistry laboratory. But the main subject in
each experiment is another person instead of physical objects or material.
The intended result of the experimenter is a subjective conviction on the part
of the other person that a given logical hypothesis leads to a given logical
conclusion. The experiment may be carried out in a conversation, or collec-
tively in a lecture, or in writing. A successful experiment ends in a subjective
conviction by a listener or reader that the hypothesis implies the conclusion.
The conviction may be incorrect either in accepting a logical falsity or in
rejecting a logical verity. The conviction may be correct, but based on faulty
reasoning. As noted, any human fallibility may be present because reasoning
is a human activity; that is, an agreement that a proof is correct and the
actual correctness of the proof are two quite independent things.

The conversation deals with a proof that the hypothesis leads to the
conclusion. The proof may consist of a single claim, "It is obvious," or a
sequence of such claims for a succession of intermediate conclusions, each of
which may serve as a hypothesis for a later conclusion. But in the final
analysis no other claim less than "It is obvious" is possible, because if one

starts to explain why "It is obvious," the explanation must lead finally to a new sub-sequence of such claims, "It is obvious," and so on. At each claim, the subject agrees or disagrees; in the first case the experiment continues, and in the second case the experiment terminates.

Mathematical notation plays no role in the proof, except in its effect on the person who is the experimental subject. What mathematical notation does is facilitate human communication and memory. It permits a succession of claims to be stated and agreed to rapidly, so that more ground can be covered for the same human effort. Mathematics also permits a person, using pencil and paper, to extend his memory for details (e.g., doing long division or simplifying an algebraic expression). It even permits humans to agree on rules for agreeing about proof claims (as in mathematical logic). In fact, the computer is itself another way of extending human effort in proof activities, with agreed rules of proof to be used in automatic theorem-proving programs.

What is a convincing proof? Clearly that depends on the person who is the experimental subject. There are many alternative conversations possible about the same hypothesis and conclusion. If there are too few steps, the leap in intuition may be too large. But if there are too many steps, human exhaustion or lack of interest may set in. So there is a balance needed. But it is a typically human problem whose resolution requires human experience and judgment.

Why bother with mathematics at all, if it only leads to subjective convictions? Because that is the only kind of reasoned conviction possible, and because the principal experimental subject who examines your program proofs is yourself! Mathematics provides language and procedure for your own peace of mind.

1.1.4   An Intuitive Approach to Program Correctness

In a small example below, we prove the correctness of a program in flowchart form, using direct analysis and deduction. We call the approach intuitive because it deals directly with program operations and does not exploit the algebraic properties of structured programs. In Chapter 6, we develop a function-theoretic approach to program correctness that utilizes these algebraic properties, but our objective here is simply to show that a proof of program correctness is possible in concrete terms.

Consider a program that is required to find the integer part of the square root, say y, of a given integer, say x, as diagrammed in Fig. 1.1. (Note that the proof method is by no means restricted to numerical problems.) First, the specification of the program needs to be stated precisely, as shown by the logical conditions attached to its entry and exit lines. The entry condi-

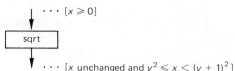

Figure 1.1

tion requires that x be zero or positive, so this particular program will not have to cope with negative values of x. The exit condition requires that y be the greatest integer equal to or less than the square root of x, and also that x be unchanged. A more general program may be required to handle any value for x, but its exit condition would merely be more complicated, and make the illustration longer.

A simple program that purports to satisfy this specification by successive incrementing is given in Fig. 1.2 (read $y := y + 1$ as "y is assigned the value $y + 1$"). Some trial and error may have gone into its invention, but an examination of initial x values 0, 1, 2, 4, 5, 9, ... seems to indicate that the program is correct. However, examining (and testing) such cases usually cannot be done exhaustively, and a more general approach is needed.

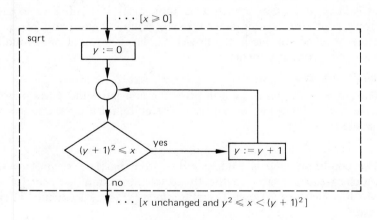

Figure 1.2

Logical entry/exit conditions can now be derived for every line in the flowchart of Fig. 1.2. After some logical invention (how is discussed later, in Chapter 6) the annotated flowchart shown in Fig. 1.3 results, where the conditions have been given short names for ease of discussion. It can now be proved that this whole set of conditions will necessarily be satisfied if only the single condition $in: [x \geq 0]$ (read "in, defined as $x \geq 0$") is satisfied.

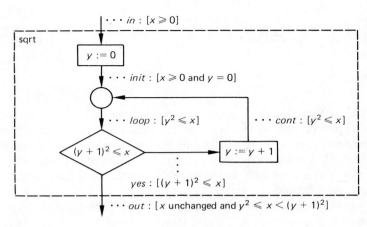

Figure 1.3

Therefore, in particular, the program will correctly compute values for x and y that satisfy the *out* condition, the specification of the program. The proof will consist of a subproof for each condition except *in*:$[x \geq 0]$, which is assumed. The sequence of subproofs is immaterial. It is sufficient to ensure that every condition is ultimately proved, assuming the truth of the immediately prior conditions in the flowchart. Thus, we state each condition followed by a proof argument:

1. *init*:$[x \geq 0$ and $y = 0]$

    The entry condition *in*:$[x \geq 0]$ gives the first part, and y has just been set to zero, giving the second part. Therefore, *init*:$[x \geq 0$ and $y = 0]$ is satisfied.

2. *loop*:$[y^2 \leq x]$

    The condition *loop* is entered either from *init*:$[x \geq 0$ and $y = 0]$ in which case *loop* is satisfied directly, or from the condition *cont*:$[y^2 \leq x]$, which is identical to *loop*. Therefore, *loop*:$[y^2 \leq x]$ is satisfied in either case.

3. *cont*:$[y^2 \leq x]$

    The condition *cont* is the exit condition when y is set to $y + 1$ with entry condition *yes*:$[(y + 1)^2 \leq x]$, so $y^2 \leq x$ (after y is set to $y + 1$), and *cont*:$[y^2 \leq x]$ is satisfied.

4. *yes*:$[(y + 1)^2 \leq x]$

    The test $(y + 1)^2 \leq x$ has just been passed successfully.

5. *out*:$[x$ unchanged and $y^2 \leq x < (y + 1)^2]$

First, an examination of the entire program shows that x is reset nowhere, and must therefore be unchanged. Second, the test $(y + 1)^2 \leq x$ has just failed, so therefore $(y + 1)^2 > x$. Finally, the entry condition $loop:[y^2 \leq x]$ for the test must still hold. The last two conditions can be combined into $y^2 \leq x < (y + 1)^2$. Therefore, condition *out* is satisfied.

The foregoing is a proof of correctness for the program, given its specification. It shows that the program will compute the correct output whenever it terminates. That the program does terminate can be seen by noting that y is incremented by 1 each time through the loop, and the loop test must eventually fail.

In this example, a key logical invention is condition 2, $loop:[y^2 \leq x]$, which holds every time the loop is entered (reentered). It is called an "invariant condition" and serves as a keystone—all of the other conditions can be derived by direct rules of reasoning from $in:[x \geq 0]$ and $loop:[y^2 \leq x]$ (once $loop:[y^2 \leq x]$ has been invented). For simple programs the invention of invariant conditions can often be done by inspection of operations. For more complex programs a systematic approach is required, as described in Chapter 6. But Chapter 6 goes beyond these ideas, to develop a theory of program correctness based on hierarchies of mathematical functions, for which invariant conditions are simply not required.

1.2   PROGRAMMING IN THE LARGE

1.2.1   Conceptual Integrity

The principal lesson of the past 25 years of programming is that software development is more difficult than it appeared to be at the outset. Without a clean and compelling design, a large software system soon becomes a jumble of confusion and frustration. Local details may be easily understood and checked, but the system gets beyond intellectual control anyway.

Fred Brooks, in *The Mythical Man-Month: Essays on Software Engineering*, states that "conceptual integrity is *the* most important consideration in system design" [p. 42] and backs it up with a dramatic recollection of his experience in managing the development of OS/360, as follows [pp. 47–48]:

> It is a very humbling experience to make a multimillion-dollar mistake, but it is also very memorable. I vividly recall the night we decided how to organize the actual writing of external specifications for OS/360. The manager of architecture, the manager of control program implementation, and I were threshing out the plan, schedule, and division of responsibilities.

The architecture manager had 10 good men. He asserted that they could write the specifications and do it right. It would take ten months, three more than the schedule allowed.

The control program manager had 150 good men. He asserted that they could prepare the specifications, with the architecture team coordinating; it would be well-done and practical, and he could do it on schedule. Furthermore, if the architecture team did it, his 150 men would sit twiddling their thumbs for ten months.

To this the architecture manager responded that if I gave the control program team the responsibility, the result would *not* in fact be on time, but would also be three months late, and of much lower quality. I did, and it was. He was right on both counts. Moreover, the lack of conceptual integrity made the system far more costly to build and change, and I would estimate that it added a year to debugging time.†

1.2.2   The Difference Between Heuristics and Rigor

The principal basis for maintaining conceptual integrity in software development is rigorous design. It was imagined in the early days of software development that *heuristic design*‡ methods were sufficient. Observation and experience seemed to be reliable guides to design, and indeed, the possibility of rigorous design methods was hardly considered. After all, it seemed a simple but tedious matter for clever people to think up all the data processing pieces that had to be done and make sure that nothing was left out. But the trouble is that such a heuristic design is usually difficult, and often virtually impossible, to prove correct. As Brooks points out, we now know better.

In order to visualize the devastation of heuristic design, imagine an important, much used, program that almost always works—the trouble is in "almost always." Such a program must be patched as errors are reported, and the patches patched, and so on, until its logic scarcely resembles the original article. In fact, the program will become highly idiosyncratic, with peculiarities that depend on the very sequence in which errors were found—a different sequence would have led to a different program. This error history may be prevented if designers are clever enough to foresee all errors of a heuristic design before implementing and releasing the

---

† Frederick P. Brooks, *The Mythical Man-Month: Essays on Software Engineering* (Reading, Mass.: Addison-Wesley, 1975).

‡ Note that *heuristic design* refers to design by trial and error, not to rigorous design of heuristic programs, as found, for example, in automatic translation of natural language.

program. But the design will still be idiosyncratic, based on the imagined error history.

In contrast, a *rigorous design* can be shown to be error free by its very form, in self-evident arguments and proofs. A rigorous design may include the form of a *state machine* that defines a closed set of system transitions, or a *recursive function* that defines a search space, or perhaps a *formal grammar* that defines all possible inputs and outputs for a program. But whatever the logical form, a rigorous design is one that can be shown to be correct, before getting into its implementation. A rigorous design will take more creativity and thought than a heuristic one, but once created a rigorous design is more stable. A rigorous design should survive its implementation, not be swamped by it, and provide a framework for the intellectual control of changes to the implementation as requirements change.

The difference between heuristics and rigor in design can be illustrated in constructing a tic-tac-toe playing program. Anyone with a pad and pencil can readily figure out what to do next in any situation. But listing all such possibilities may be impractical. So the next step might be a heuristic approach, based on introspection. The beginning of such a process (oversimplified for illustration) might be "play in priority order, if possible, center, any corner, any side." This will account for some reasonable moves but will fail in many situations, and an analysis of these situations will suggest additional criteria of play. But with each addition, a less obvious situation may still lead to a failure. After many such additions, the program may indeed be capable of perfect tic-tac-toe. But it will be difficult to prove, except for an exhaustive analysis, which itself will be hard to prove complete. As noted before, such a heuristically developed design, even though possibly correct, will be highly idiosyncratic based on the history of imagined (or real) failures encountered in play.

In Chapter 7, we contrast heuristic and rigorous designs for a change-making program and a tic-tac-toe program to illustrate this point in depth.

1.2.3 Structured Programs and Good Design

Structured programs are written for people to read and understand. At first, they may seem a little more difficult to write than unstructured programs. But a typical program uses up much more human effort being read than being written (including being read by its author), so there is great value indeed in producing readable structured programs. Readable programs are beneficiaries of good design and good style—of good precise logical expression.

Good design means finding a good solution to a problem that is often ill-defined. Therefore, there are usually two steps: (1) define a right problem, and (2) invent a good solution. A few problems (very few) are so well known and universal that a simple phrase will define them; for example, sort a linear table, find the sum of a list of numbers. Most problems need to be formulated more precisely, with respect to both what is to be done and what logical resources are available. For example, finding a sum of a list of numbers is one thing if an adder is available, another thing if an inner product operation is available, and still another if only character operations are available.

A structured program does not guarantee a good design. Structured programming introduces the possibility of good design but not the necessity. A good design provides a solution that is no more complex than the problem it solves. A good design is based on deep simplicities, not on simple-mindedness. Usually, a good design is the last thing you think of, not the first thing. A familiar example of an overcomplicated solution is the earth-centered description of the solar system. Two thousand years ago humans attempted to explain the motion of the planets with epicycles. It took another thousand years and much personal pain for people to put the sun at the center and make the explanation much simpler thereby. The moral is that if it took a thousand years for mankind's best and brightest to solve this problem, one shouldn't feel badly about taking an extra hour to think harder about a program design.

Good program design—finding deep simplicities in a complex logical task—leads to work reduction. It can reduce a 500-line program that makes sense line-by-line to 100 lines that make sense as a whole. Good design can reduce a 50,000-line program impossible to code correctly to a 20,000-line program that runs error free.

1.2.4   The Difference Between Detailing and Design

A computer program doesn't need its design—all it needs is its code. No matter what lofty ideas went into the program, if the code is right, the computer runs right. Since these facts are indisputable, it is small wonder that program designs are usually regarded as stepping stones to executing code—and throwaway stepping stones at that. There is only one difficulty with this argument; although the logic is absolutely correct, no one is smart enough to build large and complex programs that way without untold trouble and frustration.

In fact, even though the term *design* is used in programming, the term *detailing* is often more accurate. Detailing is writing a lot of details about what programs have to do, what data formats are, how program parts interact, and so on. Detailing is characterized by a preoccupation with particulars, to the exclusion of overall program structure and design. In contrast, designing is a step-by-step expansion of a set of well-defined requirements specifications into high-level, then successively lower-level, programs and subspecifications, until the level of code is reached. A program design has a hierarchical structure; it can be viewed both vertically, from requirements down to code, and horizontally, across the design at each level of detail.

Designing produces details, but detailing does not produce design.

One symptom of detailing, as opposed to design, is inflexibility. When details reveal that a project schedule and budget are jeopardized, how easy is it to subset requirements and assign new priorities to meet the challenge? When details reveal that performance is jeopardized, how easily is reanalysis undertaken? Are programming projects managed by working out mountains of details and just seeing how things come out? Or is systematic redesign used to make development means and ends meet?

Another symptom of detailing, as opposed to design, is the system-integration crunch—the frustration of program parts not going together as planned, along with the "last error" problem (a new "last error" every test run). Program parts written from detailings are based on faith in human infallibility, a notably risky proposition. The fixes undertaken in the integration crunch bring new details and new idiosyncrasies not imagined in the detailing. The more fixes, the more idiosyncratic and accidental the final result becomes.

The final symptom of detailing is the maintenance of an idiosyncratic system. The merit of the program is that it works most of the time. But discovering why it doesn't work is a major detective story. In fact, one way to solve difficult corrective maintenance is to stop using the unreliable function—the ultimate solution is to stop using the program.

In Chapter 7, we illustrate the difference between detailing and design in the construction of a program to do long division.

1.2.5   Design Validation by Top-Down Development

The necessity of top-down development in large software systems is born out of bitter experience with top-down design followed by bottom-up development. In bottom-up development, in which low-level code is written early and system integration occurs late, poor design is often hidden until late in integration, after much functional code has been written and tested only to be discarded. Conversely, in top-down development, the control programs that integrate functional code are written and tested first, and the functional code is added progressively. In fact, the development proceeds on an incremental basis, level by level, with testing and integration accomplished during the programming process rather than afterwards. At each level, required common services and data are defined and developed within the process as well.

In a software system, top-down development typically starts with a logical design for the harmonious cooperation of several programs through access to several shared data sets. For example, a financial information system may include a file maintenance program, several data entry programs (which produce transaction files for the file maintenance program), several data retrieval/report programs that access the files, system usage and billing programs, and so forth. Although each such program can be developed top-down independently, top-down system testing requires cooperation between them, for example, data entry programs providing input for the file maintenance program, which in turn creates files for data retrieval programs.

In retrospect, it is easy to see that the advantage of top-down development over bottom-up development is the advantage of a closed-loop feedback process over an open-loop process. In a bottom-up development, the programs are not tested as part of the final system until the end of development; in top-down development, they are tested in their system environment right away. If there are design or programming errors, top-down development discovers them early, when freshly programmed and when the original programmers are still on hand. But bottom-up development often leaves errors undiscovered until integration time, when the original programmers have often departed.

Top-down development is more difficult to design for than bottom-up development, but the extra effort in design is made up in integration and testing. The problem of design in top-down development is not only how the final system will look, but also how the system under development will look at every stage of its construction. Building a bridge illustrates the problem. In designing a bridge on paper, a spanning girder can be drawn first, to hang unattached until other members are drawn later to support it. But to actually construct that same bridge, a construction plan is needed that allows girders to be placed and pinned one by one in support of one another until the bridge is completed.

Building a software system bottom-up is like building a paper bridge. No construction plan is needed, only the final design, and everyone hopes it all goes together as planned. If people were infallible, especially designers, no construction plans would be needed.

Building a software system top-down is like building a real bridge. Finding the proper tops is a significant technical task. A proper top is one that executes as a partial system early in the development, and which provides the basis for adding intermediate and final programs in a continuous code/integrate/test iteration process.

1.2.6   The Basis for Software Reliability Is Design, Not Testing

It is well known that a software system cannot be made reliable by testing. If programs are well designed in both data structure and control structure, there is no contest between a programmer and a computer in finding errors; the programmer will win hands down. So the first defenses against errors are well-designed programs and preventative proofing by authors themselves.

But effective design can do far more than make errors easy to discover. Design can reduce the size of a system, reduce its interconnections, reduce the complexity of its program specifications. In short, good design makes correct systems possible out of correct programs. Since in structured programming every level of program development is conducted in identical terms (in contrast to traditional descriptions of words at the top, code at the bottom), high-level design can be scrutinized and critiqued for correctness as well as low-level design. In fact, it is extremely cost effective to validate high-level design before lower-level expansions proceed, rather than after. An important by-product of a design and validation process is traceability of requirements in every level of the design. It is this traceability that gives the flexibility to solve budget, schedule, or performance problems at the right level in the design, without having to start all over with a new detailing process.

A designer has the opportunity, using the top-down design and development discipline of structured programming, to keep the expanding design under good intellectual control, to discover the deepest simplicities possible at every level, step by step, before becoming swamped in a sea of details that make the development problem one of memorizing accidentals and oddities rather than one of clean logical design.

2
Elements of
Logical
Expression

2.1 OVERVIEW

Programming is a specialized form of creative design in writing. At first glance, it seems that programs need only be read and followed by machines and that matters of taste and style are irrelevant. But quite the opposite is true. Programs must be read and understood by people, as part of the creation process and so that they can be trusted or modified to meet changing needs. Ability in both English composition and mathematical description is a critical requirement for good programming.

In this chapter we review some elements of English, mathematics, and other means of logical expression. We first discuss good English because much of your best thinking in programming will need to be expressed for people rather than for machines. Principles for writing clear, concise English are precisely those principles required for writing clear, concise program designs. Next, we review standard concepts and terminology of formal logic, sets, relations, and functions. We also remind the reader of recursive functions, state machines, list structures, formal grammars, and regular expressions. These expressive forms allow precision and rigor in design descriptions, and permit a wide range of human creativity and imagination to be applied in complex logical situations.

2.2 GOOD ENGLISH

2.2.1 Structure and Content

It has been observed time and again that there is a high correlation between the ability for clean written expression and the ability to program computers. A Japanese programming manager put it this way at a computing conference (in Japan), "The important language for the programmer to know well is not JCL or PL/I, it is Japanese!"

This empirical observation is not hard to explain. Good English requires organization and structure to separate forests from trees. It requires logical organization as well as the right words. Effective technical communication is achieved by a combination of structure and content. A jumbled, rambling compilation of absolutely correct content may be of little value because it is simply too difficult to understand or reference. Structure reduces the amount of human effort required to understand content—structure does not make up for the lack of content, but neither does content make up for the lack of structure.

A technical composition needs to be organized into sections, sections into subsections, and so on, for human understanding. Sometimes such a hierarchical organization can be supplemented by other devices that show more complex relations among sections and their content. For example, it may be useful to incorporate a precedence diagram that shows which sections must be read prior to other sections. Occasionally, descriptions of mutual dependence may be necessary that state that two or more sections need to be understood together and that no simple ordering in their reading is possible. For example, an operations manual of a computing system usually discusses related subjects, such as data organization and instruction format, which are best understood as a group rather than as a sequence of separate topics.

Whatever way a composition is organized, whatever additional relations are described to clarify its structure, the raw materials of structure are simply the same raw materials of content itself, namely, words and diagrams. But the words and diagrams describing structure are more important to the reader and must be chosen with more care by the writer. In their structural capacity, well-chosen section headings carry content in themselves—even more content per word than the text. For example, headings such as "Introduction," "Discussion," and "Analysis," don't take much thinking to invent, and don't carry much thought to the reader. But headings such as "The Problem of Unreliable Solder Joints" or "Three Factors in Solder Joint Failure" say a good deal more to the interested reader.

In fact, the headings, subheadings, and other means to display organization to the reader provide the writer an opportunity to index and abstract the text. Usually the writer knows the content better than the reader (at least at the point in time of the writing), so the usual error is to understructure, not overstructure, because "it is all so clear." Good headings and subheadings take work to compose; in fact, composing good headings frequently forces better organization of content—to put like considerations together and to separate distinct cases otherwise jumbled together.

A good mental guide is "the rule of five," based on the well-known human ability to relate about five objects of thought (plus or minus two) into a new object of thought. Management organizations frequently follow this pattern; for example, usually a department is made up of three to seven other departments. Applied to composition structure, the rule of five suggests five (plus or minus two) sentences/paragraph, paragraphs/subheading, subheadings/heading, and so on. From the top down, these headings can tell a story in themselves in the organization of the subject matter. Exceptions prove the rule: An important sentence can be a paragraph by itself. A very regular set of topics may exceed seven in number because their regularity permits human understanding as a pattern; for example, natural collections of objects, such as counties, states, or universities, may serve as subtopics on a given occasion (even there, a contextual grouping may be better, such as by region or size).

Effective writing is based on good structure—much like a program structure—that allows the reader to execute your reasoning, maintain your perspective, and be convinced of your conclusions. If your reasoning, perspective, and conclusions don't hang together, it will be difficult to write well about them. But in this case the problem isn't in the writing after all!

2.2.2   The Context of Communication

The communication of content in text, headings, diagrams, whatever, is always carried out in some context. The primary context is natural language, but usually there are more specialized contexts, based on common experience in programming, engineering, accounting, and so forth. These contexts are defined by literature and practice; for example, the field of electrical engineering describes a certain general context for communication. These contextual domains are seldom clearly defined. They are based on human activities, organizations, and sometimes on only similarities in background and thought.

A concerted effort to define a contextual domain for discourse occurs in mathematical logic, but even there a total definition is not possible. In mathematics, physical sciences, and engineering, the contextual domains are relatively rigorous, while in the somewhat general areas of social science, management science, business practice, and so forth, broader topics involve less well-defined contexts.

Whatever the context of communication, it is vital to understand it explicitly—what is the audience of the composition? what can its members be expected to know? and what kind of reasoning is meaningful to them? Sometimes the audience is a broad one. In that case, is a single composition the best approach, or should there be separate ones? For example, a programming system may require quite separate documents for user's guides, program maintenance, and operator's guides.

Specialized contexts permit more concise compositions and conciseness is often critical to communications. But there are ways of being concise in broader contexts, too. One way is through carefully chosen structures, which permit a reader to select levels of detail by the organization of the composition, possibly with appendices to handle full details. Another is to better formulate the subject matter of the composition into subtopics that permit more concise expository treatment, one by one, even though some duplication occurs overall.

Effective writing uses its context to good advantage. Complex ideas are not easy to express, and crucial assertions often need many qualifications. But surrounding an assertion with all of its qualifications often drowns it, instead, in a sea of words. Put the assertion up front, in few words; then add the qualifications, in plain sight, but not covering up the assertion.

2.2.3   Models of Communication

The model of mathematical deduction illustrates a definite communication strategy. In order to avoid circularity in definitions and reasoning, one identifies undefined objects in discourse, and new objects are then defined in terms of undefined or previously defined objects. In this way an attempt is made to localize the appearance of undefined objects in "axioms" at the beginning (and in "rules of inference"). In broader discourses, undefined objects may be introduced anywhere. While logically disconcerting, it may not be possible to do otherwise in general subjects.

And yet, good technical writing profits from the model of mathematical deduction. The use of the "axiom–theorem–proof" model provides a strong logical persuasion arising from the deductive aspects of a composition. The difficulty with this model is motivation and understanding in a broader setting. The "theorem" is typically an answer to some problem—but is it the "right problem," or even worth knowing answers to? The "proof" often describes constructive procedures for solving a problem, subject to the problem being worth solving. So the "axiom–theorem–proof" model of mathematics is an important model of technical communication in areas where motivation and perspective have been accomplished in some other way, perhaps even earlier in the same composition.

In inductive reasoning, another strategy is represented that begins with various concrete facts and events and associates them into more general conclusions and laws. Program designs are frequently justified in terms of concrete restrictions and machine availabilities. Such a program design may solve a problem, but often the problem is not stated, being implicit in the mind of the designer. Right then, it is critical to take the time to state the problem being solved. In fact, finding the right problem is often more difficult than solving it. Thus, a very effective strategy in broad questions is a problem definition and solution sequence: What is the problem? What are the resources available? What is a good way to solve the problem with the resources available?

2.3   FORMAL LOGIC

2.3.1   Logical Propositions

Formal logic deals with human communication and mutual human beliefs about the truth of statements. It does this by providing an axiomatic calculus (a mechanical means of calculation based on a set of axioms) for deriving new beliefs about various combinations of such statements and beliefs about them. Two such systems of formal logic are discussed below, the *propositional calculus*, and (using an enlarged set of axioms) the *predicate calculus*.

A statement is called a *logical proposition*, or proposition for short; a human belief about a proposition is called its *truth value*, or value for short. The mutual beliefs may be the result of a conversation or of a written discussion read later by others. The value of a proposition is one of two possibilities, namely, *true* and *false*, for which symbols T, F, or even 1, 0, are often used. More precisely, propositions are regarded as names (aliases) for the truth values *true, false*. For example, "a circle is round" is another name for *true*, just as "2 + 4" and "six" are other names for the number called 6. Logical systems are possible with additional truth values, such as *unknown*, *undefined*, and *possibly*, but we shall restrict our attention to two-value systems.

2.3.2   The Propositional Calculus

There is no simple or universal rule in logic to decide whether a statement in natural language is a proposition or not. That decision itself reduces to a matter of human belief. But when a collection of statements is admitted as propositions, along with truth values for each, the propositional calculus provides a fixed set of ways of combining old propositions into new ones, and for calculating the truth values of the new propositions from the old values. Conversely, the propositional calculus provides ways of breaking down complex propositions into combinations of simpler propositions so that the truth values of the complex propositions can be calculated systematically from the truth values of the simpler ones.

A combination of propositions is called a *logical expression*. The common types of logical expressions are

not   For any one proposition p, its denial, denoted $\sim p$.

and   For any two propositions p, q, the assertion of both, denoted $p \wedge q$.

or   For any two propositions p, q, the assertion of at least one, denoted $p \vee q$.

equals   For any two propositions p, q, the assertion that p and q name the same logical value, denoted $p \leftrightarrow q$.

implies For any two propositions p, q, the assertion that if p is *true* then q must be *true*, denoted $p \rightarrow q$.

The truth values for these expressions, each itself a proposition, depend on the truth values of the propositions in the expressions, and are given for each possible case as axioms in *truth tables*. The truth table for these expressions, for any propositions p and q, is

Rule	p	q	*not* $\sim p$	*and* $p \wedge q$	*or* $p \vee q$	*equals* $p \leftrightarrow q$	*implies* $p \rightarrow q$
1	T	T	F	T	T	T	T
2	T	F	F	F	T	F	F
3	F	T	T	F	T	F	T
4	F	F	T	F	F	T	T

Such a truth table contains a rule (row) for each possible set of truth values of propositions in an expression. The truth table above gives truth values that seem sensible in view of the verbalizations of the expressions, but a word of warning is in order. It is the truth tables that are definitive in describing truth values of expressions and not the apparent sense of the expressions.†

Since logical expressions are themselves logical propositions, with truth values derived from the truth values of their constituent propositions, they can be used in other logical expressions to form *compound logical expressions*. Just as in compound arithmetic expressions, parentheses can be used to specify groupings and the order in which subexpressions are to be evaluated. A compound logical expression of several types of elementary expressions, such as those given above, can be evaluated a step at a time by

---

† The truth table for implies is not necessarily intuitive for the cases $p = $ F, but mathematical experience testifies to the usefulness of this definition which separates implication and causality as independent concepts (and does not address causality in any way).

replacing any innermost parenthesized expression by its truth value, as illustrated below. The leftmost inner parenthesized expression is evaluated at
each step, and the means for reaching each new expression is explained by
the truth table row invoked:

$(F \wedge (\sim T)) \vee ((F \to T) \vee (T \leftrightarrow T))$

$(F \wedge \quad\quad F\ ) \vee ((F \to T) \vee (T \leftrightarrow T))$ *not*, by Rule 1

$F \quad\quad\quad\quad \vee ((F \to T) \vee (T \leftrightarrow T))$ *and*, by Rule 4

$F \quad\quad\quad\quad \vee (\ T \quad\quad \vee (T \leftrightarrow T))$ *implies*, by Rule 3

$F \quad\quad\quad\quad \vee (\ T \quad\quad \vee\ T \quad\quad)$ *equals*, by Rule 1

$F \quad\quad\quad\quad \vee\ T$ *or*, by Rule 1

T *or*, by Rule 3

2.3.3   The Predicate Calculus

The propositional calculus deals with the analysis of propositions composed
of simpler propositions; but the simplest of the propositions are viewed as
undivided wholes. We can, however, view simple propositions as subject–
predicate structures, and, in particular, deal with statements whose subject is
unknown. Thus, instead of the proposition

A circle is round

we might consider the predicate

is round

Instead of the (*false*) proposition

$6500 < 5000$

we might consider the predicate

$salary < 5000$

or even (given values for table and minimum)

$(name\ in\ table) \wedge (salary < minimum)$

where name and salary are terms corresponding to unspecified data. (That
is, the expression has no more information content than·"(_____ in table) $\wedge$

(____ < minimum).") A useful extension to the propositional calculus that deals with such statements is the *predicate calculus*.

A statement that contains one or more *variables* (i.e., placeholders that name various possibilities), each of which may occur one or more times in the statement, is called a *predicate* (also proposition form, propositional function, or open sentence). Predicates are not necessarily propositions, because the variable may prevent assignment of a value of *true* or *false*. Such a statement may, however, become a proposition when its variables are assigned definite values. For example,

$$\text{(name in table)} \wedge \text{(salary} < \text{minimum)}$$

is not a proposition, but the assertion

$$\text{(Green, Ed in table)} \wedge (6500 < 5000)$$

is a (*false*) proposition.

It is often useful to convert predicates into propositions in more general ways, short of assigning definite values to their variables. Let $p(x)$ be a predicate that becomes a proposition when x is given a possible value. Then we define two *quantifiers* for such a statement that lead to new propositions:

there exists $(\exists x)$ (Existential quantifier.) The assertion that some possible value of x exists such that

$$p(x) = true$$

written $\exists x\, p(x)$, or $\exists x(p(x))$, or $(\exists x)(p(x))$

for all $(\forall x)$ (Universal quantifier.) The assertion that for all possible values of x

$$p(x) = true$$

written $\forall x\, p(x)$, or $\forall x(p(x))$, or $(\forall x)(p(x))$

Both $\exists x(p(x))$ and $\forall x(p(x))$ are propositions since, unlike $p(x)$, their evaluation (as *true* or *false*) doesn't depend upon the value of x. However

$$\exists x(p(x, y)) \qquad \text{and} \qquad \exists x(p(x)) \wedge q(x)$$

are *not* propositions. The former depends on the value of y; the latter depends on the value of x in $q(x)$, since $q(x)$ is not within the *scope* of the quantifier. A variable in the scope of a matching quantifier is said to be *bound*; otherwise it is said to be *free*. By binding the free variables of a predicate, we can create propositions; thus, from the examples above, we might obtain

$$\forall y(\exists x(p(x, y))) \quad \text{and} \quad \forall x(\exists x(p(x)) \wedge q(x))$$

or more simply

$$\forall y \exists x \ p(x, y) \quad \text{and} \quad \exists x \ p(x) \wedge \forall x \ q(x)$$

that are propositions.†

To illustrate this notation, we state several propositions, the plausibility of which the reader should verify, for any given $p(x)$, $q(x)$, and $r(x, y)$:

$$\forall x(\sim p(x)) \leftrightarrow \sim \exists x \ p(x)$$

$$\exists x(\sim p(x)) \leftrightarrow \sim \forall x \ p(x)$$

$$\exists x \exists y \ r(x, y) \leftrightarrow \exists y \exists x \ r(x, y)$$

$$\forall x \forall y \ r(x, y) \leftrightarrow \forall y \forall x \ r(x, y)$$

$$\forall x \ p(x) \rightarrow \exists x \ p(x)$$

$$\forall x(\sim(p(x) \wedge q(x)) \leftrightarrow \sim p(x) \vee \sim q(x))$$

$$\forall x(\sim(p(x) \vee q(x)) \leftrightarrow \sim p(x) \wedge \sim q(x))$$

One last word on notation is in order. We may wish to identify the domain of a quantifier, for example, the largest domain for which $\sqrt{x}$ is real. We recognize the domain to be $x \geq 0$, and express the proposition as

$$(\forall x, x \geq 0)(\sqrt{x} \text{ is real})$$

With a slight abbreviation in notation, we may write

$$(\forall x \geq 0)(\sqrt{x} \text{ is real})$$

In general though, the domain of a quantifier will be denoted by

$$(\forall x, p(x))(q(x)) \quad \text{or} \quad (\exists x, p(x))(q(x))$$

As an aside, these expressions are equivalent to

$$\forall x(p(x) \rightarrow q(x)) \quad \text{and} \quad \exists x(p(x) \rightarrow q(x))$$

respectively.

---

† Note $\forall x(\exists x(p(x)) \wedge q(x))$ is of the form $\forall x(r \wedge q(x))$, because $\exists x(p(x))$ is a proposition independent of x, and becomes $r \wedge \forall x \ q(x)$.

2.4   SETS AND FUNCTIONS

2.4.1   Sets

A *set* is any well-defined collection of objects, called *members* or *elements*. The relation of *membership* between a member, m, and a set, S, is written

$$m \in S$$

If m is not a member of S, we write

$$m \notin S$$

A set with no members is called the *empty set*, denoted $\emptyset$. Two sets are equal if they have the same members.

A set of elements can be listed using braces as delimiters, for example,

$$\text{fruit} = \{\text{apple, grape, orange}\}$$

The order of the members listed is immaterial, as is their duplication, for example,

$$\text{fruit} = \{\text{grape, apple, orange, apple}\}$$

since the members are still the same as above. The number of distinct elements of a set S is denoted by $|S|$, for example, $|\text{fruit}| = 3$. A set can be given by a *rule* for generating the members of a set, using a *set builder* notation, for example,

$$\text{fruit} = \{x \,|\, x = \text{apple or } x = \text{grape or } x = \text{orange}\}$$

where now the vertical bar reads "such that," and the expression is read "fruit is the name of the set containing members named x such that $x = $ apple or $x = $ grape or $x = $ orange." Given two sets, say A and B, we define their *union* $A \cup B$, *intersection* $A \cap B$, *difference* $A - B$ as follows:

$$A \cup B = B \cup A = \{x \,|\, x \in A \vee x \in B\}$$
$$A \cap B = B \cap A = \{x \,|\, x \in A \wedge x \in B\}$$
$$A - B = \{x \,|\, x \in A \wedge x \notin B\}$$

If every member of set A is also a member of a set B, we say A is a *subset* of B, written $A \subset B$. Thus,

$$A \subset A \cup B, \quad A \cap B \subset A, \quad A - B \subset A$$

The *cartesian product* of $(A1, A2, \ldots, An)$, where each element is a set name and n is some integer, is a set of lists, written

$$A1 \times A2 \times \cdots \times An = \{(a1, a2, \ldots, an) \,|\, a1 \in A1 \land a2 \in A2 \land \cdots \land an \in An\}$$

One example of a cartesian product is the familiar (x, y) rectangular coordinate system.

Note that whereas set union and intersection are commutative and associative, set difference and cartesian product are not; that is,

$$A \cup B = B \cup A \quad \text{and} \quad A \cap B = B \cap A$$
$$(A \cup B) \cup C = A \cup (B \cup C) \quad \text{and} \quad (A \cap B) \cap C = A \cap (B \cap C)$$

but

$$A - B \neq B - A \quad \text{and} \quad A \times B \neq B \times A$$
$$(A - B) - C \neq A - (B - C) \quad \text{and} \quad (A \times B) \times C \neq A \times (B \times C)$$

To illustrate the assertions about union, intersection, and difference, let

$$A = \{a, b, c, d\}$$
$$B = \{b, c, e, f\}$$
$$C = \{c, d, f, g\}$$

We have

$$A \cup B = B \cup A = \{a, b, c, d, e, f\}$$
$$A \cap B = B \cap A = \{b, c\}$$

and

$$(A \cup B) \cup C = A \cup (B \cup C) = \{a, b, c, d, e, f, g\}$$
$$(A \cap B) \cap C = A \cap (B \cap C) = \{c\}$$

but

$$A - B = \{a, d\} \quad \text{and} \quad B - A = \{e, f\}$$
$$(A - B) - C = \{a\} \quad \text{and} \quad A - (B - C) = \{a, c, d\}$$

For the assertions about cartesian product, let H be the set of heights of a group of individuals (in inches) and W be the set of their weights (in pounds). Then $H \times W$ consists of pairs of (height, weight). The absence of commutativity in cartesian products merely says that $(60, 150)$ is a quite different thing from (150, 60). To illustrate the absence of associativity, consider the following sets of strings:

$$F = \text{fruit} \quad = \{\text{apples, grapes}\}$$
$$C = \text{color} \quad = \{\text{red, yellow}\}$$
$$P = \text{package} = \{\text{crate, basket}\}$$

Then

$F \times C = \{(\text{apples, red})(\text{apples, yellow})(\text{grapes, red})(\text{grapes, yellow})\}$

$C \times P = \{(\text{red, crate})(\text{red, basket})(\text{yellow, crate})(\text{yellow, basket})\}$

and

$(F \times C) \times P = \{((\text{apples, red}), \text{crate})((\text{apples, red}), \text{basket}) \ldots\}$

$F \times (C \times P) = \{(\text{apples, (red, crate}))(\text{apples, (red, basket})) \ldots\}$

$F \times C \times P = \{(\text{apples, red, crate})(\text{apples, red, basket}) \ldots\}$

Thus, each of the 3 products just above is a set of objects, each describing packaged fruit. The first contains two ways of packaging 4 varieties; the second contains four ways of packaging 2 fruits; the third is ambiguous. They are clearly not equivalent.

2.4.2   Relations

A *relation* is a set whose members (if any) are all ordered pairs. The set composed of the first member of each pair is called the *domain*; the domain of a relation r is denoted $D(r)$. The members of $D(r)$ are called *arguments* of r. The set composed of the second member of each pair is called the *range*; the range of relation r is denoted $R(r)$. The members of $R(r)$ are called *values* of r.

Because first or second members may be duplicated in r, it is clear that

$$|D(r)| \leq |r|, \; |R(r)| \leq |r|$$

for any relation r; r is said to be a relation on the set $D(r) \cup R(r)$. Since relations are sets, they inherit set operations and properties; for example, $\emptyset$ is the empty relation, and if r and s are relations, then so are $r \cup s, r \cap s$, and $r - s$.

Relations can be classified in several useful ways:

1. r is *reflexive* if $x \in D(r)$ implies that $(x, x) \in r$, that is, r includes the relation "is the same as."

2. *r* is *symmetric* if $(x, y) \in r$ implies that $(y, x) \in r$, that is, *r* includes the relation "is the sibling of."

3. *r* is *transitive* if $(x, y) \in r$, $(y, z) \in r$ implies that $(x, z) \in r$, that is, *r* includes the relation "is the descendant of."

To illustrate, consider the relations defined by

equal $\{(x, y) \mid x = y\}$
less than $\{(x, y) \mid y < x\}$
opposite sign $\{(x, y) \mid x * y < 0\}$

We find that

equal is a reflexive relation ($7 = 7$ is *true*)

less than is not a reflexive relation ($7 < 7$ is *false*)

equal is a symmetric relation $((2/4 = 1/2) \rightarrow (1/2 = 2/4))$

less than is not a symmetric relation (it is *false* that $(2 < 7) \rightarrow (7 < 2)$)

less than is a transitive relation $(((2 < x) \wedge (x < y)) \rightarrow (2 < y))$

opposite sign is not a transitive relation (it is *false* that $((3 * (-5) < 0) \wedge ((-5) * 7 < 0) \rightarrow (3 * 7 < 0))$

The *transpose* of a relation *r*, denoted r^T, is the set of reversed ordered pairs of *r*, that is,

$$r^T = \{(x, y) \mid (y, x) \in r\}$$

It is easy to see that the union of a relation and its transpose is a symmetric relation.

2.4.3   Functions

A *function* is a relation, say *f*, such that for each $x \in D(f)$ there exists a unique element $(x, y) \in f$. We often express this as $y = f(x)$, where *y* is the unique value corresponding to *x* in the function *f*. When *x* and *y* are lists, for example of 4 and 2 elements, respectively, we may write $(y1, y2) = f(x1, x2, x3, x4)$. It is the uniqueness of *y* that distinguishes a function from other relations. It is often convenient to define a function *f* by giving its domain, $D(f)$, and a *rule* for calculating the corresponding value for each argument in the domain. A computer program may be such a rule. If a rule is given that does not suffice for the domain given, we consider it a *partial rule*, and regard the definition of the function insufficient. (Some writers use the term "partial function" for such a case, but we believe that to be a misleading phrase to describe the situation, since a function is a set, and "partial set" has no meaning.) In short, we regard function as master and rule as slave because there are many possible rules for each function.

In illustration, the function

$$f = \{(x, y) \mid x \in \{0, 1\}, y = x^2 + 3x + 2\}†$$

where $(x \in \{0, 1\})$ denotes the domain and $(y = x^2 + 3x + 2)$ denotes the rule, can also be given by enumeration as

$$f = \{(0, 2), (1, 6)\}$$

or by a set description with rule denoted by two equations:

$$f = \{(x, y) \mid x(x - 1) = 0, y - x^2 - 3x - 2 = 0\}$$

Note also that the symbols x, y are convenient place holders ("dummy variables") and irrelevant in themselves to the function f. That is, no such symbols are required at all in the enumeration of f, and an alternate description

$$f = \{(u, v) \mid u \in \{0, 1\}, v = u^2 + 3u + 2\}$$

defines the same set f of ordered pairs. Functions inherit the set operations that do not destroy the uniqueness of function values. If f, g are functions, then $f \cap g$, $f - g$ are functions, but $f \cup g$ need not be (since $(x, y) \in f$, $(x, z) \in g$ would destroy the uniqueness of function values if $y \neq z$). If f and g are functions, then the function

$$\{(x, y) \mid y = f(g(x))\}$$

is called the *function composition* of g and f and is denoted by $f \circ g$.

If a function f is reflexive, it is called an *identity function*, with $f(x) = x$ for every $x \in D(f)$. For example, of the three relations

$$\{(1, 1), (2, 2), (3, 1)\}$$

$$\{(1, 1), (2, 2), (1, 2)\}$$

$$\{(1, 1), (2, 2), (3, 3)\}$$

the first is a function but is not reflexive; the second is reflexive but is not a function; the third is both a function and reflexive and is therefore called an identity function. If the transpose of a function f is a function (it will surely

———————

† Note that the comma in the set builder notation is a synonym for logical *and* ($\wedge$), a common convention used throughout this book.

be a relation), then $f^T(f(x)) = f(f^T(x)) = x$, and f^T is called the *inverse function* of f. If the range of a function f is a one-element set, it is called a *constant function*; if the range of a function is a nonempty subset of $\{true, false\}$, it is called a *predicate function*, or simply a *predicate*. A predicate function is frequently denoted by a condition on the domain; for example,

$$p = \{(x, true) \,|\, x \geq 0\} \cup \{(x, false) \,|\, x < 0\}$$

is simply denoted by $x \geq 0$, that is, the portion of the domain for which p is *true*.

Predicate functions may be used to express rules of other functions. For example,

$$f = \{(x, y) \,|\, (x \geq 0 \rightarrow y = 3 \,|\, x < 0 \rightarrow y = 4)\}$$

In general, the rule of a function may take the form of a *conditional rule*, a sequence of (predicate → rule) pairs separated by vertical bars and enclosed in parentheses:

$$(p_1 \rightarrow r_1 \,|\, p_2 \rightarrow r_2 \,|\, \cdots \,|\, p_k \rightarrow r_k)$$

The meaning of this conditional rule is: evaluate predicates $p_1, p_2, \ldots, p_k$ in order; for the first predicate, p_i, which evaluates *true*, if any, use the rule r_i; if no predicate evaluates *true*, the rule is undefined. Note that $p \rightarrow r$ is not a logical implication; that is, we are not concerned about the truth of $p \rightarrow r$. For convenience, the conditional rule above is read "if p_1 then r_1; else if p_2 then r_2; ...; else if p_k then r_k." If p_k is the constant predicate *true* and all previous predicates are *false*, we can be assured that rule r_k will be used. For example,

$$f = \{(x, y) \,|\, x \in D, (x \text{ divisible by } 2 \rightarrow y = x/2 \,|$$

$$x \text{ divisible by } 3 \rightarrow y = x/3 \,|$$

$$true \rightarrow y = x)\}$$

Note $true \rightarrow r$ has the effect of $else \rightarrow r$ where $else$ means "if all else fails, use r."

2.4.4 Recursive Functions

A *recursively defined function*, or *recursive function* for short, is a function that is defined by using the function itself in the rule that defines it. For example, the integer function

$$\text{oddeven} = \{(x, 1) \,|\, x \text{ odd}\} \cup \{(x, 0) \,|\, x \text{ even}\}$$

can also be defined recursively, using a conditional rule, as

$$\text{oddeven} = \{(x, y) \,|\, (x \in \{0, 1\} \to y = x \,|\, x > 1 \to y = \text{oddeven } (x - 2) \,|$$
$$x < 0 \to y = \text{oddeven } (x + 2))\}$$

We can evaluate the function by repeated application of the conditional rule as follows for $x = 7$:

$$\text{oddeven}(7) = \text{oddeven}(5)$$
$$= \text{oddeven}(3)$$
$$= \text{oddeven}(1)$$
$$= 1$$

Recursive rules in themselves do not guarantee function definitions for arbitrary arguments. For example, the "definition"

$$\text{sign} = \{(x, y) \,|\, (x = 0 \to y = 0 \,|\, x \neq 0 \to y = \text{sign}(-x))\}$$

defines only the one element function

$$\text{sign} = \{(0, 0)\}$$

since repeated application for $x \neq 0$, say

$$\text{sign}(1) = \text{sign}(-1) = \text{sign}(1) = \cdots$$

never terminates in a value.

Recursive rules can be used to describe complex functions not easily defined otherwise. For example, let G be a railroad guide of connections between cities, and $C(x, y)$ be a predicate that states whether any two cities are so connected:

$$G = \{(x, y) \,|\, \text{a train runs from } x \text{ to } y\}$$
$$C(x, y) = \text{a connection exists from } x \text{ to } y$$

Then the predicate function C can be defined recursively as

$$C = \{((x, y), w) \,|\, (x \text{ and } y \text{ are cities}), w = C(x, y)\}$$

where

$$C(x, y) = ((x, y) \in G \to w = true \,|\, \exists z((x, z) \in G \wedge C(z, y)) \to w = true \,|$$
$$true \to w = false)$$

That is, $C(x, y)$ is *true* if a train runs from x to y or if a connection through some city z can be found; otherwise $C(x, y)$ is *false*. Note that the conditional rule for $C(x, y)$ can also be written as a logical proposition:

$$C(x, y) = ((x, y) \in G) \vee (\exists z((x, z) \in G \wedge C(z, y)))$$

2.4.5   Digraphs

A relation g is also called a *digraph*, defined as a set of directed *lines*, each line connecting a member of $D(g)$ to a member of $R(g)$. The term *digraph* (*directed graph*) is used to emphasize the interpretation that the ordered pairs of g are directed lines. (If g is symmetric, the lines of g can be thought of as undirected.)

In illustration, the lines of the digraph of a function are partitioned into four sets (some possibly empty) according to whether the lines originate in $D - R$ or $D \cap R$, and terminate in $D \cap R$ or $R - D$, as illustrated in Fig. 2.1. More formally, for any function f (with subscripts denoting originating and terminating partitions),

$$f = f_{D-R, D \cap R} \cup f_{D-R, R-D} \cup f_{D \cap R, D \cap R} \cup f_{D \cap R, R-D}$$

where, for example:

$$f_{D-R, D \cap R} = \{(x, y) \in f \mid x \in (D(f) - R(f)) \wedge y \in (D(f) \cap R(f))\}$$

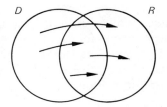

Figure 2.1

A *path* of g is a set of nodes (or members) of $D(g) \cup R(g)$, say $x_1, \ldots, x_k$, such that

$$(x_i, x_{i+1}) \in g, \, i = 1, \ldots, k - 1$$

A *cycle* of g is a path $x_1, \ldots, x_k$ such that $x_1 = x_k$. A digraph with no cycles is called *acyclic*. In further illustration, let C be the set of nodes in cycles of the digraph of function f. Then $C \subset (D \cap R)$, because each member x of a cycle must be in both $D(f)$ and $R(f)$.

2.4.6   State Machines

A *state machine* is a function whose members are ordered pairs of ordered pairs, say

$$m = \{((x,\ y),\ (u,\ v))\}$$

that is also called a transition function. These members are customarily given an interpretation denoted by

$$m = \{((\text{state, input}),\ (\text{newstate, output}))\}$$

State machines are useful in program design. For example, consider a character-by-character examination of a string for the purpose of removing excess blanks, so that on output all blank substrings have been reduced to a single member. A state machine for such a purpose can be enumerated in the following table with entries denoting (newstate, output).

	input	
state	blank	nonblank
excess	excess, λ	nonexcess, input
nonexcess	excess, input	nonexcess, input

Note that λ means the empty output here. This state machine, initialized to state "nonexcess," will remove all excess initial and interior blanks by passing the first of each string of blanks found, then ignoring the rest. This state machine can also be diagrammed as shown in Fig. 2.2, in which circles denote states and a directed line is labeled in the form input/output, the line itself showing the state transformation.

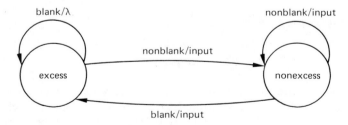

Figure 2.2

2.5 LISTS AND STRINGS

2.5.1 List Structures

A *list* is a sequence of items which are all members of a single set, called an *alphabet*. The concept of list is as important in computing as the concept of set in mathematics. Any computing process must eventually be represented by, and be described in terms of operations on, a list. The alphabet may be bits, characters, bytes (8 bits), words (e.g., 16 bits, 32 bits, etc.), or variable size sublists, as discussed below. All members of the alphabet need not be printable. The *empty list*, denoted by $\emptyset$, is a sequence of no items.

The fundamental relationship in lists is between members of the alphabet and a list, namely, being the first item, say a, of a nonempty list, say L, written

$$a = \text{head}(L), \ L \neq \emptyset$$

A nonempty list L with its first member removed is written $\text{tail}(L)$. Note that $\text{tail}(L)$ can be the empty list. An item of a list, say a, is different from a one-element list, say (a), holding that same item; $\text{head}(L)$ is an item, while $\text{tail}(L)$ is a list. If $L = \emptyset$, then $\text{head}(L)$ is undefined.

Two fundamental operations in lists are (1) adding a new item, a, to the head of a list L, written

$$a + L$$

and (2) concatenating two lists L and M, written

$$L \parallel M$$

This leads to the following identities:

$L \neq \emptyset \rightarrow \text{head}(L) + \text{tail}(L) = L$

$\text{head}(a + L) = a$

$\text{tail}(a + L) = L$

$a + L = (a) \parallel L$

A list can be structured into smaller lists, called *strings*, by the use of self-defining patterns. A simple form of self-defining pattern is to reserve certain characters as *delimiters*, which mark off the strings. For example, blanks serve as delimiters for words in ordinary English text (as do periods, commas, etc.). If the strings of the list are all disjoint, then these strings form a list of strings in a new alphabet, namely an alphabet of strings. Then, we can reapply the concepts of head, tail, + (prefix), and $\parallel$ (concatenation) to such lists of strings.

The list builder $+$, adding an item to the head of a list, permits the insertion of a list in another list by the simple device of adding a list (as an item) to a list. For example, with lists L, M, and item a, the expression

$$a + (L + M)$$

defines a list whose second member is the list L. Any such list built from lists and items is called a *list structure*. The Dewey decimal numbers form a natural coordinate system for such list structures. For example, 3.1.4 refers to the list item (possibly a list, itself) found by finding the 3rd item of the outer list structure (assumed to be a list), then the 1st item of the next inner list (also assumed to be a list), then the 4th item of this latter list. If any item cannot be found, or if any item except for the last is not a list, then 3.1.4 is undefined.

It is often convenient to be able to name lists in order to refer to them indirectly. A list name can be attached to a list by means of a colon, for example,

apple: (lettuce, 'McIntosh', 'Winesap')

indicates that apple is the name of a list of three elements, each element a string. Strings within a list may be either *names* of lists (defined elsewhere) or *literals* (usually delimited by quotes). In the list above, lettuce is the name of a list, followed by two literals.

Next, consider the set of lists defined by

apple: (lettuce, 'McIntosh', 'Winesap')

melon: (peach, 'cantaloupe', 'honeydew')

lettuce: (melon, 'iceberg', 'romaine')

A list structure is implied by the chain of names (apple, lettuce, melon, peach) that is independent of any written ordering among the named lists. For example, in the list above, apple is followed by lettuce, not melon. Using Dewey decimal notation, we have, for example,

apple.1.1.2 = 'cantaloupe'

From their context, the names apple, melon, lettuce are list names, but the referent of the name peach is undefined.

The size of a list may be used as a prefix; for example, a list of three elements may be called a 3-list. Thus, we might define a 3-list named produce as

$$\text{produce: ((lettuce, 'McIntosh', 'Winesap')}$$
$$\text{(peach, 'cantaloupe', 'honeydew')}$$
$$\text{(melon, 'iceberg', 'romaine'))}$$

Then

$$\text{produce.2} = \text{(peach, 'cantaloupe', 'honeydew')}$$

and

$$\text{produce.2.3} = \text{'honeydew'}$$

Sublists may be referred to by using ordinal identifiers, for example, $\text{apple}(2:3) = (\text{'McIntosh', 'Winesap'})$.

2.5.2   Strings and Languages

We define a *language* to be a set of strings. This may seem an unusual definition for a language, but it will prove useful because as sets, languages inherit set operations and relations, and these properties will be decisive.

Words in English (strings of characters) make up a language, say as enumerated in a specific dictionary. Sentences in English (strings of words, punctuation marks, etc.) are impractical to enumerate but are conceivable as a set. In fact, simple foreign language guides will enumerate a set of English sentences and their foreign equivalents for travel conversation. These, too, by our definition, are languages.

However, in programming, we can define languages of our own choosing with convenient internal structure among members, without having to cope with the mysteries and accidentals of languages of natural origin. And it is only sensible to use set-theoretic operations in defining such langauges. In fact, we define a *formal language* to be a set of strings that is defined exclusively by a collection of set operations and relations with no natural experience or language required in the definition. For example, consider the following two set definitions

$$D = \{0, 1, 2, 3, 4, 5, 6, 7, 8, 9\}$$
$$I = D \cup (D \times D) \cup (D \times D \times D) \cup \cdots$$

where I is a language consisting of all possible decimal integers, with the two definitions comprising the grammar of the language. In this context, the following additional terms are useful:

1. Each of the definitions is called a *production*.

2. The set names being defined (e.g., D and I) are called *phrases* (or nonterminal symbols).

3. The symbols of the language (e.g., 0, 1, 2, ..., 9) are called *terminal symbols*. The aggregate of all terminal symbols is called the *alphabet*.

4. The particular phrase (I in this example) that identifies the set that contains all strings of the language is called the *distinguished phrase*.

As further illustration, if the grammar is extended with two new productions

$$ED = \{0, 2, 4, 6, 8\}$$
$$EI = ED \cup (D \times ED) \cup (D \times D \times ED) \cup \cdots$$

and EI is identified as the distinguished phrase of the language, then the revised language consists of even decimal integers. Next, if the following production is added

$$OI = I - EI$$

and OI is defined as the distinguished phrase, then the language consists of odd integers. Finally, if

$$P = \{.\}$$

and

$$DN = (D \times \cdots \times D \times P \times \cdots \times D) \cup (D \times \cdots \times D \times P) \cup (P \times D \times \cdots \times D)$$

are added and DN is defined as the distinguished phrase, then the language consists of all decimal numbers. Note that in the final grammar, above, the productions defining I, ED, EI, and OI are superfluous.

Since languages are sets of strings, it will be useful to introduce a new set operation that is especially useful in forming languages, namely a *language product*, defined as

$$A \times\times B = \{x \mid a \in A, b \in B, x = a \parallel b\}$$

That is, the language product of two sets of strings is the set formed by concatenating each member of the first set with each member of the second set. Note the difference between $A \times B$ and $A \times\times B$. In particular, if

$$a \in A \wedge b \in B$$

then

$$(a \,\|\, b) \in A \times\times B \quad \text{but} \quad (a \,\|\, b) \notin A \times B$$

and

$$(a, b) \in A \times B \quad \text{but} \quad (a, b) \notin A \times\times B$$

Thus, elements of A and B retain their identity in $A \times B$, but that identity is lost in the language product $A \times\times B$. Note also that language product $\times\times$ is associative but not commutative:

$$A \times\times (B \times\times C) = (A \times\times B) \times\times C \quad \text{but} \quad A \times\times B \neq B \times\times A$$

In illustration of the use of the language product, we redefine the set of decimal integers, I, in a recursion

$$I = D \cup (I \times\times D)$$

in place of the infinite union used before. We can read this recursion as "an integer (I) is a decimal digit (D) or an integer followed by a decimal digit." Note in contrast that the recursion

$$I = D \cup (I \times D)$$

does *not* define the integers, but a union of list structures instead, of the form

$$I = D \cup (D \times D) \cup ((D \times D) \times D) \cup \cdots$$

In further illustration, the language of alphanumeric strings headed by an alphabetic character (the typical set of program identifiers) can be identified by the following grammar, where the first production defines the distinguished phrase:

$$ID = A \cup (ID \times\times AD)$$
$$A = \{a, b, \ldots, z\}$$
$$D = \{0, 1, \ldots, 9\}$$
$$AD = A \cup D$$

The nonrecursive (infinite union) form of ID is

$$ID = A \cup (A \times (A \cup D)) \cup (A \times (A \cup D) \times (A \cup D)) \cup \cdots$$

which is rather more cumbersome.

2.5.3   Formal Grammars

Formal grammars are often defined with more specialized notation called Backus Naur Form (BNF), summarized as follows:

1. Language product operations are denoted by juxtaposing phrases.

2. Juxtaposed phrases must be self-delimiting, often by use of angle brackets ⟨ ⟩, for example, ⟨A⟩, ⟨apple⟩, ⟨$x \geq 3$⟩ are phrases.

3. Members of the language alphabet (i.e., the set of terminal symbols) are denoted by their literal symbols.

4. The phrase definition symbol used in productions is ::=, rather than =, for example,

$$\langle \text{2-digit integers} \rangle ::= \langle \text{digit} \rangle \langle \text{digit} \rangle$$

5. The union symbol ∪ is replaced by a vertical bar |.

6. If a phrase is defined in two places within a formal grammar, the union of the resulting sets is intended (not the intersection as is customary in mathematics); for example,

$$\langle \text{integer} \rangle ::= \langle \text{digit} \rangle$$

$$\langle \text{integer} \rangle ::= \langle \text{digit} \rangle \langle \text{digit} \rangle$$

means

$$\langle \text{integer} \rangle ::= \langle \text{digit} \rangle \,|\, \langle \text{digit} \rangle \langle \text{digit} \rangle$$

7. Iterative language operations are denoted by a prefixed *, +, to mean the union of zero or more, or one or more, iterations, respectively. For example,

$$\langle \text{integer} \rangle ::= + (\langle \text{digit} \rangle)$$

defines the decimal integers, and

$$*(.)$$

defines a string of zero or more periods. A superscript used with *, + denotes maximum number of iterations, for example,

$$\langle \text{name} \rangle ::= +^5 (\langle \text{letter} \rangle) *^1 (\langle \text{digit} \rangle)$$

defines a name to be one to five letters optionally followed by a single digit. (We realize that * has been traditionally used as a suffix iteration operator, but believe the additional clarity of a prefix operator for iteration is worth the break with tradition.)

A formal grammar in which every definition is of the form

$$\langle \text{name} \rangle ::= (\text{any language expression})$$

is called a *context free grammar* (CFG). A CFG can be recursive, as illustrated for integers and identifiers above. The set of productions
(definitions) of a CFG defines a language associated with a distinguished
phrase whose definition motivates the grammar itself. For example, the
grammar for clock times {00:00, ..., 23:59} can be given in the following
form, where ⟨clocktime⟩ serves as the distinguished phrase:

$$\langle \text{clocktime} \rangle ::= \langle \text{hour} \rangle : \langle \text{minute} \rangle$$

$$\langle \text{hour} \rangle ::= 0\langle \text{digit} \rangle \,|\, 1\langle \text{digit} \rangle \,|\, 2\langle \text{digit to 3} \rangle$$

$$\langle \text{minute} \rangle ::= \langle \text{digit to 5} \rangle \langle \text{digit} \rangle$$

$$\langle \text{digit to 3} \rangle ::= 0\,|\,1\,|\,2\,|\,3$$

$$\langle \text{digit to 5} \rangle ::= \langle \text{digit to 3} \rangle \,|\,4\,|\,5$$

$$\langle \text{digit} \rangle ::= \langle \text{digit to 5} \rangle \,|\,6\,|\,7\,|\,8\,|\,9$$

If every definition is of the form

$$\langle \text{name} \rangle ::= x \langle \text{name 1} \rangle$$

where x is any character string of the alphabet and ⟨name 1⟩ possibly names
the empty string, ∅, the grammar is called a *regular grammar*.

A *syntax diagram* defines a language definition in a simple, almost self-
explanatory way by providing a "graph" with "paths" that can be taken at
will in the production. For example, the grammar for identifiers of a programming language can be diagrammed as shown in Fig. 2.3. The choice
between syntax diagrams and formal grammars depends on the use at
hand—diagrams are easier to visualize, grammars are easier to process mechanically. In fact, there is no reason why they cannot be used interchange-
ably. Grammar ideas should be used with flexibility for recording and
communicating language structures.

2.5.4   Regular Expressions

A *regular expression* is the right-hand side of a single production which
defines a language with operations of concatenation (language product),
union, and iteration. (But there is no good reason other than historical why
set intersection and difference operations should not be used in language
expressions if useful in a given context.) For example, the definition of
identifiers of a programming language can be given as the regular expression

$$\langle \text{id} \rangle ::= (A\,|\cdots|\,Z) * ((A\,|\cdots|\,Z)\,|\,(0\,|\cdots|\,9))$$

A regular expression is a compact way of describing a language.

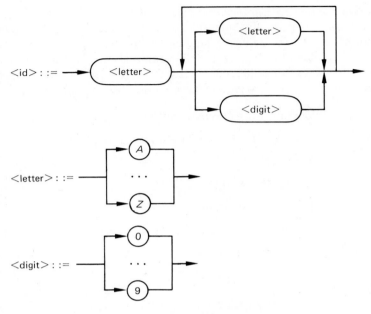

Figure 2.3

The notation of regular expressions permits several alternatives to represent identical languages, which fact may permit certain simplifications as needed, that is (where $\emptyset$ names the empty string):

$$+(A) *(A) = *(A) +(A) = +(A)$$

$$* (A) *(A) = * (A)$$

$$A *(A) = * (A)A = +(A)$$

$$A\emptyset = \emptyset A = A$$

$$* (*(A)) = * (A)$$

$$A(B|C) = (AB)|(AC), (B|C)A = (BA)|(CA)$$

$$A(BC) = (AB)C$$

$$+(A)|\emptyset = *(A)$$

There is an interesting application of regular expressions to program control structures. The instructions executed in a program form a string, and the strings formed over all possible executions form a language. The regular expressions and program control structures shown in Fig. 2.4 correspond.

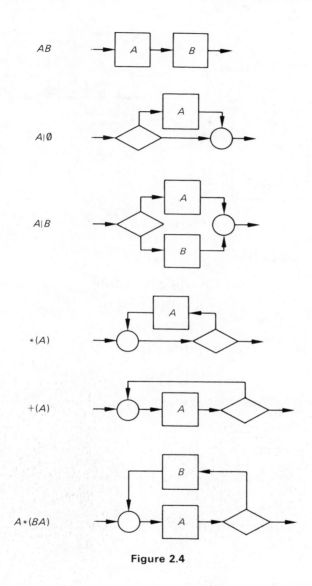

Figure 2.4

Regular expressions for complex program logic composed of these or similar structures can often be simplified, thus producing simpler program logic. For example, the program in Fig. 2.5 has regular expression (ignoring predicate values)

$$((BA)|(CA))((A *(A))|\emptyset)$$

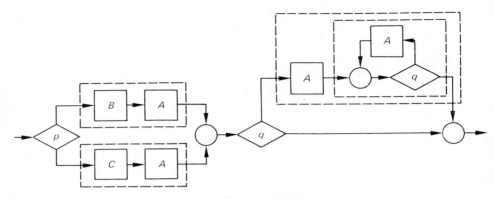

Figure 2.5

that can be simplified to

$$((BA)|(CA))(+(A)|\emptyset)$$
$$= ((BA)|(CA)) *(A)$$
$$= ((B|C)A) *(A)$$
$$= (B|C)(A *(A))$$
$$= (B|C) + (A)$$

yielding the simplified program shown in Fig. 2.6.

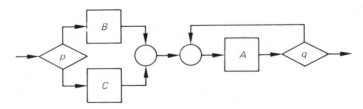

Figure 2.6

2.6 RELATED READING

We suggest the following references for readers interested in further investigation of elements of logical expression:

On good English

Barzun, Jacques, and Georgia Dunbar. *Simple and Direct: A Rhetoric for Writers.* New York: Harper & Row, 1976.

Crosby, Harry H., and George F. Estey. *College Writing—The Rhetorical Imperative.* New York: Harper & Row, 1968.

Savage, Audrey. *Straight Talk.* Pittsburgh: Stanwix House, 1971.

Strunk, W., and E. B. White. *The Elements of Style.* New York: MacMillan, 1972.

On formal logic

Bochenski, I. M. *A History of Formal Logic.* New York: Chelsea Publishing, 1970.

Chang, C., and R. C. Lee. *Symbolic Logic and Mechanical Theorem Proving.* New York: Academic Press, 1973.

Hilbert, D., and W. Ackermann. *Principles of Mathematical Logic.* New York: Chelsea Publishing, 1950.

Langer, S. *Introduction to Symbolic Logic.* New York: Dover Publishing, 1953.

On sets and functions

Burge, W. H. *Recursive Programming Techniques.* Reading, Mass.: Addison-Wesley, 1975.

Halmos, P. R. *Naive Set Theory.* Princeton: Van Nostrand, 1960.

Lipschutz, Seymour. *Set Theory and Related Topics.* Schaum's Outline Series. New York: McGraw-Hill, 1964.

Nahikian, H. M. *Topics in Modern Mathematics.* London: MacMillan, 1966.

On lists and strings

Berztiss, A. T. *Data Structures—Theory and Practice.* New York: Academic Press, 1971.

Engeler, E. *Introduction to the Theory of Computation.* New York: Academic Press, 1973.

Hopcroft, J. E., and J. D. Ullman. *Formal Languages and Their Relation to Automata.* Reading, Mass.: Addison-Wesley, 1969.

3

Elements of
Program
Expression

3.1 OVERVIEW

In this chapter we introduce language forms for the precise and concise expression of program designs. These language forms are divided between an *outer syntax*, which deals with control structure, data structure, and system/module structure, and an *inner syntax*, which deals with operations and tests on data.† Outer syntax promotes and enforces structure in program design not only with respect to control logic but also with respect to data organization and system organization.

3.2 PROCESS DESIGN LANGUAGE

3.2.1 The Idea of PDL

The development and evolution of large software systems can extend over months, years, or even decades. Throughout this time, there is a need for users and designers to communicate effectively about proposed and actual system structure and operation. For this purpose, clearly written natural language serves up to a point, but may not provide sufficient structural form to effectively define functions in a system and all their interactions. On the

---

† The terms *outer syntax* and *inner syntax* were introduced by M. V. Wilkes, "The Outer and Inner Syntax of a Programming Language," *The Computer Journal* 11 (1968): 260–263.

The concept of module structures is due to D. L. Parnas, "A Technique for Software Module Specification with Examples," *Communications of the ACM* 15, no. 5 (May 1972): 330–336.

other hand, programming languages often provide the required structural forms, but within a uniformly low level of expression so that overall design concepts become lost in a sea of details. Furthermore, programming languages introduce special syntax and implementation conventions usually not necessary at the design level.

Thus, there is a need for a language for inventing and communicating software designs, in rigorous logical terms, for use jointly by specialists and nonspecialists in software development. Such a language must be capable of expressing a continuum of design ideas—from proposals for high level system descriptions, to intermediate level operations, and even down to low level details if necessary. It must facilitate data and control logic design, as well as provide descriptive commentary; recorded designs must be easily maintained. For this purpose, we introduce some basic conventions for inventing and communicating software designs in text form, summarized as Process Design Language, or PDL. PDL is an open-ended specialization of natural language and mathematics, not a closed formal language. It permits specification of software designs from a logical point of view without getting directly into the physical storage and operations of specific computing systems. The structures of PDL are intended to facilitate discovery and insight during system and program design. PDL permits precision for human communication and for nearly direct human translation into typical procedural programming languages, as well as into procedural instructions in user's guides, operating manuals, and so forth, that are intended for human readers.

3.2.2   Outer Syntax and Inner Syntax in PDL

The principal specialization of PDL from natural language occurs in an *outer syntax* of control, data, and system structures, employing a few PDL keywords and a tabular typographic form. Outer syntax describes how operations are sequenced and controlled, how data is organized, accessed, and assigned, and how programs are defined and organized into modules. The *inner syntax* of PDL deals with data types and operations. Inner syntax is expressed in natural language or in specialized languages, such as mathematics, appropriate for the problem at hand.

The PDL outer syntax control structures are

sequence structures
    sequence
    indexed sequence (or fordo)
alternation structures
    ifthenelse

      ifthen
      indexed alternation (or case)
  iteration structures
      whiledo
      dountil
      dowhiledo

The outer syntax of data structures provides a small set of data access conventions to both named and anonymous data, specifically

  named data
      scalars
      arrays
      records
  anonymous data, organized in
      sequences
      queues
      stacks
      sets

The outer syntax of system structures defines three levels of organization: the *job*, the *procedure*, and the *module*. The job describes the highest level of program execution. Jobs are invoked on demand by an external agency (e.g., operator, scheduled clock time) and executed to completion. The procedure is the executable unit of stored programs, to be invoked and executed to completion with no internal data surviving between invocations. The module is the system unit, in which several procedures are organized to be invoked by users (jobs or other procedures) on demand, with access to a common set of data that survives between successive invocations. A procedure provides a rule for a *function*, while a module provides a rule for a *state machine*. Both procedure and module are used recursively in software system design, in wide size variations—from a three-line subprogram to a ten-thousand-line program organized into a hierarchy of smaller programs or procedures; from a module that maintains a small directory for other using procedures to a module that serves as a text processing system organized into a structure of smaller modules.

Outer and inner syntax are informal terms that point up an important distinction. Outer syntax is standard and general; since the properties of outer syntax structures are independent of program subject matter, these properties can be studied and understood once and for all. Inner syntax, on the other hand, is not so easily standardized; it encompasses a variety of expressive forms that deal directly with program subject matter and that may depend on specialized knowledge for effective communication. But note that outer syntax is not rigid; nor is inner syntax imprecise. Intelligent extensions to outer syntax control and data structures may make sense for particular problems and computer architectures, and inner syntax imposes full requirements for rigorous expression, whatever form it may assume.

3.2.3   Data Assignment in PDL

The explicit *assignment* of data is denoted by the assignment symbol ":=", as, for example, in

$$x := y + z$$

with meaning "x is assigned the value of $y + z$." The left side consists of a single data name; the right side is an expression in data names, possibly including the data name of the left side. For example,

$$x := x + 1$$
$$x := \max(x, y)$$
$$x := y$$

are assignments.

A *multiple* (concurrent) *assignment* is denoted by a list of data names on the left side of the assignment symbol and a list of expressions of the same length on the right side, as, for example,

$$x, y, z := x + y, \min(x, z), \text{abs}(z - y)$$

which means to compute the values of all expressions on the right side first, then assign these values simultaneously to the data names of the left side, respectively. For example,

$$x, y := y, x$$

exchanges the values of x and y.

3.3   OUTER SYNTAX CONTROL STRUCTURES

3.3.1   Sequence Structures

Operations carried out in a PDL *sequence* structure are written in sequence, one below another, with general form

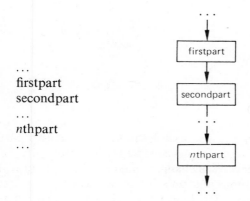

...
firstpart
secondpart
...
*n*thpart
...

where PDL text and flowchart correspond. This *program fragment* is delimited by ellipsis symbols (...) to show that it could be embedded in a larger program. Sequence is an outer syntax structure composed of component operations; namely, firstpart, secondpart, ..., *n*thpart. In the following example,

        ...
        sort transaction file;
        update inventory file with
        transactions;
        print inventory report;
        ...

the operations are specified by brief natural language statements, and the outer syntax symbol (;) serves to separate sequence parts where necessary. (Semicolons are usually omitted where each part in a sequence consistently occupies one line.) Ordinarily, no outer syntax keywords appear with operations in a sequence. However, it is sometimes useful during program design and documentation to delimit sequence parts with outer syntax **do** and **od** (**do** spelled backward) keywords, as follows.†

---

† In the PDL programs in this book, keywords are displayed in boldface format; in handwritten and typed PDL programs, keywords are ordinarily underlined for readability.

```
  . . .
do
     sort transaction file;
     update inventory file with
     transactions;
od
print inventory report;
  . . .
```

In this instance, a three-part sequence has been represented as two parts, with firstpart itself another two-part sequence indented for readability. The meaning of the original sequence is unchanged; **do** and **od** simply provide convenient delimiters for attaching comments, as we will see. As a separate example, the following sequence interchanges the values of x and y (and also sets t to the initial value of x), using explicit data assignments:

```
  . . .
t := x
x := y
y := t
  . . .
```

It is convenient to introduce a generalization of the sequence, called an *indexed sequence*, or *fordo* structure, closely patterned on the well-known do loop (e.g., "do $i = 1$ to 10;" in **PL/I**), but renamed here to identify two critical distinctions discussed below. The indexed sequence is abbreviated notation where the operations in all parts (firstpart, secondpart, ..., $n$thpart) of a fixed-length sequence are identical, although different data may be operated on in each part. PDL outer syntax keywords **for, do,** and **od** delimit the indexed sequence, written as

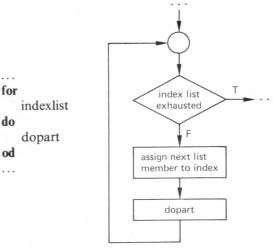

```
  . . .
for
     indexlist
do
     dopart
od
  . . .
```

where successive dopart executions carry out successive parts of the sequence. The indexlist and dopart are indented to improve readability in larger contexts. The indexlist, an inner syntax expression, defines both an index variable and a list whose values are to be successively assumed by the index. The list may be enumerated or given by a rule. For example, in

```
...
for
    i :∈ 1 to 20 by 2
do
    j := table(i) + table(i + 1)
    print j
od
...
```

i is the index, ":∈" is read "is assigned all consecutive values in the list," and "1 to 20 by 2" describes the list; in this case, i takes on consecutive values 1, 3, ..., 19. We regard the right side of an indexlist (following ":∈") as an informal specification of a list; if the specification of an arithmetic list contains no successor rule, it is assumed to be "by 1." The fordo above is an abbreviation for the following sequence:

```
j := table(1) + table(2)
print j
j := table(3) + table(4)
print j
...
j := table(19) + table(20)
print j
```

Critical distinctions between the usual do loop and the indexed sequence are (1) in the indexed sequence, the dopart cannot alter the value of the index, and (2) the value of the index is not available for use by program parts following the indexed sequence. In other forms of the do loop, the index is treated as any other variable and can be assigned new values both in the dopart and outside the loop. We regard the index in a different way—as a data item beyond control of the program once set up that can be read in the dopart, much like a local clock, but that cannot be altered in the dopart or read or altered thereafter.

As a second illustration, the indexed sequence below has an index named pointer and assigns to each member of a ten-element array named x

the sum of members from that member to the tenth member:

```
...
for
    pointer :∈ 9 to 1 by −1
do
    x(pointer) := x(pointer) + x(pointer + 1)
od
...
```

3.3.2   Alternation Structures

The *ifthenelse* structure has general form

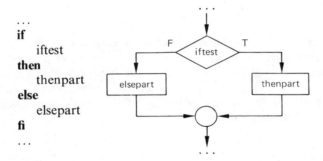

```
...
if
    iftest
then
    thenpart
else
    elsepart
fi
...
```

with outer syntax keywords **if, then, else,** and **fi** (if spelled backward) de-limiting an inner syntax predicate named iftest, an operation named thenpart to be executed when iftest evaluates *true,* and an operation named elsepart to be executed when iftest evaluates *false.* In illustration, the following ifthen-else searches either an online file or an archive file, depending on the data requested. The test and operations are given by brief natural language statements:

```
...
if
    data requested is current status
then
    search online personnel file
else
    search archive personnel file
fi
...
```

The ifthenelse below sets z to the maximum of x and y, using explicit data assignments:

```
...
if
      x > y
then
      z := x
else
      z := y
fi
...
```

If more convenient, a PDL structure can be written in linear form, for example,

if $x > y$ **then** $z := x$ **else** $z := y$ **fi**

with less readability but identical meaning as above.

The *ifthen* structure, a special case of the ifthenelse in which no operation is carried out when iftest evaluates *false*, has general form

```
...
if
      iftest
then
      thenpart
fi
...
```

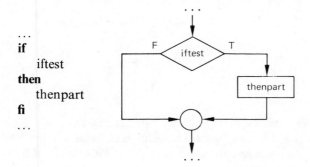

The following ifthen

```
...
if
      inventory transactions available
then
      update inventory file
fi
...
```

carries out an update process if inventory transactions are available. The ifthen below sets x to the minimum of x and y:

```
...
if
    x > y
then
    x := y
fi
...
```

The *indexed alternation,* or *case* structure, is a multibranch, multijoin control structure with general form

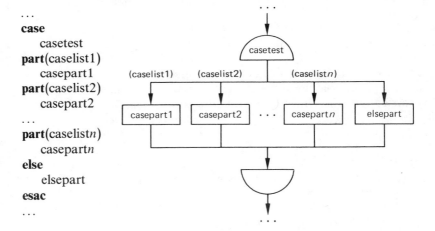

```
...
case
    casetest
part(caselist1)
    casepart1
part(caselist2)
    casepart2
...
part(caselistn)
    casepartn
else
    elsepart
esac
...
```

The case structure delimits caseparts and inner syntax casetest and caselists with outer syntax keywords **case**, **part**, **else**, and **esac** (**case** spelled backward). In execution, the casetest expression is evaluated and control flow is directed to the first casepart whose corresponding caselist (list of values or expressions) contains the current value of casetest. Caselists are scanned in ordinal sequence; for a value appearing in multiple caselists, the casepart corresponding to the first occurrence is always executed. The elsepart is optional; it handles missing casetest values when present. The indexed alternation is of interest because of the architectures of underlying physical machines (e.g., efficient use of indexed branch instructions) and because of the way program logic often seems natural to describe (e.g., expressing one of many possible alternatives, otherwise expressed as nested ifthenelse structures). In illustration, the case structure below manipulates a personnel record, based on the current value of *op*:

...
case
   op
part('add')
   add personnel record
part('delete')
   delete personnel record
part('modify')
   modify personnel record
part('display for salary', 'display for tenure')
   display personnel record
else
   display 'operation incorrectly specified'
esac
...

3.3.3 Iteration Structures

The *whiledo* structure has general form

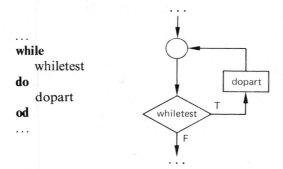

...
while
   whiletest
do
   dopart
od
...

with keywords **while**, **do**, and **od** delimiting the inner syntax whiletest, and
the dopart. The whiledo structure carries out the dopart zero or more times
as long as the whiletest evaluates to *true*. Of course, the dopart must include
modification of the whiletest condition for execution to terminate. For
example, in

...
while
   pay updates remain
do
   retrieve next pay update record
   update corresponding record in master pay file
od
...

records are updated in a master pay file as long as updates remain. Note that this structure is correct for the case where no updates exist (assuming that an end-of-file can be detected in the whiletest). In such case, the master file remains unchanged. The whiledo

```
...
while
    x > 1
do
    x := x − 2
od
...
```

converts a positive integer x into 1 if x is initially odd, into 0 if initially even; it leaves nonpositive integers unchanged.

The *dountil* structure has general form

```
...
do
    dopart
until
    untiltest
od
...
```

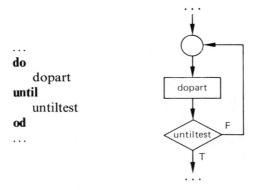

with keywords **do**, **until**, and **od** delimiting the dopart and the inner syntax untiltest. The dountil carries out an operation one or more times, including modification of the untiltest condition, until that test evaluates to *true*, as in the following example:

```
...
do
    retrieve next pay update
    update corresponding record in master pay file
until
    no pay updates remain
od
...
```

Note that this structure, unlike the whiledo, executes the dopart before evaluating the predicate; therefore it is used when at least one iteration of the dopart is required. Thus the example is correct only if at least one pay update is present. The following dountil repeatedly divides any real number x greater than or equal to 10 by 10 until its magnitude is reduced to 1 or less, and divides any real number less than 10 by 10:

```
...
do
    x := x/10
until
    x ≤ 1
od
...
```

The *dowhiledo* structure has general form

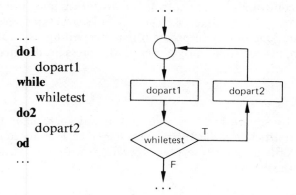

```
...
do1
    dopart1
while
    whiletest
do2
    dopart2
od
...
```

with PDL keywords **do1, while, do2,** and **od** delimiting the inner syntax whiletest, and the two doparts. For example, the following dowhiledo repeats a calculation until some resulting value is within an allowed tolerance

```
...
do1
    calculate error in value
while
    error > tolerance
do2
    calculate new value
od
...
```

and the dowhiledo below prints individual characters from a string, up to a blank character:

```
...
do1
    get next character from string
while
    character not blank
do2
    print character
od
...
```

We consider the preceding control structures to be the fundamental building blocks of programs. With the exception of extended sequence structures (sequences of more than two parts) and fordo and case structures (convenient alternatives to uniform sequences and multiple ifthenelses, respectively), the PDL control structures correspond to the simple "prime programs" to be discussed in Chapter 4. These simple structures have properties that help limit complexity in program reading, writing, and correctness demonstration, but are sufficiently powerful to express the design of any program whatsoever, as will be shown.

3.3.4   Comments

Comments, delimited by square brackets, can appear anywhere in PDL programs, but they are particularly effective when systematically attached to control structure keywords in order to explain operations within the structures. Thus for sequence structures

```
do [comment]
    firstpart
    secondpart
od [comment]
```

the **do** comment can explain the function (or action) of the sequence, that is, what firstpart followed by secondpart does, and the **od** comment can explain the status of affairs, that is, the relations holding among data objects, after the sequence has been carried out. For example (overcommenting for the sake of illustration),

```
do [set c to max(a, abs(b))]
    d := abs(b)
    c := max(a, d)
od [c = max(a, abs(b))]
```

where max produces the maximum of the two arguments and abs produces the absolute value of an argument.

Similar conventions are employed for ifthenelse:

[comment]
if
    iftest
then [comment]
    thenpart
else [comment]
    elsepart
fi [comment]

The leading comment can explain what the ifthenelse does, the **then** comment can explain what the thenpart does, the **else** comment can explain what the elsepart does, and the **fi** comment can summarize the status of data following the ifthenelse. For example (still overcommenting to illustrate),

[set x to min(a, b, c)]
if
    $a < b$
then [set x to min(a, c)]
    if $a < c$ **then** $x := a$ **else** $x := c$ **fi**
else [set x to min(b, c)]
    if $b < c$ **then** $x := b$ **else** $x := c$ **fi**
fi [$x = $ min(a, b, c)]

where min, of course, produces the minimum of its arguments.

For the whiledo form

[comment]
while
    whiletest
do [comment]
    dopart
od [comment]

the leading comment can explain what the whiledo does, the **do** comment can explain what the dopart does, and the **od** comment can summarize the state of affairs following the whiledo. To illustrate, the following initialized whiledo substitutes blanks for leading zeros in a natural number stored in an array named n:

> ...
> $i := 1$
> [remove leading zeros from n]
> **while**
> $n(i) = \text{`0'}$
> **do** [remove ith character from n, prepare to check $i + 1$ character]
> $n(i) := \text{`}\not{b}\text{'}$
> $i := i + 1$
> **od** [leading zeros removed from n]
> ...

The remaining PDL control structures are commented in similar fashion.

3.3.5   Expanding and Parsing PDL Control Structures

PDL control structures are one entry–one exit structures that can be used to expand individual operations into more and more detail, as required. Conversely, any PDL control structure can be treated as a single operation, if it is convenient to do so. For example, the PDL fragment

> ...
> **do**
>   if necessary, compute tax payment or refund
>   for next record from tax file
> **until**
>   all tax records processed
> **od**
> ...

that computes tax payments or refunds for all records in a nonempty tax file can be expanded to, or used to summarize, the PDL fragment shown in Fig. 3.1. The original dopart action appears as a comment at **do**, in Fig. 3.1, to explain the expanded dopart. Notice the cumulative indentation of PDL text to better display nesting of control structures. As a second example the fragment

> ...
> **if**
> $x > 0$
> **then**
>   convert positive x odd or even into 1 or 0
> **else**
>   convert nonpositive x odd or even into 1 or 0
> **fi**
> ...

...
do [if necessary, compute tax payment or refund
     for next record from tax file]
     read next record from tax file
     if
          tax due not equal to withholding
     then
          if
               tax due greater than withholding
          then
               compute tax payment
          else
               compute tax refund
          fi
     fi
until
     all tax records processed
od
...

Figure 3.1

converts an integer x (positive, zero, or negative) into 1 or 0 according to
whether x is initially odd or even, and can be expanded to, or regarded as a
summary of,

...
if
     $x > 0$
then [convert positive x odd or even into 1 or 0]
     while
          $x > 1$
     do
          $x := x - 2$
     od
else [convert nonpositive x odd or even into 1 or 0]
     while
          $x < 0$
     do
          $x := x + 2$
     od
fi
...

Any PDL control structure can be parsed uniquely into its constituent parts, these parts can be parsed uniquely again, and so on, until the entire program is described in a unique hierarchy of expansions. Parsing of PDL programs can be carried out directly in the program text, shown by a Dewey decimal numbering of text lines to reflect control structure hierarchy. The numbering rules are simple and standard. If a program part is itself another control structure, begin a new level of Dewey decimal numbering and number each outer and inner syntax statement in sequence (ignoring lines containing only comments). Numbering is illustrated in the PDL fragments below (with m a Dewey decimal number inherited from a containing structure):

sequence

```
        . . .
m.1    firstpart
m.2    secondpart
        . . .
m.n    nthpart
        . . .
```

ifthenelse

```
        . . .
m.1    if
m.2        iftest
m.3    then
m.4        thenpart
m.5    else
m.6        elsepart
m.7    fi
        . . .
```

whiledo

```
        . . .
m.1    while
  2        whiletest
  3    do
  4        dopart
  5    od
        . . .
```

(where a repeated digit m and the succeeding decimal point may be understood in context)

<u>dountil</u>

```
        . . .
 m.1    do
   2        dopart
   3    until
   4        untiltest
   5    od
        . . .
```

Note that more than one Dewey decimal identifier can be introduced on a single line. For example, if the firstpart of a sequence is itself an ifthen, it would be numbered

```
         . . .
 m.1.1   if
   2         iftest
   3     then
   4         thenpart
   5     fi
   2     secondpart
         . . .
```

To illustrate, the tax computation fragment previously shown has parse structure

```
            . . .
 m.1        do [if necessary, compute tax payment or refund
               for next record from tax file]
   2.1      read next record from tax file
     2.1    if
       2        tax due not equal to withholding
       3    then
         4.1    if
           2        tax due greater than withholding
           3    then
           4        compute tax payment
           5    else
           6        compute tax refund
           7    fi
       5    fi
   3        until
   4            all tax records processed
   5        od
            . . .
```

with dopart (line $m.2$) composed of a sequence (lines $m.2.1$ and $m.2.2$). The secondpart of the sequence (line $m.2.2$) is an ifthen structure (lines $m.2.2.1–m.2.2.5$), itself containing a nested ifthenelse structure. The parse structure of the oddeven fragment introduced above is

```
            . . .
   m.1      if
      2          x > 0
      3      then [convert positive x odd or even into 1 or 0]
      4.1        while
         2            x > 1
         3        do
         4            x := x − 2
         5        od
      5      else [convert nonpositive x odd or even into 1 or 0]
      6.1        while
         2            x < 0
         3        do
         4            x := x + 2
         5        od
      7      fi
            . . .
```

with thenpart (line $m.4$) and elsepart (line $m.6$) both expanding as whiledo structures (lines $m.4.1–m.4.5$ and $m.6.1–m.6.5$, respectively).

Any PDL control structure can be diagrammed as a tree to highlight its parse structure, using the following primitives:

sequence:

fordo:

ifthen:

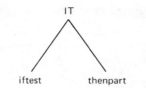

ifthenelse:

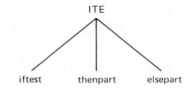

case:

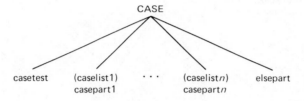

whiledo:

dountil:

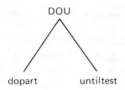

dowhiledo:

The tax computation fragment in tree form is as follows:

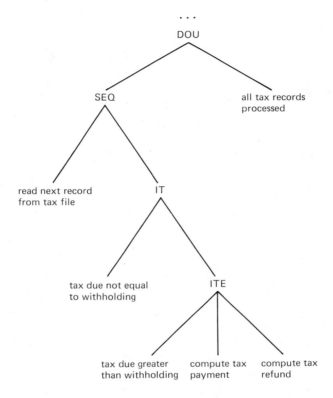

3.4   OUTER SYNTAX DATA STRUCTURES

3.4.1   Structures of Named Data

PDL provides keywords and conventions for describing collections of data and their access functions in a few special *data structures* of named and anonymous data. We begin with a discussion of named data.

Scalar.   A data structure containing a single data item with no accessible substructure is called a scalar, declared by the keyword **scalar**. PDL scalar data items are referred to by name within a PDL program and are defined separately in a data declaration prior to such use. For example,

```
...
scalar x, y, z
...
```

declares that x, y, z are each single data items. A scalar data item can be (but need not be) restricted to a given type (class of values) such as numeric, character, or logical. Data types are expressed in PDL inner syntax and are described later.

Array.   A list of PDL structures that is indexed by a Cartesian product of indexes is called an *array*. For example, the array

$$\begin{bmatrix} x(1, 1) & x(1, 2) & \ldots & x(1, n) \\ x(2, 1) & x(2, 2) & \ldots & x(2, n) \\ \ldots & \ldots & \ldots & \ldots \\ x(m, 1) & x(m, 2) & \ldots & x(m, n) \end{bmatrix}$$

is indexed by the Cartesian product $\{1, 2, \ldots, m\} \times \{1, 2, \ldots, n\}$. An array can be described as a list, or a list of lists, and so on. PDL arrays are accessed by name, and their members are accessed as illustrated by the array name followed by a parenthesized list of indexes, that is, integers and/or identifiers with integer values. The dimension of an array and the limits of each index are given in a declaration such as

$\ldots$
array $a(3)$, $b(2, 4)$, $c(3, 2, 4)$
$\ldots$

that declares a one-dimensional array of 3 members, a two-dimensional array of 8 members, and a three-dimensional array of 24 members.

The PDL assignment

$\ldots$
$a(1) := b(2, 3)$
$\ldots$

states that member $a(1)$ of a takes on the value of member $b(2, 3)$ of b; the assignment

$\ldots$
$a(1) := b$
$\ldots$

states that member $a(1)$ of a (clearly not a scalar) takes on the value of the entire array b; that is,

$$a(1) := \begin{bmatrix} b(1, 1), & b(1, 2), & b(1, 3), & b(1, 4) \\ b(2, 1), & b(2, 2), & b(2, 3), & b(2, 4) \end{bmatrix}$$

All the members of an array (or any other data structure) may have the same type of structure, for example, an array of scalars or an array of arrays, but there is no necessity for such a restriction in PDL. Also, the term *array* traditionally refers to data in the main storage of a computing system. But for design purposes, random accessed storage on disks or drums (with much longer access times) and even large main storage units are logically described as PDL arrays as well.

Record.   A *record* is a data structure that can be represented by a tree, such as

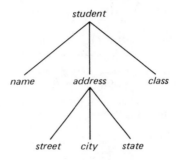

Such structures are called *Cartesian structures* because parent nodes (such as student and address above) can be identified as the Cartesian products of their descendants. Thus

$$student = (name, address, class)$$

$$address = (street, city, state)$$

A member is any node of a tree; a field is a member having no descendants. Members are named by a concatenation of node names, proceeding from the root name (i.e., the record name) and separating names with a period. In place of a node name, the ordinal position (for any fixed ordering) of the node with respect to other siblings can be used. In contexts in which there is no ambiguity, it is sufficient to use the member name alone. The names of the members in the example are

$$\begin{aligned} student.name &\quad = student.1 \quad = name \\ student.address &\quad = student.2 \quad = address \\ student.address.street &= student.2.1 = street \\ student.address.city &\quad = student.2.2 = city \end{aligned}$$

$$student.address.state = student.2.3 = state$$

$$student.class \qquad = student.3 \ = class$$

The structure of a record is given in a PDL declaration by indentation and Dewey decimal numbering, for example:

```
...
record student
    1        name
    2        address
    2.1          street
    2.2          city
    2.3          state
    3        class
...
```

3.4.2   Structures of Anonymous Data

Data structures can also be defined in which members can be accessed without individual item names. Four such data structures are defined next; namely, *sequences, stacks, queues,* and *sets*. A sequence is a familiar data structure, which can be referred to by a name as a whole but which has anonymous members, such as a deck of cards to be read, a magnetic tape file of records, or a sequence of character lines to be printed. But even though sequences have familiar realizations, this very familiarity disguises a relatively complex data structure, compared to stacks, queues, and sets. Therefore, we define stacks, queues, and sets before sequences.

List operations will be useful for defining operations with anonymous data, but we may want to view a list from either end, front or back. Therefore, we augment the ordinary list operations as follows:

List Builders.   Define list operations $+$ (plus), $\oplus$ (circle plus) to mean:

$a + b$: add member a to the front of list b

$a \oplus b$: add member b to the back of list a

List Breakers.   Define operations H^+, T^+ (head plus, tail plus), H^-, T^- (head minus, tail minus) to mean:

$$H^+(a + b) = a, \qquad T^+(a + b) = b$$
$$H^-(a \oplus b) = b, \qquad T^-(a \oplus b) = a$$

Note that $+$ is the ordinary list builder, and H^+, T^+ are the ordinary head, tail operations H, T. In what follows, H, T may be used in place of H^+, T^+.

In illustration, consider lists $a = (A\ B\ C)$, $b = (E\ F)$. Then

$$M + a = (M\ A\ B\ C)$$
$$b \oplus N = (E\ F\ N)$$
$$H^+(a) = A$$
$$T^+(b) = (F)$$
$$H^-(b) = F$$
$$T^-(a) = (A\ B)$$

(Note that (F) denotes a one-element list, F denotes a single list member.) It is easy to verify various list identities, using concatenation ($\|$) and reverse (R) operations, such as

$$H^-(a) = H^+(R(a))$$
$$T^-(a) = R(T^+(R(a)))$$
$$a \oplus b = a\ \|\ (b)$$
$$a \oplus b = R(b + R(a))$$

Stack.   A PDL *stack* is a data structure that provides for LIFO (last in, first out) access to a list by keyword **top**. On reading, **top** designates and removes the last member placed on the stack, if any; on writing, **top** designates and adds the new member to the top of the stack. The stack operations/tests in list definition form are as follows for stack a (with head (H) designating the top of the stack):

Operation/test	List definition	
$c := \textbf{top}(a)$	$c, a := H(a), T(a)$	$(a \neq \emptyset)$
$\textbf{top}(a) := d$	$d, a := d, d + a$	
$a := \textbf{empty}$	$a := \emptyset$	
$a = \textbf{empty}$	$a = \emptyset$	

where the **top** read operation fails (to execute) with an empty stack.† For example, in the program fragment

```
   ...
1  stack a
2  scalar b, c
3  top(a) := b
4  c := top(a)
   ...
```

---

† Anonymous data structures are generally not presumed to be empty on declaration; they must be assigned **empty** if so desired. However, in the small examples in this book, where context clearly indicates that a data structure is empty, no such assignment is made.

at line 1 stack a is declared; at line 3 the value of data item b is placed at the top of the stack; at line 4 the top element of the stack is assigned to c (removing it from the stack).

Queue.   A PDL *queue* is a data structure that provides for FIFO (first in, first out) access to a list by keyword **end**. On reading, **end** designates and removes the first member, if any, of the list, the only member available for reading; on writing, **end** designates and adds the member to the new last place of the list, the only place available for writing. The queue operations/tests in list definition form are as follows for queue a (with head (H) designating the end of the queue available for reading):

Operation/test	List definition	
$c := \mathbf{end}(a)$	$c, a := \mathrm{H}(a), \mathrm{T}(a)$	$(a \neq \emptyset)$
$\mathbf{end}(a) := d$	$d, a := d, a \oplus d$	
$a := \mathbf{empty}$	$a := \emptyset$	
$a = \mathbf{empty}$	$a = \emptyset$	

where the **end** read operation fails with an empty queue. For example, in the program fragment

```
       . . .
1      queue a
2      scalar b, c
3      end(a) := b
4      c := end(a)
       . . .
```

at line 1 queue a is declared; at line 3 the value of data item b is added to the end of a as its last item; at line 4 the first element of a is moved to data item c.

Set.   A PDL *set* is a data structure that provides access to an arbitrary member of a list using the keyword **member**. The set operations/tests in list definition form are (for set a)

Operation/test	List definition	
$c := \mathbf{member}(a)$	$c, a := \mathrm{H}(a), \mathrm{T}(a)$	$(a \neq \emptyset)$
$\mathbf{member}(a) := d$	$d, a := d, \mathrm{P}(d + a)$	
$a := \mathbf{empty}$	$a := \emptyset$	
$a = \mathbf{empty}$	$a = \emptyset$	

where the **member** read operation fails with an empty set, and $\mathrm{P}(x)$ is any permutation and compression (delete all duplicates) of list x. For example, in the fragment (*a* is assumed nonempty)

```
     ...
1    set a
2    scalar b, c
3    b := member(a)
4    member(a) := c
     ...
```

at line 1 set *a* is declared; at line 3 some arbitrary member of set *a* is moved into *b* (and deleted from *a*); at line 4 data item *c* is added to set *a*. Set operations have no particular access discipline, such as FIFO or LIFO, and any member at all may be produced by an assignment such as line 3, in particular not necessarily the last member added. Note that a set can contain a given member only once; that is, addition of a member already present results in no change to the set. In this, a set behaves like an index or directory with each entry unique.

Sequence. A PDL *sequence* is a data structure that provides for sequential access to a list with an implicit pointer position using keywords **current**, **next**, and **reset**. A sequence is defined to be an ordered pair of lists. The first list ("past list") designates the subsequence of members already accessed, with head minus (H^-) of the list being the most recently accessed, and so on (e.g., cards already read, lines already printed). The second list ("future list") designates the subsequence of members not yet accessed, with head plus (H^+) of the list being the next to be accessed (e.g., cards yet to be read). That is, if member *C*, of the sequence containing members (*A B C D E F G*) in order, was most recently accessed, the sequence is represented by first list (*A B C*) and second list (*D E F G*). The PDL keyword **current** refers to the last member, if any, of the first list of the sequence (member *C*, above); the keyword **next** refers to the first member, if any, of the second list of the sequence (member *D*, above). The keyword **reset** defines a new sequence that is derived from an old one, and whose first list is the empty list and whose second list is the concatenation of the two lists of the old sequence.

Given a sequence named *a*, its first and second lists are denoted by a^- and a^+, respectively, and their composition into the sequence *a* is denoted by a dot, as in

$$a = a^- . a^+$$

For example, the sequence with members (*A B C D E F G*) and pointer between *C* and *D* (*C* most recently accessed) can be written

$$a = (A\ B\ C).(D\ E\ F\ G)$$

that is,

$$a^- = (A \; B \; C)$$
$$a^+ = (D \; E \; F \; G)$$

Either a^- or a^+ can itself be replaced by a list expression, for example

$$a^- = (A) \parallel (B \; C)$$
$$a^+ = D + (E \; F \; G)$$

or

$$a = (A) \parallel (B \; C).D + (E \; F \; G)$$

The keywords **current** and **next** refer to members

$$\textbf{current}(a) = H^-(a^-)$$
$$\textbf{next}(a) = H^+(a^+)$$

Operations/tests on sequences can be defined in terms of list assignments as follows (for sequence a):

Operation/test	List definition
reset(a)	$a := \emptyset.a^- \parallel a^+$
$c := \textbf{current}(a)$	$c, a := H^-(a^-), a \qquad (a^- \neq \emptyset)$
current(a) $:= d$	$d, a := d, T^-(a^-) \oplus d.a^+$
$c := \textbf{next}(a)$	$c, a := H(a^+), a^- \oplus H(a^+).T(a^+) \qquad (a^+ \neq \emptyset)$
next(a) $:= d$	$d, a := d, a^- \oplus d.\emptyset$
$a := \textbf{empty}$	$a := a^-.\emptyset$
$a = \textbf{empty}$	$a^+ = \emptyset \qquad (\text{or, } a = a^-.\emptyset)$

where the **current** read operation fails with an empty first list, the **next** read operation fails with an empty second list. The keyword **next** implies an automatic advance along the sequence (reflected in the sizes of a^-, a^+) while the keyword **current** implies no advance. Note that writing with **next** destroys the second list of the sequence, if not already empty, but that writing with **current** preserves the second list. For that reason, the keyword **empty** refers to the second list and not the entire sequence, either in an operation or a test. That is, the test $a = \textbf{empty}$ asks if any members of a remain to be accessed by **next**.

Ordinarily, the input and output of computing are in sequential form, for example, as card input and print output. The PDL conventions make sequential input and output easy to describe by so naming files; for example,

```
    . . .
1    sequence input, output
2    c := next(input)
3    next(output) := d
    . . .
```

The keyword **next** specifies a single data item (e.g., scalar or record) to be transferred to or from a sequence. For convenience such transfers can be generalized to a list of data items using the keyword **list** as shorthand for a series of **next** operations as in

```
    . . .
1    scalar  a, b
2    record  c
        1      d
        2      e
        2.1      f
        2.2      g
3    sequence input, output
4    a, b, c := list(input)
5    list(output) := a, b, c
    . . .
```

where the **list** read operation fails if the sequence has insufficient members. At line 4 scalars a and b and all members of record c are assigned values serially read from the *input* sequence, and at line 5 the values are serially written to the *output* sequence.

3.4.3   Sequence Extensions

The sequence (and stack) data structures are generic forms that can be implemented directly in magnetic tape. But the implementation possibilities may differ in details, which can be described in list notation as variants of these generic PDL data structures. And for program designs that deal directly with physical hardware, an accurate and detailed list description of hardware operations is advisable. A physical file may have a backspace, or read backward capability, which could be described as follows,

Operation	List definition
backspace(a)	$a := T^-(a^-).H^-(a^-) + a^+ \quad (a^- \neq \emptyset)$
$c := $ **back**(a)	$c, a := H^-(a^-), T^-(a^-).H^-(a^-) + a^+ \quad (a^- \neq \emptyset)$

and other physical features will have list descriptions accordingly.

In illustration of other possibly useful operations on sequences, and their descriptions, we note the possibility of adding or deleting members of the sequence, such as follows:

Operation	List definition
addaftercurrent$(a) := d$	$d, a := d, a^- \oplus d.a^+$
$c := $ **readanddeletenext**(a)	$c, a := H(a^+), a^-.T(a^+)$ $(a^+ \neq \emptyset)$

In particular, the following operations, while a little awkward to define, are very useful in deleting a value or inserting a new value in sorted order in an already sorted list:

Operation	List definition
$c := $ **mid**(a)	$c, a := H^-(a^-), T^-(a^-).a^+$ $(a^- \neq \emptyset)$
mid$(a) := d$	$d, a := d, (T^-(a^-) \oplus d) \oplus H^-(a^-).a^+$

That is, **current**(a) is removed by the **mid** read, and d is inserted before **current**(a) by the **mid** write. To illustrate, lines 3 through 8 of the program fragment

```
      ...
1     sequence a, d [a in ascending sorted order]
2     scalar b, c, e, f, g
3     do
4          b := next(a)
5     until
6          b > c
7     od
8     mid(a) := c
9     do
10         e := next(d)
11    until
12         e = f
13    od
14    g := mid(d)
      ...
```

insert the value of c in a sorted sequence named a such that sorted order is maintained (where c is guaranteed smaller than the last member of a). Lines 9 through 14 delete the first occurrence of the value of f from a sequence named d (where f is guaranteed to occur in d).

3.4.4 Set Extensions

In addition to defining new operations for PDL data structures, it may be convenient in design to extend and specialize the data structures themselves. In illustration, we might define a *table* to be a data structure that provides access to a table of data. A table is a specialization of the set data structure, in which all members are ordered pairs. Such a specialization permits the construction of mathematical functions and relations (sets of ordered pairs) in tables, in which the first member of a pair is considered a name for the second member. Thus an anonymous data structure can be used to create named data. In addition to the set operations/tests on tables (in which members are defined as ordered pairs in every case), the table operations/tests could include the ability to deal separately with the first and second members of the ordered pairs of a table, using keywords **domain**, **range**, **argument**, and **value** of conventional meaning in functions and relations. Table operations could be given in list definition form as follows for table a, pair (c, d) of scalars, and set b:

Operation/test	List definition	
$d := \textbf{value}(a, c)$	$a, c, d := a, c, x1$	$(a \neq \emptyset)$
$\textbf{value}(a, c) := d$	$a, c, d := x2, c, d$	
$c := \textbf{argument}(a, d)$	$a, c, d := a, x3, d$	$(a \neq \emptyset)$
$\textbf{argument}(a, d) := c$	$a, c, d := x4, c, d$	
$b := \textbf{domain}(a)$	$a, b := a, \text{domain}(a)$	
$b := \textbf{range}(a)$	$a, b := a, \text{range}(a)$	
$c \in \textbf{domain}(a)$	$c \in \text{domain}(a)$	
$d \in \textbf{range}(a)$	$d \in \text{range}(a)$	
$\textbf{delete}(a, c, d)$	delete pair (c, d) from a, if present†	

where

$$x1 \in \{x \mid (c, x) \in a\}$$
$$x2 = P((c, d) + a)$$
$$x3 \in \{x \mid (x, d) \in a\}$$
$$x4 = P((c, d) + a)$$

and where a **value** read or **argument** read operation fails when the required member of a is not present ($x1$ or $x3$ are not defined). Note that operations **value**$(a, c) := d$ and **argument**$(a, d) := c$ have identical effect in table a, but

---

† The **delete**(a, c, d) operation can be expressed as a conditional rule as follows

$$(\text{H}(Q(a, (c, d)))) = (c, d) \to a, c, d := \text{T}(Q(a, (c, d))), c, d \mid true \to a, c, d := a, c, d$$

where $Q(x, y)$ is any permutation of x such that $y \notin \text{T}(Q(x, y))$.

represent two views for table building. For example, in the fragment

```
    . . .
1   table a
2     scalar c, d, e
3       value(a, c) := d
4   e := value(a, c)
    . . .
```

at line 1 table a is declared, at line 3 the ordered pair (c, d) is added to table a (that is, the name c is assigned the value d in table a), and at line 4 any value associated with name c in table a is assigned to e (if table a is empty before line 3 is executed, then d will be assigned to e in line 4, since d will be the only value associated with name c at that time).

3.4.5 Data Spaces

Thus far we have discussed PDL operations on static collections of named and anonymous data items, that is, data items that are declared in advance and exist until execution terminates. We now introduce dynamic changes in the composition of the list of data items itself, in analogy with facilities for allocation and release of storage found in some programming languages. Specifically, let S be a list of active data items declared in or passed to a program. (A declared data item becomes active when first assigned a value.) We call S a *data space*. A data space can also be changed by use of keywords **initial** and **free**, defined next.

Let each member of S name a stack of indefinite depth, with only top members accessible for program operations and tests. Then **initial** and **free** are defined as follows, where *name* refers to a declared data name:

initial *name* := *value*	If *name* is a member of S, *value* is placed on its stack; otherwise *name* is added to S and *value* is placed on its stack.
free *name*	If *name* is a member of S, the top member of its stack is removed, and if now empty, *name* is removed from S; otherwise the statement fails (to execute).

An ordinary data assignment changes the top value of a stack; an **initial** data assignment creates a new top value and makes the previous top value unavailable until a corresponding **free** statement is executed. For example, assume that x and z are active data items and that

$$S: (x: (\text{`}ab\text{'}), z: (8, 1))$$

That is, S is a list of stacks x and z, in which the top (and only) value of stack x is 'ab' and the top value of stack z is 8 (with previous value 1). Then the following sequence of operations produces the data spaces indicated (y an integer variable):

scalar y	$S: (x: (\text{`}ab\text{'}), z: (8, 1))$
$y := z$	$S: (x: (\text{`}ab\text{'}), y: (8), z: (8, 1))$
initial $y := 3$	$S: (x: (\text{`}ab\text{'}), y: (3, 8), z: (8, 1))$
$y := z$	$S: (x: (\text{`}ab\text{'}), y: (8, 8), z: (8, 1))$
free z	$S: (x: (\text{`}ab\text{'}), y: (8, 8), z: (1))$
initial $x := \text{`}cd\text{'}$	$S: (x: (\text{`}cd\text{'}, \text{`}ab\text{'}), y: (8, 8), z: (1))$
free z	$S: (x: (\text{`}cd\text{'}, \text{`}ab\text{'}), y: (8, 8))$
initial $z := 0$	$S: (x: (\text{`}cd\text{'}, \text{`}ab\text{'}), y: (8, 8), z: (0))$

Given the concept of a data space S, it is possible to invent inner syntax predicates to determine whether specified data items are currently active (i.e., members of S). For example, the predicate (using a, b, c, d as data names)

$$\text{active}(a \lor (b \land c) \lor (\sim d))$$

is *true* if a is active, or if b and c are active, or if d is not active, and is *false* otherwise.

To illustrate, consider a program to multiply nonnegative integers x and y by addition and assign their product to z. The usual assumption is that the data space is identical on entry and exit and during execution in an initialized whiledo as follows:

```
z := 0
while
    x > 0
do
    z := z + y
    x := x − 1
od
```

However, if x and y name stacks containing a single value and z is not active, the following program is an alternative to the program above:

while
    active$(x \wedge y)$
do
    if
        $\sim$ active(z)
    then
        initial $z := 0$
    else
        if
            $x = 0$
        then
            free x, y
        else
            $z := z + y$
            $x := x - 1$
        fi
    fi
od

3.5   OUTER SYNTAX SYSTEM STRUCTURES

3.5.1   Jobs and Procedures

Thus far, PDL structures have been illustrated in terms of unnamed program fragments. We now introduce named PDL programs and the means for combining them into larger program structures. We distinguish two types of named programs; namely, *jobs* and *procedures*. PDL jobs are programs intended for immediate execution; they correspond to job control language that invokes operating system facilities in batch and conversational processing. The use of jobs in a design language permits design of the highest level of control of sequential processes. The structures in a PDL job should be patterned after structures available in the target job control language. (For example, a PDL job to be translated into System/370 JCL would properly contain sequence structures but no looping structures, since JCL does not permit loops.) A job is defined by PDL text listed between keywords **job** and **boj**, with a job name following **job**.

PDL procedures are programs intended to be stored for later invocation by other programs. Procedures correspond to programs stored in system libraries for execution under operating system control. A procedure is defined by PDL text listed between keywords **proc** and **corp**, with a procedure name following **proc**. Procedures are invoked by jobs or by other procedures using PDL statements of the form "**run** name," where name identifies the procedure. To illustrate, the following job runs a program that assigns the reverse of an input queue to an output queue by use of a stack (past data declarations and parameter lists aside):

```
job printreverse
    queue inqueue, outqueue
    run reverse
boj

proc reverse [outqueue := reverse(inqueue)]
    stack a
    a := empty
    outqueue := empty
    while
        inqueue ≠ empty
    do
        top(a) := end(inqueue)
    od
    while
        a ≠ empty
    do
        end(outqueue) := top(a)
    od
corp
```

To limit complexity and enhance readability, a large PDL program can be organized not as a single procedure, but rather as a hierarchy of smaller procedures called *segments*. Segments are referenced in the hierarchy by **run** statements that appear in a procedure to invoke other named procedures, which themselves may contain additional **run** statements. For readability, segments should be limited to a quantity of text that can be easily comprehended, usually a page or less, say 10 to 50 lines or so. Parameter lists are attached to **run** statements, and corresponding parameter lists attached to **proc** keywords, to specify data items passed from a job to a procedure or between procedures. In a programming language implementation, a **run** statement can be converted into either a call (to a closed subroutine) or in-line code (possibly by "include" or "copy" facilities), depending on efficiency matters. A call makes better use of space, in-line code makes better use of time.

Similarly, although data structures can be declared within jobs or procedures, extensive collections of data can be defined in a separate *data declaration* segment, listed between keywords **data** and **atad** with a name following **data**. The data declaration is then referenced by the statement "**use** name" within the corresponding job or procedure. A large data declaration can likewise be organized as a hierarchy of declaration segments by means of "**use** name" statements to specify inclusion of other declarations, which themselves are delimited by **data** and **atad** and possibly contain additional **use** statements.

All data referenced within a PDL segment must be explicitly declared. Data structures named in a parameter list to be passed between procedures can be declared in a data segment that is then used by both procedures. In this case, data structures that are referenced by one of the procedures but that do not appear in the parameter list must not be present in the shared declaration.

Next, we distinguish between data structures appearing in the parameter list of a procedure, called *passed data*, and all other data structures declared in a procedure, called *local data*. The results of operations on passed data correspond to the function of the procedure, whereas local data operations are incidental to a particular implementation of that function.

Data passed to or from a job is called *external data* and is shown as a list of data names following the job name. For example, the job shown above could be augmented as

    job printreverse(*inqueue, outqueue*)
      queue *inqueue, outqueue*
      run reverse(*inqueue, outqueue*)
    boj

to define *inqueue* and *outqueue* as external data with respect to the job printreverse, and passed data with respect to the procedure reverse. An outside agent is required to supply or remove external data, for example, in card or tape input, or in tape or print output.

Data that is not external is called *internal data*. Such data is passed by being named in a parameter list attached to a **run** statement and is named (or renamed) in a corresponding parameter list attached to the invoked procedure. For example, for the **run** statement

    run squareroot(*root, number, bound*)

the following parameter lists correspond; the first uses the identical names, the second renames the data items:

    proc squareroot(*root, number, bound*)
    proc squareroot(*r, n, error*)

Data passed to or from a procedure and external data passed to or from a job can be further characterized as *alterable data* or *fixed data*, by the keywords **alt** and **fix**. Alterable data can be changed in an invoked segment; fixed data cannot be changed.† Alterable and fixed data usage categories are used to partition parameter lists, for better readability and control of the design process. For example,

> **run** squareroot(**alt** *root*, **fix** *number*, *bound*)
> **proc** squareroot(**alt** *root*, **fix** *number*, *bound*)

The following miniature segment-structured program reads a sequence of integers and prints a 0 or 1 for each, depending on whether the integer is even or odd. Sequences *in* and *out* are external to the job segment; they are passed data for the oddeven procedure, which also defines x as local data since it is required in the design of the oddeven function. In the invocation of the procedures positive and nonpositive, x is treated as alterable passed data:

```
job oddeven(in, out)
    sequence in, out
    run oddeven(alt out, fix in)
boj

proc oddeven(alt output, fix input)
    sequence input, output
    scalar x
    while
        input ≠ empty
    do
        x := next(input)
        if
            x > 0
        then
            run positive(alt x)
        else
            run nonpositive(alt x)
        fi
        next(output) := x
    od
corp
```

---

† It is possible to alter and restore the values of data specified as fixed, provided that the restoration is verified to be correct.

```
proc positive(alt x)
    scalar x
    while
        x > 1
    do
        x := x - 2
    od
corp

proc nonpositive(alt x)
    scalar x
    while
        x < 0
    do
        x := x + 2
    od
corp
```

3.5.2 Systems and Modules

Jobs and procedures describe data processing that, despite the operations on internal data, result ultimately in visible operations on external data. However, data processing systems ordinarily require the permanent storage of data between job executions as an integral part of their service to users. For this reason, we identify a third class of data, called *stored data*, as a subclass of internal data, and as the name implies, it is to be retained for use in subsequent job execution. For example, the files of a text processing system will be maintained as stored data. A job executed in this system will involve external data (input/output of the job), internal data (temporary working data), and stored data (the updated files). A typical data processing system will be made up of several programs, say for text entry, text retrieval, file maintenance, recovery and restart, and so on. Each job executed in such a system will call on programs of the system and convert input data into output data and a new state of stored data. In short, by regarding the job itself as part of the input, such a data processing system can be seen to behave as a finite state machine.

In contrast with a large and complex data processing system, a collection of service routines for dealing with a data object such as a directory or a disk file can be put into the same logical form, but on a smaller scale. For example, the services of a directory may be defined in separate programs to add members, delete members, find members, reclaim free space, and so on.

These programs, together with the directory, also behave as a finite state machine, under calls by other programs rather than by user jobs.

On a scale intermediate to these two examples, the mass storage subsystem of the text processing system can (possibly) be accessed through a small set of programs to put data, get data, recover space, and so on. These programs could call on the directory programs and be called on by the text processing system.

This model of a small set of programs providing service to a data object is a powerful one for organizing programs and data into data processing systems. For this reason, we define a PDL *module* to be a named collection of programs, datasets, and other modules by the syntax

```
mod name
     programs program name list
     datasets data name list
     modules module name list
dom
```

The module definition implies that data segments named after **datasets** are to be stored data and that access to this stored data is to be limited to the named programs. The named programs of a module can also define and refer to other internal and external data, as described before, and may call on services of the named modules through their programs, as identified in their corresponding module definitions.

It is evident that the text processing system, the mass storage subsystem, and the directory services outlined above can each be described and organized together in this module syntax:

```
mod textprocessor
     programs textentry, textretrieval, filemaintenance,
          recovery, restart, ...
     datasets systemdata, ...
     modules massstorage, ...
dom


mod massstorage
     programs getdata, putdata, recoverspace, ...
     datasets textfiles, archives, checkpoint, ...
     modules directoryservices, ...
dom
```

mod directoryservices
    programs addmember, deletemember, findmember, ...
    datasets directoryfiles, ...
dom
  ⋮

(PDL jobs would be used to invoke the programs of the textprocessor module.) Such a data processing system could have been described in poorly organized, difficult to understand form, as a single module. But it has been described here in better organized, more easily understood form, as a collection of interconnected modules that define system structure by higher and higher level operations on data. In fact, the term *data abstraction* is used to describe the idea of a data object that can be accessed only by a prescribed set of operations. In this case, the actual representation of the data object is immaterial to the user since the data is only manifested through the operations.

3.6   INNER SYNTAX

3.6.1   Inner Syntax Expressions

The purpose of inner syntax in PDL is to allow flexible, yet precise, data operations and tests at any point in program design, that are appropriate for the subject matter, design level, and audience. Data operations drawn from arithmetic, logic, and character processing, and data objects found in high level programming languages, such as character strings, numbers, and logical values, are useful. We use ordinary conventions in this book, denoting character strings by quotes, numbers in integer or real form, and logical values by PDL keywords **true** or **false**. Data names are (unquoted) alphanumeric strings headed by an alphabetic character.

As described in Chapter 2, logical expressions may be written using logical operators and quantifiers. The following are examples of the use of logical expressions as predicates (tests) in PDL:

there exists an unprocessed order (or, $\exists$ unprocessed order)
successful (or, *successful* = **true**)
$(x + y \leq z + limit) \wedge a \neq b$
for all transactions, $n = 128$ (or, $\forall$ transactions $(n = 128)$)
payfile $\neq$ **empty**

Assignment statements in PDL must specify a data expression whose evaluation produces a data value for assignment to a specified target identifier. For example:

Arithmetic operations (a, b, c integers)

$a := a - 2$
$a := (2*b) - (c + 2*a)/factor$ (*factor* is a variable name)
$b := b!$ (set b to the factorial of b)
$c := \text{int}(c)$ (set c to the integer part of c)

String operations (a, b, c strings, x, y integers)

$c := \text{concatenate}(a, b)$ (c becomes the string formed by
            or,   adjoining string b to string a)
$c := a \parallel b$

$c := \text{substring}(a, x, y)$ (c becomes the substring of
                                    string a that begins at character
                                    position x and has a
                                    length of y)

$x := \text{index}(a, b)$ (starting position of the first
                                    occurrence of string b in string a,
                                    if any, is assigned to x, otherwise
                                    x is assigned 0)

Ultimately, expressing data operations and tests comes down to finding suitable terms for reliable communication, taking into account context shared with the intended audience. Informal description of an operation, say "sort transaction file," may be suited to a context where the operation is well understood or need not be understood in more detail; where it is not well understood, an informal description may raise questions on details not specified, such as, in this example, questions on sort key, timing requirements, and file size.

3.6.2 Data Types

A *data type* is a set of objects to which is associated (1) a set of operations, (2) a set of tests, and (3) a convenient symbol set. For example, integer ≥ 0 is a data type with operations $+$, $*$, tests $=$, $>$, and a symbol set such as decimal or binary digit strings. A data *type specification* is denoted by the PDL keyword **type** which identifies a type name with a table of operations and tests. For example, a quite arbitrary data type, called "tricolor," could be defined with symbol set {red, white, blue}, operation "brighter of," test "brighter than," in the PDL type specification as follows:

type tricolor **defined by**

tricolor	tricolor	"brighter of"	"brighter than"
red	red	red	*false*
red	white	white	*false*
red	blue	red	*true*
white	red	white	*true*
white	white	white	*false*
white	blue	white	*true*
blue	red	red	*false*
blue	white	white	*false*
blue	blue	blue	*false*

When the data type being specified is very familiar, the table of operations and tests may be given implicitly by a name, or a reference. For example,

$$\textbf{type } \text{integer} \geq 0$$

implies a table of operations and tests that begins

integer ≥ 0	integer ≥ 0	$+$	$*$	$=$	$>$
0	0	0	0	*true*	*false*
0	1	1	0	*false*	*false*
1	0	1	0	*false*	*true*
0	2	2	0	*false*	*false*
1	1	2	1	*true*	*false*
2	0	2	0	*false*	*true*
⋮	⋮	⋮	⋮	⋮	⋮

which is well known, and can be described in more compact forms by axioms. Such data types of mathematical origin will be referred to frequently by their common names.

There are two kinds of data type specification that warrant special treatment due to their convenience—*enumerated types* and *subrange types*. An enumerated type specification is given by listing the symbol set as

$$\textbf{type } \text{weekday} = (\text{M, Tu, W, Th, F, Sa, Su})$$

with operations and tests implicit in the list form. A subrange type specification is given by listing two members of a known ordered set to signify all members from the first member to the second member; for example,

$$\textbf{type } \text{twenties} = (1920 \mathinner{\ldotp\ldotp} 1929)$$
$$\textbf{type } \text{workday} = (M \mathinner{\ldotp\ldotp} F)$$

where type twenties has members

1920, 1921, 1922, 1923, 1924, 1925, 1926, 1927, 1928, 1929

and type workday has members

M, Tu, W, Th, F

A subrange type inherits the operations and tests of its underlying ordered set that apply to the subrange.

Inner syntax *type assignments* can be appended to outer syntax data structures, as in

scalar *a*, *b*: integer

where the colon delimits the data list and integer is an inner syntax data type that implies admissible values and operations; that is, *a* and *b* are integer values for use in ordinary arithmetic operations. The following examples illustrate elementary data types; in all cases outer syntax keywords are boldface and inner syntax words are not:

scalar *a*: string(50)	(*a* is a string of length 50)
sequence *b*, *c*: string(4)	(each member of *b* and *c* is a string of length 4)
set *d*: logical	(each member of *d* takes on only values *true* or *false*)
stack *e*: string	(each member of *e* is a string of unspecified length)
queue *f*, *g*: integer ≥ 0	(each member of *f* and *g* is a nonnegative integer)
array *h*: logical	(each member of *h* takes on only values *true* or *false*)
record *k*: logical, (string, integer)	(*k* is a record with *k*.1 logical, *k*.2.1 string, and *k*.2.2 integer)

record student   (student is a record with
   1   name: nametype   typed members student.name,
   2   address   student.address.street,
   2.1   street: streettype   student.address.city,
   2.2   city: citytype   student.address.state, and
   2.3   state: statetype   student.class)
   3   class: classtype

That is, a type specification applies to every member of a structure, unless otherwise stated.

At higher levels of design, other data types may be introduced as the need arises. In particular, high-level data types can be as useful in problem solving and program design as are high-level program structures. For example, "chess board" and "chess move" may be data types that permit tests such as "black checkmate" and "white checkmate," and operations such as "chess board" + "chess move" (= new "chess board" or "illegal move"). Such tests and operations could be implemented with corresponding module definitions as before.

Even though sets, stacks, and queues have been used as outer syntax data structures, they can be regarded as data types independently if useful in a design problem. That is, sets may be regarded either as objects that contain other objects (as defined by set membership) or as objects in an algebra of sets (in which the concept of set membership plays no role at all). The first view corresponds to a data structure in which members can be stored and retrieved; the second view corresponds to a data type that permits set operations and tests. For example, a set data type would permit the use of complex set expressions in assignments, tests, and procedure arguments.

4

Structured
Programs

4.1 OVERVIEW

In Chapter 3 a small, closed set of PDL control structures was defined. But a general branching (GOTO) statement that allows the construction of arbitrarily complex control structures was not defined. The omission of such structures is justified by the *Structure Theorem*, which shows that the effect on data of any arbitrarily complex control structure can be accomplished by use of the PDL control structures alone. The Structure Theorem proof construction permits systematic transformation of programs expressed in these arbitrarily complex control structures into equivalent programs expressed in the PDL control structures. In order to make these ideas precise, this chapter introduces three fundamental concepts: *proper programs*, *prime programs*, and *program functions*.† Proper programs have one entry and one exit, and include PDL programs; their effect on data can be summarized at both the entry and the exit. Prime programs are proper programs that are irreducible in a certain sense discussed below, and include the PDL control structures. Program functions are precise and comprehensive statements of the effect of a proper program on data, from an initial *data state* at entry to a final data state at exit. Program functions are of fundamental importance in program reading, writing, and correctness validation, as described in subsequent chapters.

---

† The concept of prime programs is due to Roy A. Maddux, "A Study of Computer Program Structure," Ph.D. Thesis, University of Waterloo, Ontario, Canada, 1975.

4.2   PROGRAM EXECUTION

4.2.1   Flowchart Programs

A *flowchart* is a directed graph that depicts the flow of execution control of a program and the instructions to be executed. Each instruction of a program corresponds to a *node* in the flowchart; each possible flow of control corresponds to a line. If an instruction node has more than one out-line, it is a *control instruction*. If the execution of a control instruction affects no data except an instruction counter, it is a *pure control instruction*; otherwise the control instruction has *side effects* that change data values. (Note that if a real-time clock is part of the data, then no pure control instructions exist.) Isolation of side effects permits better human understanding of programs. Side effects can be useful in control instructions—for example, in looping (decrement and branch), in subroutine linkages (branch and link return), in implementing push down stacks—but we do not pursue those ideas further here.

If a flowchart node has a single in-line and single out-line, it is called a *function node*

where a function named f is associated with the node, typically an assignment instruction. The term function node is especially appropriate since any assignment instruction can be represented entirely by a mathematical function in its effect on data.

If a flowchart node has a single in-line and two out-lines and is a pure control instruction, it is called a *predicate node*

where a predicate named p is associated with the node. A predicate node directs the flow of execution control according to whether the predicate evaluates to *true* or *false* (T or F); it does not affect the data of a program otherwise. In this book, where labels T and F do not appear with a predicate node, the *true* out-line will always be drawn above the *false* out-line.

It is convenient to introduce one more node with a "no-op" instruction that does not change or evaluate data, with two in-lines and one out-line, called a *collecting node*:

In fact, a flowchart may join more than two in-lines at an instruction, but any number of in-lines can be depicted by a structure of multiple collecting nodes:

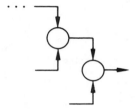

    The *control structure* of a flowchart preserves the ordering of function nodes, predicate nodes, and collecting nodes, but ignores the identity of associated functions, predicates, and predicate values. The flowchart shown in Fig. 4.1, with predicates named p and q and functions named g and h, has a control structure depicted by, say, either of the diagrams in Fig. 4.2. We note in passing that a control structure has a natural dual obtained by reversing each line and interchanging the roles of predicate and collecting nodes.

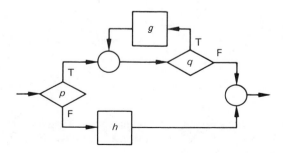

Figure 4.1

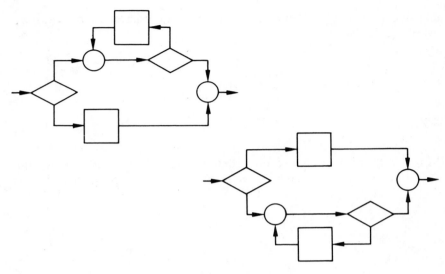

Figure 4.2

4.2.2 Proper Programs

A *proper program* is a program with a control structure that

1. has a single entry line and a single exit line, and
2. for each node, has a path through that node from the entry line to the exit line.

Condition 2 outlaws control structures such as those shown in Fig. 4.3 that have unleavable node sets (left) and unreachable node sets (right).

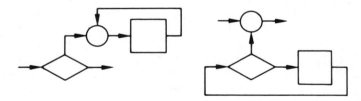

Figure 4.3

A proper program can be abstracted into a single function node for better human understanding. The function node summarizes the total effect of the data operations and tests of the proper program it represents. For

example, the proper program

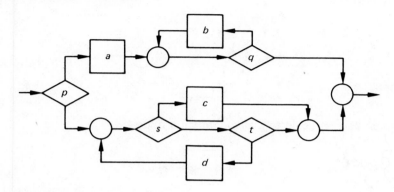

can be redescribed as

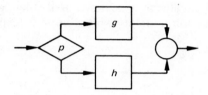

where

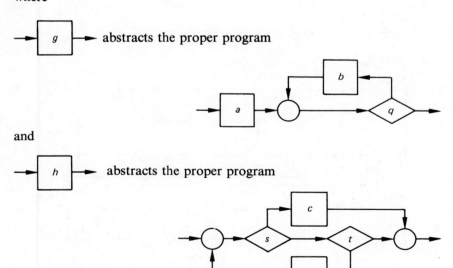

The reduced proper program

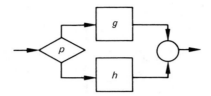

can then be abstracted to a single function node:

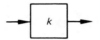

Conversely, any function node of a program can be expanded into a proper program without affecting the function of other parts of the program. For example, the function node just above could be expanded to, say

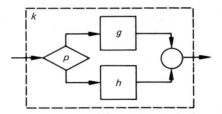

and g and h could be expanded to, say

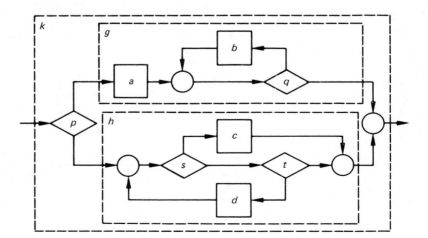

The parts of a program that are themselves proper are called *proper subprograms*. The proper subprograms of program k are g, h, a, b, c, and d. Predicates p, q, s, and t are not proper subprograms by themselves because they each have two out-lines.

4.2.3   Execution Charts and Trees

We will see that any proper program with arbitrary control structure can be expressed as an equivalent program composed of only a subset of the PDL control structures. This motivates a closer look at the concept of program equivalence. In preparation, we now introduce execution charts and execution trees, and the fundamental concept of program functions.

A flowchart program defines execution sequences along paths and cycles. These execution sequences can often be better understood in terms of a finite tree called an *execution chart* (E-chart). Given a proper flowchart, we construct its E-chart of nodes and lines in a stepwise manner as follows:

1. Start the E-chart with the entry line of the flowchart and its adjacent predicate, function, or collecting node.

2. At each step of construction, consider each *execution path* (a directed path of lines and nodes adjoined to the entry line) in the evolving E-chart. If an execution path currently terminates in a function, predicate, or collecting node not found earlier in that specific path, adjoin all of that node's out-lines (from the flowchart) and the nodes with which those out-lines connect, if any, to the execution path.

3. When all execution paths terminate in exit lines or in nodes that previously appeared on the path, the E-chart is complete.

It is clear that this procedure terminates with a finite tree since each path will eventually exhaust the nodes of the flowchart. For example, for the flowchart shown in Fig. 4.4 (with numbered collecting nodes) the above procedure generates the E-chart shown in Fig. 4.5.

The execution of a flowchart is given by executions along paths of its E-chart, with the added rule that control passes from a repeated end node back to its initial occurrence on that path. It is clear that a flowchart is loop free if and only if its E-chart has no repeated nodes as execution path end points. It is also clear that all occurrences of collecting nodes except those appearing as repeated points on a path can be suppressed; for example, the E-chart in Fig. 4.5 can be simplified as illustrated in Fig. 4.6, where only collecting node 2 has been retained.

An *execution tree* (E-tree) of a flowchart program is a tree whose paths depict all possible execution sequences of the flowchart without retracing. If loops are not present in the flowchart, then the corresponding finite E-chart is the E-tree. If loops are present in a flowchart, the E-tree is the infinite tree

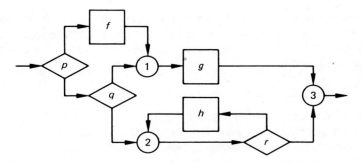

Figure 4.4

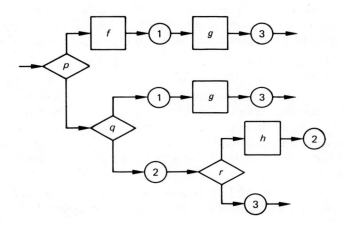

Figure 4.5

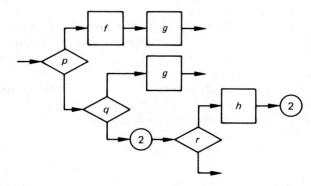

Figure 4.6

obtained by repeatedly replacing each repeated node by the subtree beginning at the first occurrence of that node earlier in the path. As a final
simplification, the first occurrence of each repeated node can itself be suppressed. For example, the flowchart

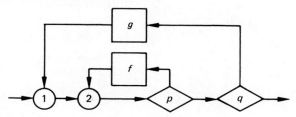

has the E-chart

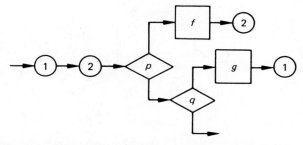

that expands to the E-tree (with collecting nodes suppressed):

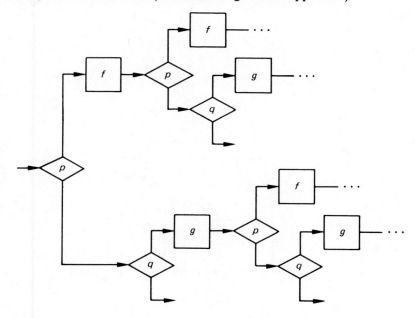

EXERCISES

1. Which of the following programs are proper?

a)

b)

c)

d)

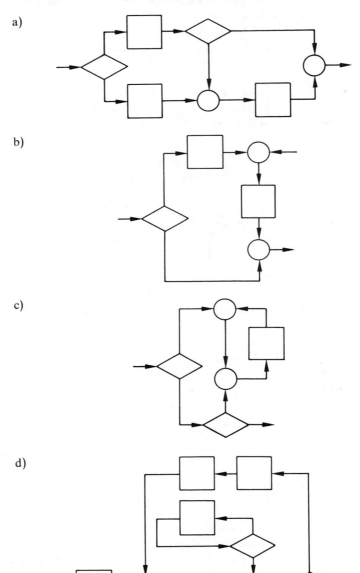

e)

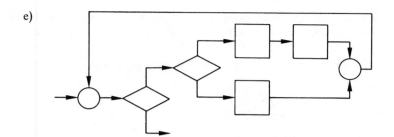

2. Enumerate the proper subprograms with more than one node in the following program:

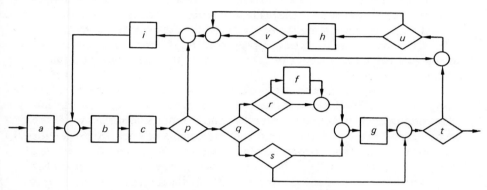

3. Given a proper program with exactly ϕ function nodes, π predicate nodes, γ collecting nodes, and λ lines, show that $\pi = \gamma$ and $\lambda = \phi + 3\pi + 1$. (*Hint:* Count heads and tails of lines and equate them.)

4. Enumerate the 16 distinct control structures for proper programs with two predicate nodes and no function nodes. (*Hint:* Two such control structures are

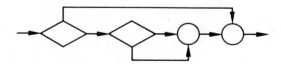

and

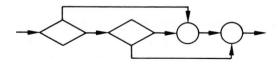

These control structures are distinct, since the collector nodes may not be interchanged.) Eight of the control structures are type CP; that is, entry is to a collector node (C), exit is from a predicate node (P). Similarly, two are type CC, two are type

PP, and four are type PC. How many of the 16 are direct combinations of one-predicate control structures? Identify the 10 control structures of the 16 that are their own duals.

5. Show that the dual of a control structure with unleavable node sets has unreachable node sets, and, conversely.

4.3   PROGRAM FUNCTIONS

4.3.1   Data Assignment

The assignment statement can be regarded as a program in its own right that transforms an initial data state into a final data state in a particularly simple way. All data not listed on the left side is to remain unchanged; the right side gives the rule for calculating the new value(s) for the data item(s) on the left side. When embedded in a larger program, the assignment statement remains well behaved; it does not change data of the larger program that it does not know about.

However, in developing the concept of assignment statements at the design level, in PDL, the behavior of assignment statements at the implementation level in language compilers and machines is instructive. At the compiler and machine level, assignment statements can fail to execute for various reasons—type incompatibility (assigning a character to integer data), arithmetic overflow (dividing by zero), structure incompatibility (assigning an array to a scalar), and so forth. At the design level, assignment statements can be used to bridge these type, finiteness, and structural problems, which are then properly handled at more detailed levels. And yet, even at the design level, assignment statements must be specified with precision, even though with flexibility.

This precision, yet flexibility, can be achieved by a simple but fundamental step. It is to understand the assignment statement as the name of a function that defines a state transition for all data known to the program containing it. The domain of the function corresponds to the initial data states that are transformed by the assignment statement into final data states. For example, in a program with data space x, y, z the assignment

$$x := y$$

corresponds to an *assignment function*, that is, a set of ordered pairs of the form

$$\{((x, y, z), (u, v, w)) \mid u = y \land v = y \land w = z\}$$

more easily written as

$$\{((x, y, z), (y, y, z))\}$$

There may be additional conditions that limit the function. For example, if x, y, z are declared as data type integer ≥ 0, then the function $x := y$ should be amended to

$$\{((x, y, z), (y, y, z)) \mid x \geq 0 \wedge y \geq 0 \wedge z \geq 0\}$$

As an alternative, a conditional rule can name the function:

$$(x \geq 0 \wedge y \geq 0 \wedge z \geq 0 \to x := y)$$

Before proceeding to more complex assignments, however, note that the letters x, y, z have quite different meanings on the two sides of the equation ($x := y$ shown in parentheses for readability)

$$(x := y) = \{((x, y, z), (y, y, z))\}$$

In the function name "$x := y$", x and y refer to names of data known to a program; on the right side, x, y, z are names of values of data. For example, given a data space (x, y, z) (meaning x is first, y second, z third) the definition

$$(x := y) = \{((u, v, w), (v, v, w))\}$$

defines the same assignment statement as before, as does

$$(x := y) = \{((y, z, x), (z, z, x))\}$$

In this context, assignments always map one data state into another, in which the names used in assignments refer to ordinal positions in the corresponding data space.

Next, consider for scalars x, y, z with data type integer ≥ 0, the assignment

$$x := y - z$$

In this case, the assignment function is

$$(x := y - z) = \{((x, y, z), (y - z, y, z)) \mid x \geq 0 \wedge y \geq 0 \wedge z \geq 0 \wedge y - z. \geq 0\}$$

That is, x must be nonnegative before and after the assignment. In particular, the function has no argument for which $y < z$. As defined, this assignment fails when $y < z$, just as real assignments fail when executing on a machine. In this way, a function definition permits flexibility for design, but also permits any degree of precision required in dealing with implementation questions.

Assignments may use functions in their definition, but these should not be confused with the assignment function itself. For example

$$x := \max(y, z)$$

makes use of a max function defined as, say

$$\max = \{((y, z), (u)) \,|\, (y \geq z \wedge u = y) \vee (z \geq y \wedge u = z)\}$$

but the assignment function is

$$(x := \max(y, z)) = \{((x, y, z), (\max(y, z), y, z))\}$$

which accounts for values of y, z, as well.

Assignments to arrays using variable indexes provide a reminder that the indexes are part of the data state, as are the array members. For example, if x is a 3-list $x(1:3)$ (that is, an array of 3 elements), the multiple assignment

$$i, x(i + 1) := x(i), i + x(i + 1)$$

is the name of a state transition function involving at least a 4-list

$$(i, x(1), x(2), x(3))$$

which includes the index. The complete expression of the assignment above is therefore given by the conditional rule

$$(i = 1 \rightarrow i, x(2) := x(1), 1 + x(2) \,|\, i = 2 \rightarrow i, x(3) := x(2), 2 + x(3))$$

(Since $x(i + 1)$ is not defined for $i > 2$, the assignment function is undefined for any initial i not 1 or 2.) In this case, the idea of an assignment function captures the correct use of assignment to arrays.

4.3.2   Program Effects on Data

An execution of a program may terminate (reach an end point) in its execution tree, and possibly every execution will terminate, even though the execution tree is itself infinite. Consider all possible executions defined by an execution tree. For each initial data state X for which execution terminates, a final data state Y is determined.† The value Y is unique, given X, so that the set of all ordered pairs $\{(X, Y)\}$ so defined is a function. We call this function the *program function* of a program. Thus, in particular, the program function of a single assignment statement is exactly the function that the assignment names, as discussed above.

---

† In this book, upper-case letters denote data states, lower-case letters denote data variables.

Given a proper program named P, we denote its program function by $[P]$ (read "bracket P"). By definition then, a program P composed of an individual function node $f = \{(X, Y)\}$

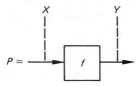

has program function

$$[P] = \{(X, Y) \mid Y = f(X)\}$$

A sequence of two functions

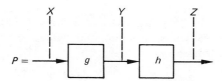

where $g = \{(X, Y)\}$, $h = \{(Y, Z)\}$, has as its program function the composition of the individual functions:

$$[P] = \{(X, Z) \mid Z = h(g(X))\}$$

The program function of a loop-free program can be described as a union of function compositions that can be derived directly from its finite E-tree. Each predicate on a path, composed with earlier functions, defines a necessary and sufficient condition for continuing on each branch of the path; the composition of all functions on the path gives the part of the program function corresponding to that path. For example, consider the flowchart program shown in Fig. 4.7. The E-chart, with end points labeled (1) to (5), is

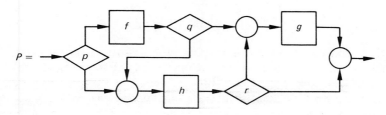

Figure 4.7

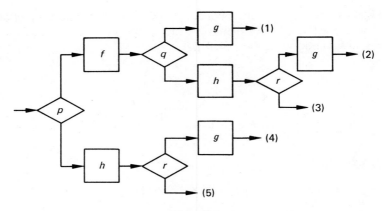

Figure 4.8

shown in Fig. 4.8. The program function is thus a union of five function compositions, each of whose domain and values are defined by a path through the E-chart; namely,

(1) $\{(X, Y) \mid p(X) \wedge q(f(X)) \wedge Y = g(f(X))\}$

(2) $\{(X, Y) \mid p(X) \wedge \sim q(f(X)) \wedge r(h(f(X))) \wedge Y = g(h(f(X)))\}$

(3) $\{(X, Y) \mid p(X) \wedge \sim q(f(X)) \wedge \sim r(h(f(X))) \wedge Y = h(f(X))\}$

(4) $\{(X, Y) \mid \sim p(X) \wedge r(h(X)) \wedge Y = g(h(X))\}$

(5) $\{(X, Y) \mid \sim p(X) \wedge \sim r(h(X)) \wedge Y = h(X)\}$

This program function can also be defined as a conditional rule:

$$[P] = \{(X, Y) \mid (p(X) \wedge q \circ f(X) \to Y = g \circ f(X) \mid$$
$$p(X) \wedge \sim q \circ f(X) \wedge r \circ h \circ f(X) \to Y = g \circ h \circ f(X) \mid$$
$$p(X) \wedge \sim q \circ f(X) \wedge \sim r \circ h \circ f(X) \to Y = h \circ f(X) \mid$$
$$\sim p(X) \wedge r \circ h(X) \to Y = g \circ h(X) \mid$$
$$\sim p(X) \wedge \sim r \circ h(X) \to Y = h(X))\}$$

The program function of a looping program can be characterized by a number of function equations in a like number of functions. In particular, for each repeated collecting node j in the E-chart of the program, define a function fj. Each fj defines the function of all nodes traversed in the E-chart from the first occurrence of collecting node j. Then, replacing each repeated collecting node with the corresponding function, we obtain a loop-free

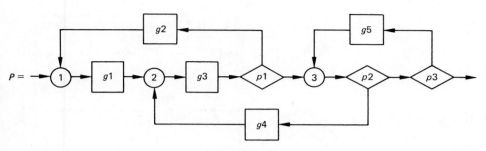

Figure 4.9

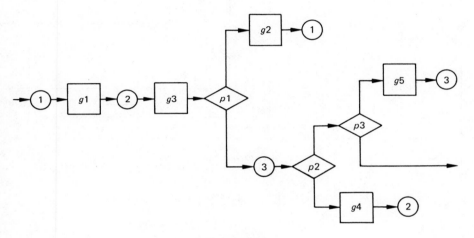

Figure 4.10

E-chart, as shown above for loop-free programs, except that the final function in each composition on a path may be one of the functions to be determined.

For example, the flowchart program P shown in Fig. 4.9 has an E-chart as shown in Fig. 4.10. To characterize the program function of P, associate $f1$, $f2$, $f3$ with collecting nodes 1, 2, 3 as shown in Fig. 4.11. Then $f1$, $f2$, $f3$ satisfy the following function equations, which can be written out by inspection, in following paths of the E-chart:

$$f1 = \{(X, Y) \mid Y = f2 \circ g1(X)\}$$
$$f2 = \{(X, Y) \mid (p1 \circ g3(X) \to Y = f1 \circ g2 \circ g3(X) \mid$$
$$\sim p1 \circ g3(X) \to Y = f3 \circ g3(X))\}$$

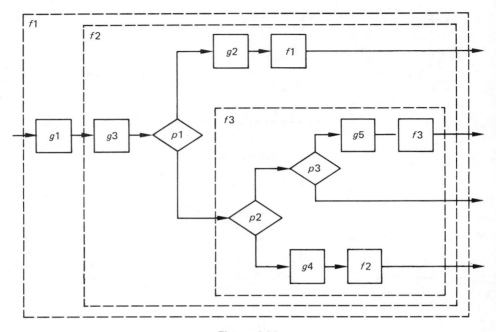

Figure 4.11

$$f3 = \{(X,\,Y)\,|\,(p2(X) \wedge p3(X) \to Y = f3 \circ g5(X)\,|$$
$$p2(X) \wedge {\sim}p3(X) \to Y = X\,|$$
$${\sim}p2(X) \to Y = f2 \circ g4(X))\}$$

If this system of equations can be solved, then the program function of P is

$$[P] = f1$$

To illustrate program functions in PDL, consider the following programs (all data items are integers). Program functions are given by sets of ordered pairs and by data assignments (within conditional rules where necessary):

a) $[x := x + y;\ y := x - y] = \{((x,\,y),\,(x + y,\,x))\}$

$$= (x,\,y := x + y,\,x)$$

b) $[\textbf{if } x > y \textbf{ then } x := y \textbf{ fi}] = \{((x,\,y),\,(\min(x,\,y),\,y))\}$

$$= (x := \min(x,\,y))$$

c) $[\textbf{while } x > 0 \textbf{ do } x := x - 1 \textbf{ od}] = \{(x, \min(0, x))\}$
$$= (x := \min(0, x))$$

d) $[\textbf{while } x \neq 0 \textbf{ do } x := x - 1 \textbf{ od}] = \{(x, 0) \mid x \geq 0\}$
$$= (x \geq 0 \rightarrow x := 0)$$

e) $[\textbf{do } x := x + 1 \textbf{ until } x > y \textbf{ od}] = \{((x, y), (\max(x + 1, y + 1), y))\}$
$$= (x := \max(x + 1, y + 1))$$

f) $[\textbf{do } x := x + 1 \textbf{ until } x \neq y \textbf{ od}] = \{((x, y), (x + 1, y)) \mid x \neq y - 1\}$
$$\cup \{((x, y), (y + 1, y)) \mid x = y - 1\}$$
$$= (x \neq y - 1 \rightarrow x := x + 1 \mid$$
$$x = y - 1 \rightarrow x := y + 1)$$

Note how a slight change in a whiletest or untiltest can change the program function. In (d), the whiledo does not terminate for $x < 0$, hence the domain is restricted to $x \geq 0$.

4.3.3 Program Equivalence

The concept of program equivalence is important in simplifying control structures for better understanding, as we will demonstrate in the Structure Theorem. We now define two types of program equivalence. If two programs have the same execution tree, they are *execution equivalent*; if they have the same program function, they are *function equivalent*. For example, the programs

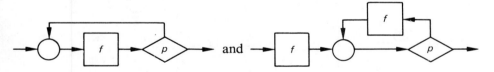

are execution equivalent, while the programs

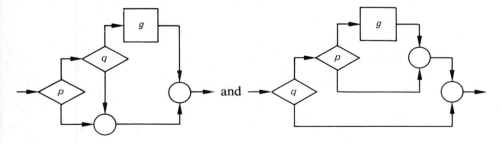

are function equivalent, but not execution equivalent. Execution equivalence implies function equivalence, but not conversely.

EXERCISES

1. Verify the assertions above about the examples of function equivalence and execution equivalence, by expanding their E-charts into execution trees and comparing them.

2. Using E-trees, verify that the following pairs are execution equivalent:

   a) **(do** g **until** p **od)**   and   **(** g; **while** ~p **do** g **od)**

   b) **(do1** g **while** p **do2** h **od)**   and   **(** g; **while** p **do** h; g **od)**

3. Construct program functions for the following programs:

a)

b)

c)

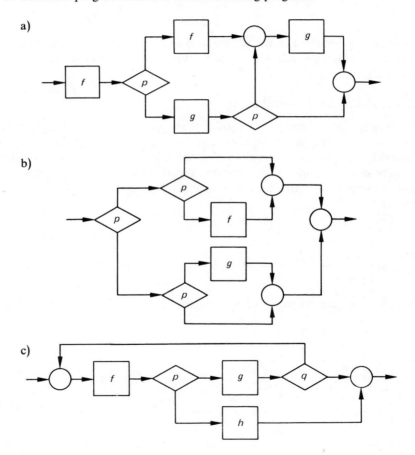

4. Given the following programs (x and y nonnegative integers), compare program P with programs Q, R, S, T, and U, and indicate whether each pair is execution equivalent, function equivalent, or neither:

$P =$ **while**
     $y > 0$
  do
     $x := x - 1$
     $y := y - 1$
  od

$Q = (x, y := x - y, 0)$

$R =$ **if**
     $y > 0$
  then
     $x := x - 1$
     $y := y - 1$
     while
        $y > 0$
     do
        $x := x - 1$
        $y := y - 1$
     od
  fi

$S =$ **if**
     $y > 0$
  then
     $x := x - 1$
     $y := y - 1$
     $x, y := x - y, 0$
  fi

$T =$ **if**
     $y > 0$
  then
     $x := x - 1$
     $y := y - 1$
  fi
     $x, y := x - y, 0$

$U =$ **if**
     $y > 0$
  then
     do
        $x := x - 1$
        $y := y - 1$
     until
        $y \le 0$
     od
  fi

5. Determine the program function of the following programs (x, y, a, b nonnegative integers; use conditional rules to define domains such that the programs terminate):

$P =$ **while**
     $x \le b$
  do
     $x := x + a$
  od

$R =$ **do**
     $x := x + a$
  until
     $x > b$
  od

$Q =$ **while**
     $x \ne b$
  do
     $x := x + a$
  od

$S =$ **do**
     $x := x + a$
  until
     $x = b$
  od

$T = $ **do1**
    $x := x + a$
  while
    $x \leq b$
  do2
    $x := x + a$
  od

$U = $ **do1**
    $x := x + a$
  while
    $x \neq b$
  do2
    $x := x + a$
  od

4.4   PROGRAM STRUCTURES

4.4.1   Prime Programs

A proper program may contain parts that are themselves proper. As defined earlier, such parts are called *proper subprograms*. A *prime program* is a proper program that has no proper subprogram of more than one node. For example, programs with control structure as shown in the left column in Fig. 4.12 are prime, while programs with control structure as shown in the right column are proper but not prime; that is, the first figure in the right column has a proper subprogram of more than one node, namely,

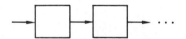

as does the second,

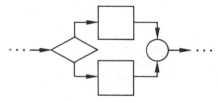

and the third:

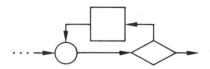

There is an infinite number of prime control structures, as Fig. 4.13 shows.

    Proper programs can be enumerated by the number of their nodes and classified as prime or not prime. The control structures of prime programs composed of 1, 2, 3, and 4 nodes are enumerated in Fig. 4.14. Of these 15 primes with up to four nodes, only seven have one or more function nodes

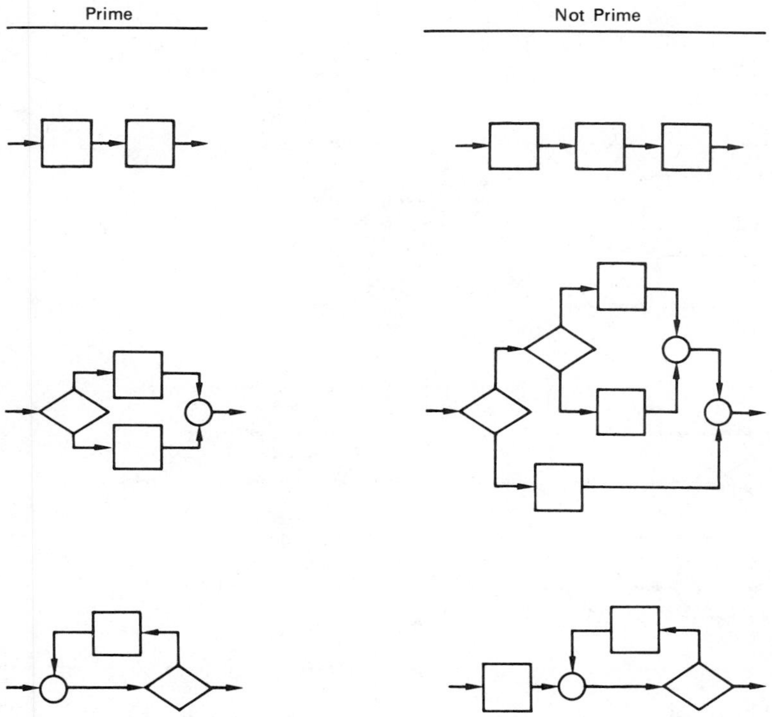

Prime   Not Prime

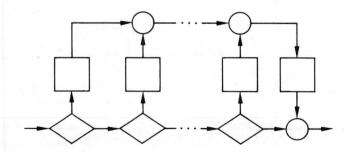

Figure 4.12

Figure 4.13

1 node

2 nodes

3 nodes

4 nodes

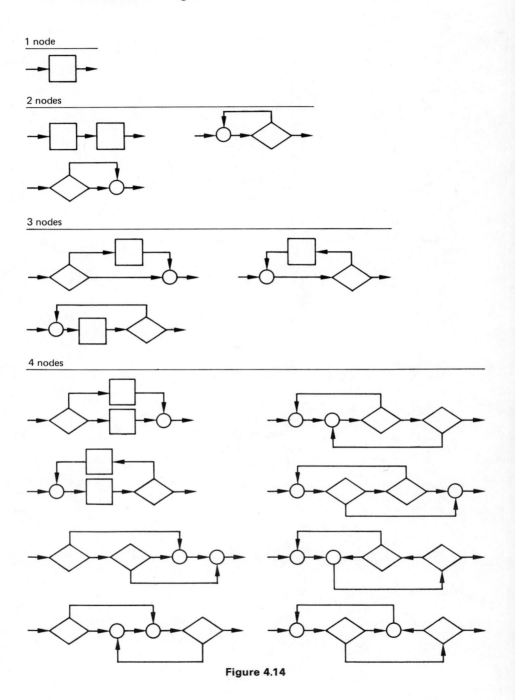

Figure 4.14

(and can thereby operate on data). These seven are given specific names below; they correspond to the control structures of PDL, as shown.†

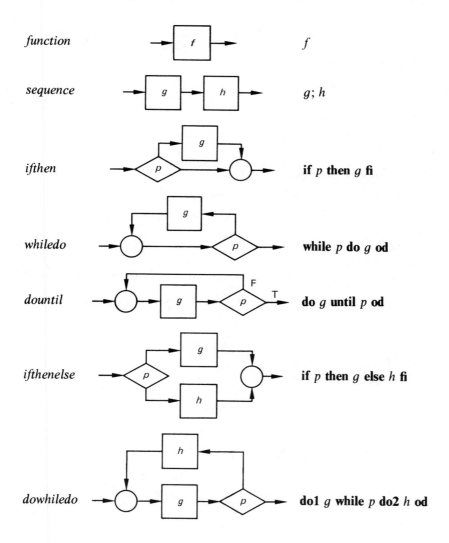

function	f
sequence	$g; h$
ifthen	**if** p **then** g **fi**
whiledo	**while** p **do** g **od**
dountil	**do** g **until** p **od**
ifthenelse	**if** p **then** g **else** h **fi**
dowhiledo	**do1** g **while** p **do2** h **od**

---

† The PDL extended sequence structure (sequence of more than two parts) and fordo and case structures (abbreviations for uniform sequences and multiple ifthenelses, respectively) do not appear in the following enumeration; however, we will find it convenient to treat them as special proper programs in the remainder of the book.

The program functions of these primes are readily derived from their functions and predicates, as shown next, where superscripts on g are interpreted as follows:

$$g^0(X) = X \quad \text{and} \quad g^k(X) = g \circ g^{k-1}(X) \qquad \text{for } k = 1, 2, \ldots$$

The program functions are†

$$[f] = f$$
$$[g; h] = \{(X, Y) \mid Y = h \circ g(X)\}$$
$$[\textbf{if } p \textbf{ then } g \textbf{ fi}] = \{(X, Y) \mid (p(X) \wedge Y = g(X))$$
$$\vee (\sim p(X) \wedge Y = X)\}$$
$$[\textbf{while } p \textbf{ do } g \textbf{ od}] = \{(X, Y) \mid \exists k \geq 0((\forall j, 0 \leq j < k)(p \circ g^j(X))$$
$$\wedge \sim p \circ g^k(X)$$
$$\wedge Y = g^k(X))\}$$

(In the outer quantified expression, the loop terminates after k iterations, with predicate p testing *true* for $k - 1$ iterations, then *false*. Note that if the domain of j is empty, the inner quantified expression is vacuously *true*.)

$$[\textbf{do } g \textbf{ until } p \textbf{ od}] = \{(X, Y) \mid \exists k > 0((\forall j, 1 \leq j < k)(\sim p \circ g^j(X))$$
$$\wedge p \circ g^k(X)$$
$$\wedge Y = g^k(X))\}$$

(The loop terminates after k iterations.)

$$[\textbf{if } p \textbf{ then } g \textbf{ else } h \textbf{ fi}] = \{(X, Y) \mid (p(X) \wedge Y = g(X))$$
$$\vee (\sim p(X) \wedge Y = h(X))\}$$
$$[\textbf{do1 } g \textbf{ while } p \textbf{ do2 } h \textbf{ od}] = \{(X, Y) \mid \exists k \geq 0((\forall j, 0 \leq j < k)(p \circ g \circ (h \circ g)^j(X))$$
$$\wedge \sim p \circ g \circ (h \circ g)^k(X)$$
$$\wedge Y = g \circ (h \circ g)^k(X))\}$$

(The loop terminates after k iterations.)

---

† These program functions can be written in an alternate form as, for example,

$$[\textbf{if } p \textbf{ then } g \textbf{ else } h \textbf{ fi}] = \{(X, Y) \mid (p(X) \rightarrow Y = g(X)$$
$$\wedge \sim p(X) \rightarrow Y = h(X))\}$$

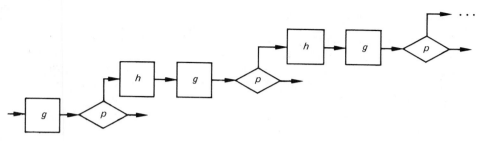

Figure 4.15

The program functions for the looping programs above are somewhat tedious to describe, but can also be visualized in terms of their E-trees. For example, the E-tree for **do1** *g* **while** *p* **do2** *h* **od** is shown in Fig. 4.15, and its program function is the union of the subfunctions defined by each terminating path. The beginning sequence of subfunctions is shown in Fig. 4.16.

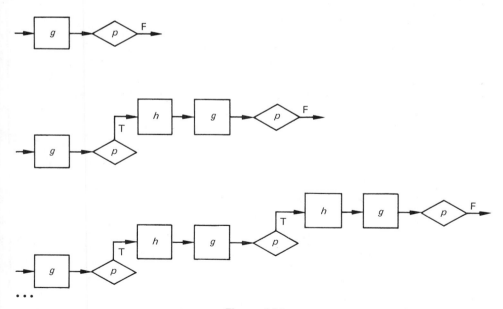

Figure 4.16

4.4.2   Compound Programs

If a function node of a prime program is replaced by another prime program, a new proper program results. We define a *compound program* to be any program obtained by replacing function nodes of a prime program by prime programs. As a special case, prime programs are considered compound programs themselves.

Compound programs can be defined with arbitrary size but limited complexity by restricting the prime programs used to a fixed set of primes called a *basis set*. Any basis set of prime programs generates a specific class of compound programs, a subset of all possible proper programs. For example, the set {sequence, ifthenelse} generates a class of loop-free programs and the set {ifthenelse, whiledo} generates a class of programs whose execution trees contain at most one distinct function node (possibly repeated) along any path. Some of these classes of compound programs are subsets of others; for example, the set {sequence, dountil} generates a subset of the programs generated by the set {sequence, ifthen, whiledo}.

Definition.   A *structured program* is a compound program constructed from a fixed basis set of prime programs.

4.4.3   The Structure Theorem

The motivation for studying compound programs is the fact that any proper program, no matter how large or complex, can be simulated in its step-by-step execution by a new compound program generated by a small basis set of prime programs. One suitable basis set consists of sequence, ifthenelse, and whiledo programs. The simulation is accomplished by using the functions and predicates of the original program, and assignments to and tests on a single new data item, namely, a "program counter." We restate these assertions more formally as a theorem:

Structure Theorem.   Any proper program is function equivalent to a structured program with basis set {sequence, ifthenelse, whiledo}, using functions and predicates of the original program and assignments and tests on one additional counter.

Proof.   Consider an arbitrary proper program, and arbitrarily number its function and predicate nodes 1, 2, ..., n, say, beginning with the first such node reached from the entry line. (If one or more collecting nodes are incident to the entry line, continue along their out-lines until a first function or predicate node is reached.) Number the exit line of the program 0. Now, attach to each out-line of each function and predicate node the number of the (unique) next function or predicate node reached, if any; otherwise (if the

exit line is reached) attach 0. Next, for each function node of the original
program numbered i, say, with function h and out-line assigned j

construct a new proper sequence program g_i (with in-line assigned i):

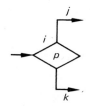

Following the execution of h, this program assigns the value j to a new label
variable L (the "program counter") not in the original program. Next, for
each predicate node numbered i, say

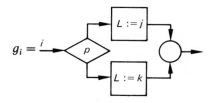

construct a new proper ifthenelse program g_i:

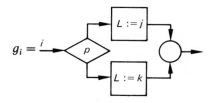

Now construct an initialized whiledo program, with dopart composed
of nested ifthenelses testing values of L from 1 to n. Each ifthenelse *true*
out-line connects to g_i, which contains a function or predicate node from the
original program. The program is shown in Fig. 4.17 (the elsepart of the
innermost ifthenelse is simply I, the identity function). The program in PDL
is shown in Fig. 4.18.

It is clear that whatever the structure of the original program, f is
function equivalent to it; moreover, f is a structured program generated by
the basis set {sequence, ifthenelse, whiledo}. This completes the proof.

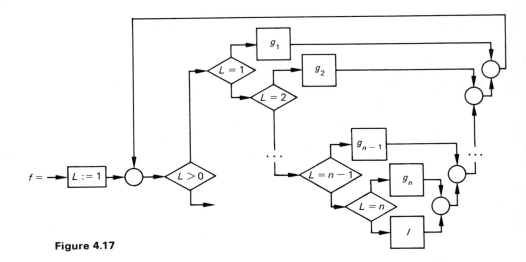

Figure 4.17

$$f = L := 1$$
   while
      $L > 0$
  do
    if
      $L = 1$
    then
      g_1
    else
      if
        $L = 2$.
      then
        g_2
      else
        . . .
        if
          $L = n - 1$
        then
          g_{n-1}
        else
          if
            $L = n$
          then
            g_n
          else
            I
          fi
        fi
        . . .
      fi
    fi
  od

Figure 4.18

In other branches of mathematics a unique representation is often a desirable goal; this does not seem to be the case in programming. Nevertheless, the existence of a representation theorem,† which is what the Structure Theorem is, still permits the resolution of questions of the completeness of a programming language simply and effectively. For example, all one needs in order to show that a new set of programs will span the set of all proper programs is the ability to represent sequence, ifthenelse, and whiledo programs in the new set. Thus, to show that the set {sequence, ifthenelse, dountil} can likewise represent all proper programs, it is sufficient to express the whiledo structure using members of that set. This can be shown in PDL text as

$$[\text{while } p \text{ do } g \text{ od}] = [\text{if } p \text{ then do } g \text{ until } \sim p \text{ od else } I \text{ fi}]$$

or in flowchart form, if

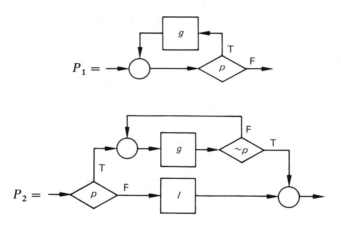

then

$$[P_1] = [P_2]$$

---

† The result of the Structure Theorem is similar to the result of representation theorems in various branches of mathematics, in which it is shown that all elements of a set, or "space," can be represented by combinations of a subset of the space. As two examples of representation theorems, three nonplanar vectors span a three-dimensional euclidean space, and the set {sin nx, cos $nx \,|\, n = 0, 1, \ldots$} spans a wide set of functions in the interval $(0, 2\pi)$—that is, the set spans a "function space." These examples refer to linear combination for representation. In the Structure Theorem it is shown that three simple classes of prime programs defined by sequence, ifthenelse, and whiledo control structures span the set of all proper programs, using substitution of prime programs for function nodes as the only rule of combination.

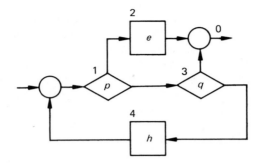

Figure 4.19

Hence sequence, ifthenelse, and dountil are sufficient control structures to represent all proper programs as well.

The constructive proof above permits a flowchart program with any arbitrary structure to be translated into a program with basis {sequence, ifthenelse, whiledo}. For example, consider the flowchart (Fig. 4.19) with function and predicate nodes and exit line as numbered. The proof construction produces the following new sequence and ifthenelse programs,

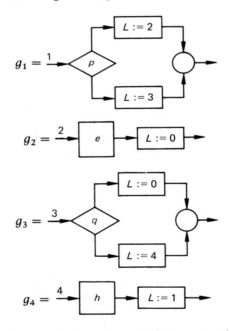

which can be combined into the structured program shown in Fig. 4.20, where each node of the original program corresponds to a case evaluation of the label variable, L. We call such a program a *label structure* program.

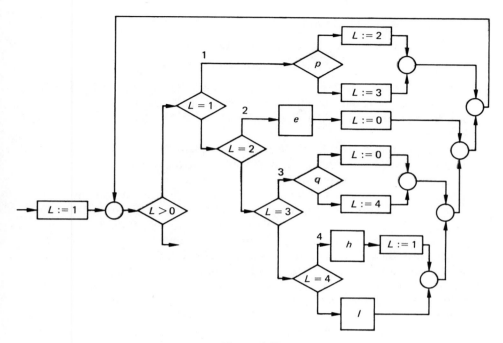

Figure 4.20

4.4.4   Recursion Structure Programs

Although structured, the programs produced in the foregoing proof of the Structure Theorem may lack clarity and efficiency. To improve on that we give a new construction for eliminating unnecessary settings and testings of the counter L.

The idea is to replace, for some given $j > 0$, all assignments $L := j$ by the program g_j. (Note that for $L = 1$, the initialization $L := 1$ preceding the whiledo must be replaced by g_1, along with any other occurrences of $L := 1$.) Since the value j will thereby never be assigned to L, the test $L = j$ can be removed from the set of ifthenelses in f. One step of this kind leads to a new sequence of programs

$$g_1', g_2', \ldots, g_{n-1}'$$

where the g's have been renumbered, if necessary. The only barrier to continuing this process is a recursive (or self) reference, that is, some g_i' has in it the assignment $L := i$. In such cases, the assignment $L := i$ cannot be eliminated, because replacing $L := i$ by g_i' reintroduces $L := i$ in the text of g_i'. We therefore can continue substitution as long as possible until either

1. all assignments to L have been eliminated except $L := 0$, or
2. every g_i' remaining contains an assignment $L := i$.

If the program is loop free, then the assignment $L := 0$ appears on every path, and the counter L and whiledo loop can be eliminated as well. What remains is a compound program that likely exhibits reasonable clarity and execution efficiency.

For example, the label structure program derived above can be improved as follows. First, choosing to substitute the program on the $L = 4$ path for the $L := 4$ assignment and to eliminate the $L = 4$ test, we get the new program shown in Fig. 4.21. (Note that on this step, programs on any of the $L = 1$, $L = 2$, $L = 3$, or $L = 4$ paths could have been substituted for the corresponding assignment to L.) We choose next to substitute the program on the $L = 3$ path for the $L := 3$ assignment and eliminate the $L = 3$ test (Fig. 4.22). Next, the program on the $L = 2$ path can be substituted for the $L := 2$ assignment and the $L = 2$ test can be eliminated (Fig. 4.23). Finally, we observe that the $L := 1$ assignment and the $L = 1$ test within the loop are unnecessary, since L is initialized to 1 and becomes 0 only on exit; thus both can be eliminated to get a final structured program (Fig. 4.24) that exhibits more clarity and efficiency. We call such a program a *recursion structure* program. Note that it may be possible to translate a given label structure

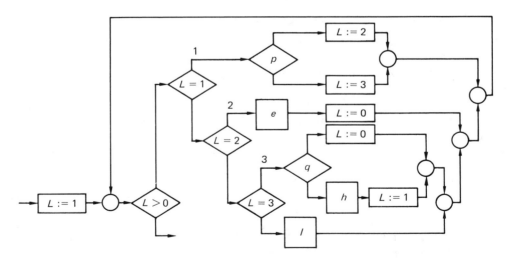

Figure 4.21

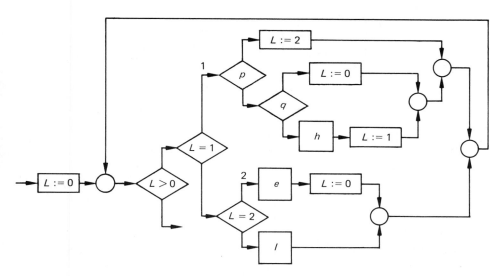

Figure 4.22

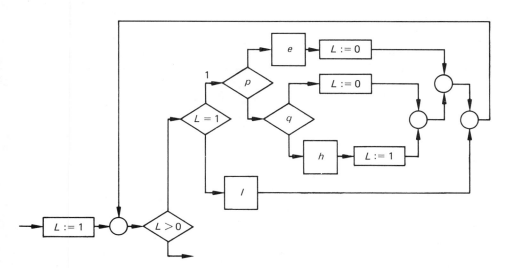

Figure 4.23

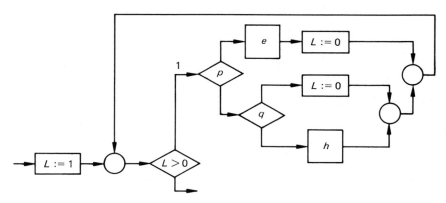

Figure 4.24

program into a number of different function equivalent, but not execution equivalent, recursion structure programs, depending on the order in which substitutions are made.

EXERCISES

1. Show that two distinct prime programs of a common program, with at least one predicate between them, are disjoint.

2. Show that there are 30 prime programs with 5 nodes. (Recall the 16 control structures with two predicate nodes and no function nodes from the exercise in Section 4.2.)

3. Carry out the construction of the Structure Theorem to produce label structure programs and then recursion structure programs for the following flowcharts:

a)

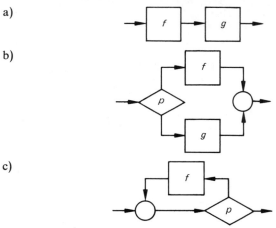

b)

c)

d)

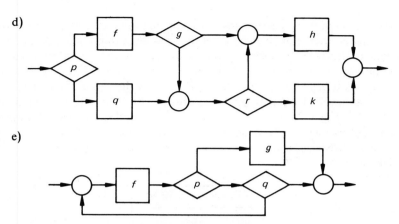

e)

4. Show that the improved construction of a recursion structure program can be continued, even when some g_i contains the assignment $L := i$, by

a) replacing g_i by the program

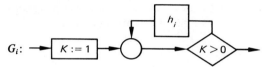

$$G_i:$$

when h_i is obtained from g_i by

1) deleting assignments $L := i$
2) adding the assignment $K := 0$ just after each assignment $L := j \ (j \neq i)$, and

b) replacing all assignments $L := i$ outside g_i by G_i.

5. Show that repeated application of the construction of Exercise 4 leads to a structured program in which the original loop on counter L is replaced by a nested set of loops on new truth values, all of which can be maintained in a single stack.

4.5   A CASE STUDY IN PROGRAM STRUCTURING

4.5.1   Prime Program Parsing

The work required to convert an arbitrary program into a structured program can often be reduced by recognizing those parts, if any, of the arbitrary program that are already structured. Recognition of structured parts can be carried out in a completely systematic manner, as described next.

The hierarchy of prime programs that make up a compound program can be found by a *prime program parse*, the process of repeatedly recognizing and replacing a prime program by a new function node, until no prime programs remain to be replaced. To expedite the parse, a sequence of any number of function nodes (not just two) can be replaced by a single function node. A *parse step* is defined by a set of *parse units* that equate named new function nodes with the prime programs they represent, and by a *reduced program* made simpler by use of the new function nodes. The last such step reduces a final prime to a single function node at the top of the hierarchy— the highest level of control structure abstraction. The flowchart program illustrated in Fig. 4.25 parses to a single function node in a series of six parse steps (a purely mechanical process, tedious for humans to work through in a program of this size) as outlined below. New function nodes in parse units are labeled

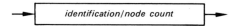

where *identification* is a number assigned in sequence, beginning with 100 for Step 1, 200 for Step 2, and so on, which names the new function, and *node count* is the number of function and predicate nodes from the original flowchart abstracted by the new function. Reduced programs corresponding to each step are shown in Figs. 4.26 through 4.31.

Step 1

Parse units:

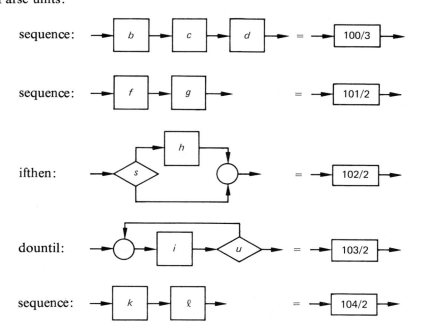

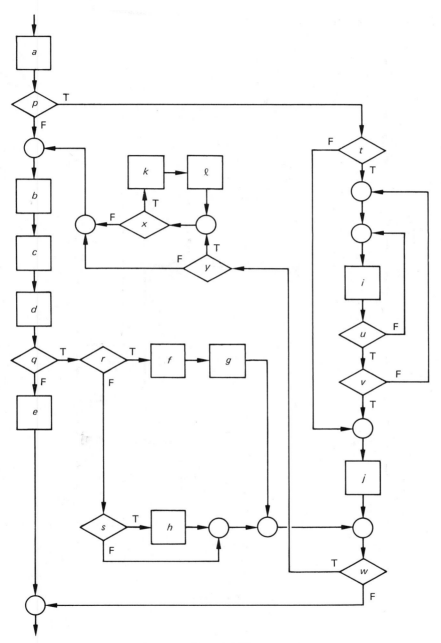

Figure 4.25

Reduced program:

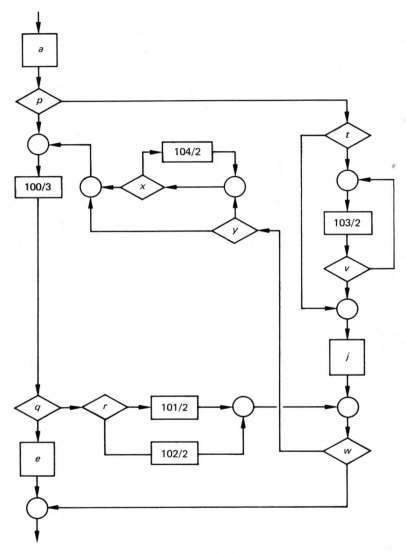

Figure 4.26

Step 2
Parse units:

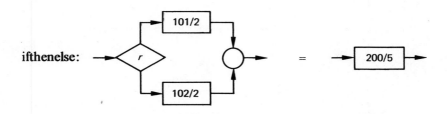

ifthenelse:

dountil:

whiledo:

Reduced program:

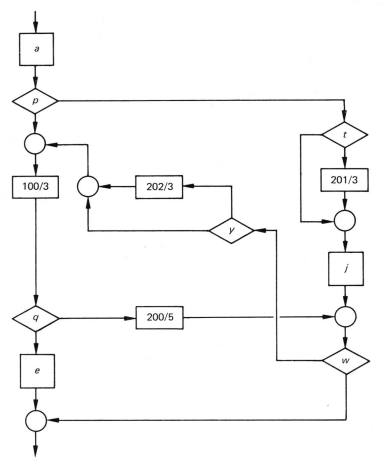

Figure 4.27

Step 3

Parse units:

ifthen:

ifthen:

Reduced program:

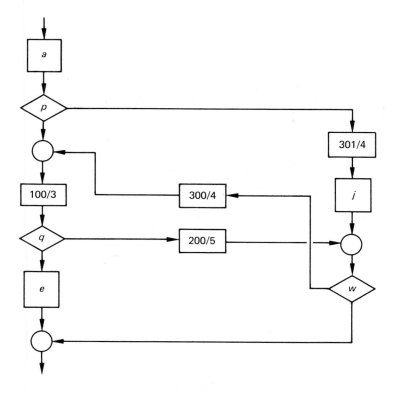

Figure 4.28

Step 4

Parse units:

sequence:

Reduced program:

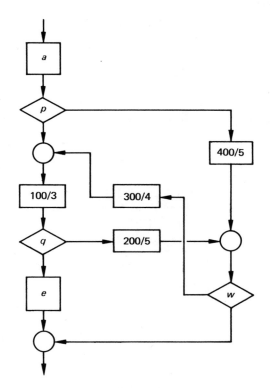

Figure 4.29

Step 5

Parse units:

> (The prime below is not a PDL prime—in fact, it has no standard name, so we call it "unnamed1".)

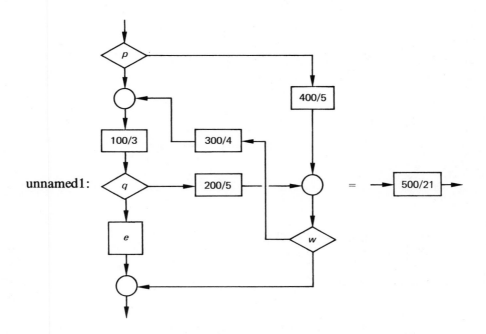

unnamed1:

Reduced program:

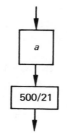

Figure 4.30

Step 6

Parse units:

sequence:

Reduced program:

Figure 4.31

Thus, the original program parses to a single function node in six steps. As a simple check on correctness, the count value of the final function node should equal the total number of function and predicate nodes in the original program—in this case 22 nodes.

4.5.2 An Improved Structuring Technique

As we have seen, the Structure Theorem proof procedure can be used to convert an arbitrary proper program into a structured program with basis {sequence, ifthenelse, whiledo}. Following the conversion, the resulting label structure program can be repeatedly simplified until it takes the form of a recursion structure program. This process can be improved by preceding the initial conversion to label structure with a special prime program parse that substitutes individual function nodes for structured portions, if any, of the arbitrary program. This reduces the work to be done in the structuring process and preserves any parts of the arbitrary program with acceptable structure.

To illustrate, the following primes compose the basis set of the parse just completed:

{sequence, ifthen, ifthenelse, dountil, whiledo, unnamed1}

However, a set of basis primes can be defined prior to parsing a program, as the only primes eligible to be recognized. In this case, the series of parse steps is called a *fixed basis parse*. For example, given the basis set {sequence, ifthen, ifthenelse, dountil, whiledo}, a fixed basis parse of the previous program would end at Step 4, since Step 5 identified a prime (unnamed1) not in the basis set.

Step 4

Reduced program:

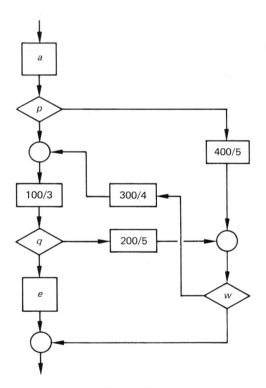

Figure 4.32

At completion of the parse, the new functions (100/3, 200/5, 300/4, 400/5) name *structured islands* in the original program. We now convert this parsed

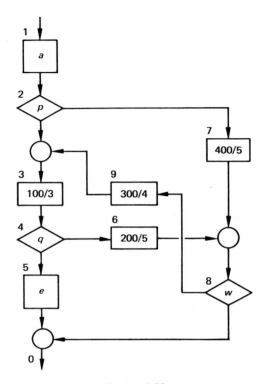

Figure 4.33

program to a label structure program and then to a recursion structure
program as usual, and finally replace the new function nodes with the
structured islands they abstract. To begin, we number the functions and
predicates of the Step 4 program in arbitrary order, and number the exit line
0 (Fig. 4.33). The label structure program (shown with a case structure, as a
simpler way to write nested ifthenelses within the dopart) appears in Fig.
4.34. We decide against substituting for an L value of 1 outside the dopart,
and reject L values of 3 and 8, whose multiple occurrences would require
duplication of structure. This leaves L values of 2, 4, 5, 6, 7, and 9. When
these substitutions and resulting case eliminations are carried out in turn,
the recursion structure program is as shown in Fig. 4.35.

Further substitutions are possible; namely, case 8 for $L := 8$ in cases 1
and 3 (creating a recursive reference in case 3), or case 3 for $L := 3$ in case 8

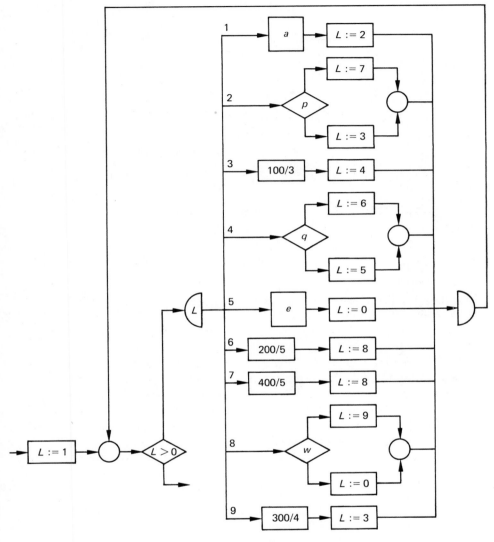

Figure 4.34

(likewise creating a recursive reference). But we elect to halt substitution with the three cases shown. In PDL, the program so far is as shown in Fig. 4.36. The final program in flowchart form can now be constructed by sub-

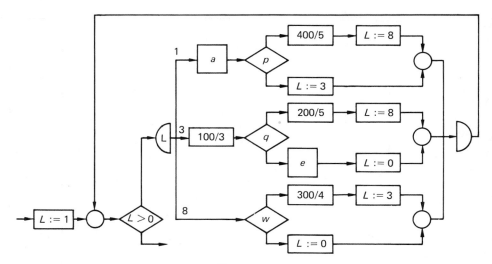

Figure 4.35

stituting structured islands named by each new function node (Fig. 4.37). To reduce the amount of consecutive PDL text, the final program can be given as a main segment that runs three segments at the next level, one for each case (Fig. 4.38).

The intertwined control logic of the original program has been unraveled into three distinct structured program parts whose execution is controlled by assignments and tests on the label variable. With complex interconnections abstracted out, the functional effect of each single entry/single exit program part can now be understood independently of the others, in a systematic manner.

```
proc main
    L := 1
    while
        L > 0
    do
        case
            L
        part(1)
            a
            if
                    p
            then
                400/5
                L := 8
            else
                L := 3
            fi
        part(3)
            100/3
            if
                    q
            then
                200/5
                L := 8
            else
                    e
                L := 0
            fi
        part(8)
            if
                    w
            then
                300/4
                L := 3
            else
                    L := 0
            fi
        esac
    od
corp
```

Figure 4.36

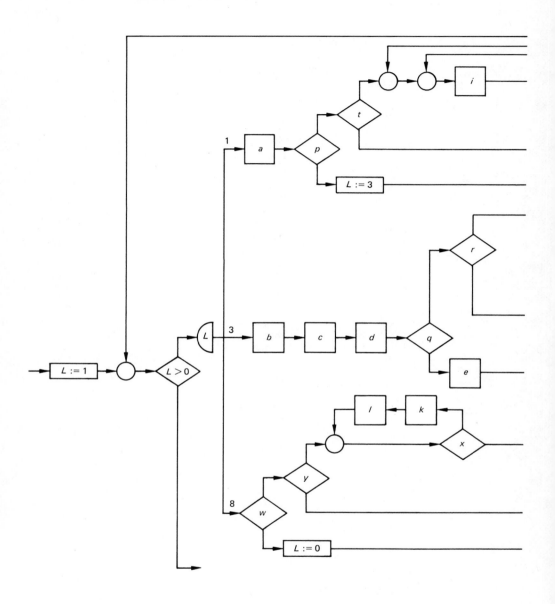

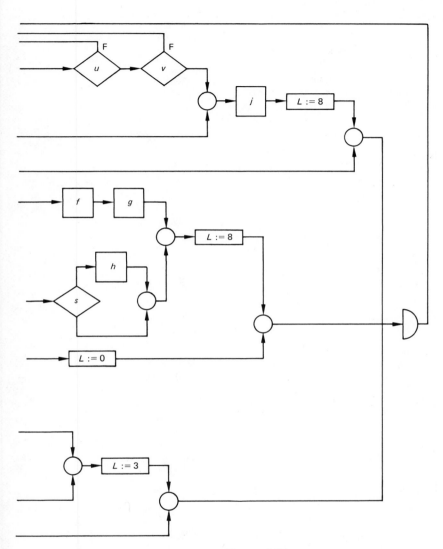

Figure 4.37

```
proc main                        proc caseone
    L := 1                           a
    while                            if
        L > 0                            p
    do                               then
        case                             if
            L                                t
        part(1)                          then
            run caseone                      do
        part(3)                              do
            run casethree                        i
        part(8)                              until
            run caseeight                        u
        esac                                 od
    od                               until
corp                                     v
                                     od
                                 fi
                                 j
                                 L := 8
                                 else
                                     L := 3
                                 fi
                             corp


proc casethree                   proc caseeight
    b                                if
    c                                    w
    d                                then
    if                                   if
        q                                    y
    then                             then
        if                                   while
            r                                    x
        then                                 do
            f                                    k
            g                                    l
        else                                 od
            if                           fi
                s                        L := 3
            then                     else
                h                        L := 0
            fi                       fi
        fi                       corp
        L := 8
    else
        e
        L := 0
    fi
corp
```

Figure 4.38

144

EXERCISES

1. Use the following flowchart to complete parts (a) through (f) below.

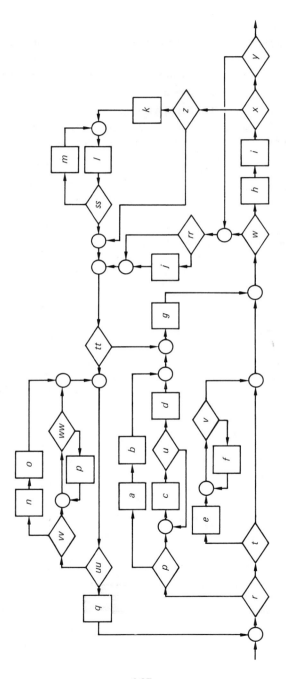

a) Perform a full parse, showing parse units and resulting parsed flowchart for each step.

b) Perform a fixed basis parse against {sequence, ifthen, ifthenelse, dountil, whiledo, dowhiledo}.

c) Diagram any structured islands identified in part (b) as tree structures.

d) Convert to a label structure program.

e) Convert to a recursion structure program.

f) Reconstruct the final structured program by expanding new function nodes according to their structured island parse histories.

5

Reading
Structured
Programs

5.1 OVERVIEW

A structured program of any size can be read and understood in a completely systematic manner, by reading and understanding its hierarchy of prime programs and their abstractions. The objective of reading prime programs is to discover their program functions. Program functions can be recorded in programs to document program design by means of *logical commentary*, which specifies special syntax and meaning for comments attached to PDL primes. When combined with the program structuring techniques described in the previous chapter, prime program reading and logical commentary permit large and complicated programs to be understood and documented. In a case study, a PL/I program with arbitrary structure and no comments becomes readily understandable after systematic structuring, reading, and writing of logical commentary.

5.2 READING FUNDAMENTALS

5.2.1 The Idea of Program Reading

The ability to read programs methodically and accurately is a crucial skill in programming. Program reading is the basis for modifying and validating programs written by others, for selecting and adapting program designs from the literature, and for verifying the correctness of one's own programs. Moreover, just as, say, good writers and engineers learn from critical study of the works of other writers and engineers, so too, good programmers become more effective through critical study of programs written by others.

There are two general reasons for reading a program: (1) the verification that a program is correct with respect to a given function, and (2) the determination of the program function of a program. The verification of a program constitutes a *design review* for its correctness. Design reviews may be used to verify other properties than correctness, such as efficiency and compatibility with implementation requirements. The determination of a program function involves a *design discovery*. Such design discovery is the difficult part of fixing an unfamiliar program, or finding out how to modify it in a simple way.

Given a well-documented program (including the program functions for its intermediate abstractions), the reading process can generally proceed top down, from overall design to successively lower levels of detail, using intermediate abstractions first as assignment statements in the overall program, then verifying the correctness of their expansions in later reading. On the other hand, given a poorly documented program, the reading process generally proceeds better bottom up, to discover the intermediate abstractions, successively at higher levels, by using those already found.

In either case, however, reading can seldom be strictly top down or bottom up. In reading the best-documented programs, one needs an occasional foray into details, if only to understand the context of documentation that is intended to precede the details. For example, a comment such as [check for special cases ...] may be ambiguous without a more local frame of reference, and the program's details may clear that up more easily than other documentation. And in reading a totally mysterious program, it is useful to back out of details periodically in order to form overall hypotheses or guesses that can help fit the details together more easily.

The process of reading a poorly documented program bottom up is called *stepwise abstraction*. Stepwise abstraction may be required in either the verification of correctness or the determination of program function. If the intended function of a program is given but intermediate abstractions are not, then the program function must be determined and compared with the intended function. If scattered intermediate abstractions are given, they can be used as anchor points, verifying them by stepwise abstraction of details below them, and using them for higher level verifications.

5.2.2   The Algebra of Structured Programs

Our discussion of program reading begins with the following Axiom of Replacement:

Let P be a proper subprogram of Q, and let the replacement of P by P' within Q result in Q'. Then

$$[P] = [P'] \rightarrow [Q] = [Q']$$

There are two important implications of this axiom: first, the truth value of any proposition involving [*Q*] is unchanged if *P* is replaced by *P'*; second, (viewing *P* as a function node and *P'* as its expansion into a prime program) prime programs can be abstracted to function nodes, and function nodes can be expanded to other prime programs, independently of their surroundings in a larger control structure. That is, large structured programs are built up from smaller ones, and small structured programs can be used to summarize larger ones. The prime program parsing and reconstruction discussed in the previous chapter was based on this axiom. In this and the following chapters, the same axiom is used to derive principles of program reading, validation, and writing. Thus, in the progression of PDL programs (Fig. 5.1), program writing is function expansion (e.g., expanding the known function named *a* into the program **while** *p* **do** *c* **od**). Program reading, the inverse of writing, is function abstraction (e.g., abstracting the known program **if** *q* **then** *h* **else** *i* **fi** into the function *d*). Program validation is comparing known functions and their expansions (e.g., is **while** *p* **do** *c* **od** equivalent to *a*, is **if** *q* **then** *h* **else** *i* **fi** equivalent to *d*?).

These expansions and abstractions are algebraic operations among structured programs. PDL prime program keywords **while-do-od, if-then-**

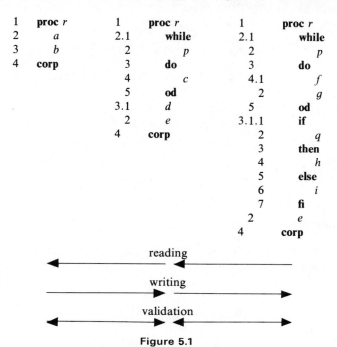

Figure 5.1

else-fi, and so on, are operators in these expressions, just as $+$, $-$, $*$, and so on, are operators in arithmetic expressions. In ordinary arithmetic, operators are eliminated when $2 + (4*3)$ is abstracted to 14, and operators are introduced when 14 is expanded into $2 + (4*3)$. This abstraction and expansion is independent of any other terms in an arithmetic expression. Likewise, the PDL program

> **if**
>> $x < 0$
>
> **then**
>> $y := -x$
>
> **else**
>> $y := x$
>
> **fi**

is an expression in an algebra of programs that can be abstracted to or expanded from

$$y := \text{abs}(x)$$

where no program operators appear. That is, their program functions are identical:

$$[\textbf{if } x < 0 \textbf{ then } y := -x \textbf{ else } y := x \textbf{ fi}] = [y := \text{abs}(x)]$$

This abstraction or expansion is independent of other parts in a program; thus in

> **if**
>> $x < 0$
>
> **then**
>> $y := -x$
>
> **else**
>> $y := x$
>
> **fi**
> $x := \min(y, z)$

abstraction of the firstpart does not affect the secondpart, and the program below is function equivalent:

$$y := \text{abs}(x)$$
$$x := \min(y, z)$$

In short, there is an algebra of structured programs that allows any structured program, no matter how large, to be considered as a compound program expression in smaller structured programs, and any compound program expression to be considered as a single term if it is convenient to do so.

This algebra of structured programs is the principal source of power for structured program reading, writing, and validation. It allows a programmer to logically divide and conquer complex processing logic, just as it allows a grade school student to methodically carry out the evaluation of complicated (for the student) arithmetic expressions. Once familiar, this algebra helps a programmer to think in wholes—in one thought to understand what a program does in every possible circumstance, not simply trace its execution for one input at a time.

5.2.3   Reading Prime Programs

One way to read a program is to mentally execute the functions and predicates on every path of the E-tree, inventing data values to stay on each path read. But for a program of any size the number of paths quickly becomes unmanageable. A sequence of only six ifthenelses contains 64 possible paths. Fortunately, we have a more effective way to read a structured program; all the functions and predicates must still be read, but with practice, they can be read and summarized once and for all, not once for each path on which they appear.

The object of reading a program or a program part is to recognize directly what it does—all in one thought—or to mentally transform it into a new one that can be recognized directly. The product of such a mental transformation is an abstraction that summarizes the possible outcomes of the program part under consideration, irrespective of its internal control structure and data operations. Thus, we can regard program reading as primarily a search for suitable abstractions.

It turns out that a prime program, particularly a small prime program such as found in PDL, is an ideal program part for abstraction. Although a PDL prime program may contain sequencing, branching, and looping, those activities are internal to its execution and are reflected by altered data on exit; the abstraction describes just this effect on data, and no more. A prime program abstraction eliminates sequencing, branching, and looping in favor of more complex, but understandable, data assignments and expressions. Control structure operators **if, do,** and so forth, are abstracted out and what remains is the program function, stated directly.

We begin reading PDL primes with a branch-free program. The sequence of assignments

$$x := x - y$$

$$y := x + y$$

creates new data values for x and y from old ones. These data relationships can be written more explicitly using a zero subscript for values in the initial data state, a one subscript for values in the data state following the first assignment, and a two subscript for values in the final data state, following the second assignment, as follows:

$$x_1 = x_0 - y_0$$
$$y_2 = x_1 + y_0$$

Note that x_1 is used on the right side of the second equation because it has appeared earlier on a left side. Then

$$x_2 = x_1$$
$$= x_0 - y_0$$

and

$$y_2 = x_1 + y_0$$
$$= (x_0 - y_0) + y_0$$
$$= x_0$$

With final values expressed in terms of initial values, the sequence program can now be represented by an equivalent sequence-free program:

$$[x := x - y; \; y := x + y] = (x, \; y := x - y, \; x)$$

Next, consider the branching program

if
  $x > y$
then
  $z := y$
else
  $z := x$
fi

Of course, such a program can always be expressed as a conditional assignment, as

$$(x > y \rightarrow z := y \mid true \rightarrow z := x)$$

But it may be useful to find a single abstraction, if possible. In this case, we recognize the ifthenelse as one that assigns x or y to z, in particular the minimum of x or y. That is

$$[\textbf{if } x > y \textbf{ then } z := y \textbf{ else } z := x \textbf{ fi}] = (z := min(x, \, y))$$

An ifthenelse abstraction is a recognition of two separate cases as part of a more general operation. If we understand what the operator min produces from arguments (x, y), then the second program is understandable directly; that is, a more complex expression in an equivalent branch-free program is a means to understanding what the branching program does. It is also a means of communicating what the branching program does to someone else, who may be more familiar with the min operator than with the ifthenelse structure. Note that abstraction does not mean vagueness, but another way of saying precisely the same thing. The abstraction above could have been written

$$z := \text{minimum of } x \text{ and } y$$

or

$$\text{assign the minimum of } x \text{ and } y \text{ to } z$$

The important point is not the written form of abstraction, but rather that it be a precise statement of a program function.

Finally, consider the looping program, for integer x

while
  $x > 1$
do
  $x := x - 2$
od

As we have seen, direct procedures exist for determining the functions of sequence programs (solving equations) and branching programs (writing conditional assignments). However, no such procedure exists for determining the functions of looping programs. But in the examination of typical loops, functions can often be determined by inspection and simple analysis of patterns of iteration. In this case, we recognize the program as one that assigns a value to x. If the initial value of x is positive, x is reduced by 2 each iteration until it becomes 1 or 0, depending on whether initial x is odd or even. If the initial value of x is negative, 0, or 1, it is not altered by the program. With a little thought, we can write the program function as

$$[\textbf{while } x > 1 \textbf{ do } x := x - 2 \textbf{ od}] = (x := \min(x, \text{oddeven}(x)))$$

where oddeven(x) is short for "1 if initially odd, 0 if initially even," and we have abstracted the whiledo into an equivalent loop-free program. We will investigate more systematic means for dealing with the functions of looping programs in Chapter 6.

5.2.4   Reading by Stepwise Abstraction

A compound program of any size can be read and understood by reading
and understanding its hierarchy of primes and their abstractions. The
process of stepwise abstraction begins at the lowest (most detailed) level, and
replaces each prime by its equivalent abstraction. To illustrate, consider the
program shown in Fig. 5.2 (given array t of n integer elements).

```
proc p(t, n, x, y)
    scalar x, y, n: integer
    array t(n): integer
    x, y := t(1), t(1)
    for
        i :∈ 2 to n
    do
        if
            t(i) > x
        then
            x := t(i)
        else
            if
                t(i) < y
            then
                y := t(i)
            fi
        fi
    od
corp
```

Figure 5.2

A quick scan reveals the overall control structure to be a sequence with
secondpart fordo, itself with dopart of nested alternations. We begin stepwise abstraction by reading the most deeply nested ifthen

```
if
    t(i) < y
then
    y := t(i)
fi
```

with hypothesized program function

$$(t(i) < y \rightarrow y := t(i) \mid t(i) \geq y \rightarrow y := y)$$

which we recognize as

$$y := \min(y, t(i))$$

Next, substituting this abstraction in the outer ifthenelse, we obtain

if
    $t(i) > x$
then
    $x := t(i)$
else
    $y := \min(y, t(i))$
fi

We note that x is increased in the thenpart if a larger $t(i)$ is found, so that we may write $x := \max(x, t(i))$ as part of the function description of this program. For the elsepart, y is decreased if a smaller $t(i)$ is found, but only if $t(i) \leq x$. What if $x < t(i) < y$? A reexamination of the overall program shows that

1. x, y are assigned the same value $t(1)$ before entry to the fordo, and
2. x is only increased, y is only decreased within the fordo.

Therefore, we conclude that $x \geq y$ on entry to the ifthenelse. Hence, if $t(i) < y$, then the ifthenelse predicate will evaluate to *false*, the ifthen predicate will evaluate to *true*, and the assignment of the smaller $t(i)$ will be made to y. Therefore, we may conclude unconditionally that $y := \min(y, t(i))$ is part of the program function. Hence, the program function of the ifthenelse program is

$$(x \geq y \rightarrow x, y := \max(x, t(i)), \min(y, t(i)))$$

We consider next the fordo prime:

for
    $i := 2$ to n
do
    $(x \geq y \rightarrow x, y := \max(x, t(i)), \min(y, t(i)))$
od

With a little thought, we form a hypothesis for the program function of the fordo, that, for initial $x \geq y$, x is the maximum of initial x and $t(2), \ldots, t(n)$ and that y is the minimum of initial y and $t(2), \ldots, t(n)$. (As we will learn in the next chapter, an inductive proof can be carried out to verify such a hypothesis.) In this case, the hypothesized function is easy to verify by a few mental executions of the fordo, and by substitution we arrive at the sequence program, with firstpart the fordo initialization

$$x, y := t(1), t(1)$$

$$(x \geq y \rightarrow x, y := \max(x, t(2), \ldots, t(n)), \min(y, t(2), \ldots, t(n)))$$

from which the overall program function of program p is simply

$$x, y := \max(t(1:n)), \min(t(1:n))$$

where $t(1:n)$ is shorthand for $t(1), \ldots, t(n)$, and a more descriptive program name might be "maxmin."

In retrospect, a little more insight than simple stepwise abstraction made this program function easy to find. It is not unusual for a program part to depend on a logical relation on entry. In this case, the program function for the ifthenelse depended on the relation $x \geq y$ on entry. We note that nesting the minimum-finding ifthen in the maximum-finding ifthenelse saves a retest for a minimum when a new maximum is found. The simpler program shown in Fig. 5.3 would be easier to abstract, as the reader may verify, but it tests for both maximum and minimum at each iteration.

```
proc maxmin(t, n, x, y)
   scalar x, y, n: integer
   array t(n): integer
   x, y := t(1), t(1)
   for
       i :∈ 2 to n
   do
       if
           t(i) > x
       then
           x := t(i)
       fi
       if
           t(i) < y
       then
           y := t(i)
       fi
   od
corp
```

Figure 5.3

As a second example of stepwise abstraction, consider the program shown in Fig. 5.4.

```
 1    proc q
 2        scalar a, b, f, g, error: real
 3        sequence input, output: real
 4        a, b := list(input)
 5        f := a*a + b*b
 6        g := 1
 7        error := abs(f − g*g)
 8        while
 9            error > .001
10        do
11            g := (g + f/g)/2
12            error := abs(f − g*g)
13        od
14        next(output) := g
15    corp
```

Figure 5.4

A quick scan reveals the control structure is a sequence with an initialized whiledo part, the inputs are scalars a and b, and the output is scalar g. We concentrate first on the whiledo on lines 8–13 and its initialization on line 7. The dopart seems a bit mysterious, particularly the assignment to g on line 11. In reading a whiledo the exit condition often provides a vital clue to the abstraction, as going from

```
 7    error := abs(f − g*g)
 8    while
 9        error > .001
10    do
11        g := (g + f/g)/2
12        error := abs(f − g*g)
13    od
```

to (by eliminating error as a variable)

```
      8    while
7, 9, 12       abs(f − g*g) > .001
     10    do
     11        g := (g + f/g)/2
     13    od
```

from which it is clear that, at exit (presuming that the whiledo terminates), $abs(f - g*g)$ must be near zero or

$$f = g^2 \quad \text{(within .001)}$$

But from the dopart, it is clear that g is being altered to satisfy this exit condition, not f. Hence, the whiledo reduces to the assignment (sqrt for square root)

6–13 $g := sqrt(f)$ $(f = g^2$ within .001)

which depends only on the whiledo predicate, the presumption of termination, and the observation that g and not f changes each iteration. In particular, it does not depend on the dopart expression $(g + f/g)/2$. The reduced program at this point is:

```
 1      proc q
 2          scalar a, b, f, g: real
 3          sequence input, output: real
 4          a, b := list(input)
 5          f := a*a + b*b
6-13        g := sqrt(f)    (within .001)
14          next(output) := g
15      corp
```

The sequence on lines 5, 6–13 creates the effect of

5–13 $g := sqrt(a*a + b*b)$ (within .001)

and as a final sequence abstraction, the function of the entire program can be written (presuming $I(input) \neq \emptyset$)

1–15 $next(output) := sqrt((H(input))^2$

$$+ (H(T(input)))^2) \quad \text{(within .001)}$$

where scalars a, b, f, g, and *error*, and the input sequence pointer, are regarded as incidental to the program function. Of course, the program function could as easily be written in English as, say,

> set the next member of the *output* sequence to the square root (within .001) of the sum of the squares of the next two members of the *input* sequence

and a more descriptive procedure name might be "distance."

EXERCISES

Read the following programs to determine their program functions:

1. **proc** *p*

    sequence *input, output*: integer [*input* composed of nonnegative integer pairs]
    scalar *a, b, c*: integer
    while
        input $\neq$ **empty**
    do
        a, b := **list**(*input*)
        c := *a*
        while
            c $\geq$ *b*
        do
            c := *c* − *b*
        od
        list(*output*) := *a, b, c*
    od
    corp

2. **proc** *q*

    sequence *input, output*: integer [*input* composed of nonnegative integer pairs]
    scalar *a, b*: integer
    while
        input $\neq$ **empty**
    do
        a, b := **list**(*input*)
        while
            a $\neq$ *b*
        do
            if
                a > *b*
            then
                a := *a* − *b*
            else
                b := *b* − *a*
            fi
        od
        next(*output*) := *a*
    od
    corp

3. **proc** *r*

    sequence *input, output*: integer [*input* composed of nonnegative integer pairs]
    scalar *a, b*: integer

```
while
    input ≠ empty
do
    a, b := list(input)
    while
        a > b
    do
        a := a − b
    od
    while
        b > a
    do
        b := b − a
    od
    next(output) := b
od
corp
```

4. **proc** *s*
```
    sequence input: character [input nonempty]
    sequence output: logical
    stack s: character
    scalar a, b: character
    scalar checking: logical
    top(s) := '#'
    checking := true
    while
        input ≠ empty ∧ checking
    do
        a := next(input)
        if
            a = '('
        then
            top(s) := ')'
        else
            if
                a = ')'
            then
                b := top(s)
                if
                    a ≠ b
                then
                    checking := false
                fi
            fi
        fi
```

```
        od
        next(output) := checking
    corp
```

5. **proc** *t*

    sequence *input*, *output*: character [*input* contains two or more characters, last
character is **eos**]

```
    scalar a, b: character
    a := next(input)
    do
        b := next(input)
        if
            a ≠ b
        then
            next(output) := a
        fi
        a := b
    until
        b = eos
    od
corp
```

6. What is the program function of exercise 5 above if the iftest is changed to $a = b$?

7. **proc** *u*

    sequence *input*, *output*: character [*input* contains two or more characters, last
character is **eos**]

```
    scalar a, b: character
    scalar i: integer
    i := 0
    a := next(input)
    do
        b := next(input)
        if
            a = b
        then
            next(output) := a
            i := i + 1
        else
            if
                i ≠ 0
            then
                list(output) := a, i + 1
                i := 0
            fi
            a := b
        fi
```

```
        until
            b = eos
        od
    corp
```

8. proc v
>   **sequence** *input*: integer [contains scalars n and k ($1 \le k \le n$) followed by array
> t of n unique elements]
>   **sequence** *output*: logical
>   **array** $t(n)$: integer
>   **scalar** $i, j, k, n, order$: integer
>   **scalar** *looking*: logical
> $n, k, t :=$ **list**(*input*)
>   *looking*, $i :=$ **true**, 0
>   **while**
> $i < n \wedge looking$
>   **do**
> $i := i + 1$
> $j, order := 0, 0$
>   **while**
> $j < n \wedge order \le k$
>   **do**
> $j := j + 1$
> $(t(j) \le t(i) \rightarrow order := order + 1)$
>   **od**
> $(order = k \rightarrow looking,$ **next**(*output*) $:=$ **false**, $t(i))$
>   **od**
>   **corp**

5.3 LOGICAL COMMENTARY IN STRUCTURED PROGRAMS

5.3.1 The Structure of Logical Commentary

We introduce the idea of logical commentary in PDL as a refinement and extension of ordinary comments found in programs. Logical commentary documents the design of a program, amid all its details, by organizing details into a hierarchy of abstractions. The principles of program reading we have applied were derived from algebraic properties of programs. The placement and intent of logical commentary are likewise determined by these algebraic properties, and the content of logical commentary is based on the abstractions of prime program reading. For poorly commented programs, the task of program reading is to invent logical commentary, and for programs already commented, to check correctness of comments and improve their clarity where possible. (In Chapter 7, we will learn how to write logical commentary during program construction.)

Two types of logical commentary are found in PDL programs, *data commentary* and *prime program commentary*. Data commentary is attached to data declarations to define the purpose and usage of data scalars or structures, as illustrated in later examples. Prime program commentary defines the prime program or prime program part to which it is attached, as illustrated below.

Two forms of prime program commentary are associated with the primes of PDL, namely, *action comments* (also called *function comments*) that describe program functions, and *status comments* that describe predicates on data states. Action comments apply to program parts that carry out the actions, that is, they define the effect on data of PDL statements within their scope. Action comments can precede any primes, as well as precede the thenparts and elseparts of alternation primes and the doparts of iteration primes. Status comments apply to program parts that produce the status, that is, they define valid predicates on the state produced by the PDL statements within their scope. Status comments can succeed sequence, alternation and iteration primes. To illustrate, the function

$$f = \{(a, b) \mid b = \text{abs}(a)\}$$

can be carried out by an ifthen prime (using a single scalar, x):

if
$\quad x < 0$
then
$\quad x := -x$
fi

The ifthen can be described by the action comment

$$x := \text{abs}(x)$$

and the thenpart by the action comment

$$\text{switch } x \text{ sign}$$

The final data state can be described by a status comment as a predicate on x, namely,

$$x \geq 0$$

and the program documented as follows. Logical commentary is delimited by square brackets, and either precedes a prime or is attached to a keyword:

$[x := abs(x)]$
if
    $x < 0$
then [switch x sign]
    $x := -x$
fi $[x \geq 0]$

If a nested prime immediately follows a keyword in a larger program, the leading comment is attached to that keyword, as in

if
    $y > 0$
then $[x := abs(x)]$
    if
        $x < 0$
    then [switch x sign]
        $x := -x$
    fi $[x \geq 0]$
fi

Note use of $:=$ operators in action comments to specify data assignments, and use of relational operators ($=$, $\leq$, $>$, etc.) in status comments to specify data properties. Of course, action and status comments can be written in any language (e.g., English or mathematical notation) suitable to a given context.

    Another convenient form of status comment expresses the final state after execution of a prime in terms of the initial state prior to execution, where initial state values are identified by a zero subscript. For example, the status comment above can be written

$$x = abs(x_0)$$

where x_0 is a constant that is the initial value of x. The subscripted items always identify data values in the entry state of the containing prime.

    The syntax and semantics of logical commentary are illustrated below for the primes of PDL. In each case, the program function of the prime is named "f-action." The miniature examples are intentionally "over commented" to fully illustrate possibilities for commentary in programs.

Sequence

Extra keywords are required to delimit sequence primes selected for commentary. A **do-od** pair is used, thus

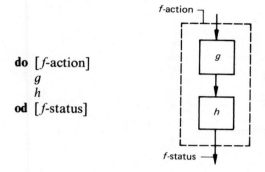

do [*f*-action]
  g
  h
od [*f*-status]

where

  f-action = [*g*; *h*],
  and
  g followed by *h* does [*f*-action] to produce [*f*-status].

(Note that the brackets in the expression [*g*; *h*] just above, and in subsequent explanations of logical commentary for the other primes, denote the program function. The brackets on *f*-action and *f*-status, of course, are logical commentary delimiters.) A sequence of any number of parts may be chosen for commentary. For example, in

  do [$x, y := y, x$]
    $x := x + y$
    $y := x - y$
    $x := x - y$
  od [$x = y_0, y = x_0$]

the sequence of assignments does action [$x, y := y, x$] to produce status [$x = y_0, y = x_0$]. The action and status could have been written in more English-like form, perhaps as [exchange(x, y)] and [x, y exchanged], respectively. For such simple sequences, either action or status may provide sufficient description. PDL keywords **proc** and **corp** can operate like a **do-od** pair, to carry action and status comments for entire programs:

> **proc** name [*f*-action]
>   *g*
>   *h*
> **corp** [*f*-status]

Fordo

Commentary is attached to fordo primes as

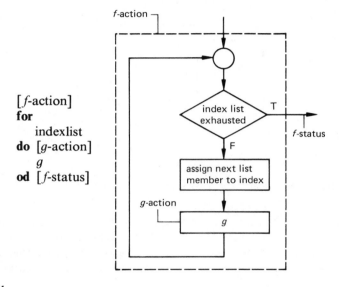

[*f*-action]
for
    indexlist
do [*g*-action]
    g
od [*f*-status]

where

> *f*-action = [**for** indexlist **do** *g* **od**],
> and
> for each consecutive indexlist member, *g* does [*g*-action],
> the sequence of *g*'s finally producing [*f*-status].

For example (*a* an array of *n* elements, int short for integer part),

> [*a* := reverse(*a*)]
> **for**
>   *i* :∈ 1 to int(*n*/2)
> **do** [exchange *a*(*i*), *a*(*n* − *i* + 1)]
>   *a*(*i*), *a*(*n* − *i* + 1) := *a*(*n* − *i* + 1), *a*(*i*)
> **od** [*a* = reverse(*a*$_0$)]

Ifthen

Commentary is attached to ifthen primes as

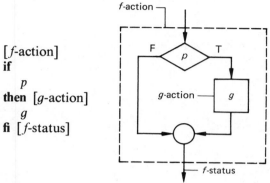

[*f*-action]
if

   p
then [*g*-action]
   g
fi [*f*-status]

where

> *f*-action = [**if** *p* **then** *g* **fi**],
> and
> when *p* is *true*, *g* does [*g*-action] to produce [*f*-status],
> and
> when *p* is *false*, [*f*-status] is *true*.

The *f*-status summarizes the data state at **fi**, whether or not *g*-action is performed. To illustrate,

$[(x > y \rightarrow x := \text{decr}(x))]$
if

   $x > y$
then $[x := \text{decr}(x)]$
   $x := x - 1$
fi $[(x_0 > y_0 \rightarrow x = \text{decr}(x_0))]$

The ifthen below is the secondpart of a sequence:

do $[x := \text{abs}(\min(y, z))]$
   $x := \min(y, z)$
   if

      $x < 0$
   then [switch sign]
      $x := -x$
   fi $[x = \text{abs}(x_0)]$
od $[x = \text{abs}(\min(y_0, z_0))]$

Note that the status comments at **fi** and **od** are not equivalent, since each summarizes the result of a different function—an ifthen at **fi**, a sequence at **od**.

Ifthenelse

Commentary is attached to ifthenelse primes as

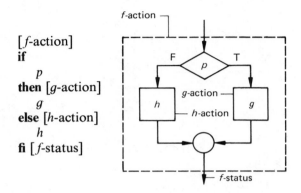

[*f*-action]
if

   p
then [*g*-action]
   g
else [*h*-action]
   h
fi [*f*-status]

where

> *f*-action = [**if** *p* **then** *g* **else** *h* **fi**],
> and
> when *p* is *true*, *g* does [*g*-action] to produce [*f*-status],
> and
> when *p* is *false*, *h* does [*h*-action] to produce [*f*-status].

The *f*-status summarizes the data state at **fi**, whether the thenpart action or the elsepart action is performed. To illustrate, for $z \geq 0$

$[z := \text{round}(z)]$
if
   $z - \text{int}(z) < .5$
then [round *z* down]
   $z := \text{int}(z)$
else [round *z* up]
   $z := \text{int}(z + 1)$
fi $[z = \text{round}(z_0)]$

Case

Logical commentary for the case, or indexed alternation, structure is a generalization of commentary for the ifthenelse:

> [*f*-action]
> **case**
> > *p*
>
> **part**(caselist1) [*g*-action]
> > *g*
>
> **...**
> **part**(caselistn) [*h*-action]
> > *h*
>
> **else** [*i*-action]
> > *i*
>
> **esac** [*f*-status]

Whiledo

Commentary is attached to the whiledo prime as

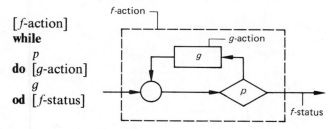

> [*f*-action]
> **while**
> > *p*
>
> **do** [*g*-action]
> > *g*
>
> **od** [*f*-status]

where

> *f*-action = [**while** *p* **do** *g* **od**],
> and
> when *p* is *true*, *g* does [*g*-action],
> and
> when *p* is *false*, [*f*-status] is *true*.

To illustrate, the add program, for $x, y \geq 0$, can be commented as

> $[x, y := x + y, 0]$
> **while**
> > $y > 0$
>
> **do** [increment *x*, decrement *y*]
> > $x, y := x + 1, y - 1$
>
> **od** $[x, y = x_0 + y_0, 0]$

Dountil

Commentary is attached to the dountil prime as

[*f*-action]
do [*g*-action]
   g
until
   p
od [*f*-status]

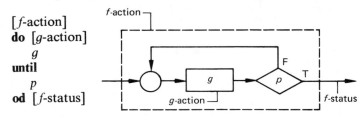

where

f-action = [**do** *g* **until** *p* **od**],
and
g does [*g*-action],
and
when *p* is *true*, [*f*-status] is *true*.

Dowhiledo

The dowhiledo prime is commented as

[*f*-action]
do1 [*g*-action]
   g
while
   p
do2 [*h*-action]
   h
od [*f*-status]

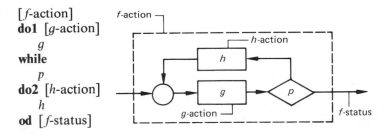

where

f-action = [**do1** *g* **while** *p* **do2** *h* **od**],
and
g does [*g*-action], *h* does [*h*-action]
and
when *p* is *false*, [*f*-status] is *true*.

Finally, we note that in writing logical commentary, various levels of rigor are possible. In situations where reliable proofs of correctness are required, logical commentary should provide self-sufficient definitions of program functions for use in proof arguments. But logical commentary that falls short of program functions can provide good documentation as well, and may be appropriate in situations where the extra effort to record program functions is not justified. Thus, in expressing the results of complex, but local, program logic, it may be useful to describe a program function only in part, by using the phrase *in part* preceding a multiple assignment statement. For example,

$$\text{in part, } x, y := y, x$$

could be used to describe an exchange program using temporary value t, with full program function

$$x, y, t := y, x, x$$

In this instance, x, y are regarded as *intentional*, and t as *incidental*, data. In practice, incidental assignments are usually omitted from logical commentary, and where the meaning is clear, *in part* may be dropped as well, to simply write

$$x, y := y, x$$

We observe, however, that in producing a well-documented program, the *in part* concept should not be applied excessively; a self-sufficient definition of the program function of each segment in a program represents a minimum practice in the use of logical commentary.

5.3.2 Logical Commentary in Stepwise Abstraction

Logical commentary makes programs intelligible by abstracting details into design. The maxmin and distance programs of Section 5.2 are shown in Figs. 5.5 and 5.6, respectively, with logical commentary based on our previous reading. The programs can be understood and checked at any level, from overall design, through intermediate abstractions, down to low-level details, if necessary. Note addition of **alt** and **fix** data usage categories to the maxmin program.

As we have seen, insights gained during program reading can be conveniently preserved in logical commentary, to better document programs for other readers. Consider stepwise abstraction and documentation of the program in Fig. 5.7, given array *table* of n integer elements.

The innermost dopart is the familiar conditional exchange, which also sets incidental variable *temp*:

$$(table(i) > table(i + 1) \rightarrow table(i), table(i + 1), temp$$
$$:= table(i + 1), table(i), table(i))$$

proc maxmin(**fix** t, n, **alt** x, y) [x, $y := \max(t(1:n))$, $\min(t(1:n))$]
  scalar x, y, n: integer
  array $t(n)$: integer
  x, $y := t(1)$, $t(1)$
  [$(x \geq y \rightarrow x$, $y := \max(x, t(2:n))$, $\min(y, t(2:n)))$]
  for
    $i :\in 2$ to n
  do [$(x \geq y \rightarrow x$, $y := \max(x, t(i))$, $\min(y, t(i)))$]
    if
      $t(i) > x$
    then
      $x := t(i)$
    else [$y := \min(y, t(i))$]
      if
        $t(i) < y$
      then
        $y := t(i)$
      fi
    fi
  od
corp [x, $y = \max(t)$, $\min(t)$]

Figure 5.5

proc distance [**next**(*output*) $:= \mathrm{sqrt}((\mathbf{H}(input))^2 + (\mathbf{H}(\mathbf{T}(input)))^2)$
           (within .001)]
  scalar a, b, f, g, *error*: real
  sequence *input*, *output*: real
  a, $b := \mathbf{list}(input)$
  do [$g := \mathrm{sqrt}(a*a + b*b)$ (within .001)]
    $f := a*a + b*b$
    $g := 1$
    error $:= \mathrm{abs}(f - g*g)$
    while
      error $> .001$
    do
      $g := (g + f/g)/2$
      error $:= \mathrm{abs}(f - g*g)$
    od [$g = \mathrm{sqrt}(f)$ (within .001)]
  od
  next(*output*) $:= g$
corp

Figure 5.6

```
1    proc r (n, table)
2        scalar n, temp: integer
3        array table(n): integer
4        for
5            j :∈ n to 2 by −1
6        do
7            for
8                i :∈ 1 to (j − 1)
9            do
10               if
11                   table(i) > table(i + 1)
12               then
13                   temp := table(i)
14                   table(i) := table(i + 1)
15                   table(i + 1) := temp
16               fi
17           od
18       od
19   corp
```

Figure 5.7

This program function can be documented in the program as

```
9    do [asort(table(i), table(i + 1))]
10       if
11           table(i) > table(i + 1)
12       then [exchange table(i), table(i + 1)]
13           temp := table(i)
14           table(i) := table(i + 1)
15           table(i + 1) := temp
16       fi [table(i) ≤ table(i + 1)]
17   od
```

where asort names an operation that ensures elements in an argument list are in ascending sorted order. For the inner fordo at lines 7–17 we observe that for each dopart execution a consecutive overlapping table pair is guaranteed to be in ascending sorted order, beginning with $(table(1), table(2))$, then $(table(2), table(3))$, and so on, up to $(table(j − 1), table(j))$. Thus, the effect of the fordo is to propagate the largest element in $table(1:j)$ to the head of $table(1:j)$, or

$$table(j) := max(table(1:j))$$

taking the final disposition of elements in $table(1:(j-1))$ as incidental. We document this insight as an action comment:

6   **do** [in part, $table(j) := \max(table(1:j))$]

Next, the outer fordo steps j from n to 2 by -1, and at each step

$$table(j) := \max(table(1:j))$$

by the analysis just above. Thus, table entries are set in the following sequence, corresponding to successive dopart executions:

$$table(n) := \max(table(1:n))$$

$$table(n-1) := \max(table(1:(n-1)))$$

$$table(n-2) := \max(table(1:(n-2)))$$

$$\ldots$$

$$table(2) := \max(table(1:2))$$

$$table(1) := \max(table(1:1))$$

```
proc sort (n, table)
    scalar
        n: integer [number of elements in table array]
        temp: integer
    array
        table(n): integer [values to be put into ascending sorted order]
    [table := asort(table)]      [asort arranges elements in an argument
                                  list in ascending sorted order]
    for
        j :∈ n to 2 by −1
    do [in part, table(j) := max(table(1:j))]
        for
            i :∈ 1 to (j − 1)
        do [asort(table(i), table(i + 1))]
            if
                table(i) > table(i + 1)
            then [exchange(table(i), table(i + 1))]
                temp := table(i)
                table(i) := table(i + 1)
                table(i + 1) := temp
            fi [table(i) ≤ table(i + 1)]
        od
    od
corp
```

Figure 5.8

That is, following the outer fordo execution, each consecutive element from *table*(2) to *table*(*n*) is greater than or equal to its predecessor, and the program function of the fordo (and the entire program) is

$$table := \text{asort}(table)$$

The fully documented program appears in Fig. 5.8. Note that the special name asort is defined to the side of the program. Control structure abstraction clarifies data usage, and data comments have been added as well.

As an exercise, try reading and writing logical commentary for the subroutine given in Fig. 5.9, with given integer arguments *n*, *table* (unique

```
1     proc s(n, table, key, i)
2         use k
3         i := 0
4         lo := 1
5         hi := n
6         while
7             lo ≤ hi ∧ i = 0
8         do
9             mid := int((lo + hi)/2)
10            if
11                key = table(mid)
12            then
13                i := mid
14            else
15                if
16                    key > table(mid)
17                then
18                    lo := mid + 1
19                else
20                    hi := mid − 1
21                fi
22            fi
23        od
24    corp

      data k
          scalar
              i, lo, hi, mid, key, n: integer
          array
              table(n): integer [unique values in ascending sorted order]
      atad
```

Figure 5.9

values in ascending sorted order), and *key*, and integer argument *i* to be found (int short for integer part).

A possible set of logical comments, including more descriptive **proc** and **data** names and **alt** and **fix** categories of data usage, appears in Fig. 5.10.

```
1    proc binary search(fix n, table, key, alt i) [(∃k(key = table(k), 1 ≤ k ≤ n)
                                                   → i := k | true → i := 0)]
2        use searchdata
3        i := 0
4        lo := 1
5        hi := n
6        [(∃k(key = table(k), lo ≤ k ≤ hi) → i := k | true → i unchanged)]
7        while
8            lo ≤ hi ∧ i = 0
9        do [(key = table(k) → i := k | key > table(k) → lo := k + 1 |
               key < table(k) → hi := k − 1), where k = int((lo + hi)/2)]
10           mid := int((lo + hi)/2)
11           if
12               key = table(mid)
13           then [finish successful search]
14               i := mid
15           else [exclude irrelevant table part from search]
16               if
17                   key > table(mid)
18               then [exclude table(lo : mid)]
19                   lo := mid + 1
20               else [exclude table(mid : hi)]
21                   hi := mid − 1
22               fi [key ∉ table(1 : (lo − 1)) ∧ key ∉ table((hi + 1) : n) since
                   table in ascending sorted order]
23           fi [table(i) = key | (i unchanged ∧ hi − lo decreased)]
24       od [table(i) = key | (hi − lo < 0 ∧ i = 0)]
25   corp

     data searchdata
         scalar
             (i [search value, to be found]
             lo [lower search bound]
             hi [higher search bound]
             mid [lookup index]
             key [given search argument]
             n [number of elements in table]): integer
         array
             table(n): integer [given array to search, unique values
                                in ascending sorted order]
         atad
```

Figure 5.10

EXERCISES

1. Read the following program and record your abstractions as logical commentary.

```
proc
   sequence
      a, b, c: integer [if not empty, a and b are each
                        in ascending sorted order]
   scalar
      akey, bkey: integer
      aleft, bleft: logical
   aleft := true
   bleft := true
   if
      a = empty
   then
      aleft := false
   else
      akey := next(a)
   fi
   if
      b = empty
   then
      bleft := false
   else
      bkey := next(b)
   fi
   while
      aleft ∨ bleft
   do
      if
         (aleft ∧ bleft ∧ akey ≤ bkey) ∨ (aleft ∧ ~bleft)
      then
         next(c) := akey
         if
            a = empty
         then
            aleft := false
         else
            akey := next(a)
         fi
      else
         next(c) := bkey
         if
            b = empty
         then
            bleft := false
```

    else
     $bkey := \textbf{next}(b)$
    fi
   fi
  od
 corp

2. Add logical commentary to the programs in exercises 1 through 8 in Section 5.2.

5.4   A CASE STUDY IN PROGRAM READING

5.4.1   The Singsort Program

Consider the PL/I program named Singsort† shown in Fig. 5.11. (Readers unfamiliar with PL/I will find the control structures of Singsort diagrammed in Fig. 5.12.) Singsort is written without indentation or comments, and contains a number of GOTO instructions and statement labels—as it stands, it is a formidable object for human understanding! But suppose we need to understand Singsort, to reliably answer critical questions on its operation and limitations, and perhaps to make some reliable modifications. How can we carry out the learning process in a systematic way? A good strategy is to first unravel Singsort's control logic, restructuring if necessary into a suitable basis set of primes, and then to read and document Singsort's functions with logical commentary. Then, with the program under intellectual control, questions and improvements can be investigated without guessing and merely hoping that we've got things right.

5.4.2   The Prime Program Parse of Singsort

Our first task in understanding Singsort is to carry out a prime program parse. Taken in reverse order, the parse steps will reveal the program's overall control structure and functions, the structure and functions of these functions, and so on, down to the individual operations and tests of the PL/I program. We begin by drawing the flowchart of Singsort, by tracing down the PL/I code, grouping sequences of statements into function nodes and inserting predicate nodes for conditional GOTO statements. At this stage, we make no particular effort to identify simple primes, although they may exist in the program in disguised form. The flowchart is shown in Fig. 5.12. Numbers in function and predicate nodes are PL/I line numbers, and state-

---

† Singsort is taken from H. Lorin, *Sorting and Sort Systems* (Reading, Mass.: Addison-Wesley, 1975) A68–70. It originally appeared in FORTRAN and ALGOL as Algorithm 347, *Communications of the ACM* 12, no. 3 (March 1969): 185–187, submitted by Richard Singleton. The method used is a variation of Algorithm 64, Quicksort, by C. A. R. Hoare, and Algorithm 271, Quickersort, by R. S. Scowen.

```
 1   SINGSORT: PROCEDURE(TOSORT, NUMBER);
 2   / * ALGORITHM 347, COMMUNICATIONS OF ACM,
     VOL 12, NO 3, P 185 */
 3   DECLARE
 4   TOSORT(*) FIXED BINARY (31, 0),
 5   PIVOT FIXED BINARY (31, 0),
 6   TEMP2 FIXED BINARY (31, 0),
 7   LIMDEX FIXED BINARY (31, 0),
 8   INITIAL FIXED BINARY (31, 0),
 9   MEDIAN FIXED BINARY (31, 0),
10   BOTIND FIXED BINARY (31, 0),
11   TOPIND FIXED BINARY (31, 0),
12   LIMITS FIXED BINARY (31, 0),
13   I FIXED BINARY (31, 0),
14   NUMBER FIXED BINARY (31, 0),
15   PARTOP FIXED BINARY (31, 0) INITIAL (1);
16   LIMITS = 20;
17   SORT: BEGIN;
18   DECLARE
19   TOPS(LIMITS) FIXED BINARY (31, 0),
20   BOTTOMS(LIMITS) FIXED BINARY (31, 0);
21   LIMDEX = 1;
22   INITIAL = PARTOP;
23   GO TO SINKTEST;
24   SPLIT: MEDIAN = TRUNC((PARTOP + NUMBER)/2);
25   PIVOT = TOSORT(MEDIAN);
26   TOPIND = PARTOP;
27   BOTIND = NUMBER;
28   IF TOSORT(PARTOP) > PIVOT THEN DO;
29   TOSORT(MEDIAN) = TOSORT(PARTOP);
30   TOSORT(PARTOP) = PIVOT;
31   PIVOT = TOSORT(MEDIAN);
32   END;
33   IF TOSORT(NUMBER) < PIVOT THEN DO;
34   TOSORT(MEDIAN) = TOSORT(NUMBER);
35   TOSORT(NUMBER) = PIVOT;
36   PIVOT = TOSORT(MEDIAN);
37   IF TOSORT(PARTOP) > PIVOT THEN DO;
38   TOSORT(MEDIAN) = TOSORT(PARTOP);
39   TOSORT(PARTOP) = PIVOT;
40   PIVOT = TOSORT(MEDIAN);
41   END;
42   END;
43   FINDSMALL: BOTIND = BOTIND − 1;
```

Figure 5.11   (Continued)

```
44    IF TOSORT(BOTIND) > PIVOT THEN GO TO FINDSMALL;
45    TEMP2 = TOSORT(BOTIND);
46    FINDLARGE: TOPIND = TOPIND + 1;
47    IF TOSORT(TOPIND) < PIVOT THEN GO TO FINDLARGE;
48    IF TOPIND < = BOTIND THEN DO;
49    TOSORT(BOTIND) = TOSORT(TOPIND);
50    TOSORT(TOPIND) = TEMP2;
51    GO TO FINDSMALL;
52    END;
53    IF BOTIND – PARTOP < NUMBER – TOPIND THEN DO;
54    TOPS(LIMDEX) = PARTOP;
55    BOTTOMS(LIMDEX) = BOTIND;
56    PARTOP = TOPIND;
57    END;
58    ELSE DO;
59    TOPS(LIMDEX) = TOPIND;
60    BOTTOMS(LIMDEX) = NUMBER;
61    NUMBER = BOTIND;
62    END;
63    LIMDEX = LIMDEX + 1;
64    SINKTEST: IF NUMBER – PARTOP > 10 THEN GO TO SPLIT;
65    IF INITIAL = PARTOP THEN DO;
66    IF PARTOP < NUMBER THEN GO TO SPLIT;
67    END;
68    DO I = PARTOP + 1 TO NUMBER BY 1;
69    PIVOT = TOSORT(I);
70    TOPIND = I – 1;
71    IF TOSORT (TOPIND) > PIVOT THEN DO;
72    SINK: TOSORT(TOPIND + 1) = TOSORT(TOPIND);
73    TOPIND = TOPIND – 1;
74    IF TOSORT(TOPIND) > PIVOT THEN GO TO SINK;
75    TOSORT(TOPIND + 1) = PIVOT;
76    END;
77    END;
78    LIMDEX = LIMDEX – 1;
79    IF LIMDEX > = 1 THEN DO;
80    PARTOP = TOPS(LIMDEX);
81    NUMBER = BOTTOMS(LIMDEX);
82    GO TO SINKTEST;
83    END;
84    END SORT;
85    END SINGSORT;
```

Figure 5.11   (Continued)

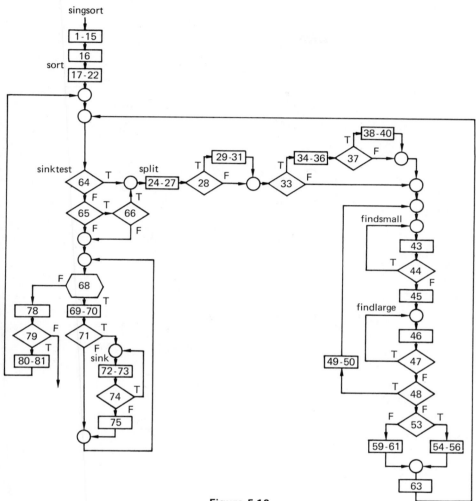

Figure 5.12

ment labels are attached to the flowchart where they appear in the PL/I code. A six-sided node (line 68) depicts the only fordo structure in the program.

Recall that a prime program parse can be determined by a series of flowchart reduction steps, each step abstracting existing primes into new function nodes. As before, it is convenient to parse sequences of more than two function nodes in a single step. A series of eight steps is required to reduce Singsort to a single node, as shown in Fig. 5.13; new function nodes

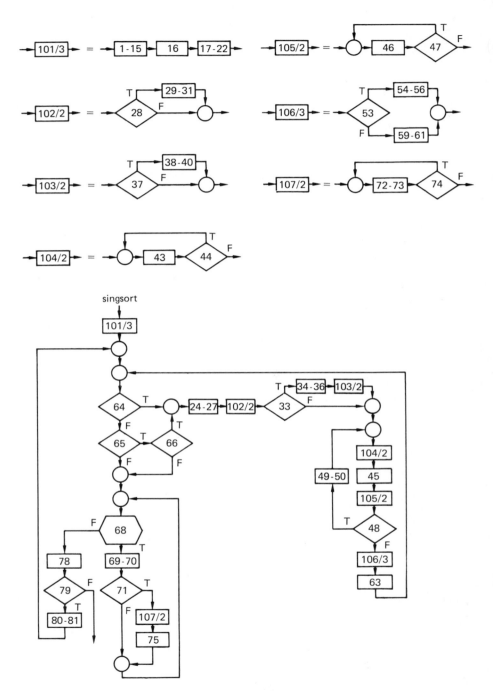

Figure 5.13   Reduction 1

182

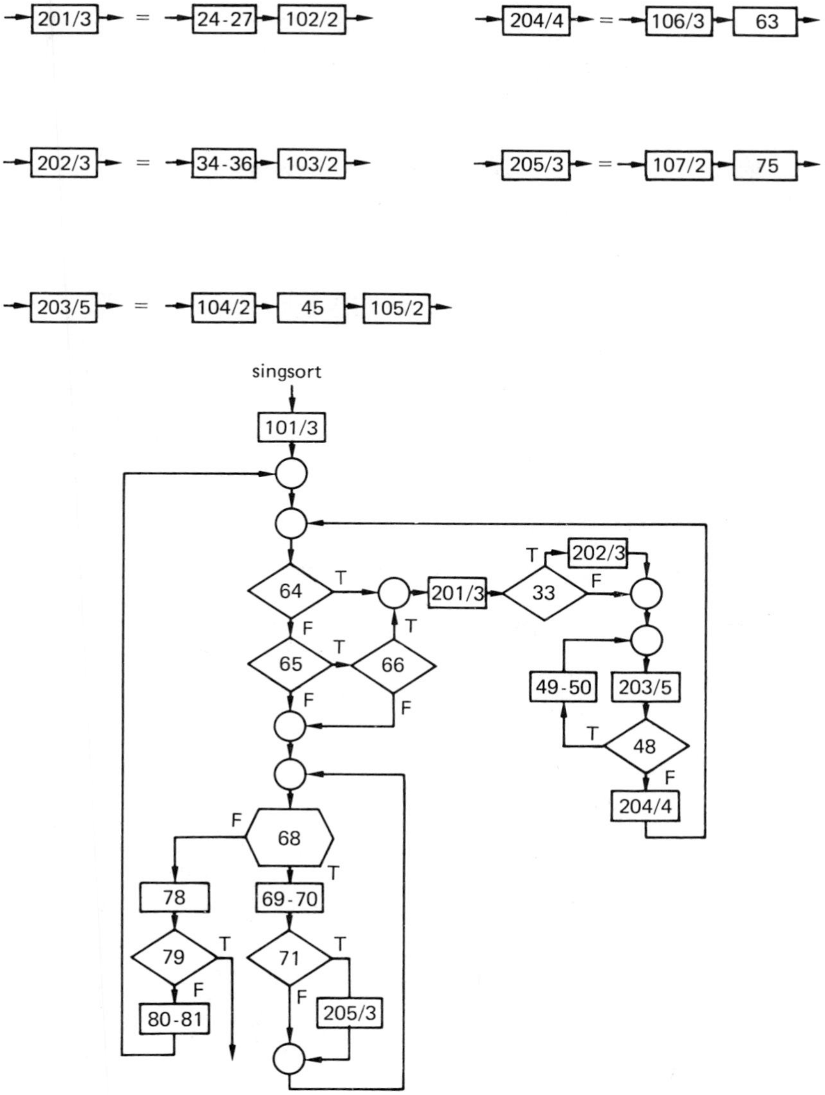

Figure 5.13   Reduction 2

Figure 5.13 (Continued)   Reduction 3

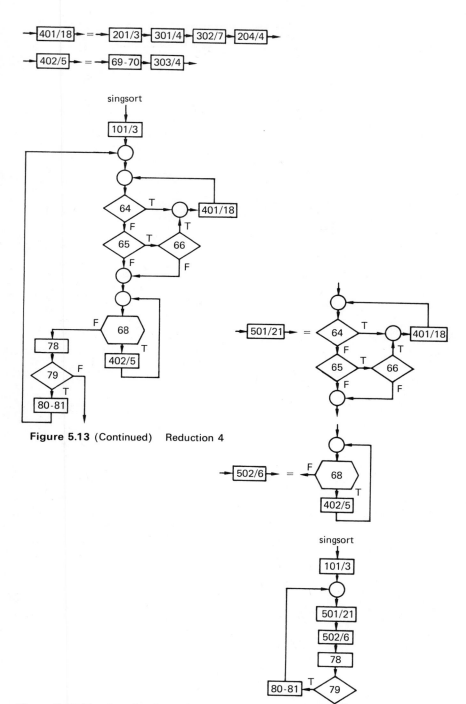

Figure 5.13 (Continued) Reduction 4

Figure 5.13 (Continued) Reduction 5

185

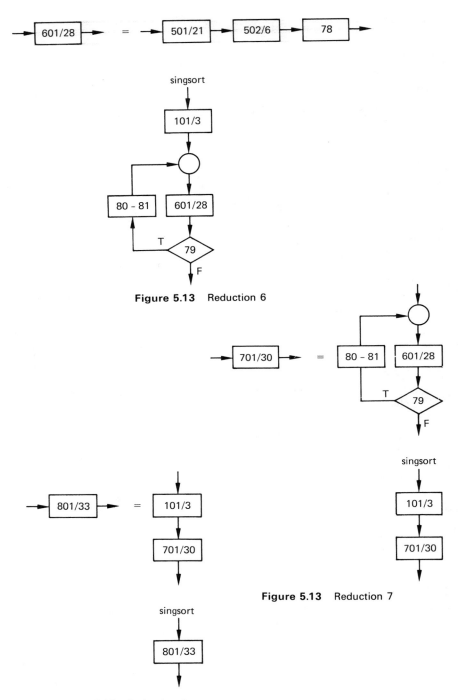

Figure 5.13 Reduction 6

Figure 5.13 Reduction 7

Figure 5.13 Reduction 8

are numbered $n01$, $n02$, ..., where n is the reduction step number. As before, each node number is followed by the number of function and predicate nodes that have been abstracted by the new node. Each successive abstraction accounts for the total of 33 nodes appearing in Fig. 5.12. This abstraction process is a purely mechanical exercise. It requires no special insight or judgment, only tracing through the flowchart to pick out primes as they show up.

In this reduction of Singsort, all abstractions are made from basis set {sequence, ifthen, ifthenelse, dountil, dowhiledo} except for the following unnamed prime:

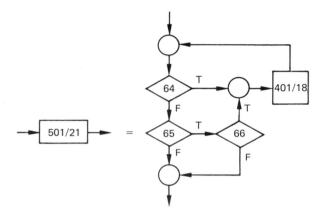

However, a simpler prime results when the individual tests are combined into a compound test

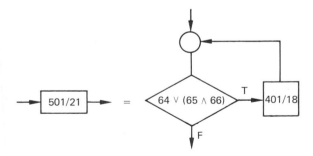

thereby adding whiledo to the basis set. Thus, Singsort has in fact control logic structured in sequence and one-predicate primes (well disguised, to be sure!) that can be expressed in PDL to produce a more readable version.

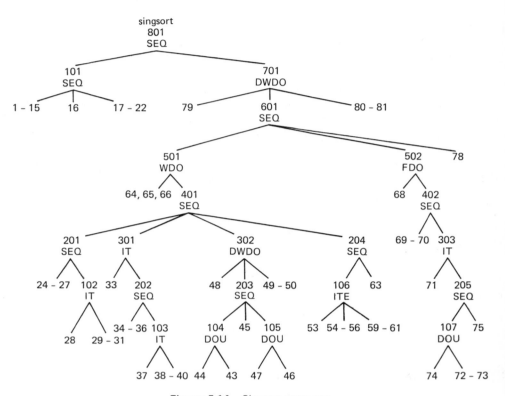

Figure 5.14   Singsort parse tree

Had our reductions turned up complex, multiple-predicate primes, we would have converted Singsort into a label structure program and then into a recursion structure program (as described in Chapter 4) to establish a simpler basis set for better understanding.

The foregoing reductions can be summarized in the prime parse tree of Singsort, given in Fig. 5.14. It can be seen that Singsort is an initialized dowhiledo program, up to eight abstractions deep, and the prime parse tree provides a simple map to the individual abstractions and their relations to the whole program. Any subtree of this prime parse tree is a candidate PDL segment—a proper program, itself. But good choice of segments requires a look at the abstractions associated with the subtrees, in order to make the best possible sense in programming terms.

5.4.3   Singsort in PDL

By inspecting its prime parse tree and reduced flowcharts in reverse order, Singsort can be readily transcribed into PDL. Transcription begins with abstraction 801, which is the sequence (101; 701). Abstraction 101 is itself the sequence (1–15; 16; 17–22) from the original program, all written in PDL, data declarations aside, as

```
801              proc singsort(tosort, number)
101    21            limdex := 1
101    22            initial := partop
                     701
801              corp
```

with a column of statement numbers on the far left delimiting the beginning and ending of each abstraction from the flowchart reductions, followed by a column of individual statement numbers from the original program. Next, abstraction 701 is a dowhiledo structure with whiletest 79, dopart1 601, and dopart2 80–81, which give the expansion

```
801              proc singsort(tosort, number)
101    21            limdex := 1
101    22            initial := partop
701                  do1
                         601
                     while
 79                      limdex ≥ 1
                     do2
 80                      partop := tops(limdex)
 81                      number := bottoms(limdex)
701                  od
801              corp
```

We continue in this fashion until all abstractions have been expanded, as shown in the final PDL program in Fig. 5.15. (Two columns are required to display the number pairs that delimit the beginning and ending of abstractions.) Note we have recorded PL/I run-time declarations as if they were declared in advance. (The PL/I variable "limits" is thereby eliminated; see lines 12, 19 and 20, and lines 4 and 14 in the PL/I program.) The PDL inner syntax word "init" is used at line 15 to indicate an initializing data declaration.

```
                        data singsortdata
                            array
                  4            tosort(number): integer
                            scalar
                  5            (pivot
                  6            temp2
                  7            limdex
                  8            initial
                  9            median
                 10            botind
                 11            topind
                 13            i
                 14            number
                 15            partop init(1)): integer
                            array
                 19            tops(20): integer
                 20            bottoms(20): integer
                        atad


         801    1      proc singsort(tosort, number)
                        use singsortdata
         101   21      limdex := 1
         101   22      initial := partop
         701          do1
  601    501             while
                 64          number − partop > 10 ∨
                 65          (initial = partop ∧
                 66          partop < number)
                        do
  401    201   24          median := truncate((partop + number)/2)
               25          pivot := tosort(median)
               26          topind := partop
               27          botind := number
         102            if
                 28          tosort(partop) > pivot
                        then
               29              tosort(median) := tosort(partop)
               30              tosort(partop) := pivot
               31              pivot := tosort(median)
  201    102            fi
         301            if
                 33          tosort(number) < pivot
```

Figure 5.15

			then
	202	34	$tosort(median) := tosort(number)$
		35	$tosort(number) := pivot$
		36	$pivot := tosort(median)$
	103		**if**
		37	$tosort(partop) > pivot$
			then
		38	$tosort(median) := tosort(partop)$
		39	$tosort(partop) := pivot$
		40	$pivot := tosort(median)$
202	103		**fi**
	301		**fi**
	302		**do1**
203	104		**do**
		43	$botind := botind - 1$
			until
		44	$tosort(botind) \leq pivot$
	104		**od**
		45	$temp2 := tosort(botind)$
	105		**do**
		46	$topind := topind + 1$
			until
		47	$tosort(topind) \geq pivot$
203	105		**od**
			while
		48	$topind \leq botind$
			do2
		49	$tosort(botind) := tosort(topind)$
		50	$tosort(topind) := temp2$
	302		**od**
204	106		**if**
		53	$botind - partop < number - topind$
			then
		54	$tops(limdex) := partop$
		55	$bottoms(limdex) := botind$
		56	$partop := topind$
			else
		59	$tops(limdex) := topind$
		60	$bottoms(limdex) := number$
		61	$number := botind$
	106		**fi**
401	204	63	$limdex := limdex + 1$
	501		**od**

Figure 5.15 (Continued)

```
502                for
    68                 i :∈ partop + 1 to number by 1
                   do
402 69                 pivot := tosort(i)
    70                 topind := i − 1
303                    if
    71                     tosort(topind) > pivot
                       then
205 107                        do
        72                         tosort(topind + 1) := tosort(topind)
        73                         topind := topind − 1
                               until
        74                         tosort(topind) ≤ pivot
    107                        od
    205 75                     tosort(topind + 1) := pivot
402 303                    fi
    502                od
    601 78             limdex := limdex − 1
                   while
        79             limdex ≥ 1
                   do2
        80             partop := tops(limdex)
        81             number := bottoms(limdex)
    701            od
    801        corp
```

Figure 5.15   (Continued)

5.4.4   Reading and Commenting Singsort

With Singsort's control structure made visible, we can now investigate the operations carried out within that structure. Our approach is to perform three types of analysis, as follows:

1. Apply the reading techniques described earlier to abstract program parts into logical commentary—action and status comments.

2. Organize the program into a perspicuous hierarchy of segments, each a page or less of PDL; segments should correspond to important abstract functions identified in the original program.

3. Perform an analysis on the resulting segment structure for fixed and altered categories of data usage, to complete the definition of **run** and **proc** statements.

As noted, Singsort's overall control structure is an initialized dowhiledo. The dowhiledo structure, abstraction 701, has dopart1 composed of a whiledo (abstraction 501), followed by a fordo (abstraction 502), followed by an assignment (line 78). Reading primes and writing logical comments can begin within the dopart1, proceeding roughly in execution sequence. For example, in abstraction 201, the sequence at lines 24–27 sets the index named *median* to the mean of *partop* and *number*, sets *pivot* to the median element of *tosort*, and initializes *topind* and *botind*. Abstraction 102 is a conditional exchange of *tosort(partop)* and *pivot*, which also sets *tosort(median)* to *tosort-(partop)*. The abstraction can be commented as follows:

$$\cdots$$

102	**if**
28	$tosort(partop) > pivot$
	then [exchange($tosort(partop)$, $pivot$),
	$tosort(median) := tosort(partop)$]
29	$tosort(median) := tosort(partop)$
30	$tosort(partop) := pivot$
31	$pivot := tosort(median)$
102	**fi** [$tosort(partop) \leq tosort(median) = pivot$]

$$\cdots$$

Nested ifthen abstractions 103 and 301 are likewise conditional exchanges, which also set new values for *tosort(median)*. The program parts read so far can be commented as shown in Fig. 5.16. Note that abstractions 102 and 103 are identical; 103 reestablishes the status of 102 if it was changed by lines 34–36. The status comment attached to **fi** at the end of abstraction 301 states that *tosort(partop)*, *tosort(median)*, and *tosort(number)* are in ascending sorted order, and that *pivot* is equivalent to *tosort(median)*. (If the *tosort* array consisted of only two or three elements, it would be sorted at this point.) The effect of the sequence 201;301 can also be expressed in a corresponding action comment as

201;301	[ascending sort $tosort(partop)$, $tosort(median)$,
	$tosort(number)$; $pivot := tosort(median)$]

To continue reading, abstraction 302 is a dowhiledo with dopart1 containing two dountil structures. The first of these, abstraction 104, searches from $tosort(botind_0 - 1)$ upward in the array (i.e., toward $tosort(1)$) for an element less than or equal to *pivot*. (Note the relations $botind_0 = number$,

$\ldots$

<pre>
201   24   median := truncate((partop + number)/2)
      25   pivot := tosort(median)
      26   topind := partop
      27   botind := number
102   if
      28   tosort(partop) > pivot
              then [exchange(tosort(partop), pivot),
                       tosort(median) := tosort(partop)]
      29   tosort(median) := tosort(partop)
      30   tosort(partop) := pivot
      31   pivot := tosort(median)
</pre>

201   102   **fi** $[tosort(partop) \leq tosort(median) = pivot]$

<pre>
      301   if
      33   tosort(number) < pivot
              then [exchange(tosort(number), pivot),
                       tosort(median) := tosort(number)]
      34   tosort(median) := tosort(number)
      35   tosort(number) := pivot
      36   pivot := tosort(median)
      103   if
      37   tosort(partop) > pivot
                  then [exchange(tosort(partop), pivot),
                           tosort(median) := tosort(partop)]
      38   tosort(median) := tosort(partop)
      39   tosort(partop) := pivot
      40   pivot := tosort(median)
</pre>

      103   **fi** $[tosort(partop) \leq tosort(median) = pivot]$
      301   **fi** $[tosort(partop) \leq tosort(median)$
              $= pivot \leq tosort(number)]$

$\ldots$

Figure 5.16

and $tosort(number) \geq pivot$.) Termination of this first dountil is guaranteed on first execution of the dopart1 since at least

$$tosort(median) = pivot$$

by the $201; 301$ abstraction above. The second dountil, abstraction 105, searches from $tosort(topind_0 + 1)$ downward in the array (i.e., toward the last $tosort$ element) for an element greater than or equal to $pivot$. (Note $topind_0 = partop$, and $tosort(partop) \leq pivot$.) Termination of this second dountil on first execution of the dopart1 is likewise guaranteed by the condition just stated. To take advantage of the mnemonic value of variable names in Singsort, we adopt the convention that the first and last positions of the array are the "top" and "bottom" of the array, respectively. Thus, the dopart1 can be commented as

```
                  . . .
104               do
    43                botind := botind − 1
                  until
    44                tosort(botind) ≤ pivot
104               od [tosort(botind) ≤ pivot, (tosort((botind + 1): number)) ≥ pivot]
    45            temp2 := tosort(botind)
105               do
    46                topind := topind + 1
                  until
    47                tosort(topind) ≥ pivot
105               od[(tosort(partop : (topind − 1))) ≤ pivot, tosort(topind) ≥ pivot]
                  . . .
```

and summarized in the following action comment:

```
    . . .
    do1 [search bottom up for next element ≤ pivot, top down
          for next element ≥ pivot]
    . . .
```

If the whiletest at line 48 of dowhiledo abstraction 302 evaluates *true*, dopart2 is carried out to exchange *tosort(topind)* and *tosort(botind)*, and the dowhiledo repeats. Termination of the dountil loops above is guaranteed from then on, but not necessarily (as before) because

$$tosort(median) = pivot$$

since the original element at *tosort(median)* may have been involved in an exchange. Instead, termination is guaranteed because

$$tosort(partop) \le pivot \quad \text{and} \quad tosort(number) \ge pivot$$

by the 201; 301 abstraction above, which is sufficient to terminate the upward and downward searches, respectively. The effect of the dowhiledo is to segregate *tosort(partop: number)* into two partitions, one with elements no

greater than *pivot*, the other with elements no less than *pivot*, by exchanges
of elements between partitions, if necessary. Termination of the dowhiledo is
assured, since *topind* and *botind* are increased and decreased, respectively, on
every iteration, and eventually, *topind* − *botind* > 0. Because *topind* and
botind are compared only when an exchange of *tosort* elements is to be made,
a small "overshoot" can occur and on exit from the dowhiledo, *topind* −
botind ≤ 2, as in the following examples:

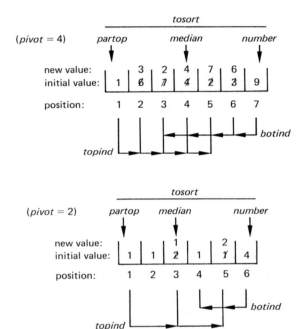

The final partition boundary can end up anywhere inside the interval
tosort((*partop* + 1):(*number* − 1)), and not necessarily at *tosort*(*median*).
Because *topind* and *botind* cross in the scanning process, on exit from the
dowhiledo *partop* and *botind* delimit the upper partition and *topind* and
number delimit the lower partition. It appears that the largest possible
partition remaining after segregating an array of *n* elements (*n* ≥ 4) has length
less than or equal to (*n* − 2).

In the commented dowhiledo fragment below, the status at **od** gives
relations that hold for the two partitions on loop termination, when the

whiletest turns *false*:

                      . . .

302   **do1** [search bottom up for next element $\leq$ *pivot*, top down for next element $\geq$ *pivot*]

203   104   **do**

        43   *botind* := *botind* − 1

                  until

        44   *tosort*(*botind*) $\leq$ *pivot*

       104   **od** [*tosort*(*botind*) $\leq$ *pivot*, (*tosort*((*botind* + 1): *number*)) $\geq$ *pivot*]

        45   *temp2* := *tosort*(*botind*)

       105   **do**

        46   *topind* := *topind* + 1

                  until

        47   *tosort*(*topind*) $\geq$ *pivot*

203   105   **od** [(*tosort*(*partop* : (*topind* − 1))) $\leq$ *pivot*, *tosort*(*topind*) $\geq$ *pivot*]

               while

        48   *topind* $\leq$ *botind*

               do2 [exchange(*tosort*(*topind*), *tosort*(*botind*))]

        49   *tosort*(*botind*) := *tosort*(*topind*)

        50   *tosort*(*topind*) := *temp2*

       302   **od** [(*tosort*(*partop* : (*topind* − 1))) $\leq$ *pivot*, (*tosort*((*botind* + 1): *number*)) $\geq$ *pivot*, *topind* > *botind*]

                      . . .

A corresponding action comment that summarizes the entire dowhiledo is

302   [segregate *tosort*(*partop* : *number*) into two partitions $\leq$ and $\geq$ *pivot*]

Consider next abstraction 106, an ifthenelse structure. The iftest compares (*botind* − *partop*) and (*number* − *topind*), and stores pointers to the smaller of these partitions in the *tops* and *bottoms* arrays. If the upper partition (delimited by *partop* and *botind*) is saved, the lower one becomes the new active partition (for possible further partitioning on the next iteration of Singsort), by setting *partop* to *topind* at line 56. If the lower partition (delimited by *topind* and *number*) is saved, the upper one becomes the new active partition, by setting *number* to *botind* at line 61. The ifthenelse of abstraction 106 can thus be commented as

$$\cdots$$

106   **if**
    53          $botind - partop < number - topind$
            then [save endpoints of upper partition, make lower new
                active partition]
    54              $tops(limdex) := partop$
    55              $bottoms(limdex) := botind$
    56              $partop := topind$
            else [save endpoints of lower partition, make upper new
                active partition]
    59              $tops(limdex) := topind$
    60              $bottoms(limdex) := number$
    61              $number := botind$
106   **fi**

$$\cdots$$

and summarized in an action comment as

106   [set $tops(limdex)$, $bottoms(limdex)$ to top, bottom pointers
        of smaller partition, set $partop$ to top, or $number$ to
        bottom pointer of larger partition]

The *tops* and *bottoms* arrays are declared with 20 elements each, so up to 20
partition boundaries can be stored. What limit does this place on the maximum possible size of the *tosort* array? This is an important question, and we
will return to it when we have learned more about Singsort's operation.

At line 63 *limdex* is incremented, and we have now read the entire
dopart of the whiledo abstraction 501.

Continuing in execution sequence, consider abstraction 502, a fordo
loop. The index *i* has initial value ($partop + 1$), and for first dopart execution
the assignments at lines 69 and 70 can be written as

$$\cdots$$

69    $pivot := tosort(partop + 1)$
70    $topind := partop$

$$\cdots$$

and the iftest at line 71 can be written as

$$\cdots$$

71    $tosort(partop) > tosort(partop + 1)$

$$\cdots$$

If this expression evaluates to *false*, no further operations are carried out in the dopart and the loop repeats, this time with

<pre>
. . .
68   pivot := tosort(partop + 2)
69   topind := partop + 1
. . .
</pre>

and so on. Thus, we conclude the fordo loop does nothing to *tosort-*
(partop : number) if the elements are already in ascending sort. So it seems
likely that the function of the thenpart, abstraction 205, is to force sorted
order for *tosort* elements scanned so far. That is, as the index *i* increments
over successive dopart executions, the thenpart assigns each *tosort(i)* not in
sorted order to that relative position in the elements already sorted which
reestablishes sorted order.

, A closer look reveals the dountil structure of abstraction 107 shifts
tosort(i − 1) to *tosort(i)*, *tosort(i − 2)* to *tosort(i − 1)*, and so on, until an
element is found with value not greater than *pivot*. No known property of
tosort(partop : number) guarantees termination of the iteration, but with further reading we learn that *topind* can be decremented to point to the element
just above *tosort(partop)*, which is guaranteed, by the partitioning abstraction 302, to be not greater than any value in the partition from *partop* to
number now being sorted. But what if the partition being sorted has first
element *tosort(1)*, since "*tosort(0)*" is not defined? Our reading so far does
not seem to provide an answer, so we leave the question open for now, and
comment the fordo structure as shown below:

<pre>
                      . . .
        502   for
            68   i :∈ partop + 1 to number by 1
                    do [ascending sort tosort(partop : i)]
        402 69   pivot := tosort(i)
            70   topind := i − 1
        303   if
            71   tosort(topind) > pivot
                      then [insert pivot in sorted position]
205 107   do
            72   tosort(topind + 1) := tosort(topind)
            73   topind := topind − 1
                          until
            74   tosort(topind) ≤ pivot
        107   od [tosort(topind) ≤ pivot, tosort(topind + 2) > pivot]
        205 75   tosort(topind + 1) := pivot
402 303   fi [tosort(partop) ≤ ··· ≤ tosort(i)]
        502   od [tosort(partop) ≤ ··· ≤ tosort(number)]
                      . . .
</pre>

Abstraction 502 can now be described by an action comment as

502   [ascending sort *tosort*(*partop*: *number*)]

Finally, at line 78, *limdex* is decremented, and we have read all of dopart1 of dowhiledo abstraction 701.

The reading so far has resulted in action comments that summarize intermediate level abstractions (sequence 201; 301, and 302, 106, and 502) of compound programs within the Singsort structure. An abstract version of Singsort can now be written using these summaries in place of the compound programs they represent, to help understand operation of the entire program, as shown in Fig. 5.17 (brackets have been dropped to emphasize that the summaries are now actions in the program, and not comments).

```
        801   1    proc singsort(tosort, number)
                     use singsort data
        101   21     limdex := 1
        101   22     initial := partop
        701          do1
    501 601            while
              64         number − partop > 10 ∨
              65         (initial = partop ∧
              66         partop < number)
                       do
401 201;301              ascending sort tosort(partop), tosort(median),
                        tosort(number); pivot := tosort(median)
        302             segregate tosort(partop: number)
                        into two partitions ≤ and ≥ pivot
        106             set tops(limdex), bottoms(limdex) to top, bottom
                        pointers of smaller partition, set partop to top,
                        or number to bottom pointer of larger partition
        401   63        limdex := limdex + 1
        501          od
        502          ascending sort tosort(partop: number)
        601   78     limdex := limdex − 1
                   while
              79     limdex ≥ 1
                   do2
              80     partop := tops(limdex)
              81     number := bottoms(limdex)
        701        od
        801   corp
```

Figure 5.17

We begin reading the reduced program above with the whiledo of abstraction 501. The dopart, abstraction 401, first sorts the endpoints and median of the active partition delimited by *partop* and *number* (abstraction 201;301), next segregates the active partition based on the value of *pivot* (abstraction 302), and finally saves the endpoints of the smaller partition and recycles the larger one for further partitioning (abstraction 106). The dopart can thus be summarized in an action comment as

   ...

do [partition the active partition, save endpoints of
     smaller, make larger new active]

   ...

Partitioning by the whiledo abstraction 501 continues until the active partition size, given by $(number - partop)$ in the first whiletest condition at line 64, drops below 10. Termination is guaranteed, since each new active partition in the loop is smaller than the previous one. What about the second whiletest condition, $(initial = partop \land partop < number)$, at lines 65 and 66? *Initial* is set to *partop* (itself initialized to 1) at line 22, and never reset. So the second condition tells us that the extent with upper boundary $partop = 1$ (i.e., extent with first element $tosort(1)$) is partitioned until $number \leq partop$ (likewise guaranteed, by reduction in successive partition sizes), and at least $tosort(1)$ and $tosort(2)$ are in sort. Remembering our open question on the fordo loop of abstraction 502, the purpose of this second condition now becomes clear. The active partition with first element $tosort(1)$ cannot be sorted by the fordo structure, as we discovered, and so is sorted by partitioning! The second whiletest condition handles this case.

What about a final status for the whiledo at **od**? A little thought reveals that all partitions produced by the whiledo are in relative ascending sort. Thus, we can define a predicate named relativesort, such that for, say, two partitions delimited by $Lo1$, $Hi1$ and $Lo2$, $Hi2$,

$$relativesort((Lo1, Hi1), (Lo2, Hi2)) \leftrightarrow Lo1 \leq Hi1 < Lo2 \leq Hi2$$
$$\land (\forall i, j) ((Lo1 \leq i \leq Hi1 \land Lo2 \leq j \leq Hi2)$$
$$\rightarrow tosort(i) \leq tosort(j))$$

Furthermore, at whiledo termination, endpoints of all partitions except for the current active partition have been saved for later processing. Thus, the whiledo can be commented as

$$\cdots$$

501   **while**
64         $number - partop > 10 \lor$
65         $(initial = partop \land$
66         $partop < number)$
        do [partition the active partition, save endpoints of
          smaller, make larger new active]

$$\cdots$$

501   **od** [relativesort(all partitions) $\land$ all except active saved $\land$
        active $\leq$ 10 elements]

$$\cdots$$

Following the whiledo abstraction 501, the current active partition is sorted by abstraction 502, and *limdex* is decremented at line 78 to complete the dopart1 of dowhiledo abstraction 701, all summarized as

$$\cdots$$

701   **do1** [for active partition > 10 or starting at *tosort*(1),
        partition, save endpoints of smaller, make larger
        new active and repeat, otherwise sort active partition]

$$\cdots$$

The dopart2 sets *partop* and *number* to the top and bottom, respectively, of the last saved partition, written in summary as

$$\cdots$$

do2 [make last saved partition new active partition]

$$\cdots$$

and the abstractions made so far permit us next to investigate the overall function of Singsort, embodied in the dowhiledo of abstraction 701.

As we have learned, dopart1 produces one partition in sorted order, and one or more partitions saved, with all partitions in relative sort. Partitions saved (counted by *limdex*) are recalled by dopart2 for further partitioning. Termination of the dowhiledo is guaranteed, whatever the size of the *tosort* array, since eventually, the partitions recalled are small enough (10 or fewer members) to be directly sorted in dopart1, thereby generating no further partitions to be saved. When *limdex* drops to 1, all partitions have been sorted, and the program terminates. Based on the foregoing analysis, the status at **od** can be written as

$$\cdots$$

od [relativesort(all partitions) $\land$ sort(partitions not
    saved) $\land$ no partitions saved]

$$\cdots$$

where "sort(partitions not saved)" is short for "every partition not currently saved is in ascending sorted order," and we are able to summarize the entire Singsort program in an action comment attached to **proc**:

proc singsort(*tosort, number*) [ascending sort *tosort* array]

This completes the derivation of Singsort's program function and the logical commentary for its prime programs. The abstracted program with derived comments appears in Fig. 5.18.

801	1		**proc** singsort(*tosort, number*) [ascending sort *tosort* array]
			use singsort data
101	21		*limdex* := 1
101	22		*initial* := *partop*
701			**do1** [for active partition > 10 or starting at *tosort*(1), partition, save endpoints of smaller, make larger new active and repeat, otherwise sort active partition]
501	601		**while**
	64		*number* − *partop* > 10 ∨
	65		(*initial* = *partop* ∧
	66		*partop* < *number*)
			do [partition the active partition, save endpoints of smaller, make larger new active]
401	201;301		ascending sort *tosort*(*partop*), *tosort*(*median*), *tosort*(*number*); *pivot* := *tosort*(*median*)
	302		segregate *tosort*(*partop* : *number*) into two partitions ≤ and ≥ *pivot*
	106		set *tops*(*limdex*), *bottoms*(*limdex*) to top, bottom pointers of smaller partition, set *partop* to top, or *number* to bottom pointer of larger partition
	401	63	*limdex* := *limdex* + 1
	501		**od** [relativesort(all partitions) ∧ all except active saved ∧ active ≤ 10 elements]
	502		ascending sort *tosort*(*partop* : *number*)
	601	78	*limdex* := *limdex* − 1
			while
	79		*limdex* ≥ 1
			do2 [make last saved partition new active partition]
	80		*partop* := *tops*(*limdex*)
	81		*number* := *bottoms*(*limdex*)
701			**od** [relativesort(all partitions) ∧ sort(partitions not saved) ∧ no partitions saved]
801			**corp**

Figure 5.18

5.4.5   A Segment Structured Singsort

The intermediate abstractions (201;301, 302, 106, 502) derived in the fore-going analysis summarize important functions in Singsort. They can be given convenient names based on their abstractions as

201;301	boundarysort
302	partition
106	save/activate
502	siftsort

and organized in a segment structure, shown as a segmented prime parse tree in Fig. 5.19, and as segmented and commented PDL in Fig. 5.20. Lists of data items in fixed- and altered-usage categories have been attached to **run** and **proc** statements (keeping all data declarations local to the top segment). The usage analysis is carried out by methodically recording data references in operations and tests of each segment, according to whether each data item is used as is or receives a new value.

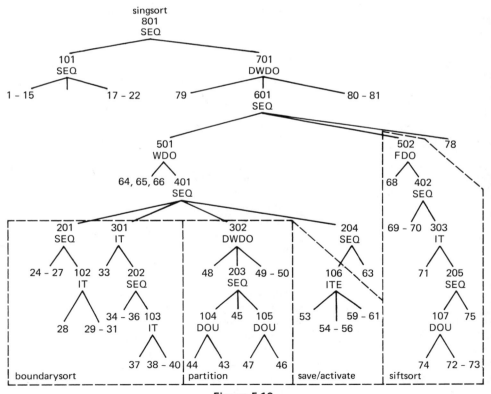

Figure 5.19

[Segment hierarchy]

singsort
  singsortdata
  boundarysort
  partition
  save/activate
  siftsort

[Segments]

data singsortdata
  array
4   *tosort(number)*: integer [array to be sorted]
  scalar
5   (*pivot* [value of active partition median for
        boundarysort]
6   *temp2*
7   *limdex* [pointer in *tops, bottoms* arrays]
8   *initial*
9   *median* [pointer to median element in active partition]
10   *botind* [pointer to bottom up exchange candidate]
11   *topind* [pointer to top down exchange candidate]
13   *i*
14   *number* [pointer to last element in active partition]
15   *partop* init(1) [pointer to first element in active
        partition]): integer
  array
19   *tops*(20): integer [pointers to first elements in saved
        partitions]
20   *bottoms*(20): integer [pointers to last elements in saved
        partitions]
atad

801 1   **proc** singsort(*tosort, number*) [ascending sort *tosort* array]
         use singsortdata
101 21 *limdex* := 1
101 22 *initial* := *partop*
701   **do1** [for active partition > 10 or starting at *tosort*(1),
             partition, save endpoints of smaller, make
             larger new active and repeat, otherwise
             sort active partition]
501 601   **while**
     64   *number − partop* > 10 ∨
     65   (*initial = partop* ∧
     66   *partop < number*)
            do [partition the active partition, save
                endpoints of smaller, make larger new active]

Figure 5.20   (Continued)

401	201;301	**run** boundarysort(**alt** *median, pivot, topind,*
		botind, tosort, **fix** *partop, number*)
	302	**run** partition(**alt** *botind, topind, tosort,*
		temp2, **fix** *pivot*)
	106	**run** save/activate(**alt** *tops, bottoms, partop,*
		number, **fix** *botind, topind, limdex*)
	401 63	*limdex* := *limdex* + 1
	501	**od** [relativesort(all partitions) ∧ all except
		active saved ∧ active ≤ 10 elements]
	502	**run** siftsort(**alt** *pivot, topind, tosort, i,* **fix**
		partop, number)
	601 78	*limdex* := *limdex* − 1
		while
	79	*limdex* ≥ 1
		do2 [make last saved partition new active partition]
	80	*partop* := *tops(limdex)*
	81	*number* := *bottoms(limdex)*
	701	**od** [relativesort(all partitions) ∧ sort(partitions
		not saved) ∧ no partitions saved]
	801	**corp**
		proc boundarysort(**alt** *median, pivot, topind, botind,*
		tosort, **fix** *partop, number*) [ascending sort *tosort(partop)*,
		tosort(median), tosort(number); pivot := *tosort(median)*]
	201 24	*median* := *truncate*((*partop* + *number*)/2)
	25	*pivot* := *tosort(median)*
	26	*topind* := *partop*
	27	*botind* := *number*
	102	**if**
	28	*tosort(partop)* > *pivot*
		then [exchange(*tosort(partop), pivot*),
		tosort(median) := *tosort(partop)*]
	29	*tosort(median)* := *tosort(partop)*
	30	*tosort(partop)* := *pivot*
	31	*pivot* := *tosort(median)*
201	102	**fi** [*tosort(partop)* ≤ *tosort(median)* = *pivot*]
	301	**if**
	33	*tosort(number)* < *pivot*
		then [exchange(*tosort(number), pivot*),
		tosort(median) := *tosort(number)*]
	34	*tosort(median)* := *tosort(number)*
	35	*tosort(number)* := *pivot*
	36	*pivot* := *tosort(median)*
	103	**if**
	37	*tosort(partop)* > *pivot*

Figure 5.20 (Continued)

```
                    then [exchange(tosort(partop), pivot),
                            tosort(median) := tosort(partop)]
        38               tosort(median) := tosort(partop)
        39               tosort(partop) := pivot
        40               pivot := tosort(median)
103              fi
301          fi [tosort(partop) ≤ tosort(median) = pivot
                    ≤ tosort(number)]
         corp


         proc partition(alt botind, topind, tosort, temp2, fix
                 pivot) [segregate tosort(partop: number) into
                 two partitions ≤ and ≥ pivot]
302          do1 [search bottom up for next element ≤ pivot, top
                 down for next element ≥ pivot]
203 104          do
        43           botind := botind − 1
                 until
        44           tosort(botind) ≤ pivot
104              od [tosort(botind) ≤ pivot, (tosort((botind + 1:
                 number)) ≥ pivot]
        45       temp2 := tosort(botind)
105              do
        46           topind := topind + 1
                 until
        47           tosort(topind) ≥ pivot
203 105          od [(tosort(partop: (topind − 1))) ≤ pivot,
                 tosort(topind) ≥ pivot]
             while
        48       topind ≤ botind
             do2 [exchange(tosort(topind), tosort(botind))]
        49       tosort(botind) := tosort(topind)
        50       tosort(topind) := temp2
302          od [(tosort(partop: (topind − 1))) ≤ pivot,
                 (tosort((botind + 1): number)) ≥ pivot,
                 topind > botind]
         corp


         proc save/activate(alt tops, bottoms, partop, number, fix botind,
                 topind, limdex) [set tops(limdex), bottoms(limdex) to top,
                 bottom pointers of smaller partition, set partop to top,
                 or number to bottom pointer of larger partition]
106          if
        53       botind − partop < number − topind
```

Figure 5.20 (Continued)

```
                             then [save endpoints of upper partition, make lower
                                    new active partition]
            54                   tops(limdex) := partop
            55                   bottoms(limdex) := botind
            56                   partop := botind
                             else [save endpoints of lower partition, make upper
                                    new active partition]
            59                   tops(limdex) := topind
            60                   bottoms(limdex) := number
            61                   number := botind
    106                      fi
                          corp


                          proc siftsort(alt pivot, topind, tosort, i, fix partop,
                                 number) [ascending sort tosort(partop:number)]
           502                for
                  68              i :∈ partop + 1 to number by 1
                              do [ascending sort tosort(partop:i)]
           402    69              pivot := tosort(i)
                  70              topind := i − 1
           303                    if
                  71                  tosort(topind) > pivot
                                  then [insert pivot in sorted position]
    205    107                        do
                  72                      tosort(topind + 1) := tosort(topind)
                  73                      topind := topind − 1
                                      until
                  74                      tosort(topind) ≤ pivot
           107                        od [tosort(topind) ≤ pivot,
                                          tosort(topind + 2) > pivot]
           205    75                  tosort(topind + 1) := pivot
    402    303                    fi [tosort(partop) ≤ ⋯ ≤ tosort(i)]
           502                od [tosort(partop) ≤ ⋯ ≤ tosort(number)]
                          corp
```

Figure 5.20

5.4.6   Open Questions

As we have learned, the save/activate segment saves top and bottom pointers
to the smaller partition, leaving the larger one for further partitioning. The
question raised earlier is still open—what limit does a capacity for saving
only 20 partitions place on the size of the array to be sorted? The largest
possible partition of an n-element array has size $n - 2$, and a series of such
lopsided partitions cannot be ruled out. Thus, in the worst case, a 42-element

array could require saving 21 partitions (each of the first 20 reducing the original array by a 2-element partition up from the bottom), thereby overflowing the save arrays.

To solve the problem, the largest partition should be saved at each step, giving a worst case (now, for nearly equal, rather than lopsided, partitions) size limit on *tosort* of $(2**(k + 1)) - 1$, where k is the size of the save arrays, in this case, $(2**21) - 1$.

There are other, less serious questions in Singsort, concerned with clarity and style, such as the following:

1. Line 45 plays no role in the search for exchange candidates within which it is embedded, and should be moved just above line 49. Then, lines 45, 49, 50 (together) make up a meaningful abstraction—exchange.

2. Two separate sorts (one for endpoints and median, another for active partitions ≤ 10 elements) could be carried out by a single sort algorithm.

3. In abstraction 502, *pivot* is used as a temporary variable, obscuring the sort function.

4. *Number* is an argument to the Singsort subroutine, but its value is changed and not restored.

5.4.7   A Stack Oriented Singsort

Our reading of Singsort has uncovered a sensible algorithm, in which we now recognize the stacking and unstacking of partitions. The *tops* and *bottoms* arrays are used as stack data structures with *limdex* as a pointer, permitting last in/first out access of stack members. Operations on these arrays (refer to Fig. 5.20) are distributed as follows:

Statement	Segment	Corresponding stack operation
21 *limdex* := 1	singsort	*tops* := **empty**; *bottoms* := **empty**
54 *tops(limdex)* := *partop*	save/activate	**top**(*tops*) := *partop*
55 *bottoms(limdex)* := *botind*	save/activate	**top**(*bottoms*) := *botind*
59 *tops(limdex)* := *topind*	save/activate	**top**(*tops*) := *topind*
60 *bottoms(limdex)* := *number*	save/activate	**top**(*bottoms*) := *number*
63 *limdex* := *limdex* + 1	singsort	none
78 *limdex* := *limdex* − 1	singsort	none
80 *partop* := *tops(limdex)*	singsort	*partop* := **top**(*tops*)
81 *number* := *bottoms(limdex)*	singsort	*number* := **top**(*bottoms*)

It is now possible to reconstruct Singsort top down as a stack-oriented algorithm. A start at reconstruction is shown below, with partition pointers *partop*, *botind*, and so on, abstracted as a 2-array called "extent," and a single stack, *s*, used to save copies of "extents":

```
    . . .
top(s) := array extent
while
    s ≠ empty
do
    active extent := top(s)
    while
        active extent > 10, etc.
    do
        larger extent, smaller extent := partition(active extent)
        top(s) := smaller extent
        active extent := larger extent
    od
    active extent := sort(active extent)
od
    . . .
```

EXERCISES

1. Finish writing and commenting the stack-oriented Singsort program above.

2. In parts (a) and (b) put the programs† into better shape for understanding by doing a prime program parse, restructuring into a simpler basis if necessary, and translating into PDL; then add logical commentary, segment, and analyze data usage for **fix** and **alt** lists:

```
a)   1    BSHELLSORT:PROCEDURE(TOSORT, NUMBER);
     2    /* ALGORITHM 201, SHELLSORT, PUBLISHED
          IN ALGOL PUBLICATION
     3    LANGUAGE, COMMUNICATIONS OF ACM,
          VOL 6, NO 8, AUGUST, 1963 */
     4    DECLARE
     5    TOSORT(*) FIXED BINARY (31, 0),
     6    DISTANCE FIXED BINARY (31, 0),
     7    LIMIT FIXED BINARY (31, 0),
     8    TEMP FIXED BINARY (31, 0),
     9    I FIXED BINARY (31, 0),
    10    J FIXED BINARY (31, 0),
    11    LOGNMBR FIXED BINARY (31, 0),
    12    NUMBER FIXED BINARY (31, 0);
    13    LOGNMBER = LOG2(NUMBER);
    14    DISTANCE = 2 ** LOGNMBER − 1;
    15    DIST: DO WHILE (DISTANCE > 0);
```

† H. Lorin, *Sorting and Sort Systems* (Reading, Mass.: Addison-Wesley, 1975) A64–65, A70–72.

```
16    LIMIT = NUMBER – DISTANCE;
17    SETS: DO J = 1 TO LIMIT BY 1;
18    ELTS: DO I = J TO 1 BY – DISTANCE;
19    IF TOSORT(I + DISTANCE) > = TOSORT(I) THEN GO TO OUT;
20    TEMP = TOSORT(I);
21    TOSORT(I) = TOSORT(I + DISTANCE);
22    TOSORT(I + DISTANCE) = TEMP;
23    END ELTS;
24    OUT: END SETS;
25    DISTANCE = DISTANCE/2;
26    END DIST;
27    END BSHELLSORT;


b)  1    STRINGSORT: PROCEDURE(TOSORT, NUMBER);
    2    /* ALGORITHM 207, COMMUNICATIONS ACM,
         VOL 5, NO 10, P 215 */
    3    DECLARE
    4    TOSORT(*) FIXED BINARY (31, 0),
    5    NUMBER FIXED BINARY (31, 0);
    6    SORT: BEGIN;
    7    DECLARE
    8    WORK(2 * NUMBER) FIXED BINARY (31, 0),
    9    TOPST FIXED BINARY (31, 0),
   10    BOTST FIXED BINARY (31, 0),
   11    LIMITS (2) FIXED BINARY (31, 0),
   12    ADVANCE FIXED BINARY (31, 0),
   13    NEXT FIXED BINARY (31, 0),
   14    LAST FIXED BINARY (31, 0),
   15    K FIXED BINARY (31, 0),
   16    PASSW FIXED BINARY (1, 0),
   17    EXTEND LABEL;
   18    INITIAL: DO I = 1 TO NUMBER BY 1;
   19    WORK(I) = TOSORT(I);
   20    END INITIAL;
   21    ODDPASS: TOPST = 1;
   22    BOTST = NUMBER;
   23    LIMITS(1) = NUMBER + 1;
   24    LIMITS(2) = 2 * NUMBER;
   25    K = 1;
   26    ADVANCE = 1
   27    PASSW = 1;
   28    FIRSTST: EXTEND = NONDOWN;
   29    NEXT = LIMITS(K);
   30    IF WORK(TOPST) > = WORK(BOTST)
         THEN GO TO BOTTOM;
   31    ELSE GO TO TOP;
   32    TOP: WORK(NEXT) = WORK(TOPST);
   33    TOPST = TOPST + 1;
   34    GO TO NEWNEXT;
```

```
35    BOTTOM: WORK(NEXT) = WORK(BOTST);
36    BOTST = BOTST − 1;
37    NEWNEXT: LAST = NEXT;
38    NEXT = NEXT + ADVANCE;
39    IF BOTST > =TOPST THEN GO TO EXTEND;
40    IF PASSW = 0 THEN IF NEXT = NUMBER + 1
      THEN GO TO EXIT;
41    ELSE GO TO ODDPASS;
42    ELSE IF NEXT = 2 * NUMBER + 1 THEN GO TO EXIT;
43    ELSE GO TO EVENPASS;
44    JDOWN: IF WORK(TOPST) > =WORK(LAST)
      THEN GO TO TOP;
45    ELSE GO TO BOTHDOWN;
46    IDOWN: IF WORK(BOTST) > =WORK(LAST)
      THEN GO TO BOTTOM;
47    ELSE GO TO BOTHDOWN;
48    NONDOWN: IF WORK(TOPST) > =WORK(LAST) THEN
49    IF WORK(BOTST) > =WORK(LAST) THEN
50    IF WORK(BOTST) > =WORK(TOPST) THEN GO TO TOP;
51    ELSE GO TO BOTTOM;
52    ELSE DO;
53    EXTEND = JDOWN;
54    GO TO TOP;
55    END;
56    ELSE DO;
57    EXTEND = IDOWN;
58    GO TO IDOWN;
59    END;
60    BOTHDOWN:
61    LIMITS(K) = NEXT;
62    IF K = 1 THEN K = 2;
63    ELSE K = 1;
64    ADVANCE = −ADVANCE;
65    GO TO FIRSTST;
66    EVENPASS: TOPST = NUMBER + 1;
67    BOTST = 2 * NUMBER;
68    LIMITS(1) = 1;
69    LIMITS(2) = NUMBER;
70    ADVANCE = 1;
71    K = 1;
72    PASSW = 0;
73    GO TO FIRSTST;
74    EXIT: DO I = 1 TO NUMBER BY 1;
75    TOSORT(I) = WORK(LIMITS (1) − 1 + I);
76    END;
77    END SORT;
78    END STRINGSORT;
```

6

The Correctness
of Structured
Programs

6.1 OVERVIEW

This chapter develops a function-theoretic basis for the correctness of structured programs. Correctness relationships are crucial: first, in program reading, to know if one is interpreting a program properly; second, in program writing, to know if one is writing a correct program; and third, in program validation, to know if a program correctly carries out its intended function.

Program correctness is defined as a correspondence between a program and its intended function. Algebraic concepts are used to reduce the problem of determining compound program correctness to the problem of determining correctness of constituent primes. The correctness verification of loop-free programs is carried out by analysis of their E-charts, and in an Iteration Recursion Lemma, the verification of looping programs is reduced to verification of equivalent loop-free programs. The Correctness Theorem summarizes verification requirements for both loop-free and looping primes. *Trace tables* and *disjoint rules* are introduced as techniques for proving program correctness, and the function-theoretic approach to verification is illustrated in several examples. *Loop invariants* are introduced for an alternate proof technique and as an aid to program documentation. A standard procedure for defining invariants is given by the Invariant Status Theorem. Finally, for insight into the design process, the derivation of correct programs is described in terms of function equations for prime programs, for which formal solutions exist.

213

6.2   VERIFYING STRUCTURED PROGRAMS

6.2.1   Verifying Correctness in Reading, Writing, and Validation

The verification questions encountered in reading, writing, and validating programs are identical.

In program reading, at each step a prime program is abstracted in the form of a hypothesis for its program function. For example, given program **if** p **then** g **else** h **fi**, we hypothesize that its program function is f. The verification task is then to show

$$f = [\text{if } p \text{ then } g \text{ else } h \text{ fi}]$$

That is, the task is to verify that the hypothesized function f is, in fact, equivalent to (or possibly a subset of) the program function of the given program.

Next, in writing or designing a program, at each step a given function is expanded into a suitable prime structure, and function and predicate components are invented that we hypothesize will produce a program function identical to the given function. For example, beginning with a given function f and hypothesizing that an equivalent function will be produced by, say, an ifthenelse structure using invented components p, g, and h, the verification task, as before, is to show

$$f = [\text{if } p \text{ then } g \text{ else } h \text{ fi}]$$

That is, the task is to verify that the given function f is equivalent to (or possibly a subset of) the program function of the invented program.

Finally, in program validation both a function and its alleged program expansion are given. So, once again, starting with the given function f, and a program, say, **if** p **then** g **else** h **fi**, we must verify that

$$f = [\text{if } p \text{ then } g \text{ else } h \text{ fi}]$$

Thus, in general, the needs for program verification (proving a program correct) are identical, whether we are engaged in program abstraction in reading, program expansion in writing, or program validation. In all three cases we seek to confirm the equivalence (or subset relationship) of two expressions, each representing the function of a program.

6.2.2   The Algebra of Correctness of Structured Programs

Program correctness is concerned with one of two questions:

Given a function f and a program P (which is claimed to implement f),

$$1. \text{ Is } f = [P]? \qquad \text{or} \qquad 2. \text{ Is } f \subset [P]?$$

That is, does P compute the correct values of f from the arguments of f?

Question 1 is called the question of *complete correctness*; question 2, of *sufficient correctness*. For complete correctness, P computes only the (correct) values of f from arguments of f (i.e., P is undefined for arguments outside of the domain of f). For sufficient correctness, P may compute values from arguments not belonging to f.

For example, for integers x, y, let

$$f = (x \geq 0 \wedge y \geq 0 \rightarrow x, \ y := x + y, \ 0)$$

$$P1 = \textbf{while } y > 0 \textbf{ do } x, \ y := x + 1, \ y - 1 \textbf{ od}$$

$$P2 = \textbf{while } y \neq 0 \textbf{ do } x, \ y := x + 1, \ y - 1 \textbf{ od}$$

Since both $P1$ and $P2$ correctly compute $f(x, y)$ for positive x, y, they satisfy the requirements for sufficient correctness, but neither satisfies the requirements for complete correctness, for they both compute values for arguments not contained in f. $P1$ accepts (i.e., terminates for) negative initial values for both x, y, and $P2$ accepts negative initial values for x. Note that $P2$ is undefined for negative initial values for y, as is f, since it does not terminate when presented with $y < 0$.

The requirement to achieve complete correctness leads to the concept of defensive programming (i.e., "defending" against unexpected inputs). In this case, the idea of defensive programming suggests a respecification of f to include the complete domain of P, with the requirement that all arguments thereby added to the domain result in "exception processing" by the program. Thus, f and P can be redefined as

$$f_1 = (x \geq 0 \wedge y \geq 0 \rightarrow x, \ y, \ z := x + y, \ 0, \ z \ | $$
$$true \rightarrow x, \ y, \ z := x, \ y, \ \text{'error'})$$

$$P3 = \textbf{if } (x < 0) \vee (y < 0) \textbf{ then } z := \text{'error'}$$
$$\textbf{else while } y > 0 \textbf{ do } x, \ y := x + 1, \ y - 1 \textbf{ od fi}$$

for complete correctness with defenses against unexpected inputs.

If P is not a prime program, its decomposition into primes provides a way to reduce the amount of reasoning required by use of the algebraic structure of P. In particular, the hierarchy of abstractions of P decomposes the proof of correctness for P into a proof of correctness for each such abstraction. For example, suppose we attempt to show that a compound program F implements a desired function f, where

$$F = \textbf{if } p \textbf{ then } G \textbf{ else } H \textbf{ fi} \tag{1}$$

and G and H are themselves programs. Rather than attempting at the outset to prove the set equality

$$f = [\textbf{if } p \textbf{ then } G \textbf{ else } H \textbf{ fi}] \tag{2}$$

which may be quite difficult (depending on the complexity of G and H), we first hypothesize functions g and h and attempt to prove the complete correctness of

$$g = [G] \quad \text{and} \quad h = [H] \tag{3}$$

If successful, we can simplify (2) above, using the Axiom of Replacement (see Section 5.2.2), and reduce the problem to proving the set equality

$$f = [\textbf{if } p \textbf{ then } g \textbf{ else } h \textbf{ fi}] \tag{4}$$

If again successful, we will have proved the complete correctness of $f = [F]$ as we set out to do. However, if any of the three programs satisfy only sufficient correctness, then program F satisfies only sufficient correctness. For example, if G computes values for arguments that are not in g, then F may compute values for arguments that are not in f.

In illustration, the subtract program (for $x, y \geq 0$)

```
SUB = while
          x > 0 ∧ y > 0
      do
          x := x − 1
          y := y − 1
      od
      if
          y > 0
      then
          x := − y
      fi
      free y
```

is intended to produce the assignment function

$$\text{sub} = [x, y := x - y, \text{free}]$$

(by repeated decrementing, then checking for sign). The four primes of SUB can be diagrammed and named as follows:

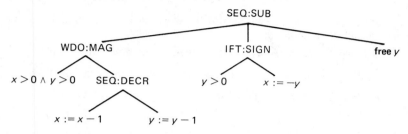

Let program functions mag, decr, sign be hypothesized for MAG, DECR, SIGN. Then there are four subproofs to a proof of correctness that

$$1. \quad \text{sub} = [\text{SUB}] \qquad \text{or} \qquad 2. \quad \text{sub} \subset [\text{SUB}]$$

These subproofs are either

1. sub = [mag; sign; **free** y]
    mag = [**while** $x > 0 \wedge y > 0$ **do** decr **od**]
    decr = [$x := x - 1$; $y := y - 1$]
    sign = [**if** $y > 0$ **then** $x := -y$ **fi**]

or

2. sub $\subset$ [mag; sign; **free** y]
    mag $\subset$ [**while** $x > 0 \wedge y > 0$ **do** decr **od**]
    decr $\subset$ [$x := x - 1$; $y := y - 1$]
    sign $\subset$ [**if** $y > 0$ **then** $x := -y$ **fi**]

Thus, the correctness of a compound program can be verified by a set of verifications of the prime programs in which the compound program is expressed.

EXERCISES

1. Given

$$P1 = \textbf{while } x \geq y \textbf{ do } x, y := y, x \textbf{ od}$$

$$P2 = \textbf{if } x \geq y \textbf{ then } x, y := y, x \textbf{ fi}$$

$$P3 = \textbf{do } x, y := y, x \textbf{ until } x \neq y \textbf{ od}$$

$$f1 = x, y := y, x$$

$$f2 = (x \neq y \rightarrow x, y := y, x)$$
$$f3 = (x \geq y \rightarrow x, y := y, x)$$

determine the correctness relationships between each program and function. (Complete, sufficient, neither?)

   2. Show a proof organization for the following program and function:

$$P = \textbf{if } x < y \textbf{ then } x, y := y, x \textbf{ fi while } y > 0 \textbf{ do } x, y := x - 1, y - 1 \textbf{ od}$$
$$f = (x \geq 0 \wedge y \geq 0 \rightarrow x, y := \text{abs}(x - y), 0)$$

6.3 THE CORRECTNESS OF PRIME PROGRAMS

6.3.1 Program Termination

As we have seen, if P is a loop-free program, then $[P]$ is determined by a finite union of function compositions defined along the paths of the E-chart of P (with or without decomposing P into constituent primes). In this case, the correctness questions can be answered directly by evaluating $[P]$ and comparing the result with the intended function of P, say f. Of course, if P and f are complicated objects, this evaluation and comparison will be complicated, too. But, nevertheless, the logical work to be done is known precisely.

   If P is not loop free, then the correctness questions are more difficult and, in general, answering them may not be possible. The correctness of a looping program depends, in part, on assurance that the program terminates. This assurance will often be based on the observation that a regularly changing variable must ultimately cause predicate evaluation to result in an exit, or perhaps that a logical predicate variable previously *true* is set *false* to permit an exit. However, even if no such observation can be made, we cannot deduce in general that the program does not terminate. In fact, it may be logically impossible (undecidable) to determine if an execution of P halts for any given initial argument, say X, of f.

   Even though the termination question is undecidable in general, we can decide to limit our consideration to programs whose termination can be established. In fact, we define a new predicate

$$\text{term}(f, P) = \text{“}P \text{ terminates for every initial state } X \in D(f)\text{”}$$

which we assume we can evaluate for any program P under consideration. In short, it's a minor sin to write a program that does not terminate, but a major sin to write one whose termination is undecidable.

6.3.2   The Iteration Recursion Lemma

The verification of the three one-predicate prime programs with loops (whiledo, dountil, dowhiledo) can be reduced to the question of termination and the verification of loop-free programs, by converting iteration into recursion. Thus, for example, instead of directly verifying that f is the program function of the terminating whiledo program

$$P = \textbf{while } p \textbf{ do } g \textbf{ od}$$

which can be extremely difficult, it is sufficient to verify that P terminates for all arguments of f and that f is the program function of the following non-looping ifthen program (with thenpart composed of dopart g followed by f)

$$Q = \textbf{if } p \textbf{ then } g; f \textbf{ fi}$$

because $[P] = [Q]$, as we show next. To illustrate this equivalence, consider the whiledo program P that adds two nonnegative integers u, v:

$$P = \textbf{while } v > 0 \textbf{ do } u, v := u + 1, v - 1 \textbf{ od}$$

We observe that P terminates and has function rule

$$f = (u, v := u + v, 0)$$

We therefore assert that P is function equivalent to

$$Q = \textbf{if } v > 0 \textbf{ then } u, v := u + 1, v - 1; u, v := u + v, 0 \textbf{ fi}$$

This can be demonstrated by an examination of two cases:

Case $\sim (v > 0)$:

$\sim (v > 0)$ and v nonnegative $\rightarrow (v = 0)$. Since the predicate $(v > 0)$ fails, both P and Q do nothing, and are therefore equivalent.

Case $(v > 0)$:

$[Q]$ is a composition of two functions, and may be determined by direct substitution, namely,

$$[u, v := u + 1, v - 1; u, v := u + v, 0] = u, v := (u + 1) + (v - 1), 0$$

with program function

$$u, v := u + v, 0$$

Therefore $[Q] = (u, v := u + v, 0) = [P]$ as was to be shown.

In other words, if we know the program function f of looping program P, we can find a recursive equation in f for a loop-free program. The solution of such a recursive equation for f may be difficult or impossible to find; but in this case we are verifying, not solving, the equation, and the recursion does not add any difficulty to the verification problem. This iteration-to-recursion possibility motivates the following Lemma.

Iteration Recursion Lemma.   Given functions f, g, h, and predicate p:

Case a (whiledo):

$$(f = [\textbf{while } p \textbf{ do } g \textbf{ od}]) \leftrightarrow$$
$$(\text{term}(f, \textbf{while } p \textbf{ do } g \textbf{ od}) \wedge$$
$$f = [\textbf{if } p \textbf{ then } g; f \textbf{ fi}])$$

Case b (dountil):

$$(f = [\textbf{do } g \textbf{ until } p \textbf{ od}]) \leftrightarrow$$
$$(\text{term}(f, \textbf{do } g \textbf{ until } p \textbf{ od}) \wedge$$
$$f = [g; \textbf{if } \sim p \textbf{ then } f \textbf{ fi}])$$

Case c (dowhiledo):

$$(f = [\textbf{do1 } g \textbf{ while } p \textbf{ do2 } h \textbf{ od}]) \leftrightarrow$$
$$(\text{term}(f, \textbf{do1 } g \textbf{ while } p \textbf{ do2 } h \textbf{ od}) \wedge$$
$$f = [g; \textbf{if } p \textbf{ then } h; f \textbf{ fi}])$$

Proof.   Case a (whiledo): Assume, first, that

$$f = [\textbf{while } p \textbf{ do } g \textbf{ od}]$$

Then term $(f, \textbf{while } p \textbf{ do } g \textbf{ od})$ is necessary, otherwise the program function $[\textbf{while } p \textbf{ do } g \textbf{ od}]$ could not equal the function f. Consider next the execution equivalent programs

$$\textbf{while } p \textbf{ do } g \textbf{ od} \qquad \text{and} \qquad \textbf{if } p \textbf{ then } g; \textbf{while } p \textbf{ do } g \textbf{ od fi}$$

whose equivalence can be seen directly, by inspection of their flowchart forms:

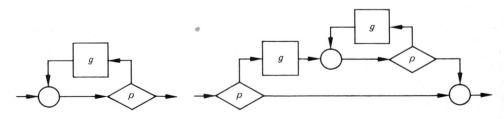

Therefore

$$[\text{while } p \text{ do } g \text{ od}] = [\text{if } p \text{ then } g; \text{ while } p \text{ do } g \text{ od fi}]$$

By hypothesis and the Axiom of Replacement, the two whiledo programs can be replaced by the single assignment program with function *f*, so that

$$f = [\text{if } p \text{ then } g; f \text{ fi}]$$

as was to be shown.

Conversely (to complete the if and only if requirement), assume

$$\text{term}(f, \text{ while } p \text{ do } g \text{ od}) \wedge f = [\text{if } p \text{ then } g; f \text{ fi}]$$

and consider the series of function equivalent programs obtained by successive substitution of the ifthen program for its program function:

if *p* then *g*; *f* fi
if *p* then *g*; if *p* then *g*; *f* fi fi
...
if *p* then *g*; if *p* then *g*; ... if *p* then *g*;
          (if *p* then *g*; *f* fi) fi ... fi fi
...

Since term(*f*, **while** *p* **do** *g* **od**) is hypothesized, the limit of this series is function equivalent to the program

if *p* then *g*; if *p* then *g*; ... if *p* then *g*; *I* fi ... fi fi

that is, identical except that the innermost ifthen is replaced by the identity function *I* because the predicate *p* must evaluate to *false* after a finite number of compositions of *g*. But this latter program is execution equivalent to

while *p* **do** *g* **od**

and hence

$$f = [\text{while } p \text{ do } g \text{ od}]$$

as was to be shown. This concludes the proof for Case a (whiledo). The proofs for Cases b and c are similar, and are left for the reader.

6.3.3   The Correctness Theorem

For convenience and reference, we assemble the requirements for verifying the correctness of prime programs with up to one predicate in a Correctness

Theorem. (Fordo and case programs are included as well.) The correctness questions noted before, namely

1. Is $f = [P]$?   (complete correctness)
2. Is $f \subset [P]$?   (sufficient correctness)

can be reasoned about and answered as corresponding set-theoretic questions. In the Correctness Theorem, we specialize these questions for various forms of program P into standard reasoning procedures for verification, based on the E-chart and Iteration Recursion Lemma discussions above. The problem of verifying a set relation is a mathematical problem. The Correctness Theorem only defines what set relations must be verified in order to prove the correctness of a program. It is still necessary to use whatever mathematical procedures and reasoning may be appropriate to demonstrate the required relationships.

The Correctness Theorem demonstrates that, aside from termination questions, all structured programs expressed in primes of up to one predicate can be verified by using only those methods of reasoning required by sequence and ifthenelse programs. The proof problems may exceed our time and patience but not our knowledge.

Correctness Theorem.   For any function f and program P, correctness is defined by a condition C for
1.   complete correctness

$$(f = [P]) \leftrightarrow (\text{term}(f, P) \wedge f = \{(X, Y) \mid C(X, Y)\})$$

2.   sufficient correctness

$$(f \subset [P]) \leftrightarrow (\text{term}(f, P) \wedge f \subset \{(X, Y) \mid C(X, Y)\})$$

where P and C are as tabulated below. Note that $\text{term}(f, P)$ is always true for loop-free programs but permits a unified treatment of loop-free and looping programs alike.

P	$C(X, Y)$
Case a (sequence):	
$g; h$	$Y = h \circ g(X)$
Case b (fordo):	
for $i :\in L(1:n)$ **do** g **od**	$Y = g_{L(n)} \circ \ldots \circ g_{L(1)}(X)$
($g_{L(k)}$ is the function of the kth dopart iteration)	
Case c (ifthen):	
if p **then** g **fi**	$(p(X) \rightarrow Y = g(X)) \wedge$ $(\sim p(X) \rightarrow Y = X)$

Case d (ifthenelse):
   if p **then** g **else** h **fi**

$(p(X) \to Y = g(X)) \wedge$
$(\sim p(X) \to Y = h(X))$

Case e (case):†
   case p **part** $(CL1)$ g ...
   part (CLn) h **else** t **esac**

$(p(X) \in CL1 \to Y = g(X)) \wedge$
$\cdots$
$(p(X) \in CLn \to Y = h(X)) \wedge$
$(p(X) \notin (CL1, \ldots, CLn) \to$

   $(CL$ short for caselist)

$Y = t(X))$

Case f (whiledo):
   while p **do** g **od**

$(p(X) \to Y = f \circ g(X)) \wedge$
$(\sim p(X) \to Y = X)$

Case g (dountil):
   do g **until** p **od**

$(p \circ g(X) \to Y = g(X)) \wedge$
$(\sim p \circ g(X) \to Y = f \circ g(X))$

Case h (dowhiledo):
   do1 g **while** p **do2** h **od**

$(p \circ g(X) \to Y = f \circ h \circ g(X)) \wedge$
$(\sim p \circ g(X) \to Y = g(X))$

Proof. In each case, the proof of the required equivalence can be found in an appropriate E-chart—the E-chart of a loop-free program itself, or for a looping program, the E-chart of its loop-free counterpart as given in the Iteration Recursion Lemma. For example, in case c (ifthen) where $P = $ **if** p **then** g **fi**, we must show

$$(f = [P]) \leftrightarrow (\text{term}(f, P) \wedge f = \{(X, Y) \,|\, C(X, Y)\})$$

or

$$(f \subset [P]) \leftrightarrow (\text{term}(f, P) \wedge f \subset \{(X, Y) \,|\, C(X, Y)\})$$

where

$$C(X, Y) = ((p(X) \to Y = g(X)) \wedge (\sim p(X) \to Y = X))$$

Since P is loop free, $\text{term}(f, P)$ is *true*, and we must show

$$(f = [P]) \leftrightarrow f = \{(X, Y) \,|\, C(X, Y)\}$$

or

$$(f \subset [P]) \leftrightarrow f \subset \{(X, Y) \,|\, C(X, Y)\}$$

† For purposes of this theorem, caselist elements are considered to be unique. Proof requirements for a case structure with non-unique caselist elements are better described by means of a conditional rule.

This will follow if we can show that

$$[P] = \{(X, Y) \mid C(X, Y)\}$$

We recall that the E-chart of P is

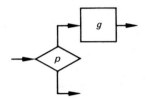

and the function definition derived from it is

$$[\text{if } p \text{ then } g \text{ fi}] = \{(X, Y) \mid (p(X) \rightarrow Y = g(X)) \wedge (\sim p(X) \rightarrow Y = X)\}$$

Thus, it follows directly that $C(X, Y)$ is the required condition, as was to be shown.

For case g (dowhiledo) where

$$P = \text{do1 } g \text{ while } p \text{ do2 } h \text{ od}$$

we must show, first for complete correctness,

$$(f = [P]) \leftrightarrow (\text{term}(f, P) \wedge f = \{(X, Y) \mid C(X, Y)\})$$

where

$$C(X, Y) = ((p \circ g(X) \rightarrow Y = f \circ h \circ g(X)) \wedge (\sim p \circ g(X) \rightarrow Y = g(X)))$$

By the Iteration Recursion Lemma, we can replace the left side $(f = [P])$ to get

$$(\text{term}(f, P) \wedge f = [Q]) \leftrightarrow (\text{term}(f, P) \wedge f = \{(X, Y) \mid C(X, Y)\})$$

where

$$Q = (g; \text{ if } p \text{ then } h; f \text{ fi})$$

Since $\text{term}(f, P)$ is common to both sides, it is sufficient to show that

$$[Q] = \{(X, Y) \mid C(X, Y)\}$$

But from the E-chart

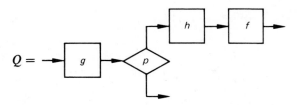

$$Q =$$

and the derived function of Q is

$$[Q] = \{(X, Y) \mid (p \circ g(X) \rightarrow Y = f \circ h \circ g(X)) \wedge (\sim p \circ g(X) \rightarrow Y = g(X))\}$$

from which it follows that $C(X, Y)$ is the required condition, as was to be shown.

Next, for sufficient correctness we must show

$$(f \subset [P]) \leftrightarrow (\text{term}(f, P) \wedge f \subset \{(X, Y) \mid C(X, Y)\})$$

Let

$$f' = [P] \tag{1}$$

Then by the complete correctness just shown

$$(f' = [P]) \leftrightarrow (\text{term}(f', P) \wedge f' = \{(X, Y) \mid C(X, Y)\}) \tag{2}$$

Since the left side is *true* by definition, the right is *true* as well; that is,

$$\text{term}(f', P) \tag{3}$$

and

$$f' = \{(X, Y) \mid C(X, Y)\} \tag{4}$$

Now for sufficient correctness, assume first that

$$f \subset [P] \tag{5}$$

From (1) and (5)

$$f \subset f' \tag{6}$$

and therefore

$$\text{term}(f', P) \rightarrow \text{term}(f, P) \tag{7}$$

From (3) and (7)

$$\text{term}(f, P) \tag{8}$$

Also from (4) and (6)

$$f \subset \{(X, Y) \mid C(X, Y)\} \tag{9}$$

Therefore, from (5), (8), and (9)

$$(f \subset [P]) \rightarrow (\text{term}(f, P) \wedge f \subset \{(X, Y) \mid C(X, Y)\}$$

Now for the converse, assume

$$\text{term}(f, P) \wedge f \subset \{(X, Y) \mid C(X, Y)\} \tag{10}$$

or in particular

$$f \subset \{(X, Y) \mid C(X, Y)\} \tag{11}$$

From (1), (4), and (11)

$$f \subset \{(X, Y) \mid C(X, Y)\} = f' = [P] \tag{12}$$

Therefore from (10) and (12)

$$\text{term}(f, P) \wedge f \subset \{(X, Y) \mid C(X, Y)\} \rightarrow f \subset [P] \tag{13}$$

The reader is invited to verify the remaining cases.

Note that the Correctness Theorem states a relationship between three objects, namely a function f, program P, and condition C, each concerned with ordered pairs (X, Y). In order to see the relationship more clearly, consider another form of the correctness questions:

1. complete correctness

$$(X, Y) \in f \leftrightarrow (X, Y) \in [P]?$$

2. sufficient correctness

$$(X, Y) \in f \rightarrow (X, Y) \in [P]?$$

and $C(X, Y)$ (with $\text{term}(f, P)$) can be used to answer them. That is, when applying $C(X, Y)$ to prove, say, $Y = h \circ g(X)$ for a sequence program, Y is derived independently from function f for argument X.

6.3.4 Working Questions for Complete Correctness

The ifthenelse correctness condition

$$C(X, Y) = ((p(X) \to Y = g(X)) \wedge (\sim p(X) \to Y = h(X)))$$

is easily put into words using the synonyms ifthenelse, iftest, thenpart, elsepart, for functions f, p, g, h, respectively. For all function arguments, we ask

> When iftest is *true* does ifthenelse equal thenpart?
>
> and
>
> when iftest is *false* does ifthenelse equal elsepart?

Such verbalizations can be used informally in program reading, writing, and validation, with the knowledge that more formal and deliberate methods of reasoning are available when needed and warranted. We verbalize the Correctness Theorem (for complete correctness) below.

For every possible argument required by a program specification:

Case a (sequence):

    sequence = [firstpart;
                    secondpart]

Does sequence equal firstpart followed by secondpart?

Case b (fordo):

    fordo = [for
                    indexlist
             do
                    dopart
             od]

Does fordo equal firstpart followed by secondpart ... followed by lastpart?

Case c (ifthen):

    ifthen = [if
                    iftest
              then
                    thenpart
              fi]

When iftest is *true* does ifthen equal thenpart?

and

when iftest is *false* does ifthen equal identity?

Case d (ifthenelse):

> ifthenelse = [**if**
> > iftest
> > **then**
> > > thenpart
> > **else**
> > > elsepart
> > **fi**]

When iftest is *true* does ifthenelse equal thenpart?

and

when iftest is *false* does ifthenelse equal elsepart?

Case e (case):

> case = [**case**
> > p
> > **part($CL1$)**
> > > casepart1
> > > . . .
> > **part(CLn)**
> > > casepart$n$
> > **else**
> > > elsepart
> > **esac**]

When $p \in CL1$ does case equal casepart1?

and

. . .

and

when $p \in CLn$ does case equal casepart$n$?

and

when $p \notin (CL1, \dots, CLn)$ does case equal elsepart?

Case f (whiledo):

> whiledo = [**while**
> > whiletest
> > **do**
> > > dopart
> > **od**]

Is loop termination guaranteed for any argument of whiledo?

and

when whiletest is *true* does whiledo equal dopart followed by whiledo?

and

when whiletest is *false* does whiledo equal identity?

Case g (dountil):

dountil = [**do**
           dopart
    until
        untiltest
    od]

Is loop termination guaranteed for any argument of dountil?

and

when untiltest after dopart is *false* does dountil equal dopart followed by dountil?

and

when untiltest after dopart is *true* does dountil equal dopart?

Case h (dowhiledo):

dowhiledo = [**do1**
           dopart1
    while
        whiletest
    do2
        dopart2
    od]

Is loop termination guaranteed for any argument of dowhiledo?

and

when whiletest after dopart1 is *true* does dowhiledo equal dopart1 followed by dopart2 followed by dowhiledo?

and

when whiletest after dopart1 is *false* does dowhiledo equal dopart1?

We will make use of these questions in the following chapter.

6.3.5 Correctness Proof Syntax

The requirements stated in the Correctness Theorem for proving prime programs suggest a standard format for the proofs themselves, for better documentation and communication of proof arguments. We give next an outer syntax of keywords and indentation for the parts of prime program proofs as extensions to PDL outer syntax, with inner syntax arguments specialized and recorded to whatever level is appropriate for the program and proof at hand.

Specifically, the Correctness Theorem requires definition of the intended function (f), the program, the proof, and the proof result, identified by keywords **function**, **program**, **proof**, and **result**, respectively. The proof outcome is specified by keywords:

> **pass** or **fail**
> **suff** or **comp** (for sufficient or complete correctness)

Proofs are written in a tabular form for any prime as follows:

> **function**
> > state or refer to intended function
>
> **program**
> > state or refer to program part
>
> **proof**
> > state or refer to proof
>
> **result**
> > **pass** or **fail**, **suff** or **comp**

The **proof** part of the proof is indented and specialized for each prime according to the form of condition $C(X, Y)$ in the Correctness Theorem, which we recast into comparisons of conditional rules in order to specify proof rules more compactly. In illustration, consider the condition C for the ifthenelse prime, namely

$$C(X, Y) = ((p(X) \to Y = g(X)) \wedge (\sim p(X) \to Y = h(X)))$$

First, since $Y = f(X)$ in $C(X, Y)$, the condition C can be restated as

$$C(X, f(X)) = ((p(X) \to f(X) = g(X)) \wedge (\sim p(X) \to f(X) = h(X)))$$

Next, the implication

$$p(X) \to f(X) = g(X)$$

can be restated as an equation between conditional rules

$$(p(X) \to f(X)) = (p(X) \to g(X))$$

or simply

$$(p \to f) = (p \to g)$$

This leads to a **proof** part for the ifthenelse of the form (with additional proof keywords, and parenthetical relations defining what is to be proved)

iftest true
  (prove $(p \to f) = (p \to g)$)
iftest false
  (prove $(\sim p \to f) = (\sim p \to h)$)

The forms for each prime follow.

Case a (sequence): $f = [g; h]$
  (prove $f = h \circ g$)

Case b (fordo): $f = [\textbf{for } i :\in L(1:n) \textbf{ do } g \textbf{ od}]$
  (prove $f = g_{L(n)} \circ \ldots \circ g_{L(1)}$)

Case c (ifthen): $f = [\textbf{if } p \textbf{ then } g \textbf{ fi}]$
  iftest true
    (prove $(p \to f) = (p \to g)$)
    pass or **fail**
  iftest false
    (prove $(\sim p \to f) = (\sim p \to I)$)
    pass or **fail**

Case d (ifthenelse): $f = [\textbf{if } p \textbf{ then } g \textbf{ else } h \textbf{ fi}]$
  iftest true
    (prove $(p \to f) = (p \to g)$)
    pass or **fail**
  iftest false
    (prove $(\sim p \to f) = (\sim p \to h)$)
    pass or **fail**

Case e (case): $f = [\textbf{case } p \textbf{ part}(CL1) \: g \ldots \textbf{part}(CLn) \: h \textbf{ else } t \textbf{ esac}]$
  part1
    (prove $(p \in CL1 \to f) = (p \in CL1 \to g)$)
    pass or **fail**
  $\ldots$
  part$n$
    (prove $(p \in CLn \to f) = (p \in CLn \to h)$)
    pass or **fail**
  elsecase
    (prove $(p \notin (CL1, \ldots, CLn) \to f) = (p \notin (CL1, \ldots, CLn) \to t)$)
    pass or **fail**

Case f (whiledo): $f = [\textbf{while } p \textbf{ do } g \textbf{ od}]$

term
  (prove term(f, P))
  pass or **fail**
whiletest true
  (prove $(p \to f) = (p \to f \circ g)$)
  pass or **fail**
whiletest false
  (prove $(\sim p \to f) = (\sim p \to I)$)
  pass or **fail**

Case g (dountil): $f = [\textbf{do } g \textbf{ until } p \textbf{ od}]$

term
  (prove term(f, P))
  pass or **fail**
untiltest true
  (prove $(p \circ g \to f) = (p \circ g \to g)$)
  pass or **fail**
untiltest false
  (prove $(\sim p \circ g \to f) = (\sim p \circ g \to f \circ g)$)
  pass or **fail**

Case h (dowhiledo): $f = [\textbf{do1 } g \textbf{ while } p \textbf{ do2 } h \textbf{ od}]$

term
  (prove term(f, P))
  pass or **fail**
whiletest true
  (prove $(p \circ g \to f) = (p \circ g \to f \circ h \circ g)$)
  pass or **fail**
whiletest false
  (prove $(\sim p \circ g \to f) = (\sim p \circ g \to g)$)
  pass or **fail**

These formats are demonstrated in the remainder of the book.

EXERCISES

1. Show that
  $(f = [\textbf{while } p \textbf{ do } g \textbf{ od}]) \to$
  $(\text{term}(f, \textbf{while } p \textbf{ do } g \textbf{ od}) \wedge$
  $f = [\textbf{if } p \textbf{ then } g \textbf{ fi } f])$
(*Hint:* Use an E-chart.)

2. For each of the programs below, form a hypothesis for [P] and verify it, assuming $(x, y \geq 0)$:

a) $P =$ **while**

$\qquad x < y$

   do

$\qquad x := y + 3$

   od

b) $P =$ **while**

$\qquad x < y$

   do

$\qquad x, y := y, x + 2$

   od

3. For each of the programs below, specify the domain (for termination), and form and verify a hypothesis for [P]:

a) $P =$ **while**

$\qquad x > y$

   do

$\qquad x, y := x - 1, y + 1$

   od

b) $P =$ **while**

$\qquad x > y$

   do

$\qquad x := x - y$

$\qquad y := x + y$

   od

4. Verify the Correctness Theorem condition $C(X, Y)$ given above for dountil and dowhiledo programs.

5. Determine $C(X, Y)$ for function f and program P, where P is defined as follows:

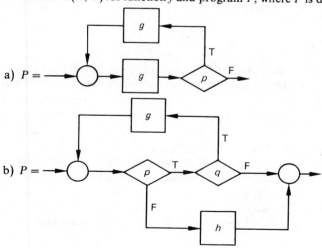

a) $P =$

b) $P =$

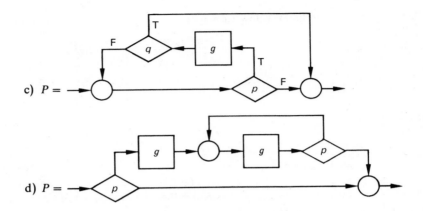

c) $P =$

d) $P =$

6.4 TECHNIQUES FOR PROVING PROGRAM CORRECTNESS

6.4.1 Trace Tables

Proving that a sequence program $G; H$ correctly implements a given function f requires verification of the set relations

$$f = [G; H] \quad \text{and} \quad f \subset [G; H]$$

The verification process, which generally involves simplifying the right-hand side, seems deceptively easy, because at first glance sequence logic seems so simple. But consider determining the program function of the following sequence of assignments:

```
1    x := x + y
2    y := x − y
3    x := x − y
```

At each assignment, one must mentally substitute the results of the preceding assignments, simplifying expressions where possible to keep what is to be remembered as manageable as possible. For a simple sequence this may be a reasonable approach, but as the sequence becomes more complex the possibility of mental error increases. Even more importantly, the reasoning process itself is unrecorded and unrepeatable. For these reasons, we introduce the concept of a *trace table* as a formal way to record reasoning about sequence programs. A trace table is defined to be a table of equations—a row corresponding to each program part of the sequence, a column corresponding to each data item assigned in the sequence. Each entry of the trace table expresses the current value of a data item, denoted as a subscripted data item, in terms of previous values of data items. Each new data value is subscripted by the row of its new assignment, with initial data values subscripted by zero. The sequence of assignments is written in a column at the left of the table, along with an optional column of row numbers. For example, the sequence above has the following trace table:

	part	x	y
1	$x := x + y$	$x_1 = x_0 + y_0$	$y_1 = y_0$
2	$y := x - y$	$x_2 = x_1$	$y_2 = x_1 - y_1$
3	$x := x - y$	$x_3 = x_2 - y_2$	$y_3 = y_2$

Note that each new value $x_1, y_1, x_2, y_2, \ldots$ is defined in terms of values with the predecessor subscripts, including the trivial definitions for items not explicitly assigned. This table of equations now permits elimination of all intermediate subscripts from final to initial subscripts, to systematically derive the program function:

$$
\begin{aligned}
x_3 &= x_2 - y_2 \qquad & y_3 &= y_2 \\
&= x_1 - (x_1 - y_1) & &= x_1 - y_1 \\
&= y_1 & &= x_0 + y_0 - y_0 \\
&= y_0 & &= x_0
\end{aligned}
$$

Thus, the program function for this sequence is simply the exchange assignment

$$x, y := y, x$$

but the reasoning is extensive enough to bear writing out and verifying.

A more familiar form of exchange is given by the sequence (with temporary data item t)

1   $t := x$
2   $x := y$
3   $y := t$

which has trace table

	part	t	x	y
1	$t := x$	$t_1 = x_0$	$x_1 = x_0$	$y_1 = y_0$
2	$x := y$	$t_2 = t_1$	$x_2 = y_1$	$y_2 = y_1$
3	$y := t$	$t_3 = t_2$	$x_3 = x_2$	$y_3 = t_2$

with derivations

$$
\begin{aligned}
t_3 &= t_2 \qquad & x_3 &= x_2 \qquad & y_3 &= t_2 \\
&= t_1 & &= y_1 & &= t_1 \\
&= x_0 & &= y_0 & &= x_0
\end{aligned}
$$

so that x, y are exchanged, all right, but t is set to x as well. In other words, this sequence has the program function

$$t, x, y := x, y, x$$

Because our interest is in exchanging x, y in this sequence, the final values of x, y are intentional, but the final value of t is incidental to the intended function. We eliminate incidental data by using PDL keywords **initial, free,** as in the sequence

1 **initial** $t := x$
2 $x := y$
3 $y := t$
4 **free** t

which has trace table

part		t	x	y
1	**initial** $t := x$	$t_1 = x_0$	$x_1 = x_0$	$y_1 = y_0$
2	$x := y$	$t_2 = t_1$	$x_2 = y_1$	$y_2 = y_1$
3	$y := t$	$t_3 = t_2$	$x_3 = x_2$	$y_3 = t_2$
4	**free** t	free	$x_4 = x_3$	$y_4 = y_3$

with derivations

$$
\begin{aligned}
x_4 &= x_3 & y_4 &= y_3 \\
&= x_2 & &= t_2 \\
&= y_1 & &= t_1 \\
&= y_0 & &= x_0
\end{aligned}
$$

and program function

$$x, y := y, x$$

as intended. Note the use of the term "free" in the table to express the disposition of t. If t had been initialized part way through the sequence instead of at the beginning, the term free would have appeared at all steps prior to initialization, as well as following the **free** statement.

The trace table can be expanded to sequences of any size for any number of data items, and its equations used in a deliberate process for eliminating intermediate data values to derive the sequence program function. In simple sequences, the trace-table operations can also be abbreviated, if reasoning can be done reliably. Even if abbreviated, trace-table operations can be redone in fully deliberate form if any doubt arises. For example, consider the following sequence and partial trace table, in which only the changed data is entered into the table.

part	w	x	y	z
1 $w := x + y$	$w_1 = x_0 + y_0$			
2 $x := y + z$		$x_2 = y_1 + z_1$		
3 $y := z + w$			$y_3 = z_2 + w_2$	
4 $z := w + x$				$z_4 = w_3 + x_3$
5 $w := y - z$	$w_5 = y_4 - z_4$			
6 $x := z - w$		$x_6 = z_5 - w_5$		
7 $y := w - x$			$y_7 = w_6 - x_6$	
8 $z := x - y$				$z_8 = x_7 - y_7$

In the derivation of assignments we make use of the fact that any blank in the trace table denotes a trivial definition for two successively subscripted variables, so that subscript elimination can be done by scanning up the appropriate column to the next entry. The derivations are

$$
\begin{aligned}
w_8 &= w_5 \\
&= y_4 - z_4 \\
&= y_3 - w_3 - x_3 \\
&= z_2 + w_2 - w_2 - x_2 \\
&= z_2 - x_2 \\
&= z_0 - y_1 - z_1 \\
&= z_0 - y_0 - z_0 \\
&= -y_0
\end{aligned}
\qquad
\begin{aligned}
x_8 &= x_6 \\
&= z_5 - w_5 \\
&= z_4 - y_4 + z_4 \\
&= 2z_4 - y_4 \\
&= 2w_3 + 2x_3 - y_3 \\
&= 2w_1 + 2x_2 - z_2 - w_2 \\
&= 2w_1 + 2y_1 + 2z_1 - z_1 - w_1 \\
&= w_1 + 2y_1 + z_1 \\
&= x_0 + y_0 + 2y_0 + z_0 \\
&= x_0 + 3y_0 + z_0
\end{aligned}
$$

$$
\begin{aligned}
y_8 &= y_7 \\
&= w_6 - x_6 \\
&= w_5 - z_5 + w_5 \\
&= 2w_5 - z_5 \\
&= 2y_4 - 2z_4 - z_4 \\
&= 2y_4 - 3z_4 \\
&= 2y_3 - 3w_3 - 3x_3 \\
&= 2z_2 + 2w_2 - 3w_2 - 3x_2 \\
&= -w_2 - 3x_2 + 2z_2 \\
&= -w_1 - 3y_1 - 3z_1 + 2z_1 \\
&= -w_1 - 3y_1 - z_1 \\
&= -x_0 - y_0 - 3y_0 - z_0 \\
&= -x_0 - 4y_0 - z_0
\end{aligned}
\qquad
\begin{aligned}
z_8 &= x_7 - y_7 \\
&= x_6 - w_6 + x_6 \\
&= 2x_6 - w_6 \\
&= 2z_5 - 2w_5 - w_5 \\
&= 2z_5 - 3w_5 \\
&= 2z_4 - 3y_4 + 3z_4 \\
&= -3y_4 + 5z_4 \\
&= -3y_3 + 5w_3 + 5x_3 \\
&= -3z_2 - 3w_2 + 5w_2 + 5x_2 \\
&= 2w_2 + 5x_2 - 3z_2 \\
&= 2w_1 + 5y_1 + 5z_1 - 3z_1 \\
&= 2w_1 + 5y_1 + 2z_1 \\
&= 2x_0 + 2y_0 + 5y_0 + 2z_0 \\
&= 2x_0 + 7y_0 + 2z_0
\end{aligned}
$$

and the program function for this sequence is

$$
w, x, y, z := -y, \; x + 3y + z, \; -x - 4y - z, \; 2x + 7y + 2z
$$

Even though the above derivation is a little tedious, it is carried out in steps that can be verified independently by another person.

6.4.2   Disjoint Rules

Proving that an ifthenelse program **if** p **then** G **else** H **fi** correctly implements a function f requires the verification of the set relations

$$f = [\text{if } p \text{ then } G \text{ else } H \text{ fi}] \qquad \text{and} \qquad f \subset [\text{if } p \text{ then } G \text{ else } H \text{ fi}]$$

The verification process will involve the comparison of conditional rules, because an ifthenelse program function can be converted exactly into the form of a conditional rule, as in

$$[\text{if } p \text{ then } G \text{ else } H \text{ fi}] = (p \rightarrow [G] \,|\, {\sim} p \rightarrow [H])$$

In the most general case, f, $[G]$, and $[H]$ may be given by conditional rules, themselves, so we consider how conditional rules of conditional rules are to be simplified, and how to compare conditional rules.

First, consider a conditional rule of conditional rules, say in illustration,

$$(p_1 \rightarrow (q_{11} \rightarrow r_{11} \,|\, q_{12} \rightarrow r_{12}) \,|\, p_2 \rightarrow (q_{21} \rightarrow r_{21} \,|\, q_{22} \rightarrow r_{22}))$$

The simple distribution of the outer p_i's into the inner rules, say as

$$(p_1 \wedge q_{11} \rightarrow r_{11} \,|\, p_1 \wedge q_{12} \rightarrow r_{12} \,|\, p_2 \wedge q_{21} \rightarrow r_{21} \,|\, p_2 \wedge q_{22} \rightarrow r_{22})$$

is not valid because of the case p_1 *true*, but neither q_{11} or q_{12} *true* while p_2 and one of q_{21}, q_{22} *true*. In this case, the original rule would be undefined, but the later one would be defined. However, if the predicate p_i's were disjoint, that is $p_1 \wedge p_2$ is *false*, then the outer p_i's can be distributed into the inner rules. We call a conditional rule with all predicates disjoint a *disjoint rule*.

As seen above, a disjoint rule can be more convenient than a conditional rule and is easy to derive by augmenting each predicate with the negation of all previous predicates. That is, the conditional rule

$$(p_1 \rightarrow r_1 \,|\, p_2 \rightarrow r_2 \,|\, p_3 \rightarrow r_3 \,|\, \ldots)$$

has identical effect as the disjoint rule

$$(p_1 \rightarrow r_1 \,|\, {\sim} p_1 \wedge p_2 \rightarrow r_2 \,|\, {\sim} p_1 \wedge {\sim} p_2 \wedge p_3 \rightarrow r_3 \,|\, \ldots)$$

Conversely, the disjoint rule

$$(q_1 \rightarrow s_1 \,|\, q_2 \rightarrow s_2 \,|\, q_3 \rightarrow s_3 \,|\, \ldots)$$

has identical effect as the conditional rule

$$(q_1 \rightarrow s_1 \,|\, q_1 \vee q_2 \rightarrow s_2 \,|\, q_1 \vee q_2 \vee q_3 \rightarrow s_3 \,|\, \ldots)$$

Note that in each predicate of this last conditional rule, any term except the last can be omitted, so that a disjoint rule may be converted into any one of many conditional rules.

In illustration of transformation to disjoint form, the conditional rule

$$(x > 0 \to z := \max(x, y) \mid y > 0 \to z := \min(x, y))$$

can be reexpressed as

$$(x > 0 \to (x > y \to z := x \mid true \to z := y) \mid y > 0 \to$$
$$(x < y \to z := x \mid true \to z := y))$$

where none of the rules are disjoint rules. We convert them to disjoint rules as

$$(x > 0 \to (x > y \to z := x \mid x \le y \to z := y) \mid$$
$$x \le 0 \land y > 0 \to (x < y \to z := x \mid x \ge y \to z := y))$$

which are equivalent to (by distributing the outer predicates into the inner rules)

$$(x > 0 \land x > y \to z := x \mid$$
$$x > 0 \land x \le y \to z := y \mid$$
$$x \le 0 \land y > 0 \land x < y \to z := x \mid$$
$$x \le 0 \land y > 0 \land x \ge y \to z := y)$$

Note the last predicate is *false* for any x, y, since it can be rewritten

$$(x \le 0 < y) \land (x \ge y)$$

and can be deleted from the disjoint rule. The remainder of the rule can be diagrammed in the x, y plane as shown in Fig. 6.1.

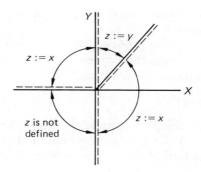

Figure 6.1

The preceding transformations can allow the manipulation and simplification of conditional rules. A disjoint rule has the property that its component rules can be permuted in any order without changing the effect of the rule. This property, along with the conversions between conditional and disjoint rules, provides a method for transforming conditional rules into simpler, equivalent ones by a three-step process; namely,

1. Given a conditional rule, convert it to an equivalent disjoint rule.
2. Transform the disjoint rule by permuting its component rules in any convenient way.
3. Convert the transformed disjoint rule back to any simpler, equivalent conditional rule.

In illustration, by reference to the diagram, the preceding three-part disjoint rule can be transformed back to a two-part conditional rule different from the original, specifically one with no min, max operations:

$$(y \geq x > 0 \rightarrow z := y \,|\, x > 0 \vee y > 0 \rightarrow z := x)$$

The verification process may require comparison of a disjoint conditional rule, say

$$(p_1 \rightarrow r_1 \,|\, p_2 \rightarrow r_2 \,|\, p_3 \rightarrow r_3)$$

with a function, say f, given by an unconditional rule. In this case, the predicates of the disjoint rule can be used to partition the domain of f, to prove, for sufficient correctness:

$$p_1(X) \rightarrow r_1(X) = f(X)$$
$$p_2(X) \rightarrow r_2(X) = f(X)$$
$$p_3(X) \rightarrow r_3(X) = f(X)$$

To prove complete correctness, the domains of the two function rules must be proved identical, as well.

Alternately, the verification process may require the comparison of two conditional rules, and, again, the disjoint form of these conditional rules will be convenient. Suppose disjoint rules

$$(p_1 \rightarrow r_1 \,|\, p_2 \rightarrow r_2 \,|\, p_3 \rightarrow r_3) \qquad \text{and} \qquad (q_1 \rightarrow s_1 \,|\, q_2 \rightarrow s_2)$$

are to be compared for complete correctness. Then it is necessary and sufficient that (1) the rules define identical domains, and (2) the rules agree on every pairwise conjunction of the predicates of the rules. That is,

$$p_1 \vee p_2 \vee p_3 = q_1 \vee q_2$$

and

$$(p_1 \wedge q_1 \rightarrow r_1) = (p_1 \wedge q_1 \rightarrow s_1)$$
$$\cdots$$
$$(p_3 \wedge q_2 \rightarrow r_3) = (p_3 \wedge q_2 \rightarrow s_2)$$

In illustration, consider the conditional rules

$$(x \geq 0 \wedge y \geq 0 \rightarrow x := x - y \,|\, x \geq 0 \wedge x + y \geq 0 \rightarrow x := x + y)$$

and

$$(x + y \geq 0 \wedge y \leq 0 \rightarrow x := x + y \,|\, x + y > 0 \wedge x \geq 0 \rightarrow x := x - y)$$

and the problem of comparing them. Step one is to convert these rules into disjoint form. The second predicate of the first rule becomes

$$\sim(x \geq 0 \wedge y \geq 0) \wedge x \geq 0 \wedge x + y \geq 0$$
$$= (x < 0 \vee y < 0) \wedge x \geq 0 \wedge x + y \geq 0$$
$$= y < 0 \wedge x \geq 0 \wedge x + y \geq 0$$

while the second predicate of the second rule becomes

$$\sim(x + y \geq 0 \wedge y \leq 0) \wedge x + y > 0 \wedge x \geq 0$$
$$= (x + y < 0 \vee y > 0) \wedge x + y > 0 \wedge x \geq 0$$
$$= y > 0 \wedge x + y > 0 \wedge x \geq 0$$

Therefore, the two rules above in disjoint form are

$$(x \geq 0 \wedge y \geq 0 \rightarrow x := x - y \,|\, y < 0 \wedge x \geq 0 \wedge x + y \geq 0 \rightarrow x := x + y)$$

and

$$(x + y \geq 0 \wedge y \leq 0 \rightarrow x := x + y \,|\, y > 0 \wedge x + y > 0 \wedge x \geq 0 \rightarrow x := x - y)$$

The comparison of these rules leads to a domain equality check, then to rule equality in four cases, which we number by the positions of their constituents in the rules.

Domain equality:

Is $(x \geq 0 \wedge y \geq 0) \vee (y < 0 \wedge x \geq 0 \wedge x + y \geq 0)$
$= (x + y \geq 0 \wedge y \leq 0) \vee (y > 0 \wedge x + y > 0 \wedge x \geq 0)$?

Case 1,1 (assignments shown in parentheses for clarity):

$$x \geq 0 \wedge y \geq 0 \wedge x + y \geq 0 \wedge y \leq 0$$
$$\text{Is } (x := x - y) = (x := x + y)?$$

Case 1,2:

$$x \geq 0 \wedge y \geq 0 \wedge y > 0 \wedge x + y > 0 \wedge x \geq 0$$
$$\text{Is } (x := x - y) = (x := x - y)?$$

Case 2,1:

$$y < 0 \wedge x \geq 0 \wedge x + y \geq 0 \wedge x + y \geq 0 \wedge y \leq 0$$
$$\text{Is } (x := x + y) = (x := x + y)?$$

Case 2,2:

$$y < 0 \wedge x \geq 0 \wedge x + y \geq 0 \wedge y > 0 \wedge x + y > 0 \wedge x \geq 0$$
$$\text{Is } (x := x + y) = (x := x - y)?$$

The domain equality can be seen in the diagram in Fig. 6.2, where L1 denotes the sector defined by the first major term of the left side, ..., R2 the sector defined by the second major term of the right side.

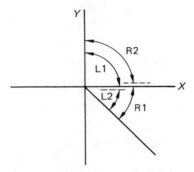

Figure 6.2

In the rule equality checks, cases 1,2 and 2,1 are evidently satisfied, because the assignments made are identical, so we investigate cases 1,1 and 2,2 in more detail. In case 1,1 the combined predicate reduces to

$$(x \geq 0 \wedge y \geq 0 \wedge x + y \geq 0 \wedge y \leq 0) = (x \geq 0 \wedge y = 0)$$

since $y \geq 0$ and $y \leq 0$. In this case

$$(x := x - y) = (x := x + y)$$

since $y = 0$. In case 2,2, the combined predicate reduces to

$$(y < 0 \wedge x \geq 0 \wedge x + y \geq 0 \wedge y > 0 \wedge x + y > 0 \wedge x \geq 0) = \textit{false}$$

since $y < 0$ and $y > 0$, and this case holds vacuously. Therefore, since the rules agree in all cases, we conclude that the rules define identical functions.

The three nonvacuous cases can be diagrammed in the X, Y plane (Fig. 6.3).

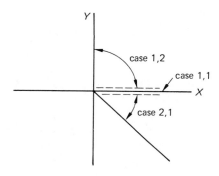

Figure 6.3

6.4.3　Case-Structured Trace Tables

The trace tables introduced before dealt with rules of a single case each, but it may be necessary to deal with sequences of conditional rules, as well. That will be easily done with disjoint rules (to which conditional rules can be readily converted). In illustration, consider a sequence of conditional rules of the form

$$(x \geq 0 \rightarrow x := x + y \,|\, true \rightarrow y := y + x)$$
$$(y \geq 0 \rightarrow y := x - y \,|\, true \rightarrow x := y - x)$$
$$(x \geq 0 \rightarrow x := x - y \,|\, true \rightarrow y := y - x)$$

which we convert into a sequence of disjoint rules:

$$(x \geq 0 \rightarrow x := x + y \,|\, x < 0 \rightarrow y := y + x)$$
$$(y \geq 0 \rightarrow y := x - y \,|\, y < 0 \rightarrow x := y - x)$$
$$(x \geq 0 \rightarrow x := x - y \,|\, x < 0 \rightarrow y := y - x)$$

There will be eight cases, each involving a simple trace table, determined by the component rule invoked in each of the three disjoint rules. We number the cases by the component rules invoked in each respective part. The condition associated with each case is given in a new column in the table, with subscripts corresponding to the points of evaluation of each predicate that makes up the total condition. Note that subscripts for conditions refer to the values previous to the assignments made in the row. Intermediate subscripts are then eliminated by substitution as was done before for the rule itself.

Case 1,1,1:

part	condition	x	y
$x := x + y$	$x_0 \geq 0$	$x_1 = x_0 + y_0$	$y_1 = y_0$
$y := x - y$	$y_1 \geq 0$	$x_2 = x_1$	$y_2 = x_1 - y_1$
$x := x - y$	$x_2 \geq 0$	$x_3 = x_2 - y_2$	$y_3 = y_2$

derivations:

condition:

$$x_0 \geq 0 \wedge y_1 \geq 0 \wedge x_2 \geq 0 = x_0 \geq 0 \wedge y_0 \geq 0 \wedge x_1 \geq 0$$
$$= x_0 \geq 0 \wedge y_0 \geq 0 \wedge x_0 + y_0 \geq 0$$
$$= x_0 \geq 0 \wedge y_0 \geq 0$$

assignments:

$$
\begin{aligned}
x_3 &= x_2 - y_2 \\
&= x_1 - (x_1 - y_1) \\
&= y_1 \\
&= y_0
\end{aligned}
\qquad
\begin{aligned}
y_3 &= y_2 \\
&= x_1 - y_1 \\
&= (x_0 + y_0) - y_0 \\
&= x_0
\end{aligned}
$$

Case 1,1,2:

part	condition	x	y
$x := x + y$	$x_0 \geq 0$	$x_1 = x_0 + y_0$	$y_1 = y_0$
$y := x - y$	$y_1 \geq 0$	$x_2 = x_1$	$y_2 = x_1 - y_1$
$y := y - x$	$x_2 < 0$	$x_2 = x_2$	$y_3 = y_2 - x_2$

derivations:

condition:

$$x_0 \geq 0 \wedge y_1 \geq 0 \wedge x_2 < 0 = x_0 \geq 0 \wedge y_0 \geq 0 \wedge x_1 < 0$$
$$= x_0 \geq 0 \wedge y_0 \geq 0 \wedge x_0 + y_0 < 0$$
$$= \textit{false}$$

assignments: Unnecessary

Case 1,2,1:

part	condition	x	y
$x := x + y$	$x_0 \geq 0$	$x_1 = x_0 + y_0$	$y_1 = y_0$
$x := y - x$	$y_1 < 0$	$x_2 = y_1 - x_1$	$y_2 = y_1$
$x := x - y$	$x_2 \geq 0$	$x_3 = x_2 - y_2$	$y_3 = y_2$

derivations:

condition:

$$x_0 \geq 0 \wedge y_1 < 0 \wedge x_2 \geq 0 = x_0 \geq 0 \wedge y_0 < 0 \wedge y_1 - x_1 \geq 0$$
$$= x_0 \geq 0 \wedge y_0 < 0 \wedge y_0 - (x_0 + y_0) \geq 0$$
$$= x_0 \geq 0 \wedge y_0 < 0 \wedge x_0 \leq 0$$
$$= x_0 = 0 \wedge y_0 < 0$$

assignments:

$$x_3 = x_2 - y_2 \qquad\qquad y_3 = y_2$$
$$= (y_1 - x_1) - y_1 \qquad\quad = y_1$$
$$= -x_1 \qquad\qquad\qquad = y_0$$
$$= -x_0 - y_0$$

Case 1,2,2:

part	condition	x	y
$x := x + y$	$x_0 \geq 0$	$x_1 = x_0 + y_0$	$y_1 = y_0$
$x := y - x$	$y_1 < 0$	$x_2 = y_1 - x_1$	$y_2 = y_1$
$y := y - x$	$x_2 < 0$	$x_3 = x_2$	$y_3 = y_2 - x_2$

derivations:

condition:

$$x_0 \geq 0 \wedge y_1 < 0 \wedge x_2 < 0 = x_0 \geq 0 \wedge y_0 < 0 \wedge y_1 - x_1 < 0$$
$$= x_0 \geq 0 \wedge y_0 < 0 \wedge y_0 - (x_0 + y_0) < 0$$
$$= x_0 \geq 0 \wedge y_0 < 0 \wedge x_0 > 0$$
$$= x_0 > 0 \wedge y_0 < 0$$

assignments:

$$x_3 = x_2 \qquad\qquad\qquad y_3 = y_2 - x_2$$
$$= y_1 - x_1 \qquad\qquad\quad = y_1 - (y_1 - x_1)$$
$$= y_0 - (x_0 + y_0) \qquad\quad = x_1$$
$$= -x_0 \qquad\qquad\qquad = x_0 + y_0$$

Case 2,1,1:

part	condition	x	y
$y := y + x$	$x_0 < 0$	$x_1 = x_0$	$y_1 = y_0 + x_0$
$y := x - y$	$y_1 \geq 0$	$x_2 = x_1$	$y_2 = x_1 - y_1$
$x := x - y$	$x_2 \geq 0$	$x_3 = x_2 - y_2$	$y_3 = y_2$

derivations:

condition:

$$x_0 < 0 \wedge y_1 \geq 0 \wedge x_2 \geq 0 = x_0 < 0 \wedge y_0 + x_0 \geq 0 \wedge x_1 \geq 0$$
$$= x_0 < 0 \wedge y_0 + x_0 \geq 0 \wedge x_0 \geq 0$$
$$= false$$

assignments: Unnecessary

Case 2,1,2:

part	condition	x	y
$y := y + x$	$x_0 < 0$	$x_1 = x_0$	$y_1 = y_0 + x_0$
$y := x - y$	$y_1 \geq 0$	$x_2 = x_1$	$y_2 = x_1 - y_1$
$y := y - x$	$x_2 < 0$	$x_3 = x_2$	$y_3 = y_2 - x_2$

derivations:

condition:

$$x_0 < 0 \wedge y_1 \geq 0 \wedge x_2 < 0 = x_0 < 0 \wedge y_0 + x_0 \geq 0 \wedge x_1 < 0$$
$$= x_0 < 0 \wedge y_0 + x_0 \geq 0 \wedge x_0 < 0$$
$$= x_0 < 0 \wedge y_0 + x_0 \geq 0$$

assignments:

$$
\begin{aligned}
x_3 &= x_2 & y_3 &= y_2 - x_2 \\
&= x_1 & &= (x_1 - y_1) - x_1 \\
&= x_0 & &= -y_1 \\
& & &= -y_0 - x_0
\end{aligned}
$$

Case 2,2,1:

part	condition	x	y
$y := y + x$	$x_0 < 0$	$x_1 = x_0$	$y_1 = y_0 + x_0$
$x := y - x$	$y_1 < 0$	$x_2 = y_1 - x_1$	$y_2 = y_1$
$x := x - y$	$x_2 \geq 0$	$x_3 = x_2 - y_2$	$y_3 = y_2$

derivations:

condition:

$$x_0 < 0 \wedge y_1 < 0 \wedge x_2 \geq 0 = x_0 < 0 \wedge y_0 + x_0 < 0 \wedge y_1 - x_1 \geq 0$$
$$= x_0 < 0 \wedge y_0 + x_0 < 0 \wedge y_0 + x_0 - x_0 \geq 0$$
$$= x_0 < 0 \wedge y_0 + x_0 < 0 \wedge y_0 \geq 0$$

assignments:

$$x_3 = x_2 - y_2 \qquad y_3 = y_2$$
$$\quad = y_1 - x_1 - y_1 \qquad = y_1$$
$$\quad = -x_1 \qquad\qquad = y_0 + x_0$$
$$\quad = -x_0$$

Case 2,2,2:

part	condition	x	y
$y := y + x$	$x_0 < 0$	$x_1 = x_0$	$y_1 = y_0 + x_0$
$x := y - x$	$y_1 < 0$	$x_2 = y_1 - x_1$	$y_2 = y_1$
$y := y - x$	$x_2 < 0$	$x_2 = x_2$	$y_3 = y_2 - x_2$

derivations:

condition:

$$x_0 < 0 \wedge y_1 < 0 \wedge x_2 < 0 = x_0 < 0 \wedge y_0 + x_0 < 0 \wedge y_1 - x_1 < 0$$
$$= x_0 < 0 \wedge y_0 + x_0 < 0 \wedge y_0 + x_0 - x_0 < 0$$
$$= x_0 < 0 \wedge y_0 + x_0 < 0 \wedge y_0 < 0$$
$$= x_0 < 0 \wedge y_0 < 0$$

assignments:

$$x_3 = x_2 \qquad\qquad y_3 = y_2 - x_2$$
$$\quad = y_1 - x_1 \qquad\quad = y_1 - (y_1 - x_1)$$
$$\quad = y_0 + x_0 - x_0 \qquad = x_1$$
$$\quad = y_0 \qquad\qquad = x_0$$

Assembling all cases, we find a function defined by a disjoint rule with six cases; namely,

$$(x \geq 0 \wedge y \geq 0 \rightarrow x, y := y, x \,|$$
$$x = 0 \wedge y < 0 \rightarrow x, y := -x - y, y \,|$$
$$x > 0 \wedge y < 0 \rightarrow x, y := -x, x + y \,|$$
$$x < 0 \wedge x + y \geq 0 \rightarrow x, y := x, -x - y \,|$$
$$x < 0 \wedge x + y < 0 \wedge y \geq 0 \rightarrow x, y := -x, x + y \,|$$
$$x < 0 \wedge y < 0 \rightarrow x, y := y, x)$$

which can be diagrammed in the x, y plane as shown in Fig. 6.4.

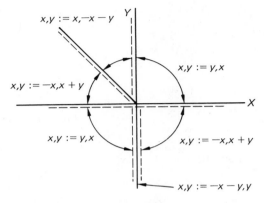

Figure 6.4

With a little thought and study of the diagram, this disjoint rule can be converted into a conditional rule such as

$(x \geq 0 \wedge y \geq 0 \rightarrow x, y := y, x\,|$
$x = 0 \rightarrow x, y := -x - y, y\,|$
$x > 0 \rightarrow x, y := -x, x + y\,|$
$y < 0 \rightarrow x, y := y, x\,|$
$x + y < 0 \rightarrow x, y := -x, x + y\,|$
$true \rightarrow x, y := x, -x - y)$

Although this example has been treated as a sequence of three conditional assignments, it could be treated as a sequence of two parts, the first part being a sequence of two parts itself. In this case, the program function of the first two conditional assignments could be derived in four cases, then combined with the third conditional assignment to get the same final result.

6.4.4 Verifying Fordo Programs

A fordo program, as described in Chapter 3, is simply an abbreviation for an extended sequence program, with an explicit data item (the index) under control of the fordo. For example, the fordo program

$Q =$ **for**
        $i :\in 1$ to 6 by 2
    do
        $s := \max(i, s + i)$
    od

is an abbreviation for the extended sequence

$$R = s := \max(1, s + 1)$$
$$s := \max(3, s + 3)$$
$$s := \max(5, s + 5)$$

In this case, the program function of Q or R can be readily determined by the trace table

part	s
$s := \max(1, s + 1)$	$s_1 = \max(1, s_0 + 1)$
$s := \max(3, s + 3)$	$s_2 = \max(3, s_1 + 3)$
$s := \max(5, s + 5)$	$s_3 = \max(5, s_2 + 5)$

with derivation

$$s_3 = \max(5, s_2 + 5)$$
$$= \max(5, \max(3, s_1 + 3) + 5)$$
$$= \max(8, s_1 + 8)$$
$$= \max(8, \max(1, s_0 + 1) + 8)$$
$$= \max(9, s_0 + 9)$$

and program function

$$s := \max(9, s + 9)$$

However, given a more general fordo program, say with parameter n

$$P_n = \textbf{for}$$
$$i :\in 1 \text{ to } n \text{ by } 2$$
$$\textbf{do}$$
$$s := \max(i, s + i)$$
$$\textbf{od}$$

where n is large—say over 100—the enumeration of the sequence and its trace table will be impractical, and we must hypothesize the program function (if not given) and verify the hypothesis, either on the basis of a clear compelling pattern or, if more rigor is needed, by mathematical induction.† Two strategies are possible in using mathematical induction to determine a fordo program function, based on the choice of the induction variable. One choice is an integer variable in the fordo list description (for example, n in the program above). The other choice is the size of the fordo list itself. In either case, the procedure is to form an induction hypothesis (an intelligent guess)

---

† See exercise 4, Section 6.4, for an alternate fordo proof technique.

of the program function as it depends on the induction variable, say k, as the hypothesis

$$H(k) = ([P_k] = h(k))$$

where $h(k)$ is the hypothesized program function of the fordo program P_k. Then, to carry out the induction, we need to show

1. $H(1)$
2. $(k \geq 1 \wedge H(k)) \rightarrow H(k + 1)$

from which we can deduce

3. $k \geq 1 \rightarrow H(k)$

It may be necessary to invent the induction variable. For example, given the program

for
    $i :\in 1$ to 100 by 2
do
    $s := \max(i, s + i)$
od

one needs to recognize the opportunity for induction by (1) generalizing the constant 100 to an induction variable with possible value 100, but other possible values 1, 2, ..., 99, or (2) generalizing the size of the fordo list to an induction variable with possible value 50, but other possible values 1, 2, ..., 49.

The choice of induction strategy depends on details of the problem. If the dopart of program P_n happened to reference n (entirely possible and legitimate), the induction should likely be on n, not on the size of the fordo list; otherwise the size of the fordo list is a natural induction variable because it states the length of the trace table. Since the dopart is independent of n in this example, we investigate the size of the fordo list as an induction variable.

First, in terms of n the size of the fordo list

$$i :\in 1 \text{ to } n \text{ by } 2 = (1, 3, \ldots)$$

say, $\text{size}(n)$, is easily seen to be

$$\text{size}(n) = (n + \text{odd}(n))/2$$

where $\text{odd}(n) = 1$ for n odd, $\text{odd}(n) = 0$ for n even. In fact, this could be proved by a separate induction on n, if necessary, but the following pattern of values is quite compelling:

n	1	2	3	4	5	6	...
size(n)	1	1	2	2	3	3	...

and size(n) can be seen to satisfy the assertions above.

Next, we enumerate program functions for list sizes 1, 2, and 3 in fordo program P_n, denoting size(n) by k. (Derivation of the function for a list of size 3 was shown above):

k	program function
1	$s := \max(1, s + 1)$
2	$s := \max(4, s + 4)$
3	$s := \max(9, s + 9)$

We notice the progression of constants in the max operands to be squares, and form the hypothesis

$$H(k) = ([P_n] = (s := \max(k**2, s + k**2))), \; k = \text{size}(n)$$

Let R be the two-assignment sequence program shown below, with the firstpart an assignment to s that is equivalent to the first k iterations of the fordo (the hypothesized program function); and secondpart an assignment to s for the $(k + 1)$ iteration. Note in the latter that the $(k + 1)$ term is $2*(k + 1) - 1 = 2*k + 1$:

$$R = s := \max(k**2, s + k**2);$$
$$s := \max(2*k + 1, s + 2*k + 1)$$

Then

1. $H(1)$ because $k = 1 \to (s := \max(1**2, s + 1**2))$
2. $(k \geq 1 \wedge H(k)) \to H(k + 1)$

In this case we need to show that $[R]$, just defined, has the value

$$[R] = s := \max((k + 1)**2, s + (k + 1)**2)$$

The trace-table equations for R are

$$s_1 = \max(k**2, s_0 + k**2)$$
$$s_2 = \max(2*k + 1, s_1 + 2*k + 1)$$

and the derivation is

$$s_2 = \max(2*k + 1, k**2 + 2*k + 1, s_0 + k**2 + 2*k + 1)$$
$$= \max((k + 1)**2, s_0 + (k + 1)**2)$$

Thus, the program function is

$$[R] = s := \max((k + 1)**2, s + (k + 1)**2)$$

which is $H(k + 1)$.

Therefore,

3. $k \geq 1 \rightarrow H(k) = ([P] = (s := \max(k**2, s + k**2)))$
that is, the hypothesized program function is correct.

The reader is invited to carry out the induction directly on n in the fordo list, in order to contrast the two treatments.

6.4.5   Direct Assertions about Program Functions

Direct assertions about program functions is a key technique in dealing with large programs and finding the right balance in mathematical proof between formal procedure and economy of effort. As discussed in Chapter 1, a mathematical proof is a repeatable experiment between two persons, the success of which depends on both using and keeping formality within allowable bounds of human attention spans. A simple program part of a large program may be better verified by a direct assertion that its program function satisfies its specification rather than by a more detailed formal proof. Such an assertion is a claim that can be recorded, agreed to or not by another person, and if need be, even verified separately on an exception basis. The level of formality should depend not only on the program itself but also on the uses to which it is put. If a life depends on its correct execution, it will be worth the formality that will require much effort. With lower stakes, an incorrect proof due to lower formality may be a reasonable calculated risk, compared to the effort required otherwise. It is important to note that no level of effort possible can guarantee the proof to be foolproof, but that even moderate levels of effort can uncover criticisms that may correct or improve the design in considerable ways.

In illustration, if a 100-line program combines 10 program parts into an abstraction of 15 lines, each of the 10 program parts (under 10 lines each) may be verified by direct assertion, leaving a 15-line program, rather than a 100-line program to be verified more formally. It should be noted here that the examples in a book such as this are usually chosen to be small, but hard for their size. In actual programming, most small program parts are easy for their size and should be treated accordingly.

For example, the procedure shown in Fig. 6.5 is intended to separate a queue of integers into its odd and even members, then put its odd members

```
 1   proc oddbeforeeven(Q) [Q := oddmembers(Q) ∥ evenmembers(Q)]
 2       queue Q, odd, even: integer
 3       scalar x: integer
 4       do [Q, odd, even := ∅, oddmembers(Q), evenmembers(Q)]
 5           initial odd, even := empty, empty
 6           while
 7               Q ≠ empty
 8           do
 9               initial x := end(Q)
10               if
11                   x odd
12               then
13                   end(odd) := x
14               else
15                   end(even) := x
16               fi
17               free x
18           od
19       od
         [Q, odd := Q ∥ odd, ∅]
20       while
21           odd ≠ empty
22       do
23           initial x := end(odd)
24           end(Q) := x
25           free x
26       od
         [Q, even := Q ∥ even, ∅]
27       while
28           even ≠ empty
29       do
30           initial x := end(even)
31           end(Q) := x
32           free x
33       od
34       free odd, even
35   corp
```

Figure 6.5

before its even members, but preserve relative order within the odd members and within the even members.

In the logical commentary, oddmembers(Q) means the list of all odd members of Q in their relative order in Q, and similarly for evenmembers(Q). We now illustrate the use of direct assertions in proving that the procedure comment provides the correct program function of the procedure. The direct assertions corresponding to the three whiledo program parts are that their logical commentary is correct (of course these program parts require study to agree or disagree with the assertions). Square brackets enclosing beginning and ending line numbers denote program functions:

$$[5\text{--}18] = (Q,odd,even := \emptyset, \text{oddmembers}(Q), \text{evenmembers}(Q))$$

$$[20\text{--}26] = (Q,odd := Q \parallel odd, \emptyset)$$

$$[27\text{--}33] = (Q,even := Q \parallel even, \emptyset)$$

Note the role of **initial, free** of item x in limiting the scope of these program functions to Q, *odd*, and *even*. Using the program functions asserted for these program parts, the procedure oddbeforeeven is now equivalent to

```
  1   proc oddbeforeeven(Q) [Q := oddmembers(Q)‖
                                    evenmembers(Q)]
  2       queue Q,odd,even: integer
  3       scalar x: integer
5-18      Q,odd,even := ∅,oddmembers(Q),evenmembers(Q)
20-26     Q,odd := Q‖odd,∅
27-33     Q,even := Q‖even,∅
 34       free odd,even
 35   corp
```

Next, a direct assertion about the program function of sequence (5–18), (20–26), (27–33) takes the form

$$[5\text{--}33] = (Q,odd,even := \text{oddmembers}(Q) \parallel \text{evenmembers}(Q), \emptyset, \emptyset)$$

For an informal proof of this assertion, one can substitute backward in the sequence, beginning with

$$[27\text{--}33] = (Q,odd,even := Q \parallel even, odd, \emptyset)$$

then replacing Q, *odd* by their assignments in [20–26] to get

$$[20\text{--}33] = (Q,odd,even := (Q \parallel odd) \parallel even, \emptyset, \emptyset)$$

and finally replacing Q, *odd, even* by their assignments in [5–18] to get

[5–33] = $(Q,odd,even := \emptyset \| oddmembers(Q) \| evenmembers(Q),\emptyset,\emptyset)$

which simplifies to the program function above.

   As a result of this last assertion, the program function of the procedure oddbeforeeven can be directly verified as

$$[oddbeforeeven(Q)] = (Q := oddmembers(Q) \| evenmembers(Q))$$

This trail of explicit direct assertions about program functions of specific program parts can be recorded and scrutinized at later times, as the product of an informal proof, and as the skeleton of a more formal proof if called for later.

EXERCISES

(All data objects are scalar integers.)

1. Determine program functions for the following sequences by means of trace tables:

   a) $y := a$
      $y := x*y + b$
      $y := x*y + c$
      $y := x*y + d$

   b) $x, y := x - y, x + y$
      $x, y := y, x$
      $x, y := x - y, x + y$

   c) $x, y, z := z, x, y$
      $x, y, z := y, z, x$
      $x, y, z := z, y, x$
      $x, y, z := y, x, z$
      $x, y, z := x, z, y$

2. Determine program functions for the following sequences by means of case structured trace tables:

   a) if $x > 0$ then $x := x - y$ else $y := x + y$ fi
      if $y > 0$ then $y := y - x$ else $x := y + x$ fi
      if $x + y > 0$ then $x, y := x - y, y - x$ fi

   b) $x, y := max(x, y), min(x, y)$
      $x, y := max(x - y, x + y), min(x - y, x + y)$
      $x, y := max(x, y), min(x, y)$

3. Determine if the fordo program

$s := 0$
for
$\quad i :\in 0$ to n by 3
do
$\quad s := \max(i, s)$
od

has program function
$s := 3*\mathrm{int}(n/3)$
by means of an inductive proof.

4. Verify the fordo program function

$$[\textbf{for } i :\in 1 \text{ to } y \textbf{ do } x := x + 2*i \textbf{ od}] = (x := x + y*(y + 1))$$

a) by induction on i, and

b) by rewriting and verifying the fordo as a sequence with whiledo secondpart:

$i := 1$
while
$\quad i \leq y$
do
$\quad x := x + 2*i$
$\quad i := i + 1$
od
free i

5. Restudy the Singsort program (Fig. 5.20) and identify the extent to which direct assertions can be used to prove it correct, what additional logical commentary is required, and what program parts should be subject to formal proof.

6.5   EXAMPLES OF PROGRAM VERIFICATION

6.5.1   Proofs of PDL Primes With Scalar Data

We illustrate next proofs of correctness for PDL prime programs with examples that operate on scalar data objects. (Fordo and case structures are not included; fordo proofs were discussed above, and case proofs are a simple generalization of ifthenelse proofs. Correctness proofs with array data and anonymous data are described in subsequent sections.) The proofs satisfy the verification requirements defined by the Correctness Theorem and are recorded in the proof syntax given in section 6.3. They are written out in complete syntactic and logical detail, to fully illustrate both the systematic process of recording data operations in trace tables and the application of logical rules of reasoning. Complete correctness is proven for each of the programs, with the exception of the dowhiledo, whose proof reveals an error.

1. Sequence proof

   function (x, y, and z logical scalars)

       $x, y, z := y, z, x$

   program ($\bar{\vee}$ indicates the *exclusive or* operation)

      1   $x := x \bar{\vee} z$
      2   $z := x \bar{\vee} z$
      3   $x := x \bar{\vee} z$
      4   $y := x \bar{\vee} y$
      5   $x := x \bar{\vee} y$
      6   $y := x \bar{\vee} y$

   proof (prove $f = h \circ g$, or in this case, that f is equivalent to the composition of six functions)[†]

part	condition	x	y	z
1	$x := x \bar{\vee} z$	$x_1 = x_0 \bar{\vee} z_0$	$y_1 = y_0$	$z_1 = z_0$
2	$z := x \bar{\vee} z$	$x_2 = x_1$	$y_2 = y_1$	$z_2 = x_1 \bar{\vee} z_1$
3	$x := x \bar{\vee} z$	$x_3 = x_2 \bar{\vee} z_2$	$y_3 = y_2$	$z_3 = z_2$
4	$y := x \bar{\vee} y$	$x_4 = x_3$	$y_4 = x_3 \bar{\vee} y_3$	$z_4 = z_3$
5	$x := x \bar{\vee} y$	$x_5 = x_4 \bar{\vee} y_4$	$y_5 = y_4$	$z_5 = z_4$
6	$y := x \bar{\vee} y$	$x_6 = x_5$	$y_6 = x_5 \bar{\vee} y_5$	$z_6 = z_5$

   derivations:

   $$
   \begin{aligned}
   x_6 &= x_5 \\
       &= x_4 \bar{\vee} y_4 \\
       &= x_3 \bar{\vee} (x_3 \bar{\vee} y_3) \\
       &= y_3 \\
       &= y_2 \\
       &= y_1 \\
       &= y_0
   \end{aligned}
   \qquad
   \begin{aligned}
   y_6 &= x_5 \bar{\vee} y_5 \\
       &= (x_4 \bar{\vee} y_4) \bar{\vee} y_4 \\
       &= x_4 \\
       &= x_3 \\
       &= x_2 \bar{\vee} z_2 \\
       &= x_1 \bar{\vee} (x_1 \bar{\vee} z_1) \\
       &= z_1 \\
       &= z_0
   \end{aligned}
   \qquad
   \begin{aligned}
   z_6 &= z_5 \\
       &= z_4 \\
       &= z_3 \\
       &= z_2 \\
       &= x_1 \bar{\vee} z_1 \\
       &= (x_0 \bar{\vee} z_0) \bar{\vee} z_0 \\
       &= x_0
   \end{aligned}
   $$

   program function:

       $x, y, z := y, z, x$

   result

       pass comp

Note that the condition column in the trace table is empty in the example, but that predicates from conditional assignments, if any, in a sequence

---

[†] The parenthetical relations defining what is to be proved for each prime are an optional part of the proof syntax, a useful reminder for the reader as well as the writer.

would be recorded there. The reduction of, say, $x_3 \triangledown (x_3 \triangledown y_3)$ to y_3 can be seen in the following table:

x	y	$x \triangledown y$	$x \triangledown (x \triangledown y)$
T	T	F	T
T	F	T	F
F	T	T	T
F	F	F	F

2. Ifthen proof

function (x an integer, abs absolute value)

$x := -\text{abs}(x)$

program (where "negate" operation not available)

```
1  if
2      x > 0
3  then
4      x := x − 2*x
5  fi
```

proof

iftest true (prove $(p \rightarrow f) = (p \rightarrow g)$)

program function:

$(x > 0 \rightarrow x := x - 2*x) = (x > 0 \rightarrow x := -x)$
$= (x > 0 \rightarrow x := -\text{abs}(x))$

pass

iftest false (prove $(\sim p \rightarrow f) = (\sim p \rightarrow I)$)

program function:

$(x \leq 0 \rightarrow x := x) = (x \leq 0 \rightarrow x := -\text{abs}(x))$

pass

result

pass comp

3. Ifthenelse proof

function (x an integer)

$x := -x$

program (where "negate" operation not available)

```
1  if
2      x > 0
3  then
4      x := x − 2*x
5  else
6      x := x + 2*abs(x)
7  fi
```

proof

    iftest true (prove $(p \rightarrow f) = (p \rightarrow g)$)

        program function:

$$(x > 0 \rightarrow x := x - 2*x) = (x > 0 \rightarrow x := -x)$$

        pass

    iftest false (prove $(\sim p \rightarrow f) = (\sim p \rightarrow h)$)

        program function:

$$(x \leq 0 \rightarrow x := x + 2*\text{abs}(x)) = (x \leq 0 \rightarrow x := -x)$$

        pass

result

    pass comp

4. Whiledo proof

    function $(x, y,$ and a integers)

$$f = (x \geq 0 \rightarrow x, y, a := 0, a*x + y, a)$$

    program

```
1  while
2      x ≠ 0
3  do
4      x, y := x − 1, y + a
5  od
```

    proof

        term

            Initial $x \geq 0$ is reduced by 1 each iteration, so eventually whiletest $x \neq 0$ fails.

            pass

whiletest true (prove $(p \rightarrow f) = (p \rightarrow f \circ g)$)

part		condition	x	y
2	$x_0 \neq 0$	$x_0 \neq 0$	$x_1 = x_0$	$y_1 = y_0$
4	$x, y := x - 1, y + a$		$x_2 = x_1 - 1$	$y_2 = y_1 + a_0$
f	$x, y, a := 0, a*x + y, a$	$x_2 \geq 0$	$x_3 = 0$	$y_3 = a_0*x_2 + y_2$

derivations:

conditions:

$$x_0 \neq 0 \wedge x_2 \geq 0 = x_0 \neq 0 \wedge x_1 - 1 \geq 0$$
$$= x_0 \neq 0 \wedge x_0 - 1 \geq 0$$
$$= x_0 \neq 0 \wedge x_0 \geq 1$$
$$= x_0 > 0$$

assignments:

$$x_3 = 0 \qquad y_3 = a_0*x_2 + y_2$$
$$= a_0*(x_1 - 1) + y_1 + a_0$$
$$= a_0*(x_0 - 1) + y_0 + a_0$$
$$= a_0*x_0 + y_0$$

program function:

$(x > 0 \rightarrow x, y, a := 0, a*x + y, a)$

which agrees with the intended function when whiletest *true*.

pass

whiletest false (prove $(\sim p \rightarrow f) = (\sim p \rightarrow I)$)

$(x = 0 \rightarrow (x \geq 0 \rightarrow x, y, a := x, a*x + y, a))$
$= (x = 0 \rightarrow x, y, a := 0, a*0 + y, a)$
$= (x = 0 \rightarrow x, y, a := x, y, a)$

that is, the identity function, as required.

pass

result

pass comp

Note in the trace table for whiletest *true*, that the whiletest and the conditional predicate of the intended function both appear in the condition column to be used in deriving a conditional predicate for the program function. The first two lines in the trace table could be combined in the case of the whiledo, but they need to be treated separately in both the dountil and the dowhiledo, as shown below. Also, scalar a is not changed in the program, and need not appear in the trace table.

5. Dountil proof

    function $(x, y,$ and a integers)

    $f = (x > 0 \rightarrow x, y, a := 0, a*x + y, a)$

    program

    ```
    1  do
    2      x, y := x − 1, y + a
    3  until
    4      x = 0
    5  od
    ```

    proof

    term

    Initial $x > 0$ is reduced by 1 each iteration, so eventually untiltest $x = 0$ becomes *true*.

    pass

    untiltest true (prove $(p \circ g \rightarrow f) = (p \circ g \rightarrow g)$)

part		condition	x	y
2	$x, y := x − 1, y + a$		$x_1 = x_0 − 1$	$y_1 = y_0 + a_0$
4	$x = 0$	$x_1 = 0$	$x_2 = x_1$	$y_2 = y_1$

    derivations:

    condition:

    $$x_1 = 0 = (x_0 − 1 = 0)$$
    $$= (x_0 = 1)$$

    assignments:

    $$x_2 = x_1 \qquad y_2 = y_1$$
    $$= x_0 − 1 \qquad = y_0 + a_0$$

    program function:

    $$(x = 1 \rightarrow x, y, a := x − 1, y + a, a)$$
    $$= (x = 1 \rightarrow x, y, a := 0, a*x + y, a)$$

    which agrees with the intended function for initial $x = 1$.

    pass

Note that a trace table is used to derive the conditional predicate of the program function, even though only one assignment is made in the program part analyzed.

untiltest false (prove $(\sim p \circ g \to f) = (\sim p \circ g \to f \circ g)$)

part		condition	x	y
2	$x, y := x - 1, y + a$		$x_1 = x_0 - 1$	$y_1 = y_0 + a_0$
4	$x = 0$	$x_1 \neq 0$	$x_2 = x_1$	$y_2 = y_1$
f	$x, y, a := 0, a*x + y, a$	$x_2 > 0$	$x_3 = 0$	$y_3 = a_0*x_2 + y_2$

derivations:

condition:

$$x_1 \neq 0 \wedge x_2 > 0 = x_0 - 1 \neq 0 \wedge x_1 > 0$$
$$= x_0 - 1 \neq 0 \wedge x_0 - 1 > 0$$
$$= x_0 \neq 1 \wedge x_0 > 1$$
$$= x_0 > 1$$

assignments:

$$x_3 = 0 \qquad y_3 = a_0*x_2 + y_2$$
$$= a_0*x_1 + y_1$$
$$= a_0*(x_0 - 1) + y_0 + a_0$$
$$= a_0*x_0 + y_0$$

program function:

$$(x > 1 \to x, y, a := 0, a*x + y, a)$$

which agrees with the intended function for initial $x > 1$.

pass

result

pass comp

6. Dowhiledo proof

function $(x, y,$ and a integers)

$$f = (x > 0 \to x, y, a := 0, a*x + y, a)$$

program

```
1  do1
2      y := y + a
3  while
4      x ≠ 1
5  do2
6      x := x - 1
7  od
```

proof

    term

       Initial $x > 0$ is reduced by 1 each iteration, so eventually whiletest $x \neq 1$ fails.

    pass

whiletest true (prove $(p \circ g \rightarrow f) = (p \circ g \rightarrow f \circ h \circ g)$)

part		condition	x	y
2	$y := y + a$		$x_1 = x_0$	$y_1 = y_0 + a_0$
4	$x \neq 1$	$x_1 \neq 1$	$x_2 = x_1$	$y_2 = y_1$
6	$x := x - 1$		$x_3 = x_2 - 1$	$y_3 = y_2$
f	$x, y, a := 0, a*x + y, a$	$x_3 > 0$	$x_4 = 0$	$y_4 = a_0*x_3 + y_3$

    derivations:

      condition:

$$x_1 \neq 1 \wedge x_3 > 0 = x_0 \neq 1 \wedge x_2 - 1 > 0$$
$$= x_0 \neq 1 \wedge x_1 - 1 > 0$$
$$= x_0 \neq 1 \wedge x_0 - 1 > 0$$
$$= x_0 \neq 1 \wedge x_0 > 1$$
$$= x_0 > 1$$

    assignments:

$$x_4 = 0 \quad y_4 = a_0*x_3 + y_3$$
$$= a_0*(x_2 - 1) + y_2$$
$$= a_0*(x_1 - 1) + y_1$$
$$= a_0*(x_0 - 1) + y_0 + a_0$$
$$= a_0*x_0 + y_0$$

    program function:

      $(x > 1 \rightarrow x, y, a := 0, a*x + y, a)$

    which agrees with the intended function for initial $x > 1$.

    pass

whiletest false (prove $(\sim p \circ g \rightarrow f) = (\sim p \circ g \rightarrow g)$)

part		condition	x	y
2	$y := y + a$		$x_1 = x_0$	$y_1 = y_0 + a_0$
4	$x = 1$	$x_1 = 1$	$x_2 = x_1$	$y_2 = y_1$

    derivations:

      condition:

$$x_1 = 1 = (x_0 = 1)$$

assignments:

$$x_2 = x_1 \qquad y_2 = y_1$$
$$\quad\;\; = x_0 \qquad\quad = y_0 + a_0$$

program function:

$$(x = 1 \rightarrow x, y, a := x, y + a, a)$$
$$= (x = 1 \rightarrow x, y, a := 1, a*1 + y, a)$$

which is not equivalent to the intended function for initial $x = 1$.

fail

result

fail

We leave correction of this program (or its intended function) as an exercise for the reader.

6.5.2 Proofs With Array Data

Correctness proofs of programs that alter both arrays and array indices proceed exactly as above, by developing proof steps in terms of function concepts, rather than program variable concepts. However, care must be taken with index variables for elements within the array. For a fixed array named a, with index variable named k, the name $a(k)$ may or may not refer to the same array element throughout program execution, since k may be assigned new values. But the name $a(k_0)$ will refer to the same element throughout execution, since k_0 is not assigned new values.

As a first illustration, consider the sequence program for integer k and n-element array a,

1   $a(k), k := a(k) + k, k + 1$
2   $a(k), k := a(k) - k, k - 1$

with hypothesized function

$$(1 \leq k < n \rightarrow k, a(k), a(k + 1) := k, a(k) + k, a(k + 1) - k - 1)$$

The trace table can be written as follows:

part	condition	a		k
1	$1 \leq k_0 \leq n_0$	(1.1) $a_1(1:k_0 - 1) = a_0(1:k_0 - 1)$		$k_1 = k_0 + 1$
		(1.2) $a_1(k_0) = a_0(k_0) + k_0$		
		(1.3) $a_1(k_0 + 1:n_0) = a_0(k_0 + 1:n_0)$		
2	$1 \leq k_1 \leq n_0$	(2.1) $a_2(1:k_1 - 1) = a_1(1:k_1 - 1)$		$k_2 = k_1 - 1$
		(2.2) $a_2(k_1) = a_1(k_1) - k_1$		
		(2.3) $a_2(k_1 + 1:n_0) = a_1(k_1 + 1:n_0)$		

An array assignment carries an implicit condition on the domain of the index value, made explicit in the condition column of the table. The notation $a(r:s)$ denotes the array part $a(r), \ldots, a(s)$ when $r \le s$. For convenience in the derivations, every array element is accounted for at each assignment in the table, not simply the element assigned. For example, lines (1.1), (1.2), (1.3) specify assignments to array elements with index values $(1:k_0 - 1)$, (k_0), $(k_0 + 1:n_0)$, respectively, even though only $a_1(k_0)$ is assigned a new value.

The condition derivation is

$$(k_0 \ge 1) \wedge (k_0 \le n_0) \wedge (k_1 \ge 1) \wedge (k_1 \le n_0)$$
$$= (k_0 \ge 1) \wedge (k_0 \le n_0) \wedge (k_0 + 1 \ge 1) \wedge (k_0 + 1 \le n_0)$$
$$= (k_0 \ge 1) \wedge (k_0 \le n_0 - 1)$$
$$= 1 \le k_0 < n_0$$

and the assignment derivation for index k is

$$k_2 = k_1 - 1$$
$$= k_0 + 1 - 1$$
$$= k_0$$

The assignment derivations for array a must express final values of array elements in terms of initial values, that is, values of a_2 in terms of a_0. Thus, subscripts for elements of both a_2 and a_0 must be expressed in terms of k_0. This requires deriving new values for both sides of the assignment equations, as follows:

(2.1) $a_2(1:k_1 - 1) = a_1(1:k_1 - 1)$
       $a_2(1:k_0) = a_1(1:k_0)$ (because $k_1 = k_0 + 1$)
            $= a_1(1:k_0 - 1), a_1(k_0)$
            $= a_0(1:k_0 - 1), a_0(k_0) + k_0$ (by (1.1), (1.2))

Note that the forms chosen from line to line in the derivation of the assignment require some insightful look-ahead in expanding and contracting array parts, in order to accommodate the proof steps required. For example, the second line just above expands into two parts that correspond to left side of equations (1.1) and (1.2), thereby permitting the derivation to proceed.

(2.2) $a_2(k_1) = a_1(k_1) - k_1$
       $a_2(k_0 + 1) = a_1(k_0 + 1) - k_0 - 1$ (because $k_1 = k_0 + 1$)
            $= a_0(k_0 + 1) - k_0 - 1$ (by (1.3))

(2.3) $a_2(k_1 + 1:n_0) = a_1(k_1 + 1:n_0)$
       $a_2(k_0 + 2:n_0) = a_1(k_0 + 2:n_0)$
            $= a_0(k_0 + 2:n_0)$ (by (1.3))

The only array elements assigned new values are $a_2(k_0)$ (from derivation (2.1)), and $a_2(k_0 + 1)$ (from derivation (2.2)), and the program function is thus

$$(1 \le k < n \to k, a(k), a(k + 1) := k, a(k) + k, a(k + 1) - k - 1)$$

which agrees with the hypothesized function given above.

As a second illustration, consider a proof for the whiledo program

```
1  while
2     i < j
3  do
4     a(i + 1), i := Σa(i : i + 1), i + 1
5  od
```

that accumulates sums forward in an n-element array named a from one specific element up to another specific element in the array, and where $\Sigma a(i : i + 1) = a(i) + a(i + 1)$. For example, for $n = 6$, $i = 2$, $j = 5$, the program produces the following mapping between arguments and values:

Name	i	j	$a(1)$	$a(2)$	$a(3)$	$a(4)$	$a(5)$	$a(6)$
Argument	2	5	$a(1)$	$a(2)$	$a(3)$	$a(4)$	$a(5)$	$a(6)$
Value	5	5	$a(1)$	$a(2)$	$a(2) + a(3)$	$a(2) + a(3)$ $+ a(4)$	$a(2) + a(3)$ $+ a(4)$ $+ a(5)$	$a(6)$

The proof is shown below. Because the hypothesized function f turns out to be a two-part conditional rule $(f1 \mid f2)$, case-structured trace tables are convenient in the whiletest *true* part of the proof, taking first $f1 \circ g$, then $f2 \circ g$.

function

$$f = (1 \le i < j \le n \to i, a(1:n) := j, (a(1:i), \Sigma a(i:i + 1), \Sigma a(i:i + 2),$$
$$\Sigma a(i:i + 3), \ldots, \Sigma a(i:j), a(j + 1:n)) \mid$$
$$i \ge j \to I)$$

Note that all elements of array a are accounted for on both the left and right sides of the multiple assignment.

program

whiledo, lines 1–5 above.

proof

term

Index i is incremented every iteration so whiletest $i < j$ will eventually fail.

pass

whiletest true (prove $(p \to f) = (p \to f \circ g)$)

Case 1 $(f1 \circ g)$:

part	condition		a	i
2	$i_0 < j_0$		$a_1(1:n_0) = a_0(1:n_0)$	$i_1 = i_0$
4	$1 \le i_1 < n_0$	(4.1)	$a_2(1:i_1) = a_1(1:i_1)$	$i_2 = i_1 + 1$
		(4.2)	$a_2(i_1 + 1) = \Sigma a_1(i_1 : i_1 + 1)$	
		(4.3)	$a_2(i_1 + 2 : n_0) = a_1(i_1 + 2 : n_0)$	
$f1$	$1 \le i_2 < j_0 \le n_0$	$(f1.1)$	$a_3(1:i_2) = a_2(1:i_2)$	$i_3 = j_0$
		$(f1.2)$	$a_3(i_2 + 1) = \Sigma a_2(i_2 : i_2 + 1)$	
		$(f1.3)$	$a_3(i_2 + 2) = \Sigma a_2(i_2 : i_2 + 2)$	
			$\ldots$	
		$(f1.4)$	$a_3(j_0) = \Sigma a_2(i_2 : j_0)$	
		$(f1.5)$	$a_3(j_0 + 1 : n_0) = a_2(j_0 + 1 : n_0)$	

derivations:

condition:

$$(i_0 < j_0) \wedge (i_1 \ge 1) \wedge (i_1 < n_0) \wedge (i_2 \ge 1)$$
$$\wedge (i_2 < j_0) \wedge (j_0 \le n_0)$$
$$= (i_0 < j_0) \wedge (i_0 \ge 1) \wedge (i_0 < n_0) \wedge (i_0 \ge 0)$$
$$\wedge (i_0 < j_0 - 1) \wedge (j_0 \le n_0)$$
$$= (i_0 \ge 1) \wedge (i_0 < j_0 - 1) \wedge (i_0 < n_0) \wedge (j_0 \le n_0)$$
$$= (i_0 \ge 1) \wedge (i_0 < j_0 - 1) \wedge (j_0 \le n_0)$$

assignments:

$i_3 = j_0$

$(f1.1)$ $a_3(1:i_2) = a_2(1:i_2)$
$a_3(1:i_1 + 1) = a_2(1:i_1 + 1)$
$a_3(1:i_0 + 1) = a_2(1:i_1), a_2(i_1 + 1)$
$\qquad = a_1(1:i_1), \Sigma a_1(i_1 : i_1 + 1)$ (by (4.1), (4.2))
$\qquad = a_0(1:i_0), \Sigma a_0(i_0 : i_0 + 1)$

$(f1.2)$ $a_3(i_2 + 1) = \Sigma a_2(i_2 : i_2 + 1)$
$a_3(i_1 + 2) = \Sigma a_2(i_1 + 1 : i_1 + 2)$
$a_3(i_0 + 2) = \Sigma(a_2(i_1 + 1), a_2(i_1 + 2))$
$\qquad = \Sigma(\Sigma a_1(i_1 : i_1 + 1),$ (by (4.2), (4.3))
$\qquad \quad a_1(i_1 + 2))$
$\qquad = \Sigma a_0(i_0 : i_0 + 2)$

$(f1.3)$ $a_3(i_2 + 2) = \Sigma a_2(i_2 : i_2 + 2)$
$a_3(i_1 + 3) = \Sigma a_2(i_1 + 1 : i_1 + 3)$

$$a_3(i_0 + 3) = \Sigma(a_2(i_1 + 1), a_2(i_1 + 2:i_1 + 3))$$
$$= \Sigma(\Sigma a_1(i_1:i_1 + 1),$$
$$a_1(i_1 + 2:i_1 + 3)) \qquad \text{(by (4.2), (4.3))}$$
$$= \Sigma a_0(i_0:i_0 + 3)$$

$(f1.4)$ $a_3(j_0) = \Sigma a_2(i_2:j_0)$
$$= \Sigma a_2(i_1 + 1:j_0)$$
$$= \Sigma(a_2(i_1 + 1), a_2(i_1 + 2:j_0))$$
$$= \Sigma(\Sigma a_1(i_1:i_1 + 1), \qquad \text{(by (4.2), (4.3))}$$
$$a_1(i_1 + 2:j_0))$$
$$= \Sigma a_0(i_0:j_0)$$

$(f1.5)$ $a_3(j_0 + 1:n_0) = a_2(j_0 + 1:n_0)$
$$= a_0(j_0 + 1:n_0) \qquad \text{(by (4.3) and } i_0 < j_0)$$

Thus, the conditional rule for case 1 is

$$((i \geq 1) \wedge (i < j - 1) \wedge (j \leq n) \rightarrow i, a(1:n) := j, (a(1:i), \Sigma a(i:i + 1),$$
$$\Sigma a(i:i + 2), \Sigma a(i:i + 3), \ldots,$$
$$\Sigma a(i:j), a(j + 1:n)))$$

Case 2 $(f2 \circ g)$:

part	condition		a	i
2	$i_0 < j_0$		$a_1(1:n_0) = a_0(1:n_0)$	$i_1 = i_0$
4	$1 \leq i_1 < n_0$	(4.1)	$a_2(1:i_1) = a_1(1:i_1)$	$i_2 = i_1 + 1$
		(4.2)	$a_2(i_1 + 1) = \Sigma a_1(i_1:i_1 + 1)$	
		(4.3)	$a_2(i_1 + 2:n_0) = a_1(i_1 + 2:n_0)$	
$f2$	$i_2 \geq j_0$	$(f2.1)$	$a_3(1:i_2) = a_2(1:i_2)$	$i_3 = i_2$
		$(f2.2)$	$a_3(i_2 + 1) = a_2(i_2 + 1)$	
		$(f2.3)$	$a_3(i_2 + 2:n_0) = a_2(i_2 + 2:n_0)$	

derivations:

condition:

$$(i_0 < j_0) \wedge (i_1 \geq 1) \wedge (i_1 < n_0) \wedge (i_2 \geq j_0)$$
$$= (i_0 < j_0) \wedge (i_0 \geq 1) \wedge (i_0 < n_0) \wedge (i_0 \geq j_0 - 1)$$
$$= (i_0 \geq 1) \wedge (i_0 = j_0 - 1) \wedge (i_0 < n_0)$$
$$= (i_0 \geq 1) \wedge (i_0 = j_0 - 1 < n_0)$$
$$= (i_0 \geq 1) \wedge (i_0 = j_0 - 1) \wedge (j_0 \leq n_0)$$

assignments:

$$i_3 = i_2$$
$$= i_1 + 1$$
$$= i_0 + 1$$
$$= j_0 - 1 + 1 \qquad \text{(by condition derivation, above)}$$
$$= j_0$$

$(f2.1)$ $a_3(1:i_2) = a_2(1:i_2)$
$$a_3(1:i_1 + 1) = a_2(1:i_1 + 1)$$
$$a_3(1:i_0 + 1) = a_2(1:i_1), a_2(i_1 + 1)$$
$$= a_1(1:i_1), \Sigma a_1(i_1:i_1 + 1) \quad \text{(by (4.1), (4.2))}$$
$$= a_0(1:i_0), \Sigma a_0(i_0:i_0 + 1)$$

$(f2.2)$ $a_3(i_2 + 1) = a_2(i_2 + 1)$
$$a_3(i_1 + 2) = a_2(i_1 + 2)$$
$$a_3(i_0 + 2) = a_1(i_1 + 2) \quad \text{(by (4.3))}$$
$$= a_0(i_0 + 2)$$

$(f2.3)$ $a_3(i_2 + 2:n_0) = a_2(i_2 + 2:n_0)$
$$a_3(i_1 + 3:n_0) = a_2(i_1 + 3:n_0)$$
$$a_3(i_0 + 3:n_0) = a_1(i_1 + 3:n_0) \quad \text{(by (4.3))}$$
$$= a_0(i_0 + 3:n_0)$$

Thus, the conditional rule for case 2 is

$$((i \geq 1) \wedge (i = j - 1) \wedge (j \leq n) \to i, a(1:n) := j, (a(1:i),$$
$$\Sigma a(i:i + 1), a(i + 2:n)))$$

Inspection reveals that the data assignments for cases 1 and 2 are identical; therefore, the conditional rules can be combined. The conditions differ only in the terms

$$i < j - 1 \quad \text{(condition 1)}$$
$$i = j - 1 \quad \text{(condition 2)}$$

which can be combined as

$$i \leq j - 1 = i < j$$

to yield

$$(i \geq 1) \wedge (i < j) \wedge (j \leq n) = 1 \leq i < j \leq n$$

The combined conditional rule is as follows:

$$(1 \leq i < j \leq n \to i, a(1:n) := j, (a(1:i), \Sigma a(i:i + 1), \Sigma a(i:i + 2),$$
$$\Sigma a(i:i + 3), \ldots, \Sigma a(i:j), a(j + 1:n)))$$

    pass
  whiletest false (prove $(\sim p \to f) = (\sim p \to I)$)
    The program function is the required identity.
    pass
result
    pass comp

In summary, we have recorded systematic proofs for sequence and whiledo programs that alter arrays. These proofs proceed along the same lines as proofs for programs that alter scalar data, but require more insight in the derivation of program functions.

6.5.3 Proofs with Anonymous Data

Correctness proofs of programs that operate on anonymous data proceed exactly as the proofs given above, except that list definitions replace the anonymous data operations. For example, the trace table of the sequence of operations

> **stack** s
> **top**$(s) := a$
> $b := $ **top**(s)

becomes (using the list operations H, T, and so on, defined in Chapter 3)

part	condition	b	s
top$(s) := a$		$b_1 = b_0$	$s_1 = a_0 + s_0$
$b := $ **top**(s)	$s_1 \neq \emptyset$	$b_2 = H(s_1)$	$s_2 = T(s_1)$

derivations:

$$s_1 \neq \emptyset \qquad\qquad b_2 = H(s_1) \qquad\quad s_2 = T(s_1)$$
$$= (a_0 + s_0 \neq \emptyset) \qquad = H(a_0 + s_0) \qquad = T(a_0 + s_0)$$
$$= a_0 \qquad\qquad\quad = s_0$$

which defines the program function

$$(a + s \neq \emptyset \to b := a)$$

or simply

$$b := a$$

since $(a + s \neq \emptyset)$ is always *true*.

In the case of a sequence data structure it is convenient to break the data column into two columns, one for each list of the sequence, as in

> **sequence** s
> **next**$(s) := a$
> $b := $ **current**(s)

which leads to the following trace table:

part	condition	b	s^-	s^+
next$(s) := a$		$b_1 = b_0$	$s_1^- = s_0^- \oplus a_0$	$s_1^+ = \emptyset$
$b := $ **current**(s)	$s_1^- \neq \emptyset$	$b_2 = H^-(s_1^-)$	$s_2^- = s_1^-$	$s_2^+ = s_1^+$

derivations:

$$
\begin{array}{llll}
s_1^- \neq \emptyset & b_2 = \text{H}^-(s_1^-) & s_2^- = s_1^- & s_2^+ = s_1^+ \\
= (s_0^- \oplus a_0 \neq \emptyset) & = \text{H}^-(s_0^- \oplus a_0) & = s_0^- \oplus a_0 & = \emptyset \\
& = a_0 & &
\end{array}
$$

which defines the program function

$$
(s^- \oplus a \neq \emptyset \rightarrow b, s := a, s^- \oplus a.\emptyset)
$$

or simply

$$
b, s := a, s^- \oplus a.\emptyset
$$

since $(s^- \oplus a \neq \emptyset)$ is always *true*.

In illustration of a simple looping program with anonymous data, consider the procedure copysequence, intended to copy one sequence into the end of another

```
1   proc copysequence(alt in, out)
2       sequence in,out
3       while
4           in ≠ empty
5       do
6           next(out) := next(in)
7       od
8   corp
```

with intended function

$$
in, out := in^- \| in^+.\emptyset, out^- \| in^+.\emptyset
$$

Note that the initial list out^+ will be destroyed by the first write to the sequence out. We now want to verify this program.

First, we observe that the dopart of the whiledo program, the single line 6, can be written as a program function in list notation, as

$$
(in^+ \neq \emptyset \rightarrow in, out := in^- \oplus \text{H}(in^+).\text{T}(in^+), out^- \oplus \text{H}(in^+).\emptyset)
$$

Then, the program can be verified in the following proof:

function

$$
f = (in, out := in^- \| in^+.\emptyset, out^- \| in^+.\emptyset)
$$

program

3 **while**
4      $in \neq$ **empty**   (that is, $in^+ \neq \emptyset$)
5 **do** $[(in^+ \neq \emptyset \rightarrow in, out := in^- \oplus H(in^+).T(in^+), out^- \oplus H(in^+).\emptyset)]$
6   **next**$(out) :=$ **next**(in)
7 **od**

proof

term

One member is removed from in^+ each iteration, so that eventually $in^+ = \emptyset$.

pass

whiletest true

part	condition	in^-	in^+	out^-	out^+
4	$in_0^+ \neq \emptyset$	$in_1^- = in_0^-$	$in_1^+ = in_0^+$	$out_1^- = out_0^-$	$out_1^+ = out_0^+$
6	$in_1^+ \neq \emptyset$	$in_2^- = in_1^- \oplus$ $H(in_1^+)$	$in_2^+ = T(in_1^+)$	$out_2^- = out_1^- \oplus$ $H(in_1^+)$	$out_2^+ = \emptyset$
f		$in_3^- = in_2^- \|$ in_2^+	$in_3^+ = \emptyset$	$out_3^- = out_2^- \|$ in_2^+	$out_3^+ = \emptyset$

derivations:

condition:

$$in_0^+ \neq \emptyset \wedge in_1^+ \neq \emptyset$$
$$in_0^+ \neq \emptyset \wedge in_0^+ \neq \emptyset$$
$$= in_0^+ \neq \emptyset$$

assignments:

$$in_3^- = in_2^- \| in_2^+ \qquad\qquad out_3^- = out_2^- \| in_2^+$$
$$= in_1^- \oplus H(in_1^+) \| T(in_1^+) \qquad = out_1^- \oplus H(in_1^+) \| T(in_1^+)$$
$$= in_0^- \oplus H(in_0^+) \| T(in_0^+) \qquad = out_0^- \oplus H(in_0^+) \| T(in_0^+)$$
$$= in_0^- \| H(in_0^+) + T(in_0^+) \qquad = out_0^- \| H(in_0^+) + T(in_0^+)$$
$$= in_0^- \| in_0^+ \qquad\qquad\qquad = out_0^- \| in_0^+$$
$$in_3^+ = \emptyset \qquad\qquad\qquad\qquad out_3^+ = \emptyset$$

program function:

$$(in^+ \neq \emptyset \rightarrow in, out := in^- \| in^+.\emptyset, out^- \| in^+.\emptyset)$$

which agrees with the intended function for whiletest *true*.

pass

whiletest false $(in^+ = \emptyset)$

program function:

$$in, out := in^- \| in^+ . \emptyset, out^- \| in^+ . \emptyset$$
$$= in^- \| \emptyset . \emptyset, out^- \| \emptyset . \emptyset$$
$$= in^- . \emptyset, out^- . \emptyset$$
$$= in^- . in^+, out^- . \emptyset$$
$$\neq in, out \; (out \neq out^- . \emptyset)$$

    fail

  result

    fail

As a result of the proof failure, it is easy to see how to correct the intended function; namely,

$$(in \neq \emptyset \to in, out := in^- \| in^+ . \emptyset, out^- \| in^+ . \emptyset \,|\, true \to in, out := in, out)$$

On the other hand, a compound program to satisfy the original intended function can be obtained by adding the assignment $out := $ **empty** either before or after the whiledo.

6.5.4 Proofs of Larger Loop-Free Primes

The program function of any loop-free program, whether prime or not, can be determined by using case-structured trace tables, incorporating the predicates of the program into the tables. In illustration, consider Fig. 6.6 that shows a three-predicate loop-free prime, say P, and what its program function might be. Our objective in dealing with a large loop-free prime such as this is to illustrate that deliberate, recordable methods of reasoning can be used on loop-free primes of large and complex structure if the need arises, either in dealing with a special programming problem or for expanding proof rules beyond the one-predicate primes.

Given a function f that program P purports to implement, we might wish to show for sufficient correctness that

$$f \subset [P]$$

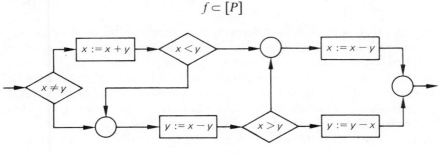

Figure 6.6

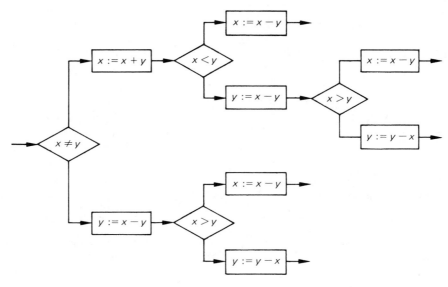

Figure 6.7

For now, we will simply derive the program function $[P]$ and note that P satisfies sufficient correctness of any subset of $[P]$. Program P has E-chart as shown in Fig. 6.7, so that the program function for P can be described by a conditional rule of five parts, one for each endpoint of the E-chart. In this case however, we note some simplification is possible since the subflowchart

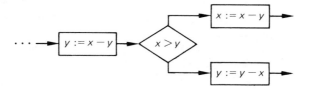

named, say S, appears in two places. We can substitute the conditional rule for the program function of S in the original E-chart, thereby reducing the paths to consider from five to three. To develop the program function for S, we create a trace table for each path of the E-chart of S. The paths can be labeled $S1$ and $S0$ in accordance with their successive predicate outcomes, 1 indicating the *true* branch and 0, the *false* branch. The first trace table for S is as follows. Where it can be done reliably, substitution of terms in the condition and assignment derivations is carried out mentally, and only the final results are shown; otherwise, full derivations are given.

path $S1$

part	condition	x	y
$y := x - y$		$x_1 = x_0$	$y_1 = x_0 - y_0$
$x > y$	$x_1 > y_1$	$x_2 = x_1$	$y_2 = y_1$
$x := x - y$		$x_3 = x_2 - y_2$	$y_3 = y_2$

derivations:

$$x_1 > y_1 = y_0 > 0 \qquad x_3 = y_0 \qquad y_3 = x_0 - y_0$$

path function:

$$(y > 0 \to x, y := y, x - y)$$

The second trace table for S is

path $S0$

part	condition	x	y
$y := x - y$		$x_1 = x_0$	$y_1 = x_0 - y_0$
$x \leq y$	$x_1 \leq y_1$	$x_2 = x_1$	$y_2 = y_1$
$y := y - x$		$x_3 = x_2$	$y_3 = y_2 - x_2$

derivations:

$$x_1 \leq y_1 = y_0 \leq 0 \qquad x_3 = x_0 \qquad y_3 = -y_0$$

path function:

$$(y \leq 0 \to x, y := x, -y)$$

Combining $S1$ and $S0$, we get $[S]$, where

$$[S] = (y > 0 \to x, y := y, x - y \,|\, y \leq 0 \to x, y := x, -y)$$

Next, we replace S by $[S]$ in the original E-chart for P to get a reduced E-chart as shown in Fig. 6.8. The reduced E-chart has three paths, $P11$, $P10$,

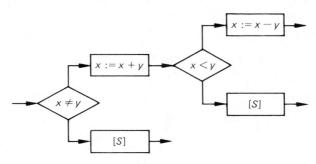

Figure 6.8

$P0$. $P11$ has no conditional rules, so a simple trace table can be used. $P10$ and $P0$ each contain $[S]$, given by a conditional rule, so each can be determined by case-structured trace tables. However, we illustrate a more informal treatment of cases in a conditional rule within a single trace table. If in doubt, a full treatment with case-structured trace tables can be used. The first of the three trace tables for P is

path $P11$

part	condition	x	y
$x \neq y$	$x_0 \neq y_0$	$x_1 = x_0$	$y_1 = y_0$
$x := x + y$		$x_2 = x_1 + y_1$	$y_2 = y_1$
$x < y$	$x_2 < y_2$	$x_3 = x_2$	$y_3 = y_2$
$x := x - y$		$x_4 = x_3 - y_3$	$y_4 = y_3$

derivations:

$$(x_0 \neq y_0) \wedge (x_2 < y_2) \qquad\qquad x_4 = x_0 \qquad y_4 = y_0$$
$$= (x_0 \neq y_0) \wedge ((x_0 + y_0) < y_0)$$
$$= (x_0 \neq y_0) \wedge (x_0 < 0)$$

path function:

$$(x \neq y \wedge x < 0 \rightarrow x, y, := x, y)$$

The second trace table for P is

path $P10$

part	condition	x	y
$x \neq y$	$x_0 \neq y_0$	$x_1 = x_0$	$y_1 = y_0$
$x := x + y$		$x_2 = x_1 + y_1$	$y_2 = y_1$
$x \geq y$	$x_2 \geq y_2$	$x_3 = x_2$	$y_3 = y_2$
$[S]$		$(y_3 > 0 \rightarrow x_4 = y_3 \mid$	$(y_3 > 0 \rightarrow y_4 = x_3 - y_3 \mid$
		$y_3 \leq 0 \rightarrow x_4 = x_3)$	$y_3 \leq 0 \rightarrow y_4 = -y_3)$

derivations:

First we derive

$$x_0 \neq y_0 \wedge x_2 \geq y_2 \qquad x_3 = x_0 + y_0 \qquad y_3 = y_0$$
$$= x_0 \neq y_0 \wedge x_0 \geq 0$$

and then

$$\text{case } (y_3 > 0) = (y_0 > 0)$$

$x_4 = y_3$	$y_4 = x_3 - y_3$
$= y_0$	$= x_0$

$$\frac{\text{case } (y_3 \le 0) = (y_0 \le 0)}{\begin{array}{ll} x_4 = x_3 & y_4 = -y_3 \\ = x_0 + y_0 & = -y_0 \end{array}}$$

path function:

$$(x \ne y \wedge x \ge 0 \to (y > 0 \to x, y := y, x \,|\, y \le 0 \to x, y := x + y, -y))$$

The third trace table for P is

path P0

part	condition		x	y
$x = y$	$x_0 = y_0$		$x_1 = x_0$	$y_1 = y_0$
$[S]$			$(y_1 > 0 \to x_2 = y_1 \,\|$	$(y_1 > 0 \to y_2 = x_1 - y_1 \,\|$
			$y_1 \le 0 \to x_2 = x_1)$	$y_1 \le 0 \to y_2 = -y_1)$

derivations:

First, we derive

$$x_0 = y_0 \qquad x_1 = x_0 \qquad y_1 = y_0$$

and then

$$\frac{\text{case } (y_1 > 0) = (y_0 > 0)}{x_2 = y_0 \qquad y_2 = x_0 - y_0}$$

$$\frac{\text{case } (y_1 \le 0) = (y_0 \le 0)}{x_2 = x_0 \qquad y_2 = -y_0}$$

path function:

$$(x = y \to (y > 0 \to x, y := y, x - y \,|\, y \le 0 \to x, y := x, -y))$$

The foregoing results for $P11$, $P10$, and $P0$ can now be combined into a single program function $[P]$ as follows, which exactly describes the operations on data carried out by program P:

$$\begin{aligned}
[P] = {}& (\text{condition } P11 \to \text{rule } P11 \,| \\
& \text{condition } P10 \to \text{rule } P10 \,| \\
& \text{condition } P0 \to \text{rule } P0) \\
= {}& ((x \ne y) \wedge (x < 0) \to x, y := x, y \,| \\
& (x \ne y) \wedge (x \ge 0) \wedge (y > 0) \to x, y := y, x \,| \\
& (x \ne y) \wedge (x \ge 0) \wedge (y \le 0) \to x, y := x + y, -y \,| \\
& (x = y) \wedge (y > 0) \to x, y := y, x - y \,| \\
& (x = y) \wedge (y \le 0) \to x, y := x, -y)
\end{aligned}$$

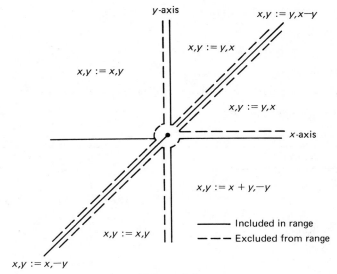

Figure 6.9

Note in passing that this program function can be diagrammed in the x, y plane as shown in Fig. 6.9.

EXERCISES

(All data objects are scalar integers unless otherwise declared.)

1. Given the program

```
if
    x > y
then
    x, y := x − y, x + y
    if
        x < y
    then
        x, y := y, x
    else
        x, y := x + y, x − y
    fi
else
    x, y := y, x
fi
```

determine the program function by
  a) analyzing the E-chart directly, and
  b) first determining an intermediate abstraction, then analyzing the E-chart.

2. Hypothesize a program function and carry out a proof of correctness for each of the following programs:

a) **while**
$$x < y + b$$
do
$$x, b, y := x + 1, b - 1, y + 1$$
od

b) **sequence** *in*: integer
while
$$in \neq \textbf{empty}$$
do
$$a := \textbf{next}(in)$$
$$x := x + a$$
od

c) **array** $t(n)$: integer
while
$$i < k$$
do
$$t(k) := (t(k) + t(k + 1))/2$$
$$k := k - 1$$
od

d) **set** $s1, s2$: integer
while
$$s1 \neq \textbf{empty}$$
do
$$\textbf{member}(s2) := \textbf{member}(s1)$$
od

e) **sequence** *in*1, *in*2, *out* [*in*1, *in*2 contain same number of members]
do
$$a, b := \textbf{next}(in1), \textbf{next}(in2)$$
if
$$a > b$$
then
$$\textbf{next}(out) := a$$
else
$$\textbf{next}(out) := b$$
fi
until
$$in1 = \textbf{empty}$$
od

f) **sequence** *in, out*: character [*in* contains ♭ character]
  scalar *a*: character
  do1
    a := **next**(*in*)
  while
    a ≠ ♭
  do2
    next(*out*) := *a*
  od

3. Verify the direct assertion made about the oddbeforeeven program (Fig. 6.5), dealing with segment [5–18]. Then, using the direct assertions for [5–18], [20–26], and [27–33], verify the direct assertion for the segment [5–33].

4. Verify the Singsort program (Fig. 5.20), using your own judgment of the extent of direct assertion required. (See Problem 5, Section 6.4.)

6.6. LOOP INVARIANTS IN CORRECTNESS PROOFS

6.6.1 Loop Invariants

We now investigate an important property of invariance in program loops, which gives deep insight in correctness proofs and logical commentary. An *invariant* of a program loop with a single predicate is a logical condition that is invariably *true* when the predicate is evaluated. For example, in the addition program $(u, v \geq 0 \rightarrow u, v := u + v, 0)$

  while
    $v \neq 0$
  do
    $u, v := u + 1, v - 1$
  od

the predicate $u + v = u_0 + v_0$ holds on entry, and furthermore holds at each iteration of the loop, and is therefore an invariant. We denote this in logical commentary as an *invariant status* comment attached to **while**:

  while $[u + v = u_0 + v_0]$
    $v \neq 0$
  do
    $u, v := u + 1, v - 1$
  od

Invariants, if known, can be used in an alternative to the verification techniques described in the Correctness Theorem, as will be shown. The placement of the invariant status between the **while** keyword and the whiletest indicates a condition that must hold, whether the whiletest evaluates to *true* or *false*. In order to prove that a predicate is an invariant for a whiledo program, it is sufficient to prove, using induction, that

1. the predicate holds on entry to the whiledo loop, and
2. if the predicate holds and the whiletest holds, then the predicate holds after the dopart is executed.

Thus, the addition program invariant holds throughout execution, since

1. $u + v = u_0 + v_0$ on entry because $u = u_0$, $v = v_0$, and
2. if $u + v = u_0 + v_0$ and $v \neq 0$, then $u + v = u_0 + v_0$ after the multiple assignment $u, v := u + 1, v - 1$.

On the other hand, if the loop terminates, the invariant still holds, and the whiletest fails (in order for the loop to terminate). That is,

$$u + v = u_0 + v_0 \wedge v = 0$$

But this implies that

$$u = u_0 + v_0 \wedge v = 0$$

and the program function can be seen to be

$$(u, v \geq 0 \rightarrow u, v := u + v, 0)$$

In general, the previous example illustrates the following idea. If q is an invariant in

$$\textbf{while } [q] \; p \; \textbf{do} \; g \; \textbf{od}$$

(with logical commentary brackets delimiting q) then

$$p \wedge q \rightarrow q \circ g \qquad \text{(by definition)} \tag{1}$$
$$\sim p \wedge q \qquad \text{(on termination, if termination ever occurs)} \tag{2}$$

Note that condition (2) above defines an automatic final status comment for the whiledo program:

$$\textbf{while } [q] \; p \; \textbf{do} \; g \; \textbf{od} \; [\sim p \wedge q]$$

6.6.2   The Invariant Status Theorem

In the addition program, the invariant shown was strong enough to characterize the program function of the whiledo loop. But weaker invariants will not be strong enough. For example, $u + v \geq u_0 + v_0$, $u + v \geq 0$, etc., are all invariants, as well, but they do not characterize the program function. In order to determine invariants strong enough to characterize program functions, we next study the whiledo program in more detail.

Invariant Status Theorem. Let

$$f = [\textbf{while } p \textbf{ do } g \textbf{ od}]$$

If $X_0 \in D(f)$, $X \in D(f)$, and $q(X) = (f(X) = f(X_0))$, then

1. q is an invariant of **while** p **do** g **od**
2. q characterizes f at loop termination, that is,

$$\sim p(X) \wedge q(X) \rightarrow X = f(X_0)$$

Proof. For (1) we prove that q is an invariant by induction, which requires proving

a) $q(X_0)$ is *true*, and
b) $q(X) \wedge p(X) \rightarrow q \circ g(X)$

First note on entry that

$$q(X_0) = (f(X_0) = f(X_0)) = true$$

so that condition (a) is satisfied. Next, to prove condition (b) we note that for $X \in D(f)$

$$p(X) \rightarrow (f(X) = f \circ g(X))$$

by the Correctness Theorem. Furthermore, since

$$q(X) = (f(X) = f(X_0))$$

by hypothesis, we can modify this implication as

$$p(X) \wedge q(X) \rightarrow (f(X_0) = f \circ g(X))$$

But the right-hand side can now be recognized as

$$q \circ g(X)$$

Therefore

$$p(X) \wedge q(X) \rightarrow q \circ g(X)$$

and condition (b) holds. Hence q is an invariant as stated.

For (2), if $\sim p(X)$ then by the definition of the whiledo program we have

$$X = f(X)$$

Furthermore, if $q(X)$, then

$$f(X) = f(X_0)$$

Therefore, by combining these last two equations,

$$X = f(X) = f(X_0)$$

or

$$\sim p(X) \wedge q(X) \rightarrow (X = f(X_0))$$

as was to be shown.

The Invariant Status Theorem permits systematic derivation of invariants. As a first illustration, recall the addition program

while
     $v \neq 0$
do
     $u, v := u + 1, v - 1$
od

with function $(u, v \geq 0 \rightarrow u, v := u + v, 0)$. The invariant $f(X) = f(X_0)$ can be derived by tabulating $f(X)$ and $f(X_0)$ for each member of the data space:

X	$f(X)$	$f(X_0)$
u	$u + v$	$u_0 + v_0$
v	0	0

and equating components of $f(X)$ and $f(X_0)$

$$u + v = u_0 + v_0$$

$$0 = 0$$

of which the first is of interest and, in fact, is identical to the invariant hypothesized above.

As a second illustration, consider deriving an invariant for a whiledo program to carry out integer division of natural numbers a and b, dividend and divisor, respectively, by repeated subtraction (given $b_0 > 0$, quotient $q_0 = 0$):

     while $a \geq b$ **do** $a, q := a - b, q + 1$ **od**

After tracing through a sample execution, say

a	b	q
13	3	0
10	3	1
7	3	2
4	3	3
1	3	4

we hypothesize the program function as

$$a, b, q := a - (a/b)*b, \ b, \ (a/b) + q$$

where integer division is assumed. We next apply the Invariant Status Theorem to derive an invariant expression for the loop, but first the reader is invited to verify an intuitive statement of the invariant invented by inspecting the program; namely, that for every iteration

$$b*q + a = a_0$$

A tabulation of $f(X)$ and $f(X_0)$ gives

X	$f(X)$	$f(X_0)$
a	$a - (a/b)*b$	$a_0 - (a_0/b_0)*b_0$
b	b	b_0
q	$(a/b) + q$	$(a_0/b_0) + q_0$

from which components can be equated to get

$$a - (a/b)*b = a_0 - (a_0/b_0)*b_0 \qquad (1)$$

$$b = b_0 \qquad (2)$$

$$(a/b) + q = (a_0/b_0) + q_0 \qquad (3)$$

This system of equations is the required invariant, but some simplification is possible,

$$a_0 - a = b*((a_0/b_0) - (a/b)) \qquad \text{(from (1) and (2))}$$
$$(a_0/b_0) - (a/b) = q - q_0 \qquad \text{(from (3))}$$

to get

$$a_0 - a = b*(q - q_0)$$

which is identical to the intuitive invariant, above, given the prescription of $q_0 = 0$.

6.6.3   Full Invariants and Limited Invariants

The last example illustrates a point we now bring out in more detail. A whiledo invariant may hold by virtue of its initialization. In particular, given

$$f = [\textbf{while } p \textbf{ do } g \textbf{ od}], \qquad X_0 \in D(f)$$

we call

$$q(X) = (f(X) = f(X_0))$$

the *full invariant* of the whiledo loop, and for any initialization of the whiledo

$$h; \textbf{ while } p \textbf{ do } g \textbf{ od}$$

we call

$$q(X) = (f(X) = f \circ h(X_0))$$

a *limited invariant* of the initialized whiledo loop.

In illustration, consider the following initialized whiledo program, which assigns nonnegative u to v ($u \geq 0 \to v := u$):

```
v := 0
while
    v < u
do
    v := v + 1
od
```

An invariant status is easy to guess and verify, as $v \leq u$, shown in the recopied program

```
v := 0
while [v ≤ u]
    v < u
do
    v := v + 1
od [v = u]
```

with final status at **od** derived from invariant $v \leq u$, and whiledo exit condition $v \geq u$.

Next consider the whiledo part of the program above; namely,

```
while
    v < u
do
    v := v + 1
od
```

that can be seen to have program function

$$v := \max(u, v)$$

The invariant status is not so easy to guess, but we know how to derive it, recalling the form of the invariant status as

$$f(u, v) = f(u_0, v_0)$$

Using this specific program function, we have the following tabulation

X	$f(X)$	$f(X_0)$
u	u	u_0
v	$\max(u, v)$	$\max(u_0, v_0)$

with equated components

$$u = u_0$$
$$\max(u, v) = \max(u_0, v_0)$$

The first equation can be used to rewrite the second equation as

$$\max(u_0, v) = \max(u_0, v_0)$$

and this second equation can be broken into two cases, according to the value of the right-hand side, defined by the following predicate expressions:

$$v_0 \leq u_0 \rightarrow (\max(u_0, v) = u_0) \rightarrow v \leq u_0$$
$$v_0 > u_0 \rightarrow (\max(u_0, v) = v_0) \rightarrow v = v_0$$

We can organize these cases, along with the first equation, into an invariant status in the recopied program:

while $[(u = u_0) \wedge (v_0 \leq u_0 \rightarrow v \leq u_0) \wedge (v_0 > u_0 \rightarrow v = v_0)]$
    $v < u$
do
    $v := v + 1$
od

When $u_0 \geq 0$, $v_0 = 0$, as for the initialized whiledo, then this invariant reduces to $(u = u_0) \wedge (v \leq u_0)$, which contains the invariant $v \leq u$ guessed above. In checking this result, the final status can now be determined as the conjunction of the invariant and the exit condition $v \geq u$, that is

$$[(u = u_0) \wedge (v_0 \leq u_0 \rightarrow v \leq u_0) \wedge (v_0 > u_0 \rightarrow v = v_0) \wedge (v \geq u)]$$

that can be simplified to

$$[(u = u_0) \wedge (v_0 \leq u_0 \rightarrow v = u_0) \wedge (v_0 > u_0 \rightarrow v = v_0)]$$

or more directly

$$[(u = u_0 \wedge v = \max(u_0, v_0)]$$

that defines the whiledo program function

$$v := \max(u, v)$$

(and not $u := \min(u, v)$, etc.).

Thus, although possibly paradoxical at first glance, the whiledo function is more complex than its initialized counterpart. In fact, the initialization of the whiledo restricts its use to a subset of the whiledo function. As a result, a limited invariant will be simpler than the full invariant of the whiledo. But the limited invariant now depends on the environment of the whiledo, whereas the full invariant does not.

EXERCISES

1. Show that the dountil program

$$f = [\text{do } g \text{ until } p \text{ od}]$$

has invariant

$$q(X) = (f(X) = f \circ g(X_0))$$

and that the dowhiledo program

$$f = [\text{do1 } g \text{ while } p \text{ do2 } h \text{ od}]$$

has invariant

$$q(X) = (f(X) = f \circ h \circ g(X_0))$$

2. Deduce the invariants of the following programs:
   a) **while** $x > 0$ **do** $x := x - 1$ **od**
   b) **while** $x \neq 0$ **do** $x := x - 1$ **od**
   c) **do** $x := x + 1$ **until** $x \geq y$ **od**
   d) **do** $x := x + 1$ **until** $x = y$ **od**

6.7 FORMULAS FOR CORRECT STRUCTURED PROGRAMS

6.7.1 The Function Equations of Structured Programs

Validation of structured programs involves repeated verification of function equations of one of the several types:

$$f = [g; h] \qquad\qquad\qquad \text{(sequence)}$$

$$f = [\text{if } p \text{ then } g \text{ fi}] \qquad\qquad \text{(ifthen)}$$

$$f = [\textbf{if } p \textbf{ then } g \textbf{ else } h \textbf{ fi}] \qquad \text{(ifthenelse)}$$

$$f = [\textbf{while } p \textbf{ do } g \textbf{ od}] \qquad \text{(whiledo)}$$

$$f = [\textbf{do } g \textbf{ until } p \textbf{ od}] \qquad \text{(dountil)}$$

$$f = [\textbf{do1 } g \textbf{ while } p \textbf{ do2 } h \textbf{ od}] \qquad \text{(dowhiledo)}$$

Conversely, the design of correct structured programs requires the repeated selection and solution of these same function equations, in each case with f a given function and unknown functions p, g, h. For example, given any function f, consider first any solution (g, h) of the equation

$$f = [g; h] \qquad \text{(sequence)}$$

Next consider any solution (p, k) of the equation

$$g = [\textbf{if } p \textbf{ then } k \textbf{ fi}] \qquad \text{(ifthen)}$$

and next any solution (q, m) of the equation

$$h = [\textbf{while } q \textbf{ do } m \textbf{ od}] \qquad \text{(whiledo)}$$

By construction, then

$$f = [g; h] = [\textbf{if } p \textbf{ then } k \textbf{ fi}; \textbf{ while } q \textbf{ do } m \textbf{ od}]$$

and this construction process can be continued indefinitely. Such programs are correct by construction in a formal way.

As surprising as it may seem, each of these function equations has a solution that can be given in closed form, if it exists at all. And it will be evident below that the existence of solutions can be easily guaranteed in equation selection during the construction process. A completely mechanical procedure for constructing a correct structured program of arbitrary structure is not now a serious design technique, because the degrees of freedom are so great that intelligence and insight are required to select reasonable solutions out of those possible. Yet, in simple design problems, as we shall see, a small amount of insight is sufficient to fix a solution. And, in any case, the form of the solutions gives a new understanding of the general design process.

The foregoing function equations have solutions for arbitrary given function f except for one case, the whiledo equation. In this one case, an existence condition is found that is both necessary and sufficient. In order to simplify the formulas for, and theorems about, these solutions, it is convenient to define a *least* solution based on subset relations. Suppose a solution

(p, g, h) has been found (one way or another) for the equation

$$f = [\textbf{if } p \textbf{ then } g \textbf{ else } h \textbf{ fi}]$$

Suppose another solution (p', g', h') has also been found, and further that p, g, h are subfunctions of p', g', h'; that is, $p \subset p'$, $g \subset g'$, $h \subset h'$, and

$$f = [\textbf{if } p' \textbf{ then } g' \textbf{ else } h' \textbf{ fi}]$$

We say that (p, g, h) is a lesser solution than (p', g', h'), and that (p, g, h) is a least solution if there exists no distinct lesser solution than it.

The formula for the ifthenelse equation is the simplest, so we begin with it, then give the ifthen solution as a variation. Next the solution for the sequence equation is given, followed by the solution for the whiledo equation.

6.7.2   The Ifthenelse Formula

Consider the ifthenelse equation

$$f = [\textbf{if } p \textbf{ then } g \textbf{ else } h \textbf{ fi}]$$

and a diagram of the function f as a set, which has been partitioned arbitrarily into two subsets, g and h:

Let p be defined as the predicate function that splits the domain of f into the domains of g and h by its values; that is, p is *true* in the domain of g and *false* in the domain of h. Then (p, g, h) as constructed solves the ifthenelse equation. This simple analysis leads to the following formula.

Ifthenelse Formula. Given any function f, (p, g, h) is a least solution of the ifthenelse equation

$$f = [\textbf{if } p \textbf{ then } g \textbf{ else } h \textbf{ fi}]$$

if and only if

$$(g, h) \text{ is a partition of } f \tag{1}$$

$$p = (D(g) \times \{true\}) \cup (D(h) \times \{false\}) \tag{2}$$

where $D(g)$, $D(h)$ are the domains of g, h, respectively.

Proof.   First, let (p, g, h) be a least solution of the ifthenelse equation

$$f = [\text{if } p \text{ then } g \text{ else } h \text{ fi}]$$

First we note that

[if p **then** g **else** h **fi]**
$$
\begin{aligned}
&= \{(X, Y) \mid (p(X) \wedge Y = g(X)) \vee (\sim p(X) \wedge Y = h(X))\} \\
&= \{(X, Y) \mid p(X) \wedge (X, Y) \in g\} \cup \{(X, Y) \mid \sim p(X) \wedge (X, Y) \in h\} \\
&\subset \{(X, Y) \mid (X, Y) \in g\} \cup \{(X, Y) \mid (X, Y) \in h\} \\
&= g \cup h
\end{aligned}
$$

Then

$f \subset g \cup h$	(as shown above)	(1.1)
$f = g \cup h$	(because (p, g, h) is a least solution)	(1.2)
$g \cap h = \emptyset$	(same reason)	(1.3)

therefore

$$(g, h) \text{ is a partition of } f \tag{1}$$

Also

$D(p) = D(f)$	(because (p, g, h) is a least solution)	(2.1)
$(X, Y) \in g \rightarrow p(X)$	(same reason)	(2.2)
$(X, Y) \in h \rightarrow \sim p(X)$		

therefore

$$p = (D(g) \times \{true\}) \cup (D(h) \times \{false\}) \tag{2}$$

and conditions (1) and (2) are seen to hold.

Conversely, suppose that conditions (1) and (2) hold. Then the program function **[if** p **then** g **else** h **fi]** can be calculated directly as

$$
\begin{aligned}
\{(X, Y) \mid (p(X) \wedge (X, Y) \in g) \vee (\sim p(X) \wedge (X, Y) \in h)\} \\
= \{(X, Y) \mid (X, Y) \in g \vee (X, Y) \in h\} \\
= g \cup h \\
= f
\end{aligned}
$$

Further, every element of p, g, h is used in this calculation, so (p, g, h) is a least solution. This completes the proof.

In illustration, consider the equation

$$z := \max(x, y) = [\text{if } p \text{ then } g \text{ else } h \text{ fi}]$$

where

$$z := \max(x, y) = \{((x, y, z), (x, y, \max(x, y)))\}$$
$$= \{((x, y, z), (x, y, x)) \mid x \geq y\}$$
$$\cup \ \{((x, y, z), (x, y, y)) \mid x < y\}$$

In this case, there is a natural partition of $z := \max(x, y)$ into subsets

$$g = \{((x, y, z), (x, y, x)) \mid x \geq y\}$$
$$h = \{((x, y, z), (x, y, y)) \mid x < y\}$$

which are, in fact, defined by conditional assignments

$$g = (x \geq y \to z := x)$$
$$h = (x < y \to z := y)$$

so that a solution is

$$z := \max(x, y) = [\textbf{if } x \geq y \textbf{ then } z := x \textbf{ else } z := y \textbf{ fi}]$$

Next, the ifthen equation

$$f = [\textbf{if } p \textbf{ then } g \textbf{ fi}]$$

can be treated as a minor variation of the ifthenelse equation that requires a solution to the equation

$$f = [\textbf{if } p \textbf{ then } g \textbf{ else } I \textbf{ fi}]$$

as follows.

Ifthen Formula. Given any function f, (p, g) is a least solution of the ifthen equation

$$f = [\textbf{if } p \textbf{ then } g \textbf{ fi}]$$

if and only if

$$(g \subset f) \wedge (f - g \subset I) \tag{1}$$
$$p = (D(g) \times \{true\}) \cup (D(f - g) \times \{false\}) \tag{2}$$

In illustration, consider the equation

$$y := \max(x, y) = [\textbf{if } p \textbf{ then } g \textbf{ fi}]$$

where

$$y := \max(x, y) = \{((x, y), (x, \max(x, y)))\}$$
$$= \{((x, y), (x, x)) \mid x \geq y\}$$
$$\cup \ \{((x, y), (x, y)) \mid x < y\}$$

and solution

$$y := \max(x, y) = [\textbf{if } x \ge y \textbf{ then } y := x \textbf{ fi}]$$

6.7.3   The Sequence Formula

Consider the sequence formula

$$f = [g; h]$$

and the diagram in Fig. 6.10 of the domains, ranges, and sample members of f, g, h (shown as lines in the diagram). In this diagram, we show two ways to reach a final value Z from an argument X; directly by means of an element $(X, Z) \in f$, and indirectly by elements $(X, Y) \in g$, $(Y, Z) \in h$. This diagram leads to the following formula.

Sequence Formula. Given any function f, (g, h) is a least solution of the sequence equation

$$f = [g; h]$$

if and only if

$$\left. \begin{aligned} D(f) &= D(g) \\ R(f) &= R(h) \\ R(g) &= D(h) \end{aligned} \right\} \tag{1}$$

$$f(X) \ne f(X') \rightarrow g(X) \ne g(X') \tag{2}$$

$$h = f \circ g^T \qquad \text{(where } g^T \text{ is the transpose of } g\text{)} \tag{3}$$

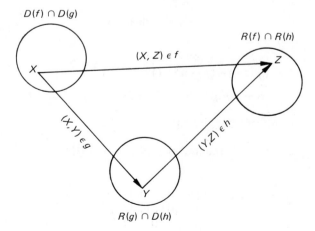

Figure 6.10

In more informal terms, condition (2) can be restated as

$$g(X) = g(X') \rightarrow f(X) = f(X') \tag{2}$$

and each level set† of g must be a subset of some level set of f; that is, the level sets of g are a refinement of the level sets of f. Condition (3) can be pictured in Fig. 6.10 as showing two alternate paths from the point Y to the point Z, the first path being the single line Y to Z (by way of h), the second path being composed of two lines Y to X (by way of g^T, since the direction is backward to g) and X to Z (by way of f).

Proof.   First, suppose that (g, h) is a least solution of the sequence equation

$$f = [g; h]$$

and recall the definition

$$[g; h] = \{(X, Z) \mid \exists Y((X, Y) \in g \wedge (Y, Z) \in h)\}$$

Then, certainly, for any solution (g, h)

$$\left. \begin{array}{l} D(f) \subset D(g) \\ R(f) \subset R(h) \\ R(g) \subset D(h) \end{array} \right\} \tag{1.1}$$

but unless each subset relation is an equality, (g, h) will not be a least solution. Therefore

$$\left. \begin{array}{l} D(f) = D(g) \\ R(f) = R(h) \\ R(g) = D(h) \end{array} \right\} \tag{1}$$

Next, we show condition (2) by contradiction. Suppose there exists X, X' such that

$$f(X) \neq f(X') \wedge g(X) = g(X') \tag{2.1}$$

Then (g, h) cannot be a solution for any function h since

$$h \circ g(X) = h \circ g(X')$$

and

$$f(X) = h \circ g(X) = h \circ g(X') = f(X')$$

but $f(X) \neq f(X')$. Therefore, by contradiction, (2.1) must be false, and

$$f(X) \neq f(X') \rightarrow g(X) \neq g(X') \tag{2}$$

---

† A level set L of function g is a set of arguments with the same value, e.g.,

$$L_y = \{x \mid (x, y) \in g\}$$

as was to be shown. Next, in order to show that condition (3) holds, we observe, if (g, h) is a least solution, that h must be characterized in the form

$$h = \{(Y, Z) \mid \exists X((X, Y) \in g \wedge (X, Z) \in f)\}$$

Now h can be rewritten as

$$h = \{(Y, Z) \mid \exists X((Y, X) \in g^T \wedge (X, Z) \in f)\}$$

so that h is seen to be the composition of g^T and f:

$$h = f \circ g^T$$

Now g^T is not necessarily a function (it is surely a relation), but we will show, with the restriction on g above, that $f \circ g^T$ is indeed a function; that is, given $(Y, Z) \in h$, $(Y, Z') \in h$, then $Z = Z'$. In order to see this, note

$$(Y, Z) \in h \rightarrow \exists X((X, Y) \in g \wedge (X, Z) \in f) \tag{3.1}$$

$$(Y, Z') \in h \rightarrow \exists X'((X', Y) \in g \wedge (X', Z') \in f) \tag{3.2}$$

and assume $Z \neq Z'$ instead. Then

$$
\begin{aligned}
(Z \neq Z') &\rightarrow f(X) \neq f(X') &&\text{(by substitution)} \\
&\rightarrow g(X) \neq g(X') &&\text{(by (2) above)} \\
&\rightarrow \quad Y \neq Y &&\text{(by substitution, using (3.1), (3.2) above)}
\end{aligned}
$$

which is a contradiction. Therefore, $f \circ g^T$ is a function whether g^T is a function or not. This completes the first part of the proof.

Conversely, suppose conditions (1), (2), and (3) hold. First, we note that the contrapositive of condition (2)

$$f(X) \neq f(X') \rightarrow g(X) \neq g(X')$$

is

$$g(X) = g(X') \rightarrow f(X) = f(X') \tag{2c}$$

Next we calculate the program function $[g; h] = h \circ g$ directly, using condition (3):

$$
\begin{aligned}
h \circ g &= (f \circ g^T) \circ g \\
&= f \circ (g^T \circ g)
\end{aligned}
$$

which we can evaluate as follows:

$$
\begin{aligned}
f \circ g^T \circ g(X) &= f \circ g^T(Y) &&\text{where } Y = g(X) \\
&= f(X') &&\text{where } Y = g(X')
\end{aligned}
$$

but, since $g(X) = Y = g(X')$, then $f(X') = f(X)$, by condition (2c), and therefore

$$h \circ g(X) = f(X), \text{ or } h \circ g = f$$

and (g, h) is a solution of the sequence equation. Condition (1) ensures that (g, h) is a least solution, because every member of g and h is required for (g, h) to be a solution. This completes the proof.

In illustration, consider the equation

$$y := \max(x, y) = [g; h]$$

Even though $y := \max(x, y)$ is more naturally expanded as an ifthen, as above, we show that a sequence solution exists, as well. Consider the candidate function

$$g = (y := x - y)$$

We can verify that condition (2) above holds:

$$(x, \max(x, y)) \neq (x', \max(x', y')) \rightarrow (x \neq x') \vee (y \neq y')$$
$$\rightarrow (x, x - y) \neq (x', x' - y')$$

Thus, h can be computed by condition (3) as follows:

$$g^T = \{((x, y), (x, x - y))\}^T$$
$$= \{((x, x - y), (x, y))\}$$

from which we see that

$$g^T = (y := x - y)$$

Therefore, by condition (3)

$$h = f \circ g^T = (y := \max(x, x - y))$$

In order to verify this mechanically derived function h, we observe

$$y := \max(x, y) = [g; h] = [y := x - y; y := \max(x, x - y)]$$

which can be verified directly by use of a trace table.

6.7.4   The Whiledo Formula

The solution of the whiledo equation proceeds as follows. First, there is an existence theorem.

Whiledo Existence Theorem. Given any function f, a solution (p, g) exists for the whiledo equation

$$f = [\textbf{while } p \textbf{ do } g \textbf{ od}]$$

if and only if

$$R(f) \subset D(f) \tag{1}$$

$$X \in R(f) \rightarrow f(X) = X \tag{2}$$

Proof. First, suppose a solution (p, g) exists for the whiledo equation. The first condition follows directly from the whiledo definition. Every value of f (i.e., every member of $R(f)$) is an argument of p, and therefore a member of $D(f)$.

Before proving the remainder of the Existence Theorem, we state and prove a useful, and surprising, Lemma.

Whiledo Predicate Lemma. If (p, g) is a least solution for the whiledo equation

$$f = [\textbf{while } p \textbf{ do } g \textbf{ od}]$$

then

$$p = ((D(f) - R(f)) \times \{true\}) \cup (R(f) \times \{false\})$$

The surprise in the Whiledo Predicate Lemma is that there is no freedom at all in the choice of the predicate of the whiledo expansion of a function.

Proof of Lemma. Suppose $X \in (D(f) - R(f))$ and $\sim p(X)$. Then, with argument X, **while** p **do** g **od** terminates after one evaluation of p without reaching $R(f)$, so (p, g) is not a solution as hypothesized. Therefore $p(X)$ is *true*. Suppose $X \in R(f)$ and $p(X)$. Then **while** p **do** g **od** can never compute value X, because it will continue to iterate, so (p, g) is not a solution as hypothesized. Therefore $p(X)$ is *false*. The foregoing two cases characterize p on the domain of f, for which a least solution p must be defined.

Continuation of Proof of Theorem. Condition (2) now follows from the Whiledo Predicate Lemma

$$X \in R(f) \rightarrow \sim p(X) \rightarrow f(X) = X$$

Conversely, suppose that

$$R(f) \subset D(f) \tag{1}$$

$$X \in R(f) \rightarrow f(X) = X \tag{2}$$

To demonstrate that some solution (p, g) exists, first define predicate p on the domain of f, $D(f)$, such that

$$X \in (D(f) - R(f)) \rightarrow p(X)$$
$$X \in R(f) \rightarrow \sim p(X)$$

Now it can be verified that (p, f) is a solution (albeit trivial) to the whiledo equation, that is

$$[\textbf{while } p \textbf{ do } f \textbf{ od}] = f$$

Note the program **while** p **do** f **od** executes f zero or one time (depending on whether the initial value X is in $R(f)$ or $(D(f) - R(f))$ and then terminates. This completes the proof of the Existence Theorem.

In illustration of the Existence Theorem, note that the add function

$$\text{add} = (x \geq 0 \wedge y \geq 0 \rightarrow x, y := x + y, 0)$$

satisfies the existence condition, for

$$D(\text{add}) = \{(x, y) \mid x, y \geq 0\}$$
$$R(\text{add}) = \{(x, y) \mid x \geq 0 \wedge y = 0\}$$

so that

$$R(\text{add}) \subset D(\text{add}) \tag{1}$$
$$(x, y) \in R(\text{add}) \rightarrow \text{add}(x, 0) = (x + 0, 0) = (x, 0) \tag{2}$$

and therefore a solution to the whiledo equation is possible. The foregoing add function destroys y. Can we amend the specification to

$$\text{add2} = (x \geq 0 \wedge y \geq 0 \rightarrow x, y := x + y, y)?$$

No! For the function add2 violates the existence condition, for example

$$D(\text{add2}) = \{(x, y) \mid x, y \geq 0\}$$
$$R(\text{add2}) = \{(x, y) \mid x \geq y \geq 0\}$$

so that

$$R(\text{add2}) \subset D(\text{add2}) \tag{1}$$

but

$$(x, y) \in R(\text{add2}) \rightarrow \text{add2}(x, y) = (x + y, y) \neq (x, y) \tag{2}$$

The seemingly slight change in specification from add to add2 means the difference between the existence or nonexistence of a whiledo program to satisfy it.

In the case of the add function, we know from the Whiledo Predicate Lemma that the *true* domain of the predicate is

$$D(\text{add}) - R(\text{add}) = \{(x, y) \,|\, x, y \geq 0\} - \{(x, y) \,|\, x \geq 0 \wedge y = 0\}$$
$$= \{(x, y) \,|\, x \geq 0 \wedge y > 0\}$$

Thus, the whiledo program to satisfy add necessarily has the form

$$\textbf{while } y > 0 \textbf{ do } g \textbf{ od}$$

where x and y are understood to be nonnegative throughout. We turn to the characterization of g next.

Whiledo Formula. Given any function f that satisfies the Whiledo Existence Theorem, (p, g) is a least solution of the whiledo equation

$$f = [\textbf{while } p \textbf{ do } g \textbf{ od}]$$

if and only if p is determined by the Whiledo Predicate Lemma and g satisfies the properties

$$D(g) = D(f) - R(f) \tag{1}$$

the graph of g is acyclic $\tag{2}$

$$X \in (D(f) - R(f)) \rightarrow f \circ g(X) = f(X) \tag{3}$$

$$g(X) \in R(f) \rightarrow g(X) = f(X) \tag{4}$$

In more informal terms, condition (3) requires that both X and $g(X)$ are in the same level set of f; hence, with condition (2) we see that g is the "parent function" for a system of trees on the level sets of f with roots in $R(f)$. Conversely, any such parent function defines a correct dopart g.

Proof of Formula. Suppose (p, g) is a least solution. For condition (1) note that g must be defined everywhere in $(D(f) - R(f))$, but need not be defined elsewhere. Condition (2) expresses termination requirements on g. For condition (3), note that $X \in (D(f) - R(f))$ implies that both X and $g(X)$ are in $D(f)$, and **while** p **do** g **od** will compute the same final value from initial values X and $g(X)$; therefore $f(X)$ and $f \circ g(X)$ must be identical, or the whiledo program computes at least one incorrect value. For condition (4), note that the whiledo program terminates (see the Whiledo Predicate Lemma) when $g(X) \in R(f)$; therefore, $g(X)$ must equal $f(X)$ to compute the correct value.

Conversely, suppose g satisfies the conditions above. In particular, the following consequences of the Whiledo Existence Theorem (E), the Whiledo Predicate Lemma (P), and the Whiledo Formula (F), are valid:

$$R(f) \subset D(f) \tag{E1}$$

$$X \in R(f) \rightarrow f(X) = X \tag{E2}$$

$$p = ((D(f) - R(f)) \times \{true\}) \cup (R(f) \times \{false\}) \tag{P}$$

$$D(g) = D(f) - R(f) \tag{F1}$$

the graph of g is acyclic $\tag{F2}$

$$X \in (D(f) - R(f)) \rightarrow f \circ g(X) = f(X) \tag{F3}$$

$$g(X) \in R(f) \rightarrow g(X) = f(X) \tag{F4}$$

Then it can be verified that the whiledo equation is satisfied by applying the Correctness Theorem. Termination of the whiledo is guaranteed by (F1) and (F2) and the condition $C(X, Y)$ is guaranteed by (F3) and (F4). Furthermore (p, g) is a least solution, p by the Whiledo Predicate Lemma, g by condition (F1). This completes the proof of the Whiledo Formula.

Returning to the add function, with program solution developed thus far

$$\text{add} = [\textbf{while } y > 0 \textbf{ do } g \textbf{ od}]$$

we note from the Whiledo Formula that if

$$g(x, y) = (u, v) \qquad (\text{i.e., } g = (x, y := u, v))$$

then, from conditions (F3) and (F4)

$$
\begin{aligned}
y > 0 \rightarrow f \circ g(X) &= f(X) && \text{(from (F3))}\\
\rightarrow \text{add} \circ g(x, y) &= \text{add}(x, y)\\
\rightarrow \text{add}(u, v) &= \text{add}(x, y)\\
\rightarrow (u + v, 0) &= (x + y, 0)
\end{aligned}
$$

$$y = 0 \rightarrow u = x + y \qquad\qquad \text{(from (F4))}$$

Thus, the program must be of the form

$$\text{add} = [\textbf{while } y > 0 \textbf{ do } x := u;\ y := x + y - u \textbf{ od}]$$

where, in addition, u must be chosen so that

$$u \geq 0,\ x + y - u \geq 0$$

because the domain of the add function is composed of nonnegative integers. A very simple, easy choice of u to satisfy these conditions is $u = x + 1$, because

$$x + 1 \geq 0 \qquad \text{(because } x \geq 0)$$
$$x + y - (x + 1) = y - 1 \geq 0 \qquad \text{(because } y > 0)$$

This choice leads to the add program seen before,

$$\textbf{while } y > 0 \textbf{ do } x := x + 1; \ y := y - 1 \textbf{ od}$$

but has been derived mechanically from the intended function except for this simple choice of the form of u above. Note u can be chosen differently, for example as $x + y$. Then the program becomes

$$\textbf{while } y > 0 \textbf{ do } x := x + y; \ y := 0 \textbf{ od}$$

which is satisfactory (if $x + y$ is available for assignment). Note also u can be chosen incorrectly, for example as 0. Then the program becomes

$$\textbf{while } y > 0 \textbf{ do } x := 0; \ y := x + y \textbf{ od}$$

and does not terminate because the graph of g is not acyclic.

EXERCISES

1. Develop corresponding formulas for the dountil and dowhiledo equations, showing also that solutions always exist for both equations.

2. Develop formulas for equations involving compound programs such as
   a) Nested whiledos

$$f = [\textbf{while } p \textbf{ do while } q \textbf{ do } g \textbf{ od od}]$$

   b) Nested ifthenelses

$$f = [\textbf{if } p \textbf{ then if } q \textbf{ then } g \textbf{ else } h \textbf{ fi else } t \textbf{ fi}]$$

7
Writing
Structured
Programs

7.1 OVERVIEW

This chapter describes function-based techniques for writing structured programs. Small structured programs and the individual segments of large ones are written by *stepwise refinement*, the process of expanding intended functions into prime programs and simpler intended functions, and then checking correctness, in a "divide, connect, and check" strategy. The process of applying stepwise refinement in segment-structured programs is known as *top-down programming*. *Stepwise reorganization* is the process whereby a program, large or small, is designed for function first to keep correctness arguments manageable, then reorganized for efficiency in small steps, each shown equivalent to its predecessor. In the examples in this chapter, correctness arguments are presented at a verbal level where appropriate, in terms of the correctness questions, and recorded more systematically where appropriate, in terms of trace tables and more formal arguments. Finally, design concepts for structured programs are illustrated in comparison of program detailing versus program design, and in heuristics versus rigor in design.

7.2 WRITING FUNDAMENTALS

7.2.1 Inventing Structured Programs

Writing structured programs is a creative mental process that requires study and practice for proficiency. As in other forms of expression, reading provides conscious and unconscious mental models for writing. Reading

301

structured programs critically, for correctness and simplicity, builds judgment and confidence for writing. In first learning to write structured programs though, a program idea may occur in thought or intuition without structured form. As a miniature illustration, reconsider the subtract program of Chapter 6 with intended function

$$(x \geq 0 \wedge y \geq 0 \rightarrow x, \ y := x - y, \ \text{free})$$

assuming no subtract operation is available and decrementing must be used. We might give a verbal description of a solution as follows. Reduce x and y each by 1 a step at a time until one of them is 0. Then the result of the subtraction, not including its sign, is the other variable; if y is 0, then x is the result but if x is 0, then $-y$ is the result required. This solution can be composed as the following PDL program (given previously):

while
   $x > 0 \wedge y > 0$
do
   $x, \ y := x - 1, \ y - 1$
od
if
   $y > 0$
then
   $x := -y$
fi
free y

with the flowchart as given in Fig. 7.1.

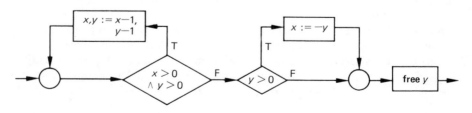

Figure 7.1

But another way of looking at this same problem might have produced instead a flowchart with function and predicate nodes connected as shown in Fig. 7.2, which is not structured in terms of PDL control structures. In fact, the firstpart of this control structure is itself a prime with two predicates. The initial PDL program above combines the tests $x > 0$ and $y > 0$ into one, and repeats the $y > 0$ test—slightly less efficient, but more understandable.

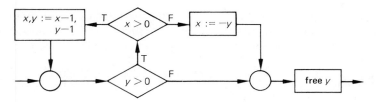

Figure 7.2

Since we want to create structured programs in the first place, we ask, What mental discipline leads to structured solutions instead of unstructured ones? The answer is to simply drop the idea of inventing individual function and predicate nodes, combined into arbitrary control structures. Instead, discipline yourself to expand an intended function directly into a PDL prime or into a simple combination of PDL primes. These are the primitives of structured program design, not individual functions and predicates. When you think in terms of these primitives, the functions and predicates you invent will be naturally combined in an evolving structured program, instead of being connected in some other way, only to be restructured later.

For example, we know that a whiledo loop requires invention of a whiletest and a dopart. In the unstructured program above, a dopart ($x, y = x - 1, y - 1$) appears in the loop, but the potential whiletest is actually a sequence of tests, forming an arbitrary control structure with two exits. The second exit is a convenient place to handle the case of $x_0 < y_0$, but this creates another arbitrary structure. This is improvising with functions and predicates; it is difficult, and often impossible, to produce large programs this way because of the complexity introduced by unrestricted branching in large primes. The required discipline is to design in terms of PDL prime programs, which can be read and verified correct at each step in the design process.

Returning to the verbal description of the structured solution with this discipline in mind, we observe that the subtract problem can be expressed as a sequence of three subproblems—(1) to calculate the magnitude of the difference between x and y; (2) to determine the sign of the difference; and (3) to free y:

> calculate magnitude of $x - y$
> determine sign
> **free** y

The sequence idea may come to mind only after some thinking about the problem, not as a first thought. The point is not top-down thinking, but top-down recording of ideas. It is difficult to write a top-level design until its expansions have been thought through, as the mind ranges over high- and low-level operations and their connections.

The firstpart of the sequence can now be expanded as a whiledo to carry out the required decrementing, and the secondpart can be expanded as an ifthen to determine the sign by finding out which variable, x or y, reached zero:

[calculate magnitude of $x - y$]
while
   $x > 0 \wedge y > 0$
do
   $x, y := x - 1, y - 1$
od
[determine sign]
if
   $y > 0$
then
   $x := -y$
fi
free y

This is an example of thinking in prime programs; it is a technique that, once mastered, can be scaled up to design programs of any size whatsoever.

7.2.2   The Discipline of Function Expansion

Structured programming is a human problem-solving process that creates logical structures for programs. But structured programming also provides a rationale for recording intermediate stages in this process, for better communication and concentration in the mental activity, itself. The principal device for structured programming is embodied in the fundamental Axiom of Replacement for structured programs, namely, replacement of functions by prime programs, as in the prime expansions of PDL:

$f = g; h$
$f = $ **if** p **then** g **else** h **fi**
$f = $ **while** p **do** g **od**
   $\dots$

In sharpening one's own mental discipline, it is important to understand the difference between program inventions that are function expansions as defined above and those that are not. In miniature illustration, suppose an initialized iteration program is constructed to be equivalent to a single function program (Fig. 7.3). That is, we are given an initial function f to expand, and have foreknowledge (for the purpose of this illustration) that the expanded design will end up as an initialized iteration.

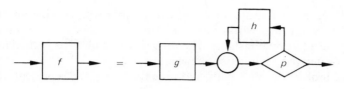

Figure 7.3

Consider two intermediate paths to construct the final design as shown in Fig. 7.4. In the YES path, f is expanded as a sequence of $g;k$, then k is expanded as the iteration **while** p **do** h **od**, while in the NO path, the iteration is developed first and the initialization is prefixed later. The NO path seems a natural one to take, but look at the consequences. While the iteration is probably the most interesting part of the design to be done, the first step on the NO path involves an unrecorded insight, namely, the function k not mentioned there; that is, the iteration "solves part of the problem," but which part is not recorded. Getting to the final design requires this unrecorded insight, so the right g can be picked later to do the initialization. Thus, there are two mental discontinuities on the NO path (the iteration doesn't do f, and the initialized iteration doesn't do the iteration),

$$f \neq [\textbf{while } p \textbf{ do } h \textbf{ od}]$$

and

$$[\textbf{while } p \textbf{ do } h \textbf{ od}] \neq [g; \textbf{while } p \textbf{ do } h \textbf{ od}]$$

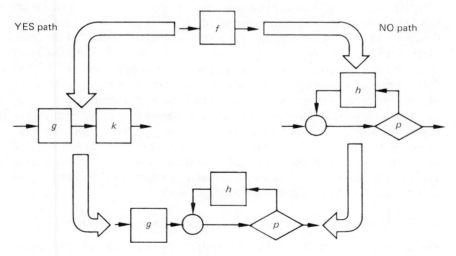

Figure 7.4

which, if recognized at all, must be held in mind while designing. It will be difficult to share this work with a colleague or conduct a design review without the additional insights. The program is structured in final form, but it was not derived by function expansions.

Now look at the YES path, and note that each step represents the same function; that is,

$$f = [g; k]$$

and

$$[g; k] = [g;\ \textbf{while}\ p\ \textbf{do}\ h\ \textbf{od}]$$

In structured programming, function equivalence is preserved, and the correctness of each step can be verified before going on to the next step, in this case by applying the sequence and then the whiledo correctness relations. If the program design is to be written in ten minutes, this may seem a moot point. But if it takes two years (and g takes 10,000 instructions, h takes 100,000 instructions), the point is not so moot.

The foregoing illustrates the reporting of a mental process that is known to the world outside your mind only by what you say or write. But there is no law against your thinking ahead. At the moment the composition

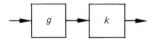

is written down, you had better know that k is going to be an iteration (in fact, an initialized iteration happens so often it is a basic pattern of thought—like a C-major arpeggio for a concert pianist). But what the discipline of writing the sequence does for you is to state what the iteration needs to do, before going into its details. And what the nondiscipline of the NO path often does is invite you into a sea of details before you even write down, or possibly think through, what that sea of details is going to do.

The YES path is a sample of function expansion of a program; that is, beginning with an intended function, a stepwise process of replacing functions by primes and simpler functions, to be carried out until, finally, all functions have been expressed in sufficient detail. Every intermediate function created plays a dual role as an intended function for expansion and as an operation in the prime structure created with it.

7.2.3   Using Program Verification in Program Design

We next present a miniature illustration of the role of correctness verification in program design. Consider a program named SUB whose design is motivated by the familiar subtraction by decrementing, where x, y are integers,

SUB = **while**
$\qquad y > 0$
$\quad$ **do**
$\qquad x, y := x - 1, y - 1$
$\quad$ **od**

and where SUB is an expansion of the intended function sub:

$$\text{sub} = (x, y := x - y, 0)$$

We will look at both questions:

1. Is sub = [SUB]?   (complete correctness)
2. Is sub $\subset$ [SUB]?   (sufficient correctness)

Be forewarned, the answer in both instances is no. But "no" is just as important a guide to design as "yes," and it is instructive to discover how it comes about. The proof is as follows:

function
$\quad$ sub = $(x, y := x - y, 0)$
program
$\quad$ SUB = **while** $y > 0$ **do** $x, y := x - 1, y - 1$ **od**

proof
$\quad$ **term**
$\qquad y$ is decremented at each iteration so whiletest $y > 0$ will eventually fail.
$\qquad$ **pass**

$\quad$ **whiletest true**

part	condition	x	y
$y > 0$	$y_0 > 0$	$x_1 = x_0$	$y_1 = y_0$
$x, y := x - 1, y - 1$		$x_2 = x_1 - 1$	$y_2 = y_1 - 1$
$x, y := x - y, 0$		$x_3 = x_2 - y_2$	$y_3 = 0$

$\qquad$ derivations:
$\qquad\quad y_0 > 0 \qquad x_3 = x_2 - y_2 \qquad\qquad\quad y_3 = 0$
$\qquad\qquad\qquad\qquad\quad = x_1 - 1 - (y_1 - 1)$
$\qquad\qquad\qquad\qquad\quad = x_0 - y_0$

program function:
$(y > 0 \rightarrow x, y := x - y, 0)$
which agrees with sub for whiletest *true.*
pass

whiletest false
The intended function is
$x, y := x - y, 0$
but the program function for $y \leq 0$ is the identity
$x, y := x, y$
and $(x - y, 0) \neq (x, y)$ as seen by counter example:
$x = y = -1: (0, 0) \neq (-1, -1)$
fail

result
fail

We see that the proof fails (for both complete and sufficient correctness)
because the domain of sub includes $y < 0$, which is not properly handled by
SUB. So we go back to redesign either SUB or sub, or both.

One way to solve the problem is to define a new subfunction of sub, say
sub1, to deal only with nonnegative y as

$$\text{sub1} = (y \geq 0 \rightarrow x, y := x - y, 0)$$

Now we will be able to show sufficient correctness, namely that

$$\text{sub1} \subset [\text{SUB}]$$

We record the proof as before:

function
$\text{sub1} = (y \geq 0 \rightarrow x, y := x - y, 0)$

program
$\text{SUB} = \textbf{while } y > 0 \textbf{ do } \overset{*}{x}, y := x - 1, y - 1 \textbf{ od}$

proof
term
y is decremented at each iteration so whiletest $y > 0$ will eventually fail.
pass

whiletest true
same as for $[\text{SUB}] = $ sub proof above
pass

whiletest false (Note $y < 0$ is now excluded.)
    The intended function is
        $x, y := x - y, 0$
    and for $y = 0$
        $(x - y, 0) = (x - 0, 0)$
               $= (x, y)$
    i.e., the required identity.
    pass

  result
    pass suff

Sufficient correctness is all that is possible for sub1, because SUB still handles negative initial values for y. What SUB computes in those cases is not described by sub1.

    The problem can also be solved by defining another new function, say sub2, to be identical with [SUB]:

$$\text{sub2} = (y \geq 0 \rightarrow x, y := x - y, 0 \,|\, y < 0 \rightarrow x, y := x, y)$$

In this case, complete correctness is satisfied. These three results are summarized in the following table of function values for arguments x, y:

function	$y \geq 0$	$y < 0$
[SUB]	$(x - y, 0)$	(x, y)
sub	$(x - y, 0)$	$(x - y, 0)$
sub1	$(x - y, 0)$	undefined
sub2	$(x - y, 0)$	(x, y)

    Still another way to achieve complete correctness is to design a new program, say SUB3, with program function identical with sub:

SUB3 = **while**
      $y > 0$
do
      $x, y := x - 1, y - 1$
od
while
      $y < 0$
do
      $x, y := x + 1, y + 1$
od

In illustration, we will give a proof of complete correctness of SUB3 for sub. First, SUB3 is a sequence of two whiledos, say

$$\text{SUB3} = \text{SUBPOS}; \text{SUBNEG}$$

where

$$\text{SUBPOS} = \textbf{while } y > 0 \textbf{ do } x, y := x - 1, y - 1 \textbf{ od}$$
$$\text{SUBNEG} = \textbf{while } y < 0 \textbf{ do } x, y := x + 1, y + 1 \textbf{ od}$$

Our hypothesized program functions are

$$\text{subpos} = (y > 0 \rightarrow x, y := x - y, 0 \mid y \le 0 \rightarrow x, y := x, y)$$
$$\text{subneg} = (y < 0 \rightarrow x, y := x - y, 0 \mid y \ge 0 \rightarrow x, y := x, y)$$

and the three propositions we need to prove are

$$\text{sub} = \text{subpos; subneg}$$
$$\text{subpos} = [\text{SUBPOS}]$$
$$\text{subneg} = [\text{SUBNEG}]$$

The proofs are independent of one another, and hence the order of proof is immaterial. Once proved, we will have completed the demonstration of $[\text{SUB3}] = \text{sub}$, since

$$[\text{SUB3}] = [\text{SUBPOS; SUBNEG}] = [\text{subpos; subneg}] = \text{sub}$$

The sequence proof is as follows:

function
   $\text{sub} = (x, y := x - y, 0)$

program
   subpos; subneg

proof
   Case 1,1 (i.e., taking part 1 of the subpos conditional rule and taking part 1 of the subneg conditional rule):

part	condition	x	y
$x, y := x - y, 0$	$y_0 > 0$	$x_1 = x_0 - y_0$	$y_1 = 0$
$x, y := x - y, 0$	$y_1 < 0$	$x_2 = x_1 - y_1$	$y_2 = 0$

   derivations:
      $y_0 > 0 \wedge y_1 < 0 = y_0 > 0 \wedge 0 < 0$
      (impossible case)

Case 1,2:

part	condition	x	y
$x, y := x - y, 0$	$y_0 > 0$	$x_1 = x_0 - y_0$	$y_1 = 0$
$x, y := x, y$	$y_1 \ge 0$	$x_2 = x_1$	$y_2 = y_1$

derivations:

$$y_0 > 0 \wedge y_1 \geq 0 \qquad x_2 = x_1 \qquad y_2 = y_1$$
$$= y_0 > 0 \wedge 0 \geq 0 \qquad = x_0 - y_0 \qquad = 0$$
$$= y_0 > 0$$

Case 2,1:

part	condition	x	y
$x, y := x, y$	$y_0 \leq 0$	$x_1 = x_0$	$y_1 = y_0$
$x, y := x - y, 0$	$y_1 < 0$	$x_2 = x_1 - y_1$	$y_2 = 0$

derivations:

$$y_0 \leq 0 \wedge y_1 < 0 \qquad x_2 = x_1 - y_1 \qquad y_2 = 0$$
$$= y_0 \leq 0 \wedge y_0 < 0 \qquad = x_0 - y_0$$
$$= y_0 < 0$$

Case 2,2:

part	condition	x	y
$x, y := x, y$	$y_0 \leq 0$	$x_1 = x_0$	$y_1 = y_0$
$x, y := x, y$	$y_1 \geq 0$	$x_2 = x_1$	$y_2 = y_1$

derivations:

$$y_0 \leq 0 \wedge y_1 \geq 0 \qquad x_2 = x_0 \qquad y_2 = y_0$$
$$= y_0 \leq 0 \wedge y_0 \geq 0 \qquad\qquad\quad = 0$$
$$= (y_0 = 0)$$

program function:

$$(y > 0 \rightarrow x, y := x - y, 0 \mid y < 0 \rightarrow x, y := x - y, 0$$
$$\mid y = 0 \rightarrow x, y := x, 0)$$

or simply,

$$x, y := x - y, 0$$

which is identical with sub, as was to be shown.

result
   pass comp

Next, the proof for subpos is as follows:

function
   subpos $= (y > 0 \rightarrow x, y := x - y, 0 \mid y \leq 0 \rightarrow x, y := x, y)$

program
   SUBPOS $=$ **while** $y > 0$ **do** $x, y := x - 1, y - 1$ **od**

proof
term
y is decremented at each iteration so whiletest $y > 0$ will eventually fail.
pass

whiletest true
Case 1:

part	condition	x	y
$y > 0$	$y_0 > 0$	$x_1 = x_0$	$y_1 = y_0$
$x, y := x - 1, y - 1$		$x_2 = x_1 - 1$	$y_2 = y_1 - 1$
subpos	$y_2 > 0$	$x_3 = x_2 - y_2$	$y_3 = 0$

derivations:

$$y_0 > 0 \wedge y_2 > 0 \qquad x_3 = x_2 - y_2 \qquad\qquad y_3 = 0$$
$$= y_0 > 0 \wedge y_1 - 1 > 0 \qquad = x_1 - 1 - (y_1 - 1)$$
$$= y_0 > 0 \wedge y_0 > 1 \qquad = x_0 - y_0$$
$$= y_0 > 1$$

Case 2:

part	condition	x	y
$y > 0$	$y_0 > 0$	$x_1 = x_0$	$y_1 = y_0$
$x, y := x - 1, y - 1$		$x_2 = x_1 - 1$	$y_2 = y_1 - 1$
subpos	$y_2 \le 0$	$x_3 = x_2$	$y_3 = y_2$

derivations:

$$y_0 > 0 \wedge y_2 \le 0 \qquad x_3 = x_2 \qquad\qquad y_3 = y_2$$
$$= y_0 > 0 \wedge y_1 - 1 \le 0 \qquad = x_1 - 1 \qquad = y_1 - 1$$
$$= y_0 > 0 \wedge y_0 \le 1 \qquad = x_0 - 1 \qquad = y_0 - 1$$
$$= (y_0 = 1)$$

program function:
$$(y > 1 \to x, y := x - y, 0 \mid y = 1 \to x, y := x - 1, y - 1)$$
$$= (y > 1 \to x, y := x - y, 0 \mid y = 1 \to x, y := x - y, 0)$$
$$= (y > 0 \to x, y := x - y, 0)$$
which agrees with subpos for whiletest *true*.
pass

whiletest false
Subpos is the identity by direct examination of its definition.
pass

result
pass comp (The domains of subpos and SUBPOS are identical.)

The proof that subneg = [SUBNEG] is symmetric with that of subpos.

In retrospect, there are several lessons in this example. First, proving correctness not only verifies correctness if it exists, but also suggests ways of redesigning for correctness if it doesn't exist. Second, complete correctness is usually more expensive in program design than sufficient correctness. If a program is well protected from unexpected inputs, sufficient correctness may be a better solution in design economy than complete correctness. Third, the creation of a correct program is more properly viewed as the creation of a correct relationship between a function and a program. If the function is given once and for all with no opportunity for negotiation, then the burden is on the program to be correct in that relationship. But such inviolate functions are in the minority for the simple reason that the program design process itself specifies all the abstract functions of a structured program, except for the highest level function of the entire program.

7.2.4 Logical Commentary in Program Writing

Up to now, logical commentary has been used to describe the abstraction of details in program reading. Given a program, we sought to discover and document its design in a hierarchy of abstractions. In writing readable programs, we reverse the process—to invent design first, details later. Logical commentary is written to record intended functions before going into their expansions (but not before thinking hard about those expansions). Logical commentary for, say, an ifthen prime and its expansion is written as

$[f\text{-action}]$ $[f\text{-action}]$
if   which   **if**
     p expands p
then   to   **then** $[g\text{-action}]$
     g-action g
fi   **fi**

For example (overcommenting for illustration)

$[x, y := \min(x, y), \max(x, y)]$ $[x, y := \min(x, y), \max(x, y)]$
if   **if**
     $x > y$ could $x > y$
then   expand   **then** $[\text{exchange } x, y]$
     exchange x, y to   **initial** $t := x$
fi $x := y$
                                             $y := t$
                                             free t
                              fi

Logical commentary carries forward through successive expansions. Thus, the final version of a program contains its own abstractions, and can be read and understood to any required level of detail. It is usually the case that some parts of a program are self-evident, and can be read and understood directly. So judgment is required to select program parts for commentary. For self-evident operations, an occasional comment will do. But more complex situations may require that every part of every prime be commented. Keep in mind that the reader is attempting to retrace your thoughts on program function and correctness. If a program is properly commented, the reader's reaction will likely be "It is obvious!" at each step along the way.

EXERCISES

1. Design programs by function expansion, with concurrent logical commentary development, for the following functions:

    a) $x, y := \text{abs}(\max(x, y)), \max(\text{abs}(x), \text{abs}(y))$
    b) $x, y, z := \max(y, z), \max(z, x), \max(x, y)$
    c) $z := \min(\max(x - y, x + y), \max(y - x, y + x))$

2. Design programs by function expansion, using logical commentary, to

    a) exchange rows and columns of an $n \times n$ array of integers,
    b) find the sum of the positive members of a set of integers, and
    c) find the largest difference between members of a stack of integers.

7.3   PROGRAMMING STRATEGIES

7.3.1   Programming by Stepwise Refinement

In practice, function expansion leads to the *stepwise refinement* of structured programs, beginning with an intended function to be programmed and a design strategy, proceeding through successive levels of expression, until the entire program has been expanded in sufficient detail. Each refinement step records an expansion of one or more functions into prime programs, or into small structured programs of manageable size, thereby introducing new functions for expansion, and so on. And, of course, the correctness of each refinement is checked, and recorded if necessary, before going on.

    The idea in stepwise refinement is to "divide, connect, and check" an intended function by reexpressing it as an equivalent structure of properly connected subfunctions, each solving part of the problem, and each simpler than the original function to further divide, connect, and check. In carrying out a refinement, look far enough ahead to feel comfortable. If a function is familiar, say, sorting a small table, further thought and elaboration may be unnecessary. If a function is not familiar, refine it far enough to feel comfortable. An evolving structured program defines a natural construction plan for allocating thought and effort to those program parts most in need of elaboration. Each refinement is taken as a working hypothesis for further investigation, to be either judged sound or amended as its implications become clear.

Stepwise refinement of a program or system of programs is undertaken only after a good general approach has been determined and critical details of data representation and algorithms have been settled. Stepwise refinement is a thought-recording process, not a thinking process. In thinking about how to write a program, many possible ideas for organizing control and data and expressing high- and low-level operations circulate in one's mind. The point is to sift through all this to record first major and then minor considerations in successive refinements. Create intermediate levels of expression that explain each step along the way. The ideal is a coherent logical description from summaries at the top, down to implementation in code.

The key to successful program design is rewriting, and more rewriting. One's first design is seldom the best idea for a program. Rethinking and reworking is the rule in good design, not the exception, and many false starts may be made before a programmer is satisfied with the logic and clarity of a design. Every effort should be made at each step to conceive and evaluate alternate designs. So the ability and willingness to redo program parts, and even whole programs, for simplicity and clarity is absolutely critical. The best debugging technique is redesigning programs into simpler and simpler forms.

Every refinement step in a design from highest to lowest, once written, should be completely rigorous, that is, capable of being shown correct. Even for PDL with operations sketched out in natural language, there is no loss of rigor in what must be proved. The idea of rigor at all levels of expression is crucial to success in structured programming. Confidence in the correctness of structured programs is built up out of checking and feeling confident about a few lines of expansion at a time. This is as true for the few lines that summarize the top of a large program, as it is for a few lines of details at the lowest level in that program. Checking for correctness is not possible if refinements are not rigorously expressed, nor is it possible in giant leaps from an intended function to a maze of details in code. Make sure every refinement is clearly expressed and of manageable size, then check it for correctness before going on.

Develop program and proof together, whether the proof is a simple mental conviction or a systematic trace table. Favor designs that are easily verified, and be critical of those that are not. Given a function to refine, develop correctness arguments in your mind ahead of time, for insight into program design. Be both writer and reader of your own programs, to put yourself in the place of someone needing to understand your work. And if the reading gets difficult and the proofs not obvious, think harder about the program. Chances are a simpler, more valuable design can be found.

7.3.2   Case Study: Air Pollution

As a first example of stepwise refinement, consider the following problem:

> Air pollution measurements have been made near the smokestack of a manufacturing plant every minute for up to 24 hours. Sixty measurements are recorded each hour, so a total of $60*n$, $1 \leq n \leq 24$, measurements are present, stored in a sequence named input. Measurement values range from zero to 1000 parts per million (ppm) of pollutant; a value of zero represents an equipment malfunction. Design a program to
>
> 1. Compute mean ppm values for each of the hours for which no malfunction occurred.
> 2. When a zero value (malfunction) is encountered, set the mean ppm value of the current hour to -1 and stop all processing for that hour, including further accumulation of violations (see item 3). However, the number of violations prior to the malfunction must be kept and printed.
> 3. Keep a count of violations per hour. A violation occurs when the pollution value is above 100 ppm for five consecutive minutes, which are not included in some previous violation. For example, 14 consecutive minutes above 100 ppm count as two violations. A violation can span hour changes, and should be assigned to the hour in which it started.
> 4. Print hourly mean values and hourly violations.

In thinking about a design strategy, it seems reasonable to read and process measurements on an hourly basis, since means and violation counts are associated with each hour of data. The mean can be directly computed for an hour's data, but the violation count for an hour is not known until the next hour's data has been checked. Thus, it makes sense to accumulate violations for all hours of data present, then print the hourly violation counts along with the means. So a possible first program, shown in Fig. 7.5, is an initialized whiledo reading and processing one hour's data from input each iteration, followed by printing results. The logical commentary is written informally in natural language, which seems an adequate level of exposition for this straightforward program.

```
1    proc air pollution [find and print means and violations for first hour to last
                         hour]
2        use airpoll
3        hour := 0
4        [find means and violations for next hour to last hour]
5        while
6            input ≠ empty
7        do
8            increment hour; read 60 measurements; find mean and violations
9        od
10       list(output) := means, violations for first hour to last hour
11   corp
```

```
     data airpoll
         scalar
             hour: integer
         sequence
             input: real [pollution measurements every minute for up to 24 hours]
             output: real [hourly means and violation counts for up to 24 hours]
     atad
```

Figure 7.5   Initial air pollution program.

As this first program is written down, we apply the sequence and whiledo correctness questions in our minds. On examination, we believe the sequence is correct, and likewise for the whiledo, since termination is assured, and for *input ≠* **empty** the whiledo (defined on line 4) equals the dopart (line 8) followed by the whiledo. Finally, for *input =* **empty**, the whiledo equals the identity. These arguments are based on operations specified informally in natural language, and, of course, are valid only up to our knowledge of the dopart, currently a working hypothesis for further refinement. Note, however, that this informality does not extend to what must be proved, nor to the necessity for doing so.

A possible elaboration for the dopart is an initialized whiledo, iterating from 1 to 60 minutes, but terminating if a malfunction is detected. The new dopart can add each minute's measurement to a running total and accumulate violations as well. The refinement is shown in Fig. 7.6, a compound program of some 29 lines. But it seems of manageable size and a reasonable next step for this program.

As the refinement was written, it was checked for correctness with the correctness questions in mind. The program thus far finds and prints means and detects malfunctions. But, as always, correctness ultimately depends on expanding the remaining function (line 8.18, "violation processing") within the existing structure.

```
1   proc air pollution [find and print means and violations for first hour
                       to last hour]
2       use airpoll
3       hour := 0
4       [find means and violations for next hour to last hour]
5       while
6           input ≠ empty
7       do [increment hour; read 60 measurements; find mean and violations]
8.1         hour := hour + 1
   2        ppm := list(input)
   3        violations(hour) := 0
   4        sum := 0
   5        malfunction := false
   6        minute := 1
   7        [find hour's sum and violations up to malfunction, if any]
   8        while
   9            minute ≤ 60 ∧ ~ malfunction
  10        do [ppm(minute) = 0 → malfunction := true | ppm(minute) ≠ 0 → add
                 ppm(minute) to sum, process for violation, increment minute]
  11            if
  12                ppm(minute) = 0
  13            then
  14                malfunction := true
  15            else
  16                sum := sum + ppm(minute)
  17                do
  18                    process ppm(minute) for violation
  19                od
  20                minute := minute + 1
  21            fi
  22        od
  23        if
  24            malfunction
  25        then
  26            means(hour) := −1
  27        else
  28            means(hour) := sum/60
  29        fi
   9    od
  10    list(output) := means, violations
  11  corp
```

data airpoll
    scalar
        hour: integer
        malfunction: logical [signals *ppm*(*minute*) = 0]
        minute: integer
        sum: real [sum of hour's measurements]
    array
        means(24): real [mean value or −1 for each hour]
        ppm(60): real [one hour's pollution measurements from *input*]
        violations(24): integer [violation count for each hour]
    sequence
        input: real [pollution measurements every minute for up to 24 hours]
        output: real [hourly means and violation counts for up to 24 hours]
atad

Figure 7.6   First air pollution refinement.

The strategy in mind for violation processing is to count consecutive measurement values over 100 ppm and to assign a violation to the proper hour if the count ever reaches 5; any measurement not over 100 will cause the count to be reset to 0, leading to the refinement shown in Fig. 7.7 (with a new data item named *over*).

In checking correctness, we observe that for *ppm*(*minute*) > 100, *over* is incremented. But what is the initial value of *over*? It has none, and this needs to be fixed. In our dividing and connecting, the division of operations between the previous refinement to process means and the current refinement to process violations was reasonable, but the connecting was faulty. *Over* must be initialized outside the hour loop, to count correctly for the first hour, written in the initial program after line 3 (using line numbers 3a and 3b to preserve numbering not affected):

    . . .
3a   *hour* := 0
3b   *over* := 0
    . . .

A good idea now is to recheck correctness from the top down. The initial program looks correct, but we realize next that *over* must also be reset in the first refinement when a malfunction is detected, since in that case a potential violation cannot straddle the following hour boundary, if any.

```
            . . .
  8.17      do [process ppm(minute) for violation]
    18.1        if
      2              ppm(minute) > 100
      3          then [increment and process violation counter]
      4              over := over + 1
      5              [if violation found, assign it to proper hour and reset over]
      6              if
      7                  over = 5
      8              then [assign violation to proper hour and reset violation counter]
      9                  if
     10                      minute ≤ 4
     11                  then [assign to previous hour]
     12                      violations(hour − 1) := violations(hour − 1) + 1
     13                  else [assign to current hour]
     14                      violations(hour) := violations(hour) + 1
     15                  fi
     16                  over := 0
     17              fi
     18          else [reset violation counter]
     19              over := 0
     20          fi
    19      od
            . . .
```

Figure 7.7   Second air pollution refinement.

Thus, initialization of *over* must be added after line 8.14

```
      . . .
  8.14a   malfunction := true
  8.14b   over := 0
      . . .
```

and now the first refinement is correct. The second refinement now appears correct as well, and the entire program has been elaborated in sufficient detail.

Finally, we note that the air pollution program is an example of a direct form of design, where the details of processing are known at the outset and the major task is to organize them into coherent refinements. Creativity is required mainly in writing for clarity and conciseness. The program itself documents the best evidence of its own correctness, and our mental correctness arguments can be duplicated by any reader, by comparing the intended function and logical commentary with the program text.

7.3.3   Top-Down Structured Programming

The stepwise refinement of large structured programs is carried out by segment structuring, in a process known as top-down structured programming. As described in Chapter 3, a segment is a small structured program, ordinarily a page or less of PDL text, say from 10 to 50 lines. A segment is delimited by **proc** and **corp**, and may refer to other segments in **run** statements. The objective in the use of segments is to control complexity, not only in clean control logic as forced by structured programming but also in limiting the extent of program text the human eye and mind need comprehend at one moment. A segment is a natural unit for recording the stepwise refinement of large programs. It is neither too large a step, leading to more complexity than can be comfortably dealt with, nor too small a step, leading to tedium and loss of continuity. A segment typically deals with a handful of data objects, prime programs, and logical comments that can be organized in the mind and written down as a coherent program. Of course, correctness proofs are still based on the prime programs found within a segment.

The segment concept is used to create large structured programs out of function specifications in a systematic way. We define a task of limited extent and complexity that we can repeat until we get a whole program written to satisfy a function specification. This task is to write a program segment that represents the entire program whose data operations may be names of *subspecifications* (subfunctions) yet to be programmed. Now we repeat this task for each of these named (but unwritten) segments. Again, we want to design a program segment to meet its subspecification, possibly with new segment names at the next level, and relegate further program details to the next level of segments. We continue to repeat this process until we have satisfied the original specification. The end result is a program, of any size whatsoever, that has been organized into a tree structure of named member segments invoked by **run** statements, each of which can be read from top to bottom without any side effects in control logic outside that particular segment.

Since each segment realizes a function, it is possible to progressively implement and test the segment control and data structures provided for newly designated segments at the next level. This is accomplished by introducing dummy versions, called *program stubs*, of the new segments before their creation. The program stubs can print messages (such as "got to segment (name) OK") and internal data values, and they can seize resources in storage and time to simulate their eventual implementation.

Several programmers may be engaged in this activity concurrently, once some initial segments are written. Each programmer can take on a separate segment and work independently within the structure of an overall program design. The hierarchical structure of the segments provides a clean interface between programmers. At any point in the programming, the segments already in existence give a precise and concise framework for the rest of the work to be done.

The air pollution program developed above can provide a miniature illustration of stepwise design, implementation, and testing, using segments, subspecifications, and program stubs. Referring to Fig. 7.6, the operation at line 8.18 is rewritten to invoke a segment at the next level

> ...
>
> 8.18   **run** violation processing (**alt** *violations, over,* **fix** *ppm, hour, minute*)
>
> ...

with subspecification, say

> If *ppm(minute)* $\leq$ 100, set *over* (the violation counter) to 0 and exit. Otherwise, add 1 to *over* and if *over* = 5, a violation has occurred (*ppm(minute)* > 100 for the last five consecutive minutes), so set *over* to 0 and add 1 to the *violations* array member corresponding to the hour in which the violation started. That is, add 1 to *violations(hour)* or *violations(hour − 1)*.

and program stub, say

> **proc** violation processing (**alt** *violations, over,* **fix** *ppm, hour, minute*)
>   **if**
>   *minute* = 1
>   **then**
>   **list**(*output*) := 'beginning to process violations for hour', *hour*
>   **fi**
> **corp**

which prints a message on the first minute of an hour.

The top segment can now be implemented and tested for correct computation of means and detection of malfunctions, and for linkage to the violation processing stub. Next, the violating processing segment can be designed to satisfy its subspecification, and then implemented and tested within an existing structure already known to execute correctly.

7.3.4   Programming by Stepwise Reorganization

The stepwise refinements of a program design record a problem-solving process that is well under control, but a process which may be known more accurately in retrospect than in prospect in complex situations. The complexity of the design task can make it difficult to practice stepwise refinement as a direct activity. Yet the benefits of stepwise refinement are substantial enough to develop new mental procedures to retain those benefits.

In program design situations where complexity makes a stepwise refinement difficult, *stepwise reorganization* may instead be possible. Stepwise reorganization is a programming strategy that arises out of concern for program correctness. The strategy is to keep complexity intellectually manageable by programming for correct function first (ignoring efficiency) by stepwise refinement, then reprogramming for efficiency later by stepwise reorganization. Specifically, the strategy is as follows:

1. *Stepwise refinement*

Use stepwise refinement to design a program with correct function, ignoring matters of efficiency. It is easier said than done for experienced programmers to ignore efficiency in creating proper function, to begin with, because the general problem-solving experience in programming is to interrelate function and efficiency. But the objective of our new mental procedure is to divide and conquer complexity, not just programs. The idea, to begin with, is to define data or control structures with regular, but often inefficient, properties. Ordinarily, designs of this type would not be considered because they do not solve the problem of computation within time and memory constraints. But they can be used to bring complex functions under intellectual control to help solve the problem of design. Efficiency in computation can then be dealt with as an additional objective.

2. *Stepwise reorganization*

Next, the program produced by stepwise refinement is reorganized for efficiency in a series of steps, each small enough so that verification of equivalent function can be done with high confidence. A reorganization step may introduce either a new control logic to process an existing data structure, or a new data structure handled by existing control logic; ordinarily, not both data and control should be changed radically in the same step. Each program version serves as a functional specification for its reorganized successor. In fact, early versions can be implemented to supply inputs for other parts of a larger system under development, once a tolerable level of efficiency has been reached. Note that stepwise reorganization is not just fine tuning, but construction of practical programs, more complex and useful than their less efficient predecessors. In practice, refinement and reorganization steps may combine in an iterative process, whereby each level of a program is designed for correctness by refinement and then reorganized for efficiency before creating further refinements.

3. *Correctness*

Just as stepwise refinement leaves a documented trail of intermediate functions and expansions, stepwise reorganization should leave a trail of structured programs of which only the first is proved correct ab initio and each of the others is proved equivalent to its predecessor. Each reorganization serves as a "verification platform" for the succeeding reorganization, and ordinarily there should be no attempt to explain ab initio why the final program is correct.

4. *Modifications*

In any subsequent modification, the necessary changes should be identified at the first program version affected, and all succeeding versions changed accordingly, with correctness demonstration proceeding as before.

7.3.5   Case Study: World Capitals

In miniature illustration of stepwise reorganization, consider a program to solve a word recognition puzzle:

> Given a list of world capital cities in no particular order and a two-dimensional table of letters, design a program to print each city name on the list that is present in the table, whether spelled horizontally (either direction), vertically (either direction), or diagonally (four possible directions), along with its starting row and column, and direction. (No more than one name starts from a location in a particular direction.) For example, the following name list and table

O	K	E	R	B	Y	L	M
A	L	D	G	O	C	E	V
R	A	S	M	N	S	M	B
T	E	L	O	N	D	O	N
D	U	B	L	H	L	R	C
W	R	S	O	P	I	K	J
A	G	I	B	X	M	U	Z
H	F	Q	G	L	A	M	V

DUBLIN

TOKYO

LONDON

ROME

BONN

PARIS

ZURICH

OSLO

LIMA

have solution:

BONN	1,5	down
LONDON	4,3	right
OSLO	4,4	up left
LIMA	5,6	down
ROME	5,7	up

The program is provided an input sequence containing the number of rows and columns in the letter table, the letter table itself, the number of names and the length of the longest name in the name list, and the name list itself.

The initial objective is a design that is obviously correct, even at the expense of efficiency if necessary. One strategy is to start at every table position and build a character string in every direction, one character at a time, and at each step look for the string in the name list. When all starting positions have been so examined, all names present will have been found and the program will terminate. The strategy is implemented in a first program shown in Fig. 7.8.

In this program, nested loops on row, column, and direction guarantee that every possible string starting from every *table* element will be tested, and printed if it appears in *namelist*.

Next, the dopart function at line 13 can be expanded in a refinement step. In generating strings for testing, one character at a time can be selected from *table* using a fixed displacement corresponding to one of the eight possible directions (shown as row, column pairs):

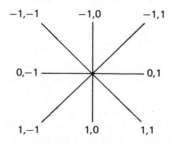

The displacements can be conveniently stored and referenced as an array named *disp* of row, column pairs, proceeding clockwise from vertical, that is, first pair is up, second pair is up right, and so on:

$$(-1, 0), (-1, 1), (0, 1), (1, 1), (1, 0), (1, -1), (0, -1), (-1, -1)$$

326 Writing Structured Programs

```
1    proc world capitals [print namelist words and locations in table, if any]
2        use capitalsdata
3        maxrow, maxcol, table, maxlist, maxname, namelist := list(input)
4        for
5            row :∈ 1 to maxrow
6        do [print namelist words and locations starting table(row), if any]
7            for
8                col :∈ 1 to maxcol
9            do [print namelist words and locations starting table(row,col), if any]
10               for
11                   dir :∈ 1 to 8
12               do
13                   print namelist word and location starting table(row,col) in direction
                     dir, if any
14               od
15           od
16       od
17   corp
```

```
data capitalsdata
    scalar
        maxrow: integer [number of rows]
        maxcol: integer [number of columns]
        maxlist: integer [number of city names in namelist]
        maxname: integer [number of characters in longest city name]
    array
        table(maxrow,maxcol): character [array of letters]
        namelist(maxlist,maxname): character [city names possibly present in
                                                           table]
    sequence
        input
        output
atad
```

Figure 7.8   Initial world capitals program.

Row and column displacements for some value of *dir*, the fordo loop index, are thus given by *disp*(*dir*,1) and *disp*(*dir*,2), respectively. A possible refinement step based on this strategy is shown in Fig. 7.9. The refinement appears correct; systematic application of horizontal and vertical displacements in the *disp* array ensures that the proper comparison strings will be built in each direction, up to the edge of *table* or to a length equal to *maxname*. This completes a stepwise refinement process. We turn to stepwise reorganization next.

In the program of Fig. 7.9, concatenating and searching for a character string can continue beyond the possibility of a match (and, in fact, beyond a match). So a first reorganization step might be to stop looking when the character string formed so far in some direction is not a left substring of any name in *namelist* (i.e., *string* fails to match the beginning of any name), and begin a new direction or new starting point. To implement, we add a new logical variable named *looking* and rewrite and renumber the expansion of

```
        . . .
12      do [print namelist word and location starting table(row, col) in direction dir, if
            any]
13.1        rowhead, colhead := row, col
   2        length, string := 1, all blanks
   3        while
   4            (1 ≤ rowhead ≤ maxrow) ∧ (1 ≤ colhead ≤ maxcol) ∧ (length ≤ maxname)
   5        do [add letter in direction to string and print with location
                if found in namelist]
   6            string(length) := table(rowhead, colhead)
   7            search for string in namelist
   8            if
   9                string found
  10            then
  11                list(output) := string, row, col, dir
  12            fi
  13            length := length + 1
  14            rowhead, colhead := rowhead + disp(dir, 1), colhead + disp(dir, 2)
  15        od
14      od
        . . .
```

```
        . . .
scalar
        rowhead: integer [row of next letter added to string]
        colhead: integer [column of next letter added to string]
        length: integer [current number of characters in string]
array
        string(maxname): character [test string for comparison with namelist
                            names]
        disp(8, 2): integer, init((−1, 0), (−1, 1), (0, 1), (1, 1), (1, 0), (1, −1),
                     (0, −1), (−1, −1) [row, column displacements for next charac-
                            ter to be added to string]
        . . .
```

Figure 7.9   First world capitals refinement.

...

12	**do** [print *namelist* word and location starting *table*(*row*, *col*) in direction *dir*, if any]
13.1	*rowhead, colhead* := *row, col*
2	*length, string* := 1, all blanks
3	*looking* := **true**
4	**while**
5	$(1 \leq rowhead \leq maxrow) \wedge (1 \leq colhead \leq maxcol) \wedge looking$
6	**do** [add letter in direction to *string*; print with location if found in *namelist* and signal end search, otherwise if left substring found continue search, else signal end search]
7	*string*(*length*) := *table*(*rowhead, colhead*)
8	search for *string* in *namelist*
9	**if**
10	*string* found
11	**then** [print *string* with location and signal end search]
12	**list**(*output*) := *string, row, col, dir*
13	*looking* := **false**
14	**else** [continue search if left substring found in *namelist*, otherwise signal end search]
15	search for left substring in *namelist*
16	**if**
17	left substring found
18	**then** [prepare to extend *string*, continue search]
19	*length* := *length* + 1
20	*rowhead, colhead* := *rowhead* + *disp*(*dir*, 1), *colhead* + *disp*(*dir*, 2)
21	**else** [signal end search]
22	*looking* := **false**
23	**fi**
24	**fi**
25	**od**
14	**od**

...

Figure 7.10   First world capitals reorganization.

line 13 as shown in Fig. 7.10. Note that it is no longer necessary to verify that the substring is less than the maximum name size.

The reorganization appears to correctly carry out the action specified on line 12. It eliminates unnecessary searches where no match is possible, but at the expense of new searches in an unsorted *namelist* for left substrings. Thus, an additional reorganization is possible to speed up the searches, by sorting *namelist* to begin with, and limiting successive searches to that partition of *namelist*, if any, that contains left substrings matching the *string* built

so far. For example, if left substring "rom" is present in *namelist*, the subsequent search with a character appended to "rom" need only scan that
partition of *namelist* whose names begin with "rom". This reorganization
adds variables *low* and *high* to denote the current active partition of *namelist*

> . . .
> **scalar**
>> *low*: integer [location of current lowest matching substring]
>> *high*: integer [location of current highest matching substring]
> . . .

and sorts *namelist* at the head of the program. *Low* and *high* are initialized at
the start of the "**for** direction" loop, and updated in a new segment named
bracket, which carries out the following subspecification:

> Set *low* and *high* to first and last *namelist* positions, respectively, of those
> names, if any, with left substrings matching *string* (of *length* characters);
> otherwise set *low* = *high* = 0.

When *low* = *high* = 0, or *low* = *high* and *string* is not found at that point in
namelist, *looking* is set **false**, and the scan continues from a new direction or
starting point, all shown in the reorganized and renumbered program of Fig.
7.11.

Is the reorganization correct? Scans of the original unsorted *namelist* in
the previous program have been replaced by searches of a partition of
matching left substrings in the sorted *namelist*. In the reorganized program,
no match is possible above or below the matching partition, and if the
matching partition reduces to one name, that name will match *string*, if any
name matches. Thus, no outcome is lost, and the search process has been
speeded up.

This strategy suggests a further improvement to perform a separate
bracket search as a special case when starting at a new table element, since a
new first character heads up strings in eight possible directions, all requiring
identical first searches. Further searches beginning with that character can
be skipped if it is not found in *namelist*; and if it is found, the searches can
begin with the second character in each direction. The reorganization, with
new scalar integers l and h, is shown (see Fig. 7.12) in a renumbered program
that requires an initial successful bracket search before building and testing
strings in each direction. Again, no possible outcome is lost (assuming there
are no one-character city names), and redundant searches have been eliminated, to produce a reasonably efficient program.

```
 1   proc world capitals [print namelist words and locations in table, if any]
 2      use capitalsdata
 3      maxrow, maxcol, table, maxlist, maxname, namelist := list(input)
 4      run sort(alt namelist, fix maxlist)
 5      for
 6         row :∈ 1 to maxrow
 7      do [print namelist words and locations starting table(row), if any]
 8         for
 9            col :∈ 1 to maxcol
10         do [print namelist words and locations starting table(row, col) if any]
11            for
12               dir :∈ 1 to 8
13            do [print namelist word and location starting table(row, col) in direc-
                  tion dir, if any]
14               low, high := 1, maxlist
15               rowhead, colhead := row, col
16               length, string := 1, all blanks
17               looking := true
18               while
19                  (1 ≤ rowhead ≤ maxrow) ∧ (1 ≤ colhead ≤ maxcol) ∧ looking
20               do [add letter in direction to string; print with location if found in
                     namelist and signal end search, otherwise if left substring found
                     continue search, else signal end search]
21                  string(length) := table(rowhead, colhead)
22                  run bracket (alt low, high, fix string, length, namelist, maxlist)
23                  if
24                     low > 0
25                  then
26                     if
27                        namelist(low) = string
28                     then [print string with location and signal end search]
29                        list(output) := string, row, col, dir
30                        looking := false
31                     else [prepare to extend string, continue search]
32                        length := length + 1
33                        rowhead, colhead := rowhead + disp(dir, 1),
                           colhead + disp(dir, 2)
34                     fi
35                  else [signal end search]
36                     looking := false
37                  fi
38               od
39            od
40         od
41      od
42   corp
```

Figure 7.11   Second world capitals reorganization.

```
1   proc world capitals [print namelist words and locations in table, if any]
2       use capitalsdata
3       maxrow, maxcol, table, maxlist, maxname, namelist := list(input)
4       run sort (alt namelist, fix maxlist)
5       for
6           row :∈ 1 to maxrow
7       do [print namelist words and locations starting table(row), if any]
8           for
9               col :∈ 1 to maxcol
10          do [print namelist words and locations starting table(row, col), if any]
11              low, high := 1, maxlist
12              length, string := 1, all blanks
13              string(length) := table(row, col)
14              run bracket (alt low, high, fix string, length, namelist, maxlist)
15              if
16                  low > 0
17              then
18                  for
19                      dir :∈ 1 to 8
20                  do [print namelist word and location starting table(row, col) in
                        direction dir, if any]
21                      rowhead, colhead := row + disp(dir, 1), col + disp(dir, 2)
22                      l, h := low, high
23                      length, looking := 2, true
24                      while
25                          (1 ≤ rowhead ≤ maxrow) ∧ (1 ≤ colhead ≤ maxcol) ∧ looking
26                      do [add letter in direction to string; print with location if found
                            in namelist and signal end search, otherwise if left substring
                            found continue search, else signal end search]
27                          string(length) := table(rowhead, colhead)
28                          run bracket (alt l, h, fix string, length, namelist, maxlist)
29                          if
30                              l > 0
31                          then
32                              if
33                                  namelist(l) = string
34                              then [print string with location and signal end search]
35                                  list(output) := string, row, col, dir
36                                  looking := false
37                              else [prepare to extend string, continue search]
38                                  length := length + 1
39                                  rowhead, colhead := rowhead + disp(dir, 1),
                                        colhead + disp(dir, 2)
40                              fi
41                          else [signal end search]
42                              looking := false
43                          fi
44                      od
45                  od
46              fi
47          od
48      od
49  corp
```

Figure 7.12 Third world capitals reorganization.

EXERCISES

Use stepwise refinement and reorganization to design programs for the intended functions described in Exercises 1–10. The function definitions may be elaborated, if necessary, to create a correspondence with their program designs.

1. Design a program to determine if an input sequence of characters is a true palindrome (reads identically in both directions), a packed palindrome (reads identically in both directions with blanks removed), or neither.

2. Consider an $m \times m$ array named *crossword*, in which each element is a number, blank, or "#", and two sequences named *across* and *down*, in which each element is a pair consisting of a square number and a word. It is alleged that *across* and *down* define a solution for the crossword. Design a program to verify this allegation.

3. Consider an $m \times m$ array named *solution*, in which each element is a letter or "#", which represents a filled-in crossword. Design a program to decompose the crossword, by numbering squares where words begin, converting letters to blanks, and creating the corresponding across and down lists of numbered words.

4. Consider an m-element array named *box*, each element an integer triple (l, w, h) of box dimensions, and an n-element array named *paper*, each element an integer pair (s, t) of paper dimensions. Design a program to determine an $m \times n$ array named *wrap*, with element values T or F for the questions of whether $box(i)$, $1 \leq i \leq m$, can be wrapped (overlap allowed) by $paper(j)$, $1 \leq j \leq n$, without cutting the paper and with box edges parallel to paper edges.

5. Given an input sequence that contains (a) numbers separated by blanks, with numbers in forms of decimal integer; fixed point; floating point (with decimal point in any location); and Roman numerals (up to 9999); and (b) possible "garbage" characters, design a program to convert numbers into standard floating point form, and print them.

6. Given a symmetric $m \times m$ array named *line*, of 0's and 1's, that defines a network among places $1, \ldots, m$ ($line(i, j) = 1$ if a line exists between i and j), design a program to print all complete subnetworks (that is, clusters of places in which every place connects to every other place).

7. Given an $m \times m$ array named *line*, of 0's and 1's, that defines the control structure of a flowchart ($line(i, j) = 1$ if node i connects to node j), design a program to list all proper control structures.

8. Given an input sequence text string named t, an input sequence substring named s, and an input sequence replacement string named r, design a program to find the first occurence of s in t, if any, and replace it by r, then print the resulting string. Consider t to wrap around, that is, the first character of t follows the last character of t.

9. Consider an input sequence named *input*, containing telegrams (words separated by blanks, word a string of nonblank characters), each telegram ending with word "zzzz," and the sequence ending with an additional "zzzz." Design a program to print each telegram, omitting "zzzz" and "stop," followed by a count of words ("zzzz" and "stop" don't count), and the word "overlength" if any word exceeds 12 characters.

10. Consider two large $n \times n$ sparse arrays (with a small fraction of nonzero members) stored in two sequences of triples (i, j, v) for (row, column, value), respectively, in sorted order (row major). Design an efficient program for minimum storage to add and multiply such arrays and put the results into another sequence. Note that addition of arrays is addition of corresponding elements; multiplication is given by the inner product of rows and columns, that is, for result c of the multiplication of arrays a and b,

$$c(i, j) = a(i, 1)*b(1, j) + \cdots + a(i, n)*b(n, j)$$

7.4   A CASE STUDY IN DETAILING AND DESIGN: LONG DIVISION

7.4.1   Detailing Versus Design

The invention of suitable abstractions for expressing and communicating design ideas is a crucial aspect of structured programming. Design abstractions can reduce the complexity of programs and their correctness proofs, and provide a foundation for stepwise refinement into further details.

Detailing is programming without the benefit of design abstractions. It is "stream-of-consciousness" programming, detailing whatever processing requirements come to mind, inventing "flags" and "counters" to control the accumulation of data assignments and tests, all with insufficient regard for the impact on program structure. Detailing leads to programs that are larger than necessary, with more data objects than necessary, and with parts that seldom fit together as hoped. On the basis of size alone, programs produced by detailing are ordinarily more difficult to prove correct, and less likely to be understood by others.

Of course, in the final stages of stepwise refinement, details of local operations must be specified, and at bottom, a stepwise-refined program is all details. But such a program contains its own design, as well, in initial and intermediate abstractions documented in logical commentary, and can be verified to be correct in steps based on levels of abstraction. But a program produced by detailing contains only its details, not its design, and documenting details after the fact rarely uncovers a coherent design.

So if you find yourself simply enumerating details at a low level and adding more and more data objects, with no end in sight, stop. Reflect on the problem at hand. Go back to definitions in the problem, and look for deeper simplicities. Search for general principles on which to base abstractions. In short, be satisfied with your design at every level before filling in its details.

7.4.2   A Long-Division Problem

In illustration of the difference between detailing and design, consider a long-division problem for a "decimal processor" with roughly the same capabilities as a human being—namely, the ability to do digit-by-digit arithmetic, and to make use of place notation for comparing decimal numbers and for multiplying by powers of 10, etc. However, in order to provide explicit instructions for the processor, the places of digits in numbers must also be made explicit as other "control numbers" that are given in the same place notation as the original numbers. And arithmetic operations will be useful in manipulating these control numbers as well.

Specifically, given two positive integers, a divisor named a of m decimal digits and a dividend b of n decimal digits, the requirement is to determine a quotient q and remainder r in decimal digit form, such that

$$b = a*q + r, 0 \leq r < a$$

The decimal processor for long division supports only a single data type, namely, strings of decimal data in ordinary positional notation. In programming the processor, decimal data strings, substrings, and individual digits may be referenced. The processor permits decimal data assignment, addition, subtraction, and arithmetic comparison. In all such operations, low-order digits are aligned, and the usual digit-by-digit, carry-and-borrow operations apply. On assignment, high-order zeros fill digit positions not explicitly assigned.

We elect to augment PDL for this processor with a special outer syntax data structure for decimal data, declared by the keyword **decimal**. For example,

$$\textbf{decimal } x(4), y(1), z(j), j(n), k(n)$$

declares strings named x, y, z, j, and k to be 4, 1, j, n, and n decimal digits, respectively. The usual convention is that the highest and lowest index values correspond to the most and least significant digits, respectively. Thus, if $x = 2946$, then

$$x(4) = 2, x(1) = 6, \text{ and } x(3{:}1) = 946.$$

Decimal strings are understood to be initialized to zero on declaration, unless otherwise specified. Arrays of decimal digit strings can be specified by multiple indexes. For example,

$$\textbf{array } u(3) \textbf{ decimal } (4)$$

declares an array named u of 3 digit strings, each with 4 digits. Thus, if $u = 3745,2165,3124$, then

$$u(2) = 2165, u(2, 3) = 1, \text{ and } u(3, 4{:}2) = 312.$$

The permissible decimal string operations of the decimal processor are summarized in the following example, for the declarations above:

$j := 4$ $(j(n:2) = 0, j(1) = 4)$

$k(1) = 1$ $(k(n:2) = 0, k(1) = 1)$

$x(j:k) := 2301$ $(x = 2301)$

$y := x(j) + 3 - x(k)$ $(y = 4)$

$z(3:k) := x(j:3)*6$ $(z = 0138)$

$z(4:1) := z(3:2)$ $(z = 0013)$

if

   $z(1) > x(j)$ $(3 > 2 = true)$

then

   $y := y*y$ (fails to execute, since $y*y = 16$, which overflows on

fi   assignment to y)

7.4.3   Detailing through Direct Experience

Long division can be accomplished by repeated subtraction of the divisor from the dividend, adding one to the quotient with each repetition. But this is inefficient, since a large number of subtract operations may be required. However, if the divisor is aligned with the proper leftmost digits of the dividend, as in grade-school long division, then quotient digits are determined from highest place down to lowest place, a more efficient process. Thus, a possible programming strategy is based directly on the digit operations of long division, as taught in grade-school arithmetic, and which correspond to operations available in the decimal processor.

The sequence of steps that produces the following display, for example,

```
            1 0 5 3
   2 1 7 |2 2 8 5 9 6
           2 1 7
           1 1 5
               0
           1 1 5 9
           1 0 8 5
               7 4 6
               6 5 1
                 9 5
```

uses divisor $a = 217$ and dividend $b = 228596$ to compute quotient $q = 1053$ and remainder $r = 95$. We can describe this long-division algorithm a step at a time in digit-by-digit operations. At each step, a new digit must be found that most nearly divides a sequence of digits by the divisor. We decide to use the name "partial dividend" for this sequence of digits. For example, with partial dividend 115 and divisor 217, the quotient digit required is 0, since 217 goes into 115 zero times; and with partial dividend 1159, the required quotient digit is 5, since 217 goes into 1159 five times but not six times. In order to get the process started, an initial partial dividend must be identified. It can be found by marking off (left to right) an equal number of digits of the dividend as are found in the divisor, if that partial dividend equals or exceeds the divisor; otherwise by marking off one more digit. If the dividend does not have enough digits to form an initial partial dividend, then the quotient is zero and the remainder is the dividend, itself. We reflect this initialization in a new display, as follows:

```
            1 0 5 3
        _____
2 1 7 | 2 2 8 5 9 6
        2 2 8            (mark off initial partial dividend)
        2 1 7            (enter 1*divisor)
        _____
        1 1 5            (subtract and bring down digit for next partial
                          dividend)
              0          (enter 0*divisor)
        _____
        1 1 5 9          (subtract and bring down digit for next partial
                          dividend)
        1 0 8 5          (enter 5*divisor)
        _____
            7 4 6        (subtract and bring down digit for next partial
                          dividend)
            6 5 1        (enter 3*divisor)
            _____
              9 5        (remainder)
```

Thus, the partial dividends are, successively, 228, 115, 1159, and 746.

Although a person might make a good guess of the next digit of the quotient at each step, a simpler, mechanical procedure is to compare successive multiples of the divisor with the partial dividend, and to back up one multiple as soon as a multiple exceeds this partial dividend. Since the same divisor will be used at each step, we decide to store a table of multiples of the divisor for use from step to step. It may be even better to build up the table of multiples as needed during the division process, since not all multiples may be needed. For example, we could define a table of multiples, say e, with 11 rows of $m + 1$ digits each for a divisor of m digits. Thus, row 1 is 0 times the divisor, row 2 is 1 times the divisor, and so on. Note that this table can be built up by addition, since multiplication is not available in the decimal processor. We can also keep track of how many multiples have been computed and stored in e at any point in the process by an index named f. Then, at each step, if more multiples are required, we can update table e and index f accordingly.

During the process each new partial dividend is formed by subtracting the correct multiple of the divisor from the previous partial dividend and bringing down the next digit from the dividend. We decide to store these partial dividends in a digit string, say g, of dimension $(m + 1)$. In terms of data, a new partial dividend is obtained by (1) subtracting a correct multiple (i.e., row of table e) from the number represented by g, (2) moving digits of g one place to the left, and (3) bringing down the correct digit from digit string b, which holds the dividend, into the low-order-digit position of g. The division process stops when a partial dividend less than the divisor has been found (possibly 0) and no more digits remain in the dividend to bring down.

The long-division strategy described above can be programmed as follows. We write a top segment first, as shown in Fig. 7.13. It runs a segment

```
proc long division(a(m:1), b(n:1), q(p:1), r(p:1))
    use long division data
    run first partial dividend
    while
        g(m + 1:1) ≠ 0
    do
        run quotient digit
    od
corp


data long division data
    decimal
        a(m:1)       [divisor]
        b(n:1)       [dividend]
        q(p:1)       [quotient, most significant digit is q(1)]
        r(p:1)       [remainder]
        g(m + 1:1)   [partial dividend]
        m            [number of digits in divisor]
        n            [number of digits in dividend]
        p            [number of digit positions for quotient and remainder,
                      assumed sufficiently large]
        f            [e array pointer]
    array e(0:10) decimal (m + 1)  [0*divisor in first row, up to 10*divisor in
                                    last row]
atad
```

Figure 7.13 Top long-division segment.

named *first partial dividend* to compute an initial g, and as long as $g \neq 0$, it runs a segment named *quotient digit* to compute a q digit, subtract, and form the next partial dividend (parameter lists not shown). The development of the first partial dividend segment, shown in Fig. 7.14, is a progression of three steps, followed by some imagined "stream-of-consciousness" thoughts by the programmer that led to the successive versions. The quotient digit segment is developed in Fig. 7.15, likewise in a series of steps.

[First step]

$$\begin{aligned}
&\textbf{proc } \text{first partial dividend}\\
&\quad\textbf{if}\\
&\qquad (m > n) \vee (m = n \wedge a(m{:}1) > b(n{:}1))\\
&\quad\textbf{then}\\
&\qquad q(p{:}1) := 0\\
&\qquad r(n{:}1) := b(n{:}1)\\
&\qquad g(m + 1{:}1) := 0\\
&\quad\textbf{else}\\
&\qquad\textbf{if}\\
&\qquad\quad m = n\\
&\qquad\textbf{then}\\
&\qquad\quad g(m{:}1) := b(n{:}1)\\
&\qquad\quad g(m + 1) := 0\\
&\qquad\quad bp := 0 \qquad [b \text{ pointer}]\\
&\qquad\textbf{else}\\
&\qquad\quad\textbf{if}\\
&\qquad\qquad b(n{:}n - m + 1) \geq a(m{:}1)\\
&\qquad\quad\textbf{then}\\
&\qquad\qquad g(m{:}1) := b(n{:}n - m + 1)
\end{aligned}$$

Programmer's thoughts. This program is getting complicated. The first thenpart is for divisor > dividend, when the partial dividend is 0, and the quotient must be set to 0 and the remainder set to the dividend. The nested thenpart is for divisor ≤ dividend, but with the same number of digits. The partial dividend here should be all the digits of the dividend. The index named bp indicates the number of digits left in the dividend. The nested elsepart is for more digits in the dividend than in the divisor. The expression $n - m + 1$ identifies the least significant digit of the m leftmost digits of b. It seems better to stop at this point and record these facts as comments before they are forgotten.

Figure 7.14   First partial dividend segment, first step.

[Second step]

> **proc** first partial dividend
>   **if**
>
> $$(m > n) \vee (m = n \wedge a(m{:}1) > b(n{:}1))$$
>
>   **then** [set quotient to 0, remainder to dividend, partial dividend
>   to 0]
> $q(p{:}1) := 0$
> $r(n{:}1) := b(n{:}1)$
> $g(m + 1{:}1) := 0$
>   **else**
>   **if**
>
> $m = n$
>
>   **then** [bring down all m digits from b into g; set b pointer to
>   indicate no more dividend digits available]
> $g(m{:}1) := b(n{:}1)$
> $g(m + 1) := 0$
> $bp := 0$
>   **else** [bring down necessary leftmost digits from b into g, set b
>   pointer to point to next available digit in dividend]
>   **if**
>
> $b(n{:}n - m + 1) \geq a(m{:}1)$ [note: $b(n - m + 1)$ identifies
>   least significant digit of the
>   leftmost m digits of b]
>
>   **then**
> $g(m{:}1) := b(n{:}n - m + 1)$

Programmer's thoughts. Now the program is more comprehensible. There are two subcases remaining to be programmed. If the high-order m digits of the dividend form a number greater than or equal to the divisor, the partial dividend must be set to these digits, otherwise the partial dividend must be set to the high-order $m + 1$ digits of the dividend. The two subcases can now be finished and the quotient digit computation initialized.

Figure 7.14 (continued)   First partial dividend segment, second step.

[Third step]

> **proc** first partial dividend
>> **if**
>>> $(m > n) \vee (m = n \wedge a(m\!:\!1) > b(n\!:\!1))$
>>
>> **then** [set quotient to 0, remainder to dividend, partial dividend to 0]
>>> $q(p\!:\!1) := 0$
>>> $r(n\!:\!1) := b(n\!:\!1)$
>>> $g(m + 1\!:\!1) := 0$
>>
>> **else**
>>> **if**
>>>> $m = n$
>>>
>>> **then** [bring down all m digits from b into g; set b pointer to indicate no more dividend digits available]
>>>> $g(m\!:\!1) := b(n\!:\!1)$
>>>> $g(m + 1) := 0$
>>>> $bp := 0$
>>>
>>> **else** [bring down necessary leftmost digits from b into g, set b pointer to point to next available digit in dividend]
>>>> **if**
>>>>> $b(n\!:\!n - m + 1) \ge a(m\!:\!1)$ [note: $b(n - m + 1)$ identifies least significant digit of the leftmost m digits of b]
>>>>
>>>> **then** [bring down m leftmost digits from b into g; set b pointer to next available dividend digit]
>>>>> $g(m\!:\!1) := b(n\!:\!n - m + 1)$
>>>>> $g(m + 1) := 0$
>>>>> $bp = n - m$
>>>>
>>>> **else** [bring down $m + 1$ leftmost digits from b into g; set b pointer to next available dividend digit]
>>>>> $g(m + 1\!:\!1) := b(n\!:\!n - m)$
>>>>> $bp := n - m - 1$
>>>>
>>>> **fi**
>>>
>>> **fi**
>>
>> **do** [initialize e array and qp, the quotient pointer]
>>> $f := 0$
>>> $e(f, m + 1\!:\!1) := 0$
>>> $qp := 0$
>>
>> **od**
>>
>> **fi**
>
> **corp**

added data items:
> qp [quotient pointer]
> bp [dividend pointer]

Figure 7.14 (continued)   First partial dividend segment, third step.

[First step]　　　　　**proc** quotient digit
$$qp := qp + 1$$
$$i := 0$$
while
$$e(i, m + 1{:}1) \le g(m + 1{:}1)$$
do
$$i := i + 1$$
if
$$i > f$$
then
$$f := f + 1$$
$$e(f, m + 1{:}1) := e(f - 1, m + 1{:}1) + a(m{:}1)$$
fi
od
$$g(m + 1{:}1) := g(m + 1{:}1) - e(i - 1, m + 1{:}1)$$
$$q(qp) := i - 1$$

Programmer's thoughts. This program is also getting complicated and could benefit from some logical commentary while the operations are still fresh in mind. The whiledo loop must search for (and compute if necessary) the first row of table e that exceeds the partial result g. The partial result is then reduced by the proper row of e (the $(i - 1)$ row, since i corresponds to the first row of e that exceeds the partial result) and the current quotient digit is set to $i - 1$.

Figure 7.15　Quotient digit segment, first step.

[Second step]　　　　**proc** quotient digit
$$qp := qp + 1$$
$$i := 0$$
while
$$e(i, m + 1{:}1) \le g(m + 1{:}1)$$
do [increment i; ensure ith row of e is available]
$$i := i + 1$$
if
$$i > f$$
then [set f to point to ith row of e; set ith row to next
　　　　multiple of divisor]
$$f := f + 1$$
$$e(f, m + 1{:}1) := e(f - 1, m + 1{:}1) + a(m{:}1)$$
fi
od [correct multiple is row $i - 1$ of e]
do [subtract correct multiple of divisor from partial
　　　dividend and assign quotient digit]
$$g(m + 1{:}1) := g(m + 1{:}1) - e(i - 1, m + 1{:}1)$$
$$q(qp) := i - 1$$　　　　　　　　[Note: Most significant digit of
od　　　　　　　　　　　　　　　q is $q(1)$.]

Programmer's thoughts. The program is now more understandable. It can be completed by computing a new partial dividend for the next iteration of the top segment. If no digits remain in the dividend, then the remainder must be set to the partial dividend (possibly 0) and the partial dividend set to 0 to terminate the program.

Figure 7.15 (continued)　Quotient digit segment, second step.

[Third step]

proc quotient digit
   $qp := qp + 1$
   $i := 0$
   while
      $e(i, m + 1{:}1) \leq g(m + 1{:}1)$
   do [increment i; ensure ith row of e is available]
      $i := i + 1$
      if
         $i > f$
      then [set f to point to ith row of e; set ith row to next multiple of
          divisor]
         $f := f + 1$
         $e(f, m + 1{:}1) := e(f - 1, m + 1{:}1) + a(m{:}1)$
      fi
   od [correct multiple is row $i - 1$ of e]
   do [subtract correct multiple of divisor from partial dividend and assign
      quotient digit]
      $g(m + 1{:}1) := g(m + 1{:}1) - e(i - 1, m + 1{:}1)$
      $q(qp) := i - 1$ [Note: Most significant digit of q is $q(1)$.]
   od
   while
      $bp > 0 \wedge a(m{:}1) > g(m + 1{:}1)$
   do [move partial dividend left one position and bring down next digit from
      dividend; possibly assign 0 quotient digit]
      $g(m + 1{:}2) := g(m{:}1)$
      $g(1) := b(bp)$
      $bp := bp - 1$
      if
         $a(m{:}1) > g(m + 1{:}1)$
      then
         $qp := qp + 1$
         $q(qp) := 0$
      fi
   od
   if
      $bp = 0$
   then [set remainder to partial dividend, partial dividend to 0]
      $r(m + 1{:}1) := g(m + 1{:}1)$
      $g(m + 1{:}1) := 0$
   fi
corp

added data item:
   i [e table pointer]

Figure 7.15 (continued)   Quotient digit segment, third step.

We now have a program for long division that has been written out to the last detail. But if the program is correct, how will we ever know it? (In fact, it contains a number of logical errors.) The correctness arguments will involve at least as many details as the program itself and are sure to tax intellectual control without an extensive and organized approach. If important, the proofs can be done, but is it worth the effort?

Although the process of grade school long division is well known and easy to describe, the foregoing program is not. In fact, the foregoing programming process illustrates how *not* to program long division. It represents an undisciplined mental process, which ignores important aspects of stepwise refinement and which compiles complexities with little thought to their impact on intellectual control. The programs were not created by expanding intended functions and then checking correctness, and the logical commentary was added after the fact, in an attempt to make sense out of all the details. In our rush to combine function and efficiency, it was easy to digress into the discussion of storing multiples of the divisor and of computing such multiples only on demand by addition, but it was unwise to do so at that point in the development. But the major flaw in the foregoing development was in accepting the inherent complexity of dealing with strings of digits in a way so easy for a person but which requires so much housekeeping for a computer. We jumped into programming by "stream of consciousness," with our heads full of the familiar digit-by-digit operations, without pausing to think of abstractions that could organize, or even circumvent, all those details. We turn now to a better way to formulate the long-division process.

7.4.4   Design through Stepwise Refinement

Chastened by the excursion into detailing, we now look for suitable abstractions that can be combined into a provable program. To begin, we return to the definition of integer division and write the following intended function, for divisor a, dividend b $(a, b > 0$, int short for integer part):

$$q, r := \text{int}(b/a), b - \text{int}(b/a)*a$$

We know (and can prove) that this function can be carried out by the program below

```
scalar a, b, q, r: integer
q, r := 0, b
[q, r := q + int(r/a), r - int(r/a)*a]
while
    a ≤ r
do
    q, r := q + 1, r - a
od
```

that treats a, b, q, r as scalar integers and ignores for the moment details of decimal digit representation. (In fact, we had this division-by-subtraction strategy in mind all along, but lost ourselves in the details of the more efficient grade-school implementation.) This program is inefficient; for example, a quotient of 946 requires 946 subtractions. But by grade-school long division, the same quotient could be obtained in just $9 + 4 + 6 = 19$ subtractions. Is there a way to systematically reorganize the program into grade-school long division? The answer is yes.

First, with a little thought on the mathematics underlying grade school long division, we rewrite the earlier example, $228596 \div 217$, as follows, where we recognize that the required digit alignments can be obtained quite simply, by multiplying divisor multiples by the proper power of ten:

divisor multiples		partial dividends	quotient terms
		228596	
$1*217*10**3$	$=$	217000	$1*10**3 = 1000$
		11596	
$0*217*10**2$	$=$	0	$0*10**2 = 000$
		11596	
$5*217*10**1$	$=$	10850	$5*10**1 = 50$
		746	
$3*217*10**0$	$=$	651	$3*10**0 = 3$
		95	1053

Thus, the problem can be described as a series of four individual division operations, each using the divisor multiplied by a power of ten, and each producing a quotient digit that, when multiplied by the same power of ten, results in a quotient term. The sum of individual quotient terms is the desired quotient. This appears to be a useful abstraction, since the decimal processor can deal with powers of ten by simply shifting digits. Since each quotient term is computed in the same manner, we propose a fordo fragment, indexing from highest quotient place, say $10**h$, down to lowest quotient place, $10**0$. The dopart is composed of the integer division program above, with test and operations adjusted by the required power of ten:

```
...
set h such that a*10**h ≤ b < a*10**(h + 1)
q, r := 0, b
[q, r := q + int(r/a), r − int(r/a)*a]
for
    i :∈ h to 0 by −1
do [q, r := q + int(r/a*10**i)*10**i, r − int(r/a*10**i)*a*10**i]
    while
        a*10**i ≤ r
    do
        q, r := q + 10**i, r − a*10**i
    od
od [b = a*q + r, 0 ≤ r < a]
...
```

Now it remains to determine the value of the parameter h, which is the number of zeros required to pad the divisor to the size of the dividend. This can be done by the following fragment:

```
...
do [set h such that a*10**h ≤ b < a*10**(h + 1)]
    h := 0
    while
        a*10**h ≤ b
    do
        h := h + 1
    od
    h := h − 1
od [a*10**h ≤ b < a*10**(h + 1)]
...
```

We are now able to combine these abstractions into a program that carries out the required digit-by-digit determination of q, as shown in Fig. 7.16.

```
 1   proc long division (a, b, q, r) [q, r := int(b/a), b − int(b/a)*a]
 2      scalar a, b, q, r: integer [a, b > 0]
 3      do [set h such that a*10**h ≤ b < a*10**(h + 1)]
 4         h := 0
 5         while
 6            a*10**h ≤ b
 7         do
 8            h := h + 1
 9         od
10         h := h − 1
11      od
12      q, r := 0, b
13      [q, r := q + int(r/a), r − int(r/a)*a]
14      for
15         i :∈ h to 0 by −1
16      do [q, r := q + int(r/a*10**i)*10**i, r − int(r/a*10**i)*a*10**i]
17         while
18            a*10**i ≤ r
19         do
20            q, r := q + 10**i, r − a*10**i
21         od
22      od [b = a*q + r, 0 ≤ r < a]
23   corp
```

Figure 7.16   New long-division program.

The program part of lines 3 through 11 that computes a value for h is correct by direct inspection. Index h is initialized to 0 and is incremented (if at all) until eventually $a*10**h > b$, and we are guaranteed that, on exit from the loop, h is the largest integer such that $a*10**(h − 1) ≤ b$. Note that if $a > b$, h is assigned −1, and the fordo on lines 14 through 22 is not executed. In this case, the assignment on line 12 sets q and r to 0 and b, respectively, as required. Next, the whiledo of lines 17 through 21 has proof as follows:

function
$$f = (q, r := q + int(r/a*10**i)*10**i, r − int(r/a*10**i)*a*10**i)$$

program
    whiledo (lines 17–21)

proof
    term
        r decreased by $a*10**i$ each iteration so whiletest $a*10**i ≤ r$ will eventually fail.
    pass

whiletest true $(a*10**i \leq r)$

part	condition	q	r
$a*10**i \leq r$	$a*10**i \leq r_0$	$q_1 = q_0$	$r_1 = r_0$
$q, r := q + 10**i,$		$q_2 = q_1 + 10**i$	$r_2 = r_1 - a*10**i$
$r - a*10**i$			
f		$q_3 = q_2$	$r_3 = r_2$
		$+ \text{int}(r_2/a*10**i)*$	$- \text{int}(r_2/a*10**i)*$
		$10**i$	$a*10**i$

derivations:
  condition:
$$a*10**i \leq r_0$$

  assignments:
$$q_3 = q_2 + \text{int}(r_2/a*10**i)*10**i$$
$$= q_1 + 10**i + \text{int}((r_1 - a*10**i)/a*10**i)*10**i$$
$$= q_0 + 10**i + \text{int}((r_0 - a*10**i)/a*10**i)*10**i$$
$$r_3 = r_2 - \text{int}(r_2/a*10**i)*a*10**i$$
$$= r_1 - a*10**i - \text{int}((r_1 - a*10**i)/a*10**i)*a*10**i$$
$$= r_0 - a*10**i - \text{int}((r_0 - a*10**i)/a*10**i)*a*10**i$$

But $\text{int}((r_0 - a*10**i)/a*10**i) = \text{int}(r_0/a*10**i) - 1$, so
$$q_3 = q_0 + 10**i + \text{int}(r_0/a*10**i)*10**i - 10**i$$
$$= q_0 + \text{int}(r_0/a*10**i)*10**i$$
$$r_3 = r_0 - a*10**i - \text{int}(r_0/a*10**i)*a*10**i + a*10**i$$
$$= r_0 - \text{int}(r_0/a*10**i)*a*10**i$$

program function:
$$(a*10**i \leq r \rightarrow q, r := q + \text{int}(r/a*10**i)*10**i,$$
$$r - \text{int}(r/a*10**i)*a*10**i)$$

which agrees with the intended function for whiletest *true*.
  pass

whiletest false $(a*10**i > r)$
  for $a*10**i > r$, $\text{int}(r/a*10**i) = 0$
  and $q, r := q, r$ as is required.
  pass

result
  pass
    given $a, r > 0$
  comp

Next, the proof for the fordo of lines 14 through 22 is as follows:

function
$$f = (q, r := q + \text{int}(r/a), r - \text{int}(r/a)*a)$$

program
fordo (lines 14–22)

proof (where d_h names the quantity $\text{int}(r_0/a*10**h)$,
d_{h-1} names $\text{int}(r_1/a*10**(h-1))$, ..., d_0 names
$\text{int}(r_h/a*10**(0)))$

i	part	q	r
h	$q, r := q + \text{int}(r/a*10**i)$ $*10**i,$ $r - \text{int}(r/a*10**i)$ $*a*10**i$	$q_1 = q_0 + d_h$ $*10**h$	$r_1 = r_0 - d_h$ $*a*10**h$
$h-1$	$q, r := q + \text{int}(r/a*10**i)$ $*10**i,$ $r - \text{int}(r/a*10**i)$ $*a*10**i$	$q_2 = q_1 + d_{h-1}$ $*10**(h-1)$	$r_2 = r_1 - d_{h-1}$ $*a*10**(h-1)$
...	...	...	...
0	$q, r := q + \text{int}(r/a*10**i)$ $*10**i,$ $r - \text{int}(r/a*10**i)$ $*a*10**i$	$q_{h+1} = q_h + d_0$ $*10**(0)$	$r_{h+1} = r_h - d_0$ $*a*10**(0)$

derivations (the leading digit of $10**h$ identifies the highest place
of q, by definition):
$$q_{h+1} = q_0 + (d_h*10**h) + (d_{h+1}*10**(h-1))$$
$$+ \cdots + (d_0*10**(0))$$
$$= q_0 + \text{int}(r_0/a)$$
$$r_{h+1} = r_0 - ((d_h*10**h) + (d_{h-1}*10**(h-1))$$
$$+ \cdots + (d_0*10**(0)))*a$$
$$= r_0 - \text{int}(r_0/a)*a$$

program function:
$$q, r := q + \text{int}(r/a), r - \text{int}(r/a)*a$$

result
pass
given $a, r > 0$
comp

Finally, q, r are initialized to 0, b on line 12 (and handle the case for $a > b$), and the function of the program part on lines 12 through 22 is thus

$$q, r := \text{int}(b/a). \ b - \text{int}(b/a)*a$$

as is required.

We have now developed an abstract program that does decimal long division correctly. Local abstract operations in the program can now be reorganized into operations available in the decimal processor with high confidence that correctness is preserved. First, the program part of lines 3 through 11 that computes h can be programmed as follows, using a decimal string named $shift$:

```
...
do [set h such that a*10**h ≤ b < a*10**(h + 1)]
    h := 0
    shift(p:1) := 0
    shift(m:1) := a(m:1)
    while
        shift(p:1) ≤ b(n:1)
    do
        h := h + 1
        shift(p:2) := shift(p − 1:1)
        shift(1) := 0
    od
    h := h − 1
od
...
```

Next, the fordo loop of lines 13 through 22 can be programmed as follows:

```
...
[q, r := q + int(r/a), r − int(r/a)*a]
for
    i ∈ h to 0 by −1
do [q, r := q + int(r/a*10**i)*10**i, r − int(r/a*10**i)*a*10**i]
    shift(p:1) := 0
    shift(m + i:1 + i) := a(m:1)
    while
        shift(p:1) ≤ r(p:1)        [a*10**i ≤ r]
    do [q, r := q + 10**i, r − a*10**i]
        q(i + 1) := q(i + 1) + 1
        r(p:1) := r(p:1) − shift(p:1)
    od
od [b = a*q + r, 0 ≤ r < a]
...
```

proc long division($a(m:1)$, $b(n:1)$, $q(p:1)$, $r(p:1)$) [q, $r := \text{int}(b/a)$,
    $b - \text{int}(b/a)*a$]
  use long-division data
  do [set h such that $a*10**h \leq b < a*10**(h + 1)$]
    $h := 0$
    $shift(p:1) := 0$
    $shift(m:1) := a(m:1)$
    while
      $shift(p:1) \leq b(n:1)$
    do
      $h := h + 1$
      $shift(p:2) := shift(p - 1:1)$
      $shift(1) := 0$
    od
    $h := h - 1$
  od
  do [q, $r := 0$, b]
    $q(p:1) := 0$
    $r(p:1) := 0$
    $r(n:1) := b(n:1)$
  od
  [q, $r := q + \text{int}(r/a)$, $r - \text{int}(r/a)*a$]
  for
    $i :\in h$ to 0 by -1
  do [q, $r := q + \text{int}(r/a*10**i)*10**i$, $r - \text{int}(r/a*10**i)*a*10**i$]
    $shift(p:1) := 0$
    $shift(m + i:1 + i) := a(m:1)$
    while
      $shift(p:1) \leq r(p:1)$ [$a*10**i \leq r$]
    do [q, $r := q + 10**i$, $r - a*10**i$]
      $q(i + 1) := q(i + 1) + 1$
      $r(p:1) := r(p:1) - shift(p:1)$
    od
  od [$b = a*q + r$, $0 \leq r < a$]
corp

data long-division data
  decimal
    $a(m:1)$ [divisor, $a > 0$]
    $b(n:1)$ [dividend, $b > 0$]
    $q(p:1)$ [quotient, $q(1)$ is low order quotient digit]
    $r(p:1)$ [remainder]
    $shift(p:1)$ [temporary]
    h [divisor alignment value]
    m [number of digits in divisor]
    n [number of digits in dividend]
    p [number of digit positions for q, r, and *shift*,
      assumed sufficiently large]
atad

Figure 7.17 Final long-division program.

The resulting program is shown in Fig. 7.17, with all abstract operations translated into operations of the decimal processor. Note that these abstractions, which treat a, b, q, r as scalars, appear in the program as logical commentary to document its design.

To summarize our experience with long division, we first tried creating a program out of an accumulation of details. When the complexity of all those details made correctness difficult to determine, we adopted an abstract view of the problem that yielded a compact design, easier to understand and verify. This design was proven correct and then expanded into operations of the decimal processor, with design abstractions carried into the expansion as logical commentary.

7.5   A CASE STUDY IN HEURISTICS AND RIGOR: MAKING CHANGE

7.5.1   Heuristics Versus Rigor

In many cases, a function to be programmed is quite straightforward, even though filling in the details may be somewhat tedious. In such cases, we can simply write a structured program, using a direct form of design for the implementation of the function by means of a self-evident rule. For example, the air pollution program was a product of direct design. However, in some cases, a rule for implementing a function may not be so evident, and an indirect design approach may be required. In these cases, we distinguish between heuristic and rigorous design methods.

A rigorous design is, by definition, a design that admits a self-sufficient argument for its correctness. In contrast, a heuristic design, by definition, admits no known self-sufficient argument for its correctness. As with any mathematical argument, a proof of the correctness of a rigorous design may be faulty, because of the fallibility of its designer. And indeed, a heuristic design may be absolutely correct, even though no self-sufficient argument for its correctness is known. But as mathematical experience shows, a rigorous design will usually be correct, with reasonable care on the part of its designers, and a heuristic design for a complex functional requirement will usually lead to errors in some executions of the design. For example, a heuristic design to prevent deadlock among a set of interrelated asynchronous processes, when it fails, will permit deadlock; a heuristic design to handle all possible expressions in a programming language will break down when it encounters an expression it cannot handle. Much current software is heuristically designed, and then patched and repatched as experience uncovers failures.

However, our interest in rigor, rather than heuristics, in design goes deeper than correctness considerations, to the stability and integrity of the design itself. A rigorous design survives its implementation and maintenance, whereas a heuristic design may not. In this connection, the illustration of Chapter 1 is worth recalling. Imagine a program written heuristically that encounters errors in executions and that is fixed as each error is discovered. After some time, such a program will become highly idiosyncratic, depending on the errors actually encountered. If the same errors occurred in a different sequence, the resulting patched up program would be different. Thus, the idiosyncracy depends on the sequence of errors, as well as on the errors themselves. To continue the illustration, imagine next a designer who conceives a heuristic design, but with great foresight, imagines every possible error before testing the program and fixes the design for each error anticipated. The program will be error free, but it will still be highly idiosyncratic, based on the error-removal sequence. If another programmer writes an error-free program in the same way, the second program may be entirely different from the first one.

In contrast, a rigorous design begins with a compelling simplicity that admits a self-sufficient argument for its correctness, and the implementation is defined as an elaboration of this design. The design will survive the implementation, even though mistakes may be made in carrying out the implementation. The origin of a rigorous design is a creative human mind. How such a design is to be invented is beyond our power to describe. But its value is unmistakable. There are several patterns of rigorous design that recur in programming, most notably in the systematic use of *state machines*, *formal grammars*, and *recursive functions*. In what follows, we use recursive functions to illustrate the distinction between heuristics and rigor, first in design of a program to make change, and second in design of a program to play tic-tac-toe.

7.5.2   A Change-Making Problem

Programs that deal with extensive combinatorial computation can often be designed more easily and surely by the discovery of a recursive property of the desired computation.

As a first illustration, consider the problem of making change. A subprogram is required for a microprocessor application, to compute change in vending machines for the Soviet system of coins, with kopeck denominations 1, 2, 3, 5, 10, 15, 20, and 50. Specifically, the subprogram is given three data items:

x (change to make, $x > 0$)

$q(1:8)$ (initial quantities of coins on hand, $q(1) = |1\text{'s}|$, $q(2) = |2\text{'s}|$, ..., $q(8) = |50\text{'s}|$)

result   (outcome of change-making operation, *true* or *false*)

If change can be made, the program is to reduce q by the required number of coins in each denomination and set *result* to *true*. Otherwise, if change cannot be made, q must remain unchanged and *result* set to *false*. The program will be "burned-in" to read-only memory, so errors can be fixed only at great expense, by recalling the machines and replacing memories. Thus, there is substantial economic motivation to produce a correct program.

7.5.3   A Heuristic Approach and Its Difficulties

On first thought the problem seems simple enough, and a reasonable design strategy might emerge as follows. Make change out of as many 50's as possible, then as many 20's as possible, and so on, down to 1's, if necessary. At any point, if the change left to make is 0, the coins on hand can be reduced by the number of coins used, and *result* set to *true*. The number of 50's possible is limited by $q(8)$, the quantity on hand, and by x itself, since we must have (using an array $n(1:8)$, with structure identical to q, for number of coins in change)

$$50*n(8) \le x$$

Now returning $n(8)$ 50's means the change yet to be made is

$$x - 50*n(8)$$

and we have a new change making problem, using only 20's, 15's, 10's, 5's, 3's, 2's, and 1's (since no more 50's can help, or are available, by the choice of $n(8)$). This strategy leads to the program of Fig. 7.18 (min for minimum, int for integer part).

Is the program correct? As a first test case, if we attempt to make change for, say, 67 kopecks with 20 coins of each denomination on hand, the program makes correct change:

	1's	2's	3's	5's	10's	15's	20's	50's		
x	$q(1)$	$q(2)$	$q(3)$	$q(4)$	$q(5)$	$q(6)$	$q(7)$	$q(8)$	*result*	
67	20	20	20	20	20	20	20	20		
17	20	20	20	20	20	20	20	19		(one 50 used)
2	20	20	20	20	20	19	20	19		(one 15 used)
0	20	19	20	20	20	19	20	19	*true*	(one 2 used)

But what if fewer coins are on hand, as in the following test case where, for

```
proc changemaker(alt x, q, result)
    scalar x: integer
    scalar result: logical
    array q(8), n(8): integer
    n(8) := min(int(x/50), q(8))
    x := x − (50*n(8))
    n(7) := min(int(x/20), q(7))
    x := x − (20*n(7))
    ...
    n(2) := min(int(x/2), q(2))
    x := x − (2*n(2))
    n(1) := min(x, q(1))
    x := x − n(1)
    if
        x = 0
    then
        q := q − n
        result := true
    else
        result := false
    fi
corp
```

Figure 7.18   First heuristic change program.

$x = 60$, the program produces

	1's	2's	3's	5's	10's	15's	20's	50's		
x	q(1)	q(2)	q(3)	q(4)	q(5)	q(6)	q(7)	q(8)	result	
60	1	0	1	1	0	8	4	3		
10	1	0	1	1	0	8	4	2		(one 50 used)
5	1	0	1	0	0	8	4	2		(one 5 used)
2	1	0	0	0	0	8	4	2		(one 3 used)
1	0	0	0	0	0	8	4	2	false	(one 1 used)

when in fact change can be made as

	1's	2's	3's	5's	10's	15's	20's	50's		
x	q(1)	q(2)	q(3)	q(4)	q(5)	q(6)	q(7)	q(8)	result	
60	1	0	1	1	0	8	4	3		
0	1	0	1	1	1	8	1	3	true	(three 20's used)

Thus, the program as it stands may add one too many 50's to the change and thereby prevent change from being made. Are there similar cases for other denominations? Yes, as the following test case demonstrates for 20's,

	1's	2's	3's	5's	10's	15's	20's	50's		
x	$q(1)$	$q(2)$	$q(3)$	$q(4)$	$q(5)$	$q(6)$	$q(7)$	$q(8)$	result	
30	0	0	3	0	0	4	5	2		
10	0	0	3	0	0	4	4	2		(one 20 used)
1	0	0	0	0	0	4	4	2	false	(three 3's used)

when in fact change can be made as

	1's	2's	3's	5's	10's	15's	20's	50's		
x	$q(1)$	$q(2)$	$q(3)$	$q(4)$	$q(5)$	$q(6)$	$q(7)$	$q(8)$	result	
30	0	0	3	0	0	4	5	2		
0	0	0	3	0	0	2	5	2	true	(two 15's used)

We elect at this point to fix the problems for 50's and 20's, so as to know how to handle other similar cases that may arise. First, a fix-up for the 50's problem is to make change with one less 50, if possible, when change cannot be made initially, as shown in Fig. 7.19.

But now we realize that the 50's fix-up is itself complicated, and in fact makes fixing the 20's problem more difficult. Furthermore, similar problems may exist with other denominations not yet tested. The attempt to fix the original program for these failures has weakened our confidence in the initial design. In fact, we are well on the way to a heuristic design that is correct only up to the last failure discovered.

7.5.4   A Rigorous Solution and Its Expansion

Our heuristic approach of thinking up cases to program has clearly led to difficulties. Heuristic thinking can work in simple situations, but the change problem is turning out to be more complex than anticipated. A rigorous treatment is required, one that will solve the problem once and for all, for every possible case, and that can be proven to be correct.

A little reflection reveals that each time a coin is added to the change, a new problem of exactly the same type results, with a new amount of change to be made and a new quantity of coins left on hand. Furthermore, the new problem is smaller than the old, that is, closer to the final outcome. This stepwise reduction to smaller and smaller problems suggests that a recursive function can be defined to capture all possibilities for making change from any initial problem.

```
proc changemaker(alt x, q, result)
   scalar x, xsave, correct50: integer
   scalar result, looking: logical
   array q(8), n(8): integer
   xsave := x
   correct50 := 0
   looking := true
   while
      looking
   do
      n(8) := min(int(x/50), q(8)) − correct50
      x := x − (50∗n(8))
      n(7) := min(int(x/20), q(7))
      x := x − (20∗n(7))
      . . .
      n(2) := min(int(x/2), q(2))
      x := x − (2∗n(2))
      n(1) := min(x, q(1))
      x := x − n(1)
      if
         x = 0
      then
         q := q − n
         result := true
         looking := false
      else
         if
            n(8) ≥ 1 ∧ correct50 = 0
         then
            correct50 := 1
            x := xsave
         else
            result := false
            looking := false
         fi
      fi
   od
corp
```

Figure 7.19   Second heuristic change program.

It is not always easy to invent a recursive function. The idea is to define a function that, when applied to a set of arguments (in this case, x and q), will yield a new set of arguments to which the function can subsequently be applied, and so on, until the final outcome is known. One strategy for inventing recursive functions is to recognize that with each reduction, if a desired outcome was possible for the old problem, the desired outcome should still be possible for the new problem. The desired outcome for the change problem is "change possible," or cp for short. If cp is *true* (or *false*) for the original problem, it should be likewise *true* (or *false*) for each reduced problem, until the ultimate truth or falsity of cp is known.

A recursive definition for the function named change possible (cp) can be written as follows, with line numbers in a column on the left:

```
1    cp(x, q(1), ..., q(8)) =
2         (x = 0
3         ∨ (x ≥ 50 ∧ q(8) ≥ 1 ∧ cp(x − 50, q(1), ..., q(8) − 1))
4         ∨ (x ≥ 20 ∧ q(7) ≥ 1 ∧ cp(x − 20, q(1), ..., q(7) − 1, q(8)))
...        ...
10        ∨ (x ≥ 1 ∧ q(1) ≥ 1 ∧ cp(x − 1, q(1) − 1, ..., q(8))))
```

The expression on line 1 names the function and its arguments. Line 2 defines cp *true* if $x = 0$, that is, no change has to be made. If $x \neq 0$, one of the expressions on lines 3 through 10 may be *true*, leading to a recursive reference to cp with a reduced problem as argument. Otherwise, cp must be *false*. Change making is a numerical problem, but surprisingly, this recursive function was discovered by posing a logical problem, "Is change possible?", whose evaluation will produce the desired numerical result as a byproduct.

The recursive definition for cp defines a "change tree" for every list, $(x, q(1), ..., q(8))$, such that $(x, q(1), ..., q(8))$ is the root of the tree, and if the list $(y, r(1), ..., r(8))$ is a node in the tree, then every reduced problem of this list is also a node in the tree. For example, if $y \geq 50 \wedge r(8) \geq 1$, then the reduced problem $(y − 50, r(1), ..., r(8) − 1)$ is also a node, and so on. Then, it can be seen that $cp(x, q(1), ..., q(8)) = true$ if and only if the change tree defined by $(x, q(1), ..., q(8))$ contains a node $(y, r(1), ..., r(8))$ such that $y = 0$. In illustration, the change tree for the last test case above

	1's	2's	3's	5's	10's	15's	20's	50's
x	$q(1)$	$q(2)$	$q(3)$	$q(4)$	$q(5)$	$q(6)$	$q(7)$	$q(8)$
30	0	0	3	0	0	4	5	2

is given in Fig. 7.20 in outline (indented) form. Decremented denominations are in bold type in each reduced problem, and line numbers are shown in a

1	(30, 0, 0, 3, 0, 0, 4, 5, 2)
2	(10, 0, 0, 3, 0, 0, 4, **4**, 2)
3	(7, 0, 0, **2**, 0, 0, 4, 4, 2)
4	(4, 0, 0, **1**, 0, 0, 4, 4, 2)
5	(1, 0, 0, **0**, 0, 0, 4, 4, 2)
6	(15, 0, 0, 3, 0, 0, **3**, 5, 2)
7	(0, 0, 0, 3, 0, 0, **2**, 5, 2)
8	(12, 0, 0, **2**, 0, 0, 3, 5, 2)
9	(9, 0, 0, **1**, 0, 0, 3, 5, 2)
10	(6, 0, 0, **0**, 0, 0, 3, 5, 2)
11	(27, 0, 0, **2**, 0, 0, 4, 5, 2)
12	(7, 0, 0, 2, 0, 0, 4, **4**, 2)
13	(4, 0, 0, **1**, 0, 0, 4, 4, 2)
14	(1, 0, 0, **0**, 0, 0, 4, 4, 2)
15	(12, 0, 0, 2, 0, 0, **3**, 5, 2)
16	(9, 0, 0, **1**, 0, 0, 3, 5, 2)
17	(6, 0, 0, **0**, 0, 0, 3, 5, 2)
18	(24, 0, 0, **1**, 0, 0, 4, 5, 2)
19	(4, 0, 0, 1, 0, 0, 4, **4**, 2)
20	(1, 0, 0, **0**, 0, 0, 4, 4, 2)
21	(9, 0, 0, 1, 0, 0, **3**, 5, 2)
22	(6, 0, 0, **0**, 0, 0, 3, 5, 2)
23	(21, 0, 0, **0**, 0, 0, 4, 5, 2)
24	(1, 0, 0, 0, 0, 0, 4, **4**, 2)
25	(6, 0, 0, 0, 0, 0, **3**, 5, 2)

Figure 7.20   Change tree for (30, 0, 0, 3, 0, 0, 4, 5, 2) in outline form.

column on the left. Nodes on lines 2, 6, and 11 are adjacent to the root node on line 1; nodes on lines 12, 15, and 18 are adjacent to the node on line 11, etc. One node (line 7) has $y = 0$, so that cp(30, 0, 0, 3, 0, 0, 4, 5, 2) = *true*, as found above. But the subtree on lines 11 through 25, with root at line 11, has no node with $y = 0$, so that cp(27, 0, 0, 2, 0, 0, 4, 2) = *false*. Note that the tree contains duplicated nodes; for example, the nodes on lines 10, 17, 22, and 25 are all identical.

In the heuristic design of Fig. 7.19, a strategy for an imagined subset of reduced problems was defined, with unimagined cases added as failures were discovered. No such fix-up is required here; in fact, the correctness of the cp function is self-evident. Every possible combination of coins is embodied in the function and enumerated in the tree. If change can be made for some initial amount, it can be made by one (or more) of these combinations. Thus, the change problem is equivalent to searching a tree for a desired outcome. There is no guarantee against errors in writing the required tree-search program, but its function is now known precisely, and thus its correctness can be determined.

There is no straightforward way to program recursive functions. In fact, some recursive functions cannot be programmed at all, and no general mathematical theory exists for deciding in advance whether a particular recursive function can or cannot be programmed. But in this case the change function definition always reduces the total number of coins considered in the recursions; this finite, monotonic property puts change in a class of recursive functions that can indeed be programmed.

Our interest now is to write a program that searches the change tree defined by $(x, q(1), \ldots, q(8))$ for a node $(y, r(1), \ldots, r(8))$, with $y = 0$. If such a node is found, the change required is given by the path to that node. If no such node exists, then change cannot be made. Since the outcome of a path is known only by proceeding to its end (change possible or not), it makes sense to carry out a depth-first search. The tree is deepest toward the smaller denominations; thus, for efficiency, the search should begin with the largest denomination and work depth-first toward the smallest. Furthermore, even though the tree contains duplicate nodes, it is sufficient to visit only the first occurrence of such a node, since the value of cp is the same for subsequent occurrences.

Nodes can be generated as needed, rather than computed and stored in advance. The tree is traversed by following paths and backing up, if necessary, to branch to other paths. That is, when nodes on a path are exhausted without making change, the program must retrace to a node where the subpath of the next smaller denomination can be explored. This "depth-first, largest-to-smallest denomination" strategy is similar to the heuristic design above, but it is systematically applied to the entire tree. Thus, in retrospect, the original heuristic solution is now seen to traverse only one possible path in the change tree.

In order to simplify record keeping during the search of the change tree, we adjoin an additional "denomination value," i, to the list $(x, q(1), \ldots, q(8))$. Thus, a typical node of the augmented change tree is of the form $(x, q(1), \ldots, q(8), i)$. The meaning of i is that denomination i is the next candidate to be used in forming a reduced problem. For example, if $i = 8$, the candidate problem is

$$(x - 50, q(1), \ldots, q(8) - 1, 8)$$

(Of course, unless $x \geq 50$, $q(8) \geq 1$, this list does not represent a reduced problem.) At each point of the search, the next smaller denomination is found by decrementing i. Next, in order to further simplify the search, we permit i to be decremented to 0, meaning all denominations for the corresponding x, q have been tried for creating candidate reduced problems.

The state of the search of the change tree will be recorded in a stack named *nodestack*, which maintains the path from the root of the change tree down to the next node to be examined for reduced problems. Going down the tree adds members to the stack; going across the tree preserves the size of the stack; backing up the tree deletes members from the stack. The search begins with a stack of a single member, the root of the change tree; a complete search of all nodes in the change tree results in an empty stack; the discovery that change possible is *true* results in a stack from which change can be computed.

Finally, in order to design a provable program to carry out the search, we define a "virtual" sequence of search states, called "tour," that is ordered by the depth-first, largest-to-smallest denomination principle. A search state will be a stack (*nodestack*), and the sequence tour is defined as follows:

1. The first member of the sequence tour is a stack with a single element, the triple (x, q, m) where x, q defines the root of the change tree, and m is the index of the maximum denomination (in this case, 8).

2. The last member of the sequence tour is the empty stack, and the empty stack has no successor (so the first empty stack in the sequence is the last member).

3. For any nonempty stack of the sequence tour, the next member is the stack determined by the following three-part rule. If the topmost element of *nodestack* is denoted by (x, q, i), the next member is determined in the following order of priority:

    a) depth-first: next level, same denomination if possible.

    If (y, r) is a reduced problem defined by (x, q, i) (that is, $x \geq q(i) \wedge q(i) \geq 1 \rightarrow y = x - q(i)$, $r = (q(1), \ldots, q(i) - 1, \ldots, q(8)))$, form the next member of tour by adding (y, r, i) to the stack.

    b) largest-to-smallest: current level, next smaller denomination, if possible.

    If (x, q, i) does not define a reduced problem (as in case (a) above) but $i > 0$, form the next member of tour by replacing (x, q, i) by $(x, q, i - 1)$ on the top of the stack.

    c) back up: previous level, next smaller denomination, if possible.

    If $i = 0$, form the next member of tour by removing the top member from the stack and replacing the new top member (x, q, i) (if any) with $(x, q, i - 1)$.

It is clear, by construction, that the stacks of the sequence tour have only elements of the form (y, r, i), where (y, r) defines a node in the change tree defined by the initial (x, q). Furthermore, the stacks of the sequence are necessarily distinct, because rules 3b and 3c decrement the denomination index monotonically. Finally, every unique node (y, r) in the change tree defined by the initial (x, q) will be represented in an element (y, r, i) of some stack in the sequence tour. This is so because reduced problems (y, r) will be found in depth-first, largest-to-smallest denomination order by rule 3, beginning with the root of the change tree given by rule 1.

The program of Figure 7.21 searches the sequence tour of stacks for a reduced problem (y, r) such that $y = 0$. The search takes the form of an initialized whiledo program, and its proof of correctness will involve the standard forms for the sequence and the whiledo. In particular, the search is carried out by a program part of the form

$$h; F$$

where

$$F = \textbf{while } p \textbf{ do } g \textbf{ od}$$

and where the following definitions apply:

1. $[h]$: initialize *nodestack* to the first member of the search sequence tour, namely, a stack with a single element (x, q, m).

2. $[F]$: transform *nodestack* either into the first member of the search sequence tour from here on with topmost element (y, r, i) such that $y = 0$ or into the empty stack if no such topmost element exists.

3. $[g]$: transform the current member of the search sequence tour into the next member, according to rules 3a, b, c, above.

4. p: provide termination of the whiledo when a member of the range of $[F]$ is found.

Note that the whiledo program function $[F]$ deals solely with transformations on *nodestack*. The argument of $[F]$ is an initial *nodestack*, the first member of the sequence tour, and the value of $[F]$ is the final *nodestack*, the last member of the sequence tour. To emphasize this functional property, local variables *cng*, *coins*, k are used for *nodestack* elements in the whiledo, in place of x, q, i.

The program can be verified informally as follows:

1. nextnode segment: By inspection, the nested alternations carry out $[g]$.

2. changemaker segment: The whiledo proof (Fig. 7.22) is the only one not obvious.

The changemaker program of Fig. 7.21, while transparent to the foregoing search strategy, is somewhat awkward in its explicit and complete construction of the member stacks of the sequence tour. For example, the procedure nextnode stacks and unstacks an element (x, q, i) predictably at the end of each invocation and the beginning of the next. The reorganized

```
1    proc changemaker(alt x, q, result) [if change can be made for x, set to 0, reduce
            q by coins used, and set result to true; else set result to false]
2       use changedata
3       do [h: initialize nodestack to the first member of the search sequence tour,
            namely, a stack with a single element (x, q, m)]
4          nodestack := empty
5          top(nodestack) := x, q, m
6       od
7       cng := x
8       [F: transform nodestack either into the first member of the search sequence
            tour from here on with topmost element (y, r, i) such that y = 0 or into the
            empty stack if no such topmost element exists]
9       while
10         nodestack ≠ empty ∧ cng > 0
11      do [g: transform the current member of the search sequence tour into the
            next member, according to rules 3a, b, c]
12         run nextnode (alt nodestack, cng, coins, k, fix val)
13      od
14      if
15         nodestack ≠ empty
16      then
17         x, q, i := top(nodestack)
18         result := true
19      else
20         result := false
21      fi
22   corp

     data changedata
        stack
           nodestack [element is (x, q, i)]
        array
           coins(8): integer [local value of q in whiledo]
           q(8): integer [elements are numbers of coins on hand, i.e., |1's|, ...,
                          |50's|]
           val(8): integer init (1, 2, 3, 5, 10, 15, 20, 50) [elements are monetary values
                                               of corresponding q elements]
        scalar
           cng: integer [local value of x in whiledo]
           i: integer [problem index]
           k: integer [local problem index in whiledo]
           m: integer init (8) [number of denominations]
           result: logical [value of change possible function, true or false]
           x: integer [change to be made]
        atad
```

Figure 7.21   Changemaker program.

```
1     proc nextnode(alt nodestack, cng, coins, k, fix, val) [g: transform the current
              member of the search sequence tour into the next member, according to
              rules 3a, b, c]
2         cng, coins, k := top(nodestack) [stack read, factored out of implementation
                                              of 3a, b, c below]
3         if
4            k > 0
5         then
6            if
7                cng ≥ val(k) ∧ coins(k) ≥ 1
8            then [3a. depth-first: next level, same denomination]
9                top(nodestack) := cng, coins, k
10               cng, coins(k) := cng − val(k), coins(k) − 1
11               top(nodestack) := cng, coins, k
12           else [3b. largest-to-smallest: current level, next smaller denomination]
13               k := k − 1
14               top(nodestack) := cng, coins, k
15           fi
16        else
17           if
18               nodestack ≠ empty
19           then [3c. back up: previous level, next smaller denomination]
20               cng, coins, k := top(nodestack)
21               k := k − 1
22               top(nodestack) := cng, coins, k
23           fi
24        fi
25     corp
```

Figure 7.21   (continued)

changemaker program (named changemaker1) of Fig. 7.23 eliminates such unnecessary stacking and unstacking of nodes, but must provide a whiledo loop exit criteria in the logical variable named *looking*. The program consists of a single segment, and local variables *cng*, *coins*, *k* used in the whiledo of the changemaker program have been replaced by variables *x*, *q*, *i*. Initial *x*, *q* are saved in *xs*, *qs*, and restored prior to exit, if necessary. Note that with unnecessary stacking and unstacking eliminated, the search state of the sequence tour now involves *x*, *q*, *i*, as well as *nodestack*.

Figures 7.24 and 7.25 show PL/I implementations of the changemaker and reorganized changemaker (changemaker1) subprograms, along with some test results for changemaker.† (The programs that invoke change-maker and changemaker1 and print test results are not shown.) The change-

---

† Programs coded and tested by Larry I. Schwartz.

function

  F: transform *nodestack* either into the first member of the search sequence tour from here on with topmost element (y, r, i) such that $y = 0$ or into the empty stack if no such topmost element exists.

program

  whiledo, lines 9–13.

proof

  term

    The whiletest eventually fails, either because a node is encountered such that $cng = 0$, or the sequence tour is exhausted. The length of tour is finite, since (1) stacks of tour are distinct, by definition, and (2) each stack is of finite depth, because the corresponding path in the change tree is of finite depth.

    pass

  whiletest true (*nodestack* $\neq$ **empty** $\wedge$ *cng* > 0)

    $g \circ F = F$ because F, when applied to the sequence tour as modified by g, produces the same effect as F applied to the original sequence tour.

    pass

  whiletest false (*nodestack* $=$ **empty** $\vee$ *cng* $= 0$)

    The identity is required, since the transformation defined by F is complete.

    pass

result

  pass

Figure 7.22

maker, nextnode, and changemaker1 program designs and implementations are cross-referenced for better readability and correctness checking. Line numbers from the PDL text appear in the PL/I programs in a column on the left, next to the corresponding PL/I statements. Alternately, cross-referencing can be accomplished by duplicating logical commentary and abstract operations from the PDL in the PL/I programs.

7.5.5   Redefining the Problem

Finally, reflecting on the original problem statement, we note that the vending machine manufacturer may be better off with the original heuristic algorithm. It doesn't always make change when possible, but the manufacturer may find it a better solution because it might require a simpler microprocessor. And besides, a vending machine customer never really knows whether change is possible or not! In this case, the program and its program function should be examined more closely to make sure of their properties and adequacy for the task.

```
1    proc changemaker1(alt x, q, result) [if change can be made for x, set x to 0,
         reduce q by coins used, and set result to true; else set result to false]
2        use changedata
3        xs, qs := x, q
4        nodestack := empty
5        i, looking := m, true
6        [F: transform nodestack either into the first member of the search sequence
         tour from here on with topmost element (y, r, i) such that y = 0 or into the
         empty stack (and set looking to false) if no such topmost element exists]
7        while
8            x > 0 ∧ looking
9        do [g: transform the current member of the search sequence tour into the
             next member according to rules 3a, b, c, and set looking to false if the
             member is empty]
10           if
11               i > 0
12           then
13               if
14                   x ≥ val(i) ∧ q(i) ≥ 1
15               then [3a. depth-first: next level, same denomination]
16                   top(nodestack) := x, q, i
17                   x, q(i) := x − val(i), q(i) − 1
18               else [3b. largest-to-smallest: current level, next smaller
                     denomination]
19                   i := i − 1
20               fi
21           else
22               if
23                   nodestack ≠ empty
24               then [3c. back up: previous level, next smaller denomination]
25                   x, q, i := top(nodestack)
26                   i = i − 1
27               else[signal tour is exhausted]
28                   looking := false
29               fi
30           fi
31       od
32       if
33           x = 0
34       then
35           result := true
36       else
37           x, q, := xs, qs
38           result := false
39       fi
40   corp
```

added data items for changedata:

      scalar *xs*: integer [saved initial value of *x*]
      scalar *looking*: logical [signals tour is exhausted]
      array *qs*(8): integer [saved initial values of *q*]

Figure 7.23 Reorganized changemaker program.

366   Writing Structured Programs

[Changemaker segment]

```
1       CHANGEMAKER: PROC(X,Q,RESULT);
        /* IF CHANGE CAN BE MADE FOR X, SET X TO 0, REDUCE Q BY
           REQUIRED COINS, AND SET RESULT TRUE; OTHERWISE LEAVE X AND
           Q UNCHANGED AND SET RESULT FALSE.                          */

        %INCLUDE /* DATA DECLARATIONS */ CMDATA;

4       STACK_INDEX = 0;
5       STACK_INDEX = STACK_INDEX + 1;
        STACK.X(STACK_INDEX) = X;
        STACK.Q(STACK_INDEX,*) = Q;
        STACK.I(STACK_INDEX) = M;
7       CNG = X;
9       DO WHILE (STACK_INDEX > 0   &   CNG > 0);
12        CALL NEXT_NODE;
          CALL PRINT_STACK(STACK,STACK_INDEX,CNG,COINS,K);
13      END;
14      IF
15        STACK_INDEX > 0
16      THEN
          DO;
17        X = STACK.X(STACK_INDEX);
          Q = STACK.Q(STACK_INDEX,*);
          I = STACK.I(STACK_INDEX);
          STACK_INDEX = STACK_INDEX - 1;
18        RESULT = '1'B; /* TRUE */
          END;
19      ELSE
20        RESULT = '0'B; /* FALSE */

        RETURN;
```

[Cmdata segment]

```
DECLARE                     /* STACK VARIABLES              */
 1 STACK(50)
 .2 X
 .2 Q(8)
 .2 I
 .STACK_INDEX
;

DECLARE                     /* ARRAY VARIABLES              */
 COINS(8)
        /* LOCAL VALUES OF Q IN DOWHILE                     */
 .Q(8)
        /* ELEMENTS ARE # OF COINS ON HAND, I.E., |1S|,...,|50S| */
 .VAL(8)                    INIT((1,2,5,10,15,20,50)
        /* ELEMENTS ARE MONETARY VALUES OF CORRESPONDING Q ELEM'S*/
;

DECLARE                     /* SCALAR VARIABLES             */
 CNG
        /* LOCAL VALUE OF X IN DOWHILE                      */
 .I
        /* PROBLEM INDEX                                    */
 .K                         FIXED BIN
        /* LOCAL PROBLEM INDEX IN DOWHILE                   */
 .M                         INIT(8)
        /* NUMBER OF DENOMINATIONS                          */
 .RESULT                    BIT(1)
        /* VALUE OF CHANGE POSSIBLE FUNCTION, TRUE OR FALSE */
 .X
        /* CHANGE TO BE MADE                                */
;
```

Figure 7.24 Changemaker in PL/I with test results.

[Nextnode segment]

```
 1    NEXT_NODE: PROCEDURE;

 2    CNG = STACK.X(STACK_INDEX);
      COINS = STACK.Q(STACK_INDEX,*);
      K = STACK.I(STACK_INDEX);
      STACK_INDEX = STACK_INDEX - 1;
 3    IF
 4      K > 0
 5    THEN
 6      IF
 7        CNG >= VAL(K) & COINS(K) >= 1
 8      THEN
          DO;
 9          STACK_INDEX = STACK_INDEX + 1;
            STACK.X(STACK_INDEX) = CNG;
            STACK.Q(STACK_INDEX,*) = COINS;
            STACK.I(STACK_INDEX) = K;
10          CNG = CNG - VAL(K);
            COINS(K) = COINS(K) - 1;
11          STACK_INDEX = STACK_INDEX + 1;
            STACK.X(STACK_INDEX) = CNG;
            STACK.Q(STACK_INDEX,*) = COINS;
            STACK.I(STACK_INDEX) = K;
          END;
12      ELSE
          DO;
13          K = K - 1;
14          STACK_INDEX = STACK_INDEX + 1;
            STACK.X(STACK_INDEX) = CNG;
            STACK.Q(STACK_INDEX,*) = COINS;
            STACK.I(STACK_INDEX) = K;
          END;
16    ELSE
17      IF
18        STACK_INDEX > 0
19      THEN
          DO;
            PUT SKIP EDIT('BACKING UP') (A);
20          CNG = STACK.X(STACK_INDEX);
            COINS = STACK.Q(STACK_INDEX,*);
            K = STACK.I(STACK_INDEX);
            STACK_INDEX = STACK_INDEX - 1;
21          K = K - 1;
22          STACK_INDEX = STACK_INDEX + 1;
            STACK.X(STACK_INDEX) = CNG;
            STACK.Q(STACK_INDEX,*) = COINS;
            STACK.I(STACK_INDEX) = K;
          END;

25    END NEXT_NODE;
```

Figure 7.24   (continued)

[Changemaker test results]

```
TEST 1:   CHANGE NEEDED = 90.       MAKE CHANGE EXACTLY, WITHOUT BACKING.

COIN QUANTITIES ON HAND:
     5 OF VALUE   1        5 OF VALUE    2       5 OF VALUE   3       1 OF VALUE    5
     5 OF VALUE  10        5 OF VALUE   15       0 OF VALUE  20       5 OF VALUE   50

WORKING   X   I   Q1 Q2 Q3 Q4 Q5 Q6 Q7 Q8      STACK    X   I   Q1 Q2 Q3 Q4 Q5 Q6 Q7 Q8
         40   8   5  5  5  1  5  5  0  4                2   40   8   5  5  5  1  5  5  0  4
                                                       1   90   8   5  5  5  1  5  5  0  5

WORKING   X   I   Q1 Q2 Q3 Q4 Q5 Q6 Q7 Q8      STACK    X   I   Q1 Q2 Q3 Q4 Q5 Q6 Q7 Q8
         40   7   5  5  5  1  5  5  0  4                2   40   7   5  5  5  1  5  5  0  4
                                                       1   90   8   5  5  5  1  5  5  0  5

WORKING   X   I   Q1 Q2 Q3 Q4 Q5 Q6 Q7 Q8      STACK    X   I   Q1 Q2 Q3 Q4 Q5 Q6 Q7 Q8
         40   6   5  5  5  1  5  5  0  4                2   40   6   5  5  5  1  5  5  0  4
                                                       1   90   8   5  5  5  1  5  5  0  5

WORKING   X   I   Q1 Q2 Q3 Q4 Q5 Q6 Q7 Q8      STACK    X   I   Q1 Q2 Q3 Q4 Q5 Q6 Q7 Q8
         25   6   5  5  5  1  5  4  0  4                3   25   6   5  5  5  1  5  4  0  4
                                                       2   40   6   5  5  5  1  5  5  0  4
                                                       1   90   8   5  5  5  1  5  5  0  5

WORKING   X   I   Q1 Q2 Q3 Q4 Q5 Q6 Q7 Q8      STACK    X   I   Q1 Q2 Q3 Q4 Q5 Q6 Q7 Q8
         10   6   5  5  5  1  5  3  0  4                4   10   6   5  5  5  1  5  3  0  4
                                                       3   25   6   5  5  5  1  5  4  0  4
                                                       2   40   6   5  5  5  1  5  5  0  4
                                                       1   90   8   5  5  5  1  5  5  0  5

WORKING   X   I   Q1 Q2 Q3 Q4 Q5 Q6 Q7 Q8      STACK    X   I   Q1 Q2 Q3 Q4 Q5 Q6 Q7 Q8
         10   5   5  5  5  1  5  3  0  4                4   10   5   5  5  5  1  5  3  0  4
                                                       3   25   6   5  5  5  1  5  4  0  4
                                                       2   40   6   5  5  5  1  5  5  0  4
                                                       1   90   8   5  5  5  1  5  5  0  5

WORKING   X   I   Q1 Q2 Q3 Q4 Q5 Q6 Q7 Q8      STACK    X   I   Q1 Q2 Q3 Q4 Q5 Q6 Q7 Q8
          0   5   5  5  5  1  4  3  0  4                5    0   5   5  5  5  1  4  3  0  4
                                                       4   10   5   5  5  5  1  5  3  0  4
                                                       3   25   6   5  5  5  1  5  4  0  4
                                                       2   40   6   5  5  5  1  5  5  0  4
                                                       1   90   8   5  5  5  1  5  5  0  5

RESULT = TRUE

COIN QUANTITIES ON HAND:
     5 OF VALUE   1        5 OF VALUE    2       5 OF VALUE   3       1 OF VALUE    5
     4 OF VALUE  10        3 OF VALUE   15       0 OF VALUE  20       4 OF VALUE   50
```

Figure 7.24   (continued)

```
TEST 2:  CHANGE NEEDED = 10.     CAN'T MAKE CHANGE, EVEN WITH BACKING.

COIN QUANTITIES ON HAND:
  1 OF VALUE  1         0 OF VALUE   2      2 OF VALUE   3       0 OF VALUE   5
  0 OF VALUE 10         0 OF VALUE  15      0 OF VALUE  20       0 OF VALUE  50

WORKING  X  I  Q1 Q2 Q3 Q4 Q5 Q6 Q7 Q8       STACK  X  I  Q1 Q2 Q3 Q4 Q5 Q6 Q7 Q8
        10  7   1  0  2  0  0  0  0  0               1 10  7   1  0  2  0  0  0  0  0

WORKING  X  I  Q1 Q2 Q3 Q4 Q5 Q6 Q7 Q8       STACK  X  I  Q1 Q2 Q3 Q4 Q5 Q6 Q7 Q8
        10  6   1  0  2  0  0  0  0  0               1 10  6   1  0  2  0  0  0  0  0

WORKING  X  I  Q1 Q2 Q3 Q4 Q5 Q6 Q7 Q8       STACK  X  I  Q1 Q2 Q3 Q4 Q5 Q6 Q7 Q8
        10  5   1  0  2  0  0  0  0  0               1 10  5   1  0  2  0  0  0  0  0

WORKING  X  I  Q1 Q2 Q3 Q4 Q5 Q6 Q7 Q8       STACK  X  I  Q1 Q2 Q3 Q4 Q5 Q6 Q7 Q8
        10  4   1  0  2  0  0  0  0  0               1 10  4   1  0  2  0  0  0  0  0

WORKING  X  I  Q1 Q2 Q3 Q4 Q5 Q6 Q7 Q8       STACK  X  I  Q1 Q2 Q3 Q4 Q5 Q6 Q7 Q8
        10  3   1  0  2  0  0  0  0  0               1 10  3   1  0  2  0  0  0  0  0

WORKING  X  I  Q1 Q2 Q3 Q4 Q5 Q6 Q7 Q8       STACK  X  I  Q1 Q2 Q3 Q4 Q5 Q6 Q7 Q8
         7  3   1  0  1  0  0  0  0  0               2  7  3   1  0  1  0  0  0  0  0
                                                    1 10  3   1  0  2  0  0  0  0  0

WORKING  X  I  Q1 Q2 Q3 Q4 Q5 Q6 Q7 Q8       STACK  X  I  Q1 Q2 Q3 Q4 Q5 Q6 Q7 Q8
         4  3   1  0  0  0  0  0  0  0               3  4  3   1  0  0  0  0  0  0  0
                                                    2  7  3   1  0  1  0  0  0  0  0
                                                    1 10  3   1  0  2  0  0  0  0  0

WORKING  X  I  Q1 Q2 Q3 Q4 Q5 Q6 Q7 Q8       STACK  X  I  Q1 Q2 Q3 Q4 Q5 Q6 Q7 Q8
         4  2   1  0  0  0  0  0  0  0               3  4  2   1  0  0  0  0  0  0  0
                                                    2  7  3   1  0  1  0  0  0  0  0
                                                    1 10  3   1  0  2  0  0  0  0  0

WORKING  X  I  Q1 Q2 Q3 Q4 Q5 Q6 Q7 Q8       STACK  X  I  Q1 Q2 Q3 Q4 Q5 Q6 Q7 Q8
         4  1   1  0  0  0  0  0  0  0               3  4  1   1  0  0  0  0  0  0  0
                                                    2  7  3   1  0  1  0  0  0  0  0
                                                    1 10  3   1  0  2  0  0  0  0  0

WORKING  X  I  Q1 Q2 Q3 Q4 Q5 Q6 Q7 Q8       STACK  X  I  Q1 Q2 Q3 Q4 Q5 Q6 Q7 Q8
         3  1   0  0  0  0  0  0  0  0               4  3  1   0  0  0  0  0  0  0  0
                                                    3  4  1   1  0  0  0  0  0  0  0
                                                    2  7  3   1  0  1  0  0  0  0  0
                                                    1 10  3   1  0  2  0  0  0  0  0

WORKING  X  I  Q1 Q2 Q3 Q4 Q5 Q6 Q7 Q8       STACK  X  I  Q1 Q2 Q3 Q4 Q5 Q6 Q7 Q8
         3  0   0  0  0  0  0  0  0  0               4  3  0   0  0  0  0  0  0  0  0
                                                    3  4  1   1  0  0  0  0  0  0  0
                                                    2  7  3   1  0  1  0  0  0  0  0
BACKING UP                                          1 10  3   1  0  2  0  0  0  0  0

WORKING  X  I  Q1 Q2 Q3 Q4 Q5 Q6 Q7 Q8       STACK  X  I  Q1 Q2 Q3 Q4 Q5 Q6 Q7 Q8
         4  0   1  0  0  0  0  0  0  0               3  4  0   1  0  0  0  0  0  0  0
                                                    2  7  3   1  0  1  0  0  0  0  0
BACKING UP                                          1 10  3   1  0  2  0  0  0  0  0

WORKING  X  I  Q1 Q2 Q3 Q4 Q5 Q6 Q7 Q8       STACK  X  I  Q1 Q2 Q3 Q4 Q5 Q6 Q7 Q8
         7  2   1  0  1  0  0  0  0  0               2  7  2   1  0  1  0  0  0  0  0
                                                    1 10  3   1  0  2  0  0  0  0  0

WORKING  X  I  Q1 Q2 Q3 Q4 Q5 Q6 Q7 Q8       STACK  X  I  Q1 Q2 Q3 Q4 Q5 Q6 Q7 Q8
         7  1   1  0  1  0  0  0  0  0               2  7  1   1  0  1  0  0  0  0  0
                                                    1 10  3   1  0  2  0  0  0  0  0

WORKING  X  I  Q1 Q2 Q3 Q4 Q5 Q6 Q7 Q8       STACK  X  I  Q1 Q2 Q3 Q4 Q5 Q6 Q7 Q8
         6  1   0  0  1  0  0  0  0  0               3  6  1   0  0  1  0  0  0  0  0
                                                    2  7  1   1  0  1  0  0  0  0  0
                                                    1 10  3   1  0  2  0  0  0  0  0

WORKING  X  I  Q1 Q2 Q3 Q4 Q5 Q6 Q7 Q8       STACK  X  I  Q1 Q2 Q3 Q4 Q5 Q6 Q7 Q8
         6  0   0  0  1  0  0  0  0  0               3  6  0   0  0  1  0  0  0  0  0
                                                    2  7  1   1  0  1  0  0  0  0  0
BACKING UP                                          1 10  3   1  0  2  0  0  0  0  0

WORKING  X  I  Q1 Q2 Q3 Q4 Q5 Q6 Q7 Q8      .STACK  X  I  Q1 Q2 Q3 Q4 Q5 Q6 Q7 Q8
         7  0   1  0  1  0  0  0  0  0               2  7  0   1  0  1  0  0  0  0  0
BACKING UP                                          1 10  3   1  0  2  0  0  0  0  0

WORKING  X  I  Q1 Q2 Q3 Q4 Q5 Q6 Q7 Q8       STACK  X  I  Q1 Q2 Q3 Q4 Q5 Q6 Q7 Q8
        10  2   1  0  2  0  0  0  0  0               1 10  2   1  0  2  0  0  0  0  0

WORKING  X  I  Q1 Q2 Q3 Q4 Q5 Q6 Q7 Q8       STACK  X  I  Q1 Q2 Q3 Q4 Q5 Q6 Q7 Q8
        10  1   1  0  2  0  0  0  0  0               1 10  1   1  0  2  0  0  0  0  0

WORKING  X  I  Q1 Q2 Q3 Q4 Q5 Q6 Q7 Q8       STACK  X  I  Q1 Q2 Q3 Q4 Q5 Q6 Q7 Q8
         9  1   0  0  2  0  0  0  0  0               2  9  1   0  0  2  0  0  0  0  0
                                                    1 10  1   1  0  2  0  0  0  0  0

WORKING  X  I  Q1 Q2 Q3 Q4 Q5 Q6 Q7 Q8       STACK  X  I  Q1 Q2 Q3 Q4 Q5 Q6 Q7 Q8
         9  0   0  0  2  0  0  0  0  0               2  9  0   0  0  2  0  0  0  0  0
BACKING UP                                          1 10  1   1  0  2  0  0  0  0  0

WORKING  X  I  Q1 Q2 Q3 Q4 Q5 Q6 Q7 Q8       STACK  X  I  Q1 Q2 Q3 Q4 Q5 Q6 Q7 Q8
        10  0   1  0  2  0  0  0  0  0               1 10  0   1  0  2  0  0  0  0  0

WORKING  X  I  Q1 Q2 Q3 Q4 Q5 Q6 Q7 Q8       STACK  X  I  Q1 Q2 Q3 Q4 Q5 Q6 Q7 Q8
        10  0   1  0  2  0  0  0  0  0

RESULT = FALSE

COIN QUANTITIES ON HAND:
  1 OF VALUE  1         0 OF VALUE   2      2 OF VALUE   3       0 OF VALUE   5
  0 OF VALUE 10         0 OF VALUE  15      0 OF VALUE  20       0 OF VALUE  50
```

```
TEST 3:  CHANGE NEEDED = 38.        MAKE CHANGE BY BACKING.

COIN QUANTITIES ON HAND:
     0 OF VALUE  1      4 OF VALUE  2      0 OF VALUE  3      1 OF VALUE  5
     0 OF VALUE 10      2 OF VALUE 15      0 OF VALUE 20      0 OF VALUE 50

WORKING  X    I   Q1 Q2 Q3 Q4 Q5 Q6 Q7 Q8    STACK      X    I   Q1 Q2 Q3 Q4 Q5 Q6 Q7 Q8
         38   7    0  4  0  1  0  2  0  0               1   38   7    0  4  0  1  0  2  0  0

WORKING  X    I   Q1 Q2 Q3 Q4 Q5 Q6 Q7 Q8    STACK      X    I   Q1 Q2 Q3 Q4 Q5 Q6 Q7 Q8
         38   6    0  4  0  1  0  2  0  0               1   38   6    0  4  0  1  0  2  0  0

WORKING  X    I   Q1 Q2 Q3 Q4 Q5 Q6 Q7 Q8    STACK      X    I   Q1 Q2 Q3 Q4 Q5 Q6 Q7 Q8
         23   6    0  4  0  1  0  1  0  0               2   23   6    0  4  0  1  0  1  0  0
                                                       1   38   6    0  4  0  1  0  2  0  0

WORKING  X    I   Q1 Q2 Q3 Q4 Q5 Q6 Q7 Q8    STACK      X    I   Q1 Q2 Q3 Q4 Q5 Q6 Q7 Q8
          8   6    0  4  0  1  0  0  0  0               3    8   6    0  4  0  1  0  0  0  0
                                                       2   23   6    0  4  0  1  0  1  0  0
                                                       1   38   6    0  4  0  1  0  2  0  0

WORKING  X    I   Q1 Q2 Q3 Q4 Q5 Q6 Q7 Q8    STACK      X    I   Q1 Q2 Q3 Q4 Q5 Q6 Q7 Q8
          8   5    0  4  0  1  0  0  0  0               3    8   5    0  4  0  1  0  0  0  0
                                                       2   23   6    0  4  0  1  0  1  0  0
                                                       1   38   6    0  4  0  1  0  2  0  0

WORKING  X    I   Q1 Q2 Q3 Q4 Q5 Q6 Q7 Q8    STACK      X    I   Q1 Q2 Q3 Q4 Q5 Q6 Q7 Q8
          8   4    0  4  0  1  0  0  0  0               3    8   4    0  4  0  1  0  0  0  0
                                                       2   23   6    0  4  0  1  0  1  0  0
                                                       1   38   6    0  4  0  1  0  2  0  0

WORKING  X    I   Q1 Q2 Q3 Q4 Q5 Q6 Q7 Q8    STACK      X    I   Q1 Q2 Q3 Q4 Q5 Q6 Q7 Q8
          3   4    0  4  0  0  0  0  0  0               4    3   4    0  4  0  0  0  0  0  0
                                                       3    8   4    0  4  0  1  0  0  0  0
                                                       2   23   6    0  4  0  1  0  1  0  0
                                                       1   38   6    0  4  0  1  0  2  0  0

WORKING  X    I   Q1 Q2 Q3 Q4 Q5 Q6 Q7 Q8    STACK      X    I   Q1 Q2 Q3 Q4 Q5 Q6 Q7 Q8
          3   3    0  4  0  0  0  0  0  0               4    3   3    0  4  0  0  0  0  0  0
                                                       3    8   4    0  4  0  1  0  0  0  0
                                                       2   23   6    0  4  0  1  0  1  0  0
                                                       1   38   6    0  4  0  1  0  2  0  0

WORKING  X    I   Q1 Q2 Q3 Q4 Q5 Q6 Q7 Q8    STACK      X    I   Q1 Q2 Q3 Q4 Q5 Q6 Q7 Q8
          3   2    0  4  0  0  0  0  0  0               4    3   2    0  4  0  0  0  0  0  0
                                                       3    8   4    0  4  0  1  0  0  0  0
                                                       2   23   6    0  4  0  1  0  1  0  0
                                                       1   38   6    0  4  0  1  0  2  0  0

WORKING  X    I   Q1 Q2 Q3 Q4 Q5 Q6 Q7 Q8    STACK      X    I   Q1 Q2 Q3 Q4 Q5 Q6 Q7 Q8
          1   2    0  3  0  0  0  0  0  0               5    1   2    0  3  0  0  0  0  0  0
                                                       4    3   4    0  4  0  0  0  0  0  0
                                                       3    8   4    0  4  0  1  0  0  0  0
                                                       2   23   6    0  4  0  1  0  1  0  0
                                                       1   38   6    0  4  0  1  0  2  0  0

WORKING  X    I   Q1 Q2 Q3 Q4 Q5 Q6 Q7 Q8    STACK      X    I   Q1 Q2 Q3 Q4 Q5 Q6 Q7 Q8
          1   1    0  3  0  0  0  0  0  0               5    1   1    0  3  0  0  0  0  0  0
                                                       4    3   2    0  4  0  0  0  0  0  0
                                                       3    8   4    0  4  0  1  0  0  0  0
                                                       2   23   6    0  4  0  1  0  1  0  0
                                                       1   38   6    0  4  0  1  0  2  0  0

WORKING  X    I   Q1 Q2 Q3 Q4 Q5 Q6 Q7 Q8    STACK      X    I   Q1 Q2 Q3 Q4 Q5 Q6 Q7 Q8
          1   0    0  3  0  0  0  0  0  0               5    1   0    0  3  0  0  0  0  0  0
                                                       4    3   2    0  4  0  0  0  0  0  0
                                                       3    8   4    0  4  0  1  0  0  0  0
                                                       2   23   6    0  4  0  1  0  1  0  0
                                                       1   38   6    0  4  0  1  0  2  0  0

BACKING UP

WORKING  X    I   Q1 Q2 Q3 Q4 Q5 Q6 Q7 Q8    STACK      X    I   Q1 Q2 Q3 Q4 Q5 Q6 Q7 Q8
          3   1    0  4  0  0  0  0  0  0               4    3   1    0  4  0  0  0  0  0  0
                                                       3    8   4    0  4  0  1  0  0  0  0
                                                       2   23   6    0  4  0  1  0  1  0  0
                                                       1   38   6    0  4  0  1  0  2  0  0
```

Figure 7.24   (continued)

WORKING

X	I	Q1	Q2	Q3	Q4	Q5	Q6	Q7	Q8
3	0	0	4	0	0	0	0	0	0

STACK

	X	I	Q1	Q2	Q3	Q4	Q5	Q6	Q7	Q8
4	3	0	0	4	0	0	0	0	0	0
3	8	4	0	4	0	1	0	0	0	0
2	23	6	0	4	0	1	0	1	0	0
1	38	6	0	4	0	1	0	2	0	0

BACKING UP

WORKING

X	I	Q1	Q2	Q3	Q4	Q5	Q6	Q7	Q8
8	3	0	4	0	1	0	0	0	0

STACK

	X	I	Q1	Q2	Q3	Q4	Q5	Q6	Q7	Q8
3	8	3	0	4	0	1	0	0	0	0
2	23	6	0	4	0	1	0	1	0	0
1	38	6	0	4	0	1	0	2	0	0

WORKING

X	I	Q1	Q2	Q3	Q4	Q5	Q6	Q7	Q8
8	2	0	4	0	1	0	0	0	0

STACK

	X	I	Q1	Q2	Q3	Q4	Q5	Q6	Q7	Q8
3	8	2	0	4	0	1	0	0	0	0
2	23	6	0	4	0	1	0	1	0	0
1	38	6	0	4	0	1	0	2	0	0

WORKING

X	I	Q1	Q2	Q3	Q4	Q5	Q6	Q7	Q8
6	2	0	3	0	1	0	0	0	0

STACK

	X	I	Q1	Q2	Q3	Q4	Q5	Q6	Q7	Q8
4	6	2	0	3	0	1	0	0	0	0
3	8	2	0	4	0	1	0	0	0	0
2	23	6	0	4	0	1	0	0	0	0
1	38	6	0	4	0	1	0	2	0	0

WORKING

X	I	Q1	Q2	Q3	Q4	Q5	Q6	Q7	Q8
4	2	0	2	0	1	0	0	0	0

STACK

	X	I	Q1	Q2	Q3	Q4	Q5	Q6	Q7	Q8
5	4	2	0	2	0	1	0	0	0	0
4	6	2	0	3	0	1	0	0	0	0
3	8	2	0	4	0	1	0	0	0	0
2	23	6	0	4	0	1	0	1	0	0
1	38	6	0	4	0	1	0	2	0	0

WORKING

X	I	Q1	Q2	Q3	Q4	Q5	Q6	Q7	Q8
2	2	0	1	0	1	0	0	0	0

STACK

	X	I	Q1	Q2	Q3	Q4	Q5	Q6	Q7	Q8
6	2	2	0	1	0	1	0	0	0	0
5	4	2	0	2	0	1	0	0	0	0
4	6	2	0	3	0	1	0	0	0	0
3	8	2	0	4	0	1	0	0	0	0
2	23	6	0	4	0	1	0	1	0	0
1	38	6	0	4	0	1	0	2	0	0

WORKING

X	I	Q1	Q2	Q3	Q4	Q5	Q6	Q7	Q8
0	2	0	0	0	1	0	0	0	0

STACK

	X	I	Q1	Q2	Q3	Q4	Q5	Q6	Q7	Q8
7	0	2	0	0	0	1	0	0	0	0
6	2	2	0	1	0	1	0	0	0	0
5	4	2	0	2	0	1	0	0	0	0
4	6	2	0	3	0	1	0	0	0	0
3	8	2	0	4	0	1	0	0	0	0
2	23	6	0	4	0	1	0	1	0	0
1	38	6	0	4	0	1	0	2	0	0

RESULT = TRUE

COIN QUANTITIES ON HAND:

0 OF VALUE 1	0 OF VALUE 2	0 OF VALUE 3	1 OF VALUE 5
0 OF VALUE 10	0 OF VALUE 15	0 OF VALUE 20	0 OF VALUE 50

END OF RUN.

Figure 7.24   (continued)

[Changemaker1 segment]

```
        CHANGEMAKER1: PROC(X,Q,RESULT);
           /* IF CHANGE CAN BE MADE FOR X, SET X TO 0, REDUCE Q BY
              REQUIRED COINS, AND SET RESULT TRUE; OTHERWISE LEAVE X
              AND Q UNCHANGED AND SET RESULT FALSE.                    */

           %INCLUDE /* DATA DECLARATIONS */ CM1DATA;

   3       XS = X;
           QS = Q;
   4       STACK_INDEX = 0;
   5       I = M;
           LOOKING = '1'B;
   7       DO WHILE (X > 0  &  LOOKING);
  10          IF
  11             I > 0
  12          THEN
  13             IF
  14                X >= VAL(I) & Q(I) >= 1
  15             THEN
                     DO;
  16                     STACK_INDEX = STACK_INDEX + 1;
                         STACK.X(STACK_INDEX) = X;
                         STACK.Q(STACK_INDEX,*) = Q;
                         STACK.I(STACK_INDEX) = I;
  17                     X = X - VAL(I);
                         Q(I) = Q(I) - 1;
                     END;
  18             ELSE
  19                I = I - 1;
  21          ELSE
  22             IF
  23                STACK_INDEX > 0
  24             THEN
                     DO;
  25                     X = STACK.X(STACK_INDEX);
                         Q = STACK.Q(STACK_INDEX,*);
                         I = STACK.I(STACK_INDEX);
                         STACK_INDEX = STACK_INDEX - 1;
  26                     I = I - 1;
                         PUT FILE(SYSPRINT) SKIP(2)
                             EDIT('BACKUP: X=',X ,'   I=',I, '   Q=',Q       )
                                 (A,        F(2),A,    F(2),A     ,8 F(3));
                     END;
  27             ELSE
  28                LOOKING = '0'B;
           CALL PRINT_STACK(STACK,STACK_INDEX,X,Q,I);
  31       END;
  32       IF
  33          X = 0
  34       THEN
  35          RESULT = '1'B;
  36       ELSE
             DO;
  37             X = XS;
                 Q = QS;
  38             RESULT = '0'B;
             END;
           RETURN;

        END CHANGEMAKER1;
```

Figure 7.25   Reorganized changemaker in PL/I.

[Cm1data segment]

```
DECLARE                        /* STACK VARIABLES                      */
  1 STACK(50)
   .2 X
   .2 Q(6)
   .2 I
  .STACK_INDEX
;

DECLARE                        /* ARRAY VARIABLES                      */
  Q(8)
       /* ELEMENTS ARE # OF COINS ON HAND, I.E., |1S|,....,|50S| */
  .QS(8)
       /* SAVED COPY OF Q                                        */
  .VAL(8)            INIT(1,2,3,5,10,15,20,50)
       /* ELEMENTS ARE MONETARY VALUES OF CORRESPONDING Q ELEM'S*/
;

DECLARE                        /* SCALAR VARIABLES                     */
  1
       /* PROBLEM INDEX                                          */
  .LOOKING            BIT(1)
       /* SIGNALS TOUR IS EXHAUSTED                              */
  .M                  INIT(8)
       /* NUMBER OF DENOMINATIONS                                */
  .RESULT             BIT(1)
       /* VALUE OF CHANGE POSSIBLE FUNCTION, TRUE OR FALSE       */
  .X   /* CHANGE TO BE MADE                                      */
  .XS  /* SAVED COPY OF X                                        */
;
```

Figure 7.25   (continued)

7.6 ANOTHER CASE STUDY IN HEURISTICS AND RIGOR: TIC-TAC-TOE

7.6.1 Tic-Tac-Toe

The game of tic-tac-toe provides an example for illustrating the difference between rigor and heuristics—one that has practical meaning for today's software design problems. Tic-tac-toe is simple enough to develop a rigorous strategy for play, but complicated enough that many program designers, faced with a comparable problem in software, will settle for a heuristic strategy. While a heuristic strategy is more easily developed, such a strategy becomes more complex and ad hoc as experience develops failures; but a rigorous strategy provides a coherent, permanent plan from which continued optimization can be carried out in a well-controlled manner. There is a crucial difference between fixing a program whose design has failed and increasing the efficiency of a correct design by rigorous stepwise program refinement or reorganization. In the first case the design has been degraded, with more potential danger, while in the second it has been better implemented with no lingering liability.

In what follows, we illustrate three approaches to programming tic-tac-toe. The first, a casual solution, enumerates possible board situations and responses, but is soon overwhelmed by the sheer number of possibilities. The second, a heuristic solution, develops rules for play similar to rules humans use; for example, "win if possible, otherwise play in priority order, center square, any corner square, any side square." Such a design accounts for some reasonable moves but fails in many situations, thus suggesting additional criteria of play, leading to fixing the design, uncovering other failures, and more fixing. The resulting design may be capable of perfect tic-tac-toe, but it will be difficult to prove it, short of exhaustive analysis, itself hard to prove complete, and so on. The third approach utilizes a recursive function for the best possible outcome of any game, which can be used to design a program capable of playing perfect tic-tac-toe.

7.6.2 A Direct Approach

We all know how to play tic-tac-toe from childhood experience. How do we program it? More precisely, how do we program a player, say taking the side of ×, to find the best move from any possible point in a game, when either × or Ø plays first? For example, the player may be asked to take over play initiated by someone else. A reasonable start, if × has the first move to any of the nine squares, is to place an × token in the center square, and we know from experience that correct play from here on leads to a draw. If Ø has the first move to any of the nine squares, the best choice for × is still the center square (if it is open); otherwise, a corner square, and we have covered all possible 0- and 1-token boards (no moves entered and one move entered).

Next, consider 2-token boards. With an × move to the center square and an Ø move, some positions lead to wins, some to draws, some to losses; for example, an Ø move to a corner square

leads to at least a draw because × can force a draw, as shown next, and win if Ø does not block at every Ø move:

But for an Ø move to a side square

an × win can be forced by going to an opposite corner square

	∅	
	×	
×		

→

∅	∅	
	×	
×		

→

×	∅	∅
	×	
×		

and × can win on the next move, no matter how ∅ responds. By symmetry, we have now covered all 2-token boards if we moved to the center square first.

But what if we were asked to take the seat of an × player who had started on a side square, and ∅ replied to the center? The situation is

	×	
	∅	

Some diagramming shows

	×	×
	∅	

→

∅	×	×
	∅	

→

∅	×	×
	∅	
		×

→

∅	×	×
	∅	∅
		×

→

∅	×	×
×	∅	∅
		×

will get at least a draw. Similarly, if ∅ replied to an adjacent corner

∅	×	

the forced set of moves

∅	×	
	×	

→

∅	×	
	×	
	∅	

→

∅	×	
	×	
×	∅	

→

∅	×	∅
	×	
×	∅	

→

∅	×	∅
	×	×
×	∅	

will get at least a draw. Are there other side cases? Yes, for example,

	×	
∅		

and a win can be forced by going to

where × can win on the next move no matter how Ø responds. Another corner case is

and a win can be forced from here by going to

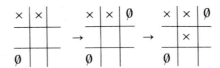

Still another side case is

from which a draw can be guaranteed, as follows:

Are there any other side cases? No, by symmetry, as the following board shows:

1	×	6
2	4	7
3	5	8

We have considered cases 1 through 5 for the Ø move and cases 6, 7, 8 are similar by symmetry to cases 1, 2, 3, respectively.

Next, what about the 2-token boards beginning with a corner square?

×	3	6
1	4	7
2	5	8

The cases, with symmetry accounted for, are 1, 2, 4, 5, 8 for which we determine

×	×	
∅		

gets a win

×	×	
∅		

gets a win

×		×
	∅	

gets at least a draw

×		
	×	
	∅	

gets a win

×		×
	∅	

gets a win

By this time, we have done considerable investigation, hoping no mistakes have been made, and have covered cases of 0-, 1-, and 2-token boards. We have covered

$$1 + 9 + 9*8 = 82$$

cases so far (somewhat overstated, with symmetrical cases included). The number of distinct boards to consider for 0, 1, 2, ..., 8 tokens present is

$$1 + \frac{9}{1} + \frac{9*8}{1*1} + \frac{9*8*7}{1*1*2} + \frac{9*8*7*6}{1*1*2*2} + \cdots + \frac{9*8*7*6*5*4*3*2}{1*1*2*2*3*3*4*4} = 5920$$

cases to be covered (somewhat overstated, with winning boards included), giving approximately 82/5920 < 2% of cases considered thus far, so we are not getting very far very fast! In fact, it is now apparent that this approach will not lead to any practical program design at all.

7.6.3   A Heuristic Approach

Since enumerating next moves has turned out impractical, we now attempt to develop a strategy for finding the best next moves where "best" is defined by some heuristic evaluation of the current board status. Specifically, consider a strategy defined by the following program, with array argument named b (for board):

```
proc tictactoe(b)
    run winifpossible
    if
        ~ win
    then
        run bestmove
    fi
corp
```

The winifpossible segment can examine each of the eight lines on a board (three across, three down, two diagonal) to determine if a win is possible in one move for ×. If not, the bestmove segment can determine the best move to make according to the following strategy. For any line on the board, a win is possible for × if the line is blank or contains one × but no $\emptyset$'s (any line with two ×'s and no $\emptyset$ would have been found by the winifpossible segment). A reasonable heuristic strategy is to identify those lines where a win is still possible and play the square where the greatest number of such lines intersect (in case of ties, choosing, say, the first such square looking left to right, top to bottom). Thus, when a play is made to a square on two or more winning lines, a multiple threat may be created, which leads to a win. For an empty board, the line intersection counts for each square are

3	2	3
2	4	2
3	2	3

(i.e., four lines intersect at the center square, three at each corner square, and two at each side square). This corresponds to the intuitive strategy of "play center square if possible, otherwise a corner, otherwise a side" often used by tic-tac-toe players.

In terms of data, we can represent any current board status in a one-dimensional array named b as follows, numbering squares across, then down, with possible element values $\times$, $\emptyset$ or $\flat$ (for blank):

Array b

$$
\begin{matrix}
 & \text{board} \\
 & \text{columns}
\end{matrix}
$$

$$
\text{board rows}
\left\{
\begin{matrix}
b(1) & b(2) & b(3) \\
\\
b(4) & b(5) & b(6) \\
\\
b(7) & b(8) & b(9)
\end{matrix}
\right.
$$

Triples of square numbers composing each of the eight lines on the board can be defined in a two-dimensional array named *line*, where the first three rows list the square numbers on board rows, the next three rows list the square numbers on board columns, and last two rows list the square numbers on board diagonals:

Array *line*

		1	2	3	
line numbers	1	1	2	3	square numbers
assigned to	2	4	5	6	on *b* rows
b rows	3	7	8	9	
line numbers	4	1	4	7	square numbers
assigned to	5	2	5	8	on *b* columns
b columns	6	3	6	9	
line numbers	7	1	5	9	square numbers
assigned to	8	3	5	7	on *b* diagonals
b diagonals					

The winifpossible segment will require a two-dimensional array that defines the three board line configurations for which a win is possible for $\times$ on the next move. We name the array *wp* (for win pattern):

Array *wp*

	1	2	3
1	♭	×	×
2	×	♭	×
3	×	×	♭

win possible patterns

With these data structures in mind, the winifpossible segment can be defined as shown in Fig. 7.26 (data declarations and parameter list not shown).

Next, the bestmove segment will require an array similar to the *wp* array, but containing board line patterns for best moves, given that a win is not possible. We name the array *bp* (for best pattern):

Array *bp*

	1	2	3
1	♭	♭	♭
2	×	♭	♭
3	♭	×	♭
4	♭	♭	×

best move patterns

Lines (see definition of **array** *line*, above) that intersect at each board square can be defined in a two-dimensional array of line numbers named *intersect*. For example, the line numbers of those lines that intersect at square 5 (center square) are 2 (middle row), 5 (middle column), 7 (upper left to lower right diagonal), and 8 (lower left to upper right diagonal). A zero value in the array indicates that no third or fourth line intersects that particular square:

Array *intersect*

b array square numbers

	1	2	3	4
1	1	4	7	0
2	1	5	0	0
3	1	6	8	0
4	2	4	0	0
5	2	5	7	8
6	2	6	0	0
7	3	4	8	0
8	3	5	0	0
9	3	6	7	0

line numbers that intersect at given square

proc winifpossible
    win := **false**
    i := 0
    while
        i ≤ 8 ∧ ~ *win*
    do [(*i* + 1 line of board = any win pattern → *win* := **true**)]
        i := *i* + 1
        j := 0
        while
            j ≤ 3 ∧ ~ *win*
        do [(ith line of board = *j* + 1 win pattern → *win* := **true**)]
            j := *j* + 1
            if
                $b(line(i, 1)) = wp(j, 1)$ ∧
                $b(line(i, 2)) = wp(j, 2)$ ∧
                $b(line(i, 3)) = wp(j, 3)$
            then
                win := **true**
            fi
        od
    od
    if
        win
    then [win game by placing third × in blank square of *i*th line of board]
        if
            $b(line(i, 1)) = ♭$
        then
            $b(line(i, 1)) := ×$
        else
            if
                $b(line(i, 2)) = ♭$
            then
                $b(line(i, 2)) = ×$
            else
                $b(line(i, 3)) := ×$
            fi
        fi
    fi
corp

Figure 7.26   Winifpossible segment.

The status of each line of the board can be recorded in an array named *best*,

$$best(1:8)$$

recording a 1 for each element of *best* for which the corresponding board line matches any *bp* array pattern, recording a 0 otherwise. Finally, a one-dimensional array named *tot* (for totals), numbered identically to the *b* array, can be used to store intersecting line status (1 or 0) totals for each square:

Array *tot*

$tot(1)$	$tot(2)$	$tot(3)$
$tot(4)$	$tot(5)$	$tot(6)$
$tot(7)$	$tot(8)$	$tot(9)$

Based on these data definitions, the bestmove segment can be defined as shown in Fig. 7.27. Note that two additional segments named findbestlines and makemove are required at the next level, as shown in Figs. 7.28 and 7.29.

With these data structures and program segments in hand, we now try out some test cases. For example, given the first board below (× moves next) our heuristic strategy gets a win for × :

	Ø	×	Ø
×	Ø		
×		Ø	

→

	Ø	×	Ø
×	Ø		
×		Ø	

Next, given a board where a win is not possible on the next move (best pattern intersection totals shown in blank squares) our heuristic strategy likewise gets a win:

Ø	Ø	2
1	×	2
2	1	2

→

Ø	Ø	×
	×	

→

Ø	Ø	×
Ø	×	1
2	1	2

→

Ø	Ø	×
Ø	×	
×		

But what if from the second board above, Ø made a smarter move as follows, blocking the × win and permitting a win for Ø:

Ø	Ø	×
1	×	2
Ø	0	1

→

Ø	Ø	×
	×	×
Ø		

→

Ø	Ø	×
Ø	×	×
Ø		

```
proc bestmove
  run findbestlines
  for
    i :∈ 1 to 9
  do [tot(i) := sum of best pattern line intersections for ith square]
    tot(i) := 0
    for
      j :∈ 1 to 4
    do
      if
        intersect(i, j) ≠ 0
      then
        if
          best(intersect(i, j)) = 1
        then
          tot(i) := tot(i) + 1
        fi
      fi
    od
  od
  max, move := 0, 0
  [set move to blank square number with largest tot array value]
  for
    k :∈ 1 to 9
  do
    if
      tot(k) > max ∧ b(k) = ᛒ
    then
      max, move := tot(k), k
    fi
  od
  run makemove
corp
```

Figure 7.27 Bestmove segment.

It now occurs to us that this situation can arise frequently; for example, in play from an empty board, our heuristic strategy likewise permits a win for $\emptyset$:

$$
\begin{array}{|c|c|c|}
\hline 3 & 2 & 3 \\ \hline 2 & 4 & 2 \\ \hline 3 & 2 & 3 \\ \hline \end{array} \rightarrow
\begin{array}{|c|c|c|}
\hline & & \\ \hline & \times & \\ \hline & & \\ \hline \end{array} \rightarrow
\begin{array}{|c|c|c|}
\hline \emptyset & 1 & 2 \\ \hline 1 & \times & 2 \\ \hline 2 & 2 & 2 \\ \hline \end{array} \rightarrow
\begin{array}{|c|c|c|}
\hline \emptyset & & \times \\ \hline & \times & \\ \hline & & \\ \hline \end{array} \rightarrow
\begin{array}{|c|c|c|}
\hline \emptyset & 1 & \times \\ \hline 1 & \times & 2 \\ \hline \emptyset & 1 & 1 \\ \hline \end{array} \rightarrow
\begin{array}{|c|c|c|}
\hline \emptyset & & \times \\ \hline & \times & \\ \hline \emptyset & & \\ \hline \end{array} \rightarrow
\begin{array}{|c|c|c|}
\hline \emptyset & 1 & \times \\ \hline \times & \times & \\ \hline \emptyset & 1 & 1 \\ \hline \end{array} \rightarrow
\begin{array}{|c|c|c|}
\hline \emptyset & & \times \\ \hline \times & \times & \\ \hline \emptyset & & \\ \hline \end{array}
$$

```
proc findbestlines
    for
        i :∈ 1 to 8
    do [(ith line of board = any best pattern → best(i) := 1 | true → best(i) := 0)]
        best(i) := 0
        for
            j :∈ 1 to 4
        do
            if
                b(line(i, 1)) = bp(j, 1) ∧
                b(line(i, 2)) = bp(j, 2) ∧
                b(line(i, 3)) = bp(j, 3)
            then
                best(i) := 1
            fi
        od
    od
corp
```

Figure 7.28   Findbestlines segment.

```
proc makemove
    if
        move ≠ 0
    then [make best move]
        b(move) := ×
    else [make first available move]
        k := 1
        while
            k ≤ 9 ∧ move = 0
        do
            if
                b(k) = ♭
            then
                move := k
            else
                k := k + 1
            fi
        od
        b(move) := ×
    fi
corp
```

Figure 7.29   Makemove segment.

The problem is easy to solve, though, by adding a procedure to block possible wins on the next move by $\emptyset$, before looking for a best move for $\times$. A new array for checking losing patterns is required, which we name *loss*:

Array *loss*

	1	2	3
1	♭	$\emptyset$	$\emptyset$
2	$\emptyset$	♭	$\emptyset$
3	$\emptyset$	$\emptyset$	♭

} loss possible patterns

The reorganized top segment is as follows:

```
proc tictactoe(b)
    run winifpossible
    if
        ~ win
    then
        run blockloss
        if
            ~ blocking
        then
            run bestmove
        fi
    fi
corp
```

The blockloss segment is shown in Fig. 7.30. (The bestmove, findbestlines, and makemove segments are unaffected by the fix.)

We now have a program that, if correct (no minor assumption at this point!), wins if possible and defends against possible losses before building threats of its own. Thus, for an empty board, the program now produces, for example,

3	2	3
2	4	2
3	2	3

$\rightarrow$

(tic-tac-toe grid with $\times$ in center)

$\rightarrow$

$\emptyset$	1	2
1	$\times$	2
2	2	2

$\rightarrow$

(grid with $\times$ in center)

$\rightarrow$

(grid with $\emptyset$ top-left, $\times$ top-right, $\times$ center)

$\rightarrow$

(grid with $\emptyset$ top-left, $\times$ top-right, $\times$ center, $\times$ middle-left, $\emptyset$ bottom-left)

$\rightarrow$

$\emptyset$	1	$\times$
$\times$	$\times$	$\emptyset$
$\emptyset$	1	0

$\rightarrow$

$\emptyset$	$\times$	$\times$
$\times$	$\times$	$\emptyset$
$\emptyset$		

$\rightarrow$

$\emptyset$	$\times$	$\times$
$\times$	$\times$	$\emptyset$
$\emptyset$	$\emptyset$	

```
proc blockloss
    blocking := false
    i := 0
    while
        i ≤ 8 ∧ ~blocking
    do [(i + 1 line of board = any loss pattern → blocking := true)]
        i := i + 1
        j := 0
        while
            j ≤ 3 ∧ ~blocking
        do [(ith line of board = j + 1 loss pattern → blocking := true)]
            j := j + 1
            if
                b(line(i, 1)) = loss(j, 1) ∧
                b(line(i, 2)) = loss(j, 2) ∧
                b(line(i, 3)) = loss(j, 3)
            then
                blocking := true
            fi
        od
    od
    if
        blocking
    then [make blocking move in ith line]
        if
            b(line(i, 1)) = ♭
        then
            b(line(i, 1)) := ×
        else
            if
                b(line(i, 2)) = ♭
            then
                b(line(i, 2)) = ×
            else
                b(line(i, 3)) = ×
            fi
        fi
    fi
corp
```

Figure 7.30 Blockloss segment.

which gets a tie, where the initial program produced a loss. Does the fixed-up program always win if possible? With a little thought, we realize the answer is no, since given the following board, for example, the new program still permits a win for ∅:

```
2 2 2         . . .        1 1 ∅        × . ∅        × . ∅        × . ∅        × . ∅
1 3 2   →   . × .   →    1 × 1   →   . × .   →   . × .   →   . × .   →   . × ∅
∅ 1 2       ∅ . .        ∅ 1 1        ∅ . .        ∅ . ∅        ∅ × ∅        ∅ × ∅
```

But if the program had played × to a side square from the third board above, a tie would have resulted instead of a loss:

```
× ∅         × ∅          × ∅         ∅ × ∅        ∅ × ∅
. × .   →   . × .   →   . × .   →   . × .   →   × × .
∅ . .       ∅ ∅ .        ∅ ∅ ×        ∅ ∅ ×        ∅ ∅ ×
```

So here is a new problem to be solved, perhaps by reorganizing the block loss segment just added to anticipate this "double threat" in its symmetrical forms and to block possible losses. But it is sure to bring more complication to an already complicated program, and there is no guarantee that we have found all failure cases. In fact, we are well on the way, once again, to an idiosyncratic program that is correct only up to the last known failure.

7.6.4 A Rigorous Design for Tic-Tac-Toe

Having seen the complexities of a heuristic approach to tic-tac-toe, we now look for a rigorous treatment, using a recursive function. A convenient function appears to be one that defines the outcome from any possible situation with perfect play by both players from there on (not assuming perfect play up to that point, of course). Then the basic idea of the recursion will be to reformulate perfect play from any point as a perfect move followed by perfect play thereafter. But before defining the recursion in more detail, some preliminary simplifications and abstractions will be convenient.

First, we consider only the × player problem, in order to keep the definitions below free of player designation. (The ∅ player problem is obtained simply by interchanging ∅'s and ×'s on the board.) Next, we will use informal abstractions of data types with convenient operations, tests, and orderings for later programming into more concrete data types. In particular, we define data types named outcome, square, and board as follows:

1. outcome (o ∈ outcome)

outcome = {win, draw, lose}   (1.1)
operation − (minus) is defined as   (1.2)

o	− o
win	lose
draw	draw
lose	win

transitive relation > (greater than) is defined as   (1.3)

win > draw > lose

2. square (s ∈ square)

square = {×, ♭, ∅}   (2.1)
operation − (minus) is defined as   (2.2)

s	− s
×	∅
♭	♭
∅	×

3. board (b ∈ board)

board = {b | **array** b(3, 3) ∧ (b(i, j) ∈ square,   (3.1)
           1 ≤ i ≤ 3, 1 ≤ j ≤ 3)}
operation − (minus) is defined as   (3.2)

$$-b = \begin{bmatrix} -b(1,1) & -b(1,2) & -b(1,3) \\ -b(2,1) & -b(2,2) & -b(2,3) \\ -b(3,1) & -b(3,2) & -b(3,3) \end{bmatrix}$$

Next, we define a function named value, to be redefined recursively later, directly as follows:

value = {(b, o) | b ∈ board, o ∈ outcome; o is the outcome
                  to × player in situation defined by b with
                  × player to move, if possible, and with
                  perfect play by both players from this point on}

For example,

$$\text{value}\left(\ \begin{array}{|c|c|c|}\hline \ & \ & \ \\\hline \ & \ & \ \\\hline \ & \ & \ \\\hline\end{array}\ \right) = \text{draw} \qquad \text{value}\left(\begin{array}{|c|c|c|}\hline \times & & \emptyset \\\hline & \times & 0 \\\hline & & \\\hline\end{array}\right) = \text{win}$$

$$\text{value}\left(\begin{array}{|c|c|c|}\hline \times & \times & \emptyset \\\hline \times & & \\\hline \emptyset & & \emptyset \\\hline\end{array}\right) = \text{lose} \qquad \text{value}\left(\begin{array}{|c|c|c|}\hline \times & \emptyset & \emptyset \\\hline \emptyset & \times & \times \\\hline \times & & \emptyset \\\hline\end{array}\right) = \text{draw}$$

In order to define value recursively, we further define a function named result and a predicate named end, both with domain board:

$$\text{result} = \{(b, o)\,|\,o = \text{win, draw, or lose, respectively,} \qquad (3.3)$$
$$\text{if b has more, equal, or less} \times \text{lines}$$
$$\text{than } \emptyset \text{ lines}\}$$

$$\text{end} = \{(b, z)\,|\,z = \textit{true} \text{ if b has no blanks or at least} \qquad (3.4)$$
$$\text{one} \times \text{line or } \emptyset \text{ line, otherwise } z = \textit{false}\}$$

We also define a data type named move, with associated functions legal and newboard:

4. move (m ∈ move)

$$\text{move} = \{(i, j)\,|\,1 \le i \le 3,\ 1 \le j \le 3\} \qquad (4.1)$$
$$\text{legal} = \{((b, m), z)\,|\,b \in \text{board, } m \in \text{move,} \qquad (4.2)$$
$$z = (b(m) = \flat)\}$$
$$\text{newboard} = \{((b, m), c)\,|\,b \in \text{board, } m \in \text{move,} \qquad (4.3)$$
$$c \in \text{board, and } c(m) = \times,$$
$$c(i, j) = b(i, j) \text{ for } (i, j) \ne m\}$$
$$\text{(newboard(b, m) will be abbreviated as } b + m)$$

Then, for example,

$$\text{result}\left(\ \begin{array}{|c|c|c|}\hline \ & \ & \ \\\hline \ & \ & \ \\\hline \ & \ & \ \\\hline\end{array}\ \right) = \text{draw} \qquad \text{result}\left(\begin{array}{|c|c|c|}\hline \times & \times & \times \\\hline \times & \times & \times \\\hline \times & \times & \times \\\hline\end{array}\right) = \text{win}$$

$$\text{result}\left(\begin{array}{|c|c|c|}\hline \times & \times & \times \\\hline \emptyset & \emptyset & \emptyset \\\hline \emptyset & \emptyset & \emptyset \\\hline\end{array}\right) = \text{lose} \qquad \text{result}\left(\begin{array}{|c|c|c|}\hline \times & \emptyset & \emptyset \\\hline \emptyset & \times & \times \\\hline \times & \times & \emptyset \\\hline\end{array}\right) = \text{draw}$$

$$\text{end}\left(\begin{array}{|c|c|}\hline & \\ \hline & \\ \hline\end{array}\right) = \textit{false} \qquad \text{end}\left(\begin{array}{|c|c|c|}\hline \times & \times & \times \\ \hline \times & \times & \times \\ \hline \times & \times & \times \\ \hline\end{array}\right) = \textit{true}$$

$$\text{legal}\left(\begin{array}{|c|c|}\hline \times & \emptyset \\ \hline & \\ \hline\end{array}, (2, 2)\right) = \textit{true} \qquad \text{legal}\left(\begin{array}{|c|c|}\hline \times & \emptyset \\ \hline & \\ \hline\end{array}, (1, 2)\right) = \textit{false}$$

$$\text{newboard}\left(\begin{array}{|c|c|}\hline \times & \emptyset \\ \hline & \\ \hline\end{array}, (2, 2)\right) = \begin{array}{|c|c|}\hline \times & \emptyset \\ \hline & \times \\ \hline\end{array}$$

$$\text{newboard}\left(\begin{array}{|c|c|}\hline \times & \emptyset \\ \hline & \\ \hline\end{array}, (1, 2)\right) = \begin{array}{|c|c|}\hline \times & \times \\ \hline & \\ \hline\end{array}$$

Note that the result, end, legal, and newboard functions are defined for any members of board and move, not just ones that can arise in legal tic-tac-toe play.

Now the value function can be redefined with the following recursive rule, as we explain next:

value(b) = (end(b) → result(b) |
 ~ end(b) → max{− value(− (b + m)) | legal(b, m)})

The first term of this conditional rule deals with the case that no move is required of the $\times$ player and gives the outcome directly. The second term requires that the $\times$ player select a perfect move to maximize the outcome possible from b by a choice of a specific value of m from the legal moves available. In particular, working from the inner terms out,

$$\text{value}(-(b + m))$$

is the outcome (win, lose, or draw) for the $\emptyset$ player if the $\times$ player chooses move m in board b; next,

$$-\text{value}(-(b + m))$$

is the outcome for the $\times$ player; finally, the best outcome possible for a legal move by the $\times$ player is

$$\text{max}\{-\text{value}(-(b + m)) \mid \text{legal}(b, m)\}$$

Any m that achieves this maximum will be a perfect move, as required. For example,

$$\text{value}\left(\begin{array}{ccc} \times & \times & \emptyset \\ \times & \emptyset & \emptyset \\ \times & \emptyset & \end{array}\right) = \text{win},$$

because

$$\text{end}\left(\begin{array}{ccc} \times & \times & \emptyset \\ \times & \emptyset & \emptyset \\ \times & \emptyset & \end{array}\right) = \textit{true} \quad \text{and} \quad \text{result}\left(\begin{array}{ccc} \times & \times & \emptyset \\ \times & \emptyset & \emptyset \\ \times & \emptyset & \end{array}\right) = \text{win}$$

Also,

$$\text{value}\left(\begin{array}{ccc} \times & \times & \emptyset \\ \times & \emptyset & \emptyset \\ & & \end{array}\right) = \max\left(-\text{value}\left(\begin{array}{ccc} \emptyset & \emptyset & \times \\ \emptyset & \times & \times \\ \emptyset & & \end{array}\right), \ -\text{value}\left(\begin{array}{ccc} \emptyset & \emptyset & \times \\ \emptyset & \times & \times \\ & \emptyset & \end{array}\right),\right.$$

$$\left.-\text{value}\left(\begin{array}{ccc} \emptyset & \emptyset & \times \\ \emptyset & \times & \times \\ & & \emptyset \end{array}\right)\right)$$

$$= \max(-\text{lose}, \ -\text{win}, \ -\text{win})$$

where the first of the max operands can be seen to be $(-\text{lose})$ through the next application of the recursion, and the other two operands seen to be $(-\text{win})$ by two applications of the recursion. Therefore,

$$\text{value}\left(\begin{array}{ccc} \times & \times & \emptyset \\ \times & \emptyset & \emptyset \\ & & \end{array}\right) = \max(\text{win}, \text{lose}, \text{lose})$$

$$= \text{win}$$

by the choice of the first operand, namely move(3, 1).

In general, the recursion defines a tree of moves by both players, each path in the tree ending when either an × line or $\emptyset$ line arises, or when the board becomes full. In fact, this recursive rule defines outcomes for boards that cannot arise from legal play, for example,

$$\text{value}\left(\begin{array}{ccc} \times & \times & \times \\ \times & \times & \times \\ \emptyset & \emptyset & \emptyset \end{array}\right) = \text{win}$$

Such an extension does no harm, avoids the cumbersome question of defining a domain of board values reachable by legal play, and allows a simpler function definition.

We can translate the recursive rule for the value function directly into program form, as shown in Fig. 7.31 (with data as defined above), assigning value(b) to the name *val*. The program produces an assignment to *val* of win, draw, or lose, that is, it evaluates the recursive function for a given board. The corresponding next move can then be determined as a reorganization of this program, as we will see.

The program is an ifthenelse, just as specified by the recursive rule. The thenpart gives the value of *val* directly; the elsepart is a sequence that finds the maximum required by the rule, using an initialized fordo followed by the assignment of the maximum to *val*. Within the dopart of the fordo, the ifthen considers only legal moves, and invokes the procedure recursively. The **initial, free** operations on b, which bracket the procedure call, save and restore the situation known at the point of the call. Note that the fordo provides implicit **initial, free** operations on m that save and restore move choices. The **initial, free** operations on v, bracketing the major elsepart, save and restore the maximum found so far for each call of the procedure.

```
proc tictactoe
    if
        end(b)
    then
        val := result(b)
    else
        initial v := lose
        for
            m :∈ move
        do
            if
                legal(b, m)
            then
                initial b := -(b + m)
                run tictactoe
                free b
                v := max(v, -val)
            fi
        od
        val := v
        free v
    fi
corp
```

Figure 7.31   Tictactoe program.

An informal proof of the correctness of tictactoe can be carried out in two inductions on the number of nonblanks in b, say $|b|$, the first induction to show termination, the second induction to show the correctness of the assignment to val. First, if $|b| = 9$, the predicate end(b) is *true* and tictactoe terminates. Also, if tictactoe terminates for any initial b such that $|b| = i > 0$, then tictactoe terminates for any b such that $|b| = i - 1$, since $|b|$ is increased by 1 in the elsepart. Therefore, tictactoe terminates for any b such that $|b| = 9, 8, \ldots, 0$, that is, for any b. Second, if $|b| = 9$, tictactoe assigns result(b) to val as required; also if tictactoe assigns the correct value to val for any initial b such that $|b| = i > 0$, then tictactoe assigns the correct value to val for any b such that $|b| = i - 1$, since val is assigned either result(b) (in the thenpart) or the maximum required by the recursive rule (in the elsepart). In more detail, this last requirement is to show that the elsepart program

```
initial v := lose
for
    m ∈ move
do
    if
        legal(b, m)
    then
        initial b := −(b + m)
        run tictactoe
        free b
        v := max(v, −val)
    fi
od
val := v
free v
```

has program function

$$val := \text{value}(b)$$

under the following hypothesis:

1. tictactoe assigns value(b') to val for any b' such that $|b'| = i > 0$
2. end(b) is *false*
3. $|b| = i - 1$

From the recursive definition of value, it will be sufficient to show that this elsepart program has program function

$$val := \max\{-\text{value}(-(b + m)) \mid \text{legal}(b, m)\}$$

The initialized fordo computes and assigns this maximum to v, because only legal moves m in b are considered, and at each invocation $|-(b+m)| = i$, so by hypothesis (1) above (where $b' = -(b+m)$) val is assigned value$(-(b+m))$ by tictactoe, and the assignment

$$v := \max(v, -val)$$

then accumulates the maximum as required. Note that this copy of v is undisturbed by the recursive calls of tictactoe, because each such call initializes and frees its own copy of v.

The move required can be determined as a by-product of the execution of this procedure. It will be a move m at which v achieves its maximum during the topmost invocation of the procedure (whose execution may be interrupted several times by further recursive invocations of the procedure). A simple way of determining this is to introduce a level count on the depth of the stack v, and to update a new data item, say *nextmove*, with the value of m whenever this level count is 1 and a new maximum value has been found.

This procedure, while readily understood and proved correct, can be made more efficient in various ways. First, the maximum finding fordo can be terminated whenever a value of win has been found for v. Second, any look ahead conceivable (including a heuristic look ahead) for determining val can be added at the beginning of the elsepart of the program. If val is not determined by such a look ahead, the remainder of the elsepart (presently the entire elsepart) will determine it correctly. This look ahead need not be complete, of course, and would be invoked with a possible speedup at each level of recursion. For example, a win next move, a forced loss by opponent's next move, and a forced win on the second move could be programmed. In fact, even in these cases, the look ahead need not be complete (but needs to be correct). This example illustrates a general idea for improving the efficiency of a design while ensuring its continued correctness, namely to use a correct design as a basis for stepwise reorganization that introduces speedup parts in a fail-safe way.

EXERCISES

1. Reorganize the design of the recursive tictactoe program to determine the required move, as described above.

2. Introduce heuristic speedups to the program design of exercise 1, to
   a) win next move,
   b) force loss by opponent's next move, and
   c) force win on second move,

   while assuring program correctness with each addition.

Index